ENERGY CRISIS IN
INDIA

ENERGY CRISIS IN
INDIA

A COMMENTARY ON INDIA'S ELECTRICITY SECTOR

DR SHREE RAMAN DUBEY

PARTRIDGE
A Penguin Random House Company

To order additional copies of this book, contact
Partridge India
000 800 10062 62
orders.india@partridgepublishing.com

www.partridgepublishing.com/india

CONTENTS

SECTION-A

SECTION-B

SECTION-C

ABSTRACT

India's quest for clean survival despite Energy Crisis, Economic Recession and merry go-round Liberalized Energy Policies are opening prospective avenues for Green Power across the country.

Why India is facing energy crisis? Can the least developed countries invariably battling with energy crisis and poverty develop the clean energy industry and sustained renewable energy markets?

Increasing share of renewable in countries with energy mix least diversified due to resources, geographical constraints and other national factors are the challenges ahead. Moreover the ice of National commitments for alleviating poverty in India with Global objectives of electrifying all villages is never melting down bridging the gap between abundant potential utilization and undercapitalized renewable resources.

Unfortunately all the reforms implemented in India to improve accessibility of electricity in rural areas are dwindling between the philosophy of business and service.

Will Renewable Energy translate the Destiny of India? Will LED light up India? Will Solar Power substitute Fossil Power in India?

Why did the monopoly of "Public Enterprises ended in Indian Power Sector?

PURPOSE

Energy is indispensable to life.

What is our obligation as citizen of the world? The question is "Are we citizens first?" or "Are we consumers first?"

Facts are facts. We should not kill the facts. Killing fact is as good as crime. The transparency in resolving national crisis is always going to be in the right direction of national development. An effort big or small which adds to national betterment must be encouraged at any level of commitment.

Can you think of life without energy? This is a study primarily to share the voices of Indian citizens who experience the gains and losses with and without power to their homes. There is no fun in flaming the blames in the sector.

An integrated system is the call of the day now in India.

Unity Vs Diversity is part and parcel of existence. Need Vs Greed the equilibrium is invariably essential.

Population Vs Service is a national challenge to any form, size and style of government across the world.

India is trying to shine with frozen limbs.

India is driven by "Political Mix". The policies are guided by "Government Mix". The "Economic Mix" impacts our growth and development. Amidst this is the emerging "Energy Mix".

India is today sailing in "Era of Mix". History in times to come will salute this phase of transition India is undergoing. The greatest turbulence is in energy sector.

Crisis Vs Surplus dreams yet to be realized in the electricity sector. What went wrong in policy earlier is not that important than what is going wrong today?

New Policies should not hold the legacy of unsuccessful stories in the power sector in India. Though amendments are being enacted after long debates and discussions but the apprehensions are still at the grass roots.

Training Vs Awareness the gap is vast. More and more programs are to be implemented to educate the society in India. The Institutions have to take the leading role in grooming and developing the young generations in India.

Industrialization Vs Modernization continually brings in technological changes in society. Infrastructure is becoming key to elevating standards of living, health and happiness.

Energy is no doubt enriching lives all over the world. How will Indians benefit by revamping the energy sector?

Profile Vs Pattern of energy speaks of supply and demand gap from dawn to dusk.

Where Energy is heading in India? This is throughout the day on the lips of every citizen in India. Will all the Rural Villages become Smart Cities in the coming decades? Can we have a power system absolutely free from problems and issues in the coming years?

Can we get rid of "Black Out in India" completely? Who can design an integrated power system of that kind for India?

This analytical study was undertaken for unearthing the possible opportunities which can help society as a whole in efficiently utilizing the reserves of natural resources, economically consuming electrical energy and simultaneously conserving the power equally to save energy for betterment of human living on this earth.

The task of designing the methodology of study and implementing it with limited resources was the challenge in front of me. Not limiting it to be useful only for academic values, made it more difficult assignment to be judiciously undertaken.

Moreover my focus was towards all the stakeholders of the energy and power sector in the country. I had to seriously endeavor to see that the outcome of the study should add value to the whole process of research.

It may be a crude research but the base findings can substantially bring in enormous insight to any beginner trying to understand the energy crisis in India.

"Drain of Energy" is "Drain of Life". Let us all understand this. "Energy on Earth" is for everybody today and tomorrow. It is our responsibility to balance the living. Energy Saving is equally important as energy generation. How to be successful in preserving energy?

My readers no doubt might be thinking of way forward in the sector. Are we really meeting the aspirations of key stakeholders in the power sector?

What should be the next wave of reforms in the power sector?

Congratulations!

To The Team

Energy Crisis in India

Project ID-710159

I congratulate the entire team for eloquently placing the commentary on Indian Electricity Sector. This unique presentation expresses the integrated dedication of all the members involved right from compilation to release of the book.

The team will be light to the world as this commentary promises to alleviate darkness from the mankind's living.

With Regards

Dr Shree Raman Dubey

PREFACE

Respected My Dear Readers

Let us take the challenge of excelling in the new millennium living.

Let us aim to place India in the list of nations with surplus power, infrastructure, wealth, healthiness, prosperity, literacy, smart cities, power to all and so on, so that India rises to shine forever.

I hope very sooner every citizen of India will have access to electricity.

Electricity is today's life line. Every nation has to craft an optimal solution for global power crisis.

"Energy Crisis in India", An Analytical Approach, Indian Case Study is an attempt in designing an optimal energy model for India. This is a model reflecting the possible solutions pertaining to the gaps encouraging the power crisis in India.

I more or less can say that this book has covered the saga of Indian Electricity Sector from 2005 to 2015 very closely. One can say this is the period of new dawn in the history of electricity in India. For the reason that the year

2003 initiated the electricity reforms & restructuring and 2012 was the mandate of the government to make power available to all.

With the above background this study no doubt shall always remain an inciting research in analyzing India's Energy Sector.

How to understand the limitation of business and services in the electricity sector? The power supply chain is supported by different roles of power utilities.

To have an understandable insight right from the source of electricity generation units to switching of power by consumers in home, markets and industries for the readers the current issues and concerns of the power sector has been studied in field with immense sincerity and dedication.

I being a Technocrat associated with the Energy Sector in India have always felt that the majority of consumers are not educated on many policy to supply related matters of the power sector.

All the citizens of India may not have an opportunity to carry out field research investigating the issues causing energy crisis in India. Awareness helps you to understand the challenges of the government in delivering these services through different models of power utilities.

Energy consumption to conservation is the responsibility of one and all. With all these turbulence in mind I decided to practically find the facts of perception the Indian citizens are having for the power utilities.

After having a deeper study of the ailing sector I could design questionnaires which would be instrumental in probing out the realities from end users, intermediate and beneficiaries linked to the entire electricity supply chain.

I assure that any reader with the bent of mind to reform the sector will surely gain something from this narration on energy crisis in India.

You can take me as a spokesman of the people of India. Though this field study has been done in limited districts of India yet it represents more or less the same environment of business and services. The valuable suggestions of the consumers are the voices of the well wisher citizens of India.

They had lot to tell right from the village panchyat to national parliament. The floor of the parliament is hardly looking into the subsidy leaks of the nation. This way there are numerous bitter truths and religiously indispensable in the whole process of reformation analysis.

I salute the democratic rights of the nations who prosper with the voice of citizens. Are the services to citizens an obligatory binding on the nation?

The readers are certainly going to understand the subject of policy vs reality as they pick up the analytics of the whole debate on the energy sector.

I have toiled to tailor out a tool of investigation to bring the gaps of the energy sector. Power is leader in the energy sector. Hence the concentration of this study is concentric to issues pertaining to the electricity in India.

This field report no doubt will be useful to similar people working in this area. The findings are promising avenues to all.

I have willingly not reproduced national or global statistics in the form of pie-charts with %, histograms, bar charts, percentage share of energy portfolio, power consumption by market segmentation, energy intensity, per capita consumption of electricity, or data from the AGM reports of Corporate, summary reports of consultants, performance reports of power utilities, sensex reports of investors, with figures and forecasts only for the sake of my readers development.

I wish that my readers after going through this commentary can willingly explore, discover, review and compare the substance for better learning and awareness.

The purpose of this book is not to arrive at the exact figures against the parameters but to understand the gaps between the problems and solution of the sector.

Dr Shree Raman Dubey
BE. MBA. Ph.D
10th May, 2015.

DEDICATION

I owe everything to my parents.

Every father and mother dream of their son's contribution to the World.

Today is Mother's Day and with her divine blessings and grace I sincerely dedicate this book to the society for a better and happy living.

In my perception, "Man's journey on this Earth appears to be for unfolding the mysteries of the Universe in subsequent phases so that the beauty of Life continuously inspires us to excel in living again and again outperforming the old with the new against all odds of several cyclic fall and rise in quest for survival."

Dr Shree Raman Dubey
10th May, 2015.

ACKNOWLEDGEMENT

I honestly begin with, saluting my country for this indelible opportunity, I dedicate this piece of small effort to the citizens of India for enriching their awareness on the core sector which fuels and sustains our daily living.

At the very outset, I would like to express heartfelt thanks and gratitude to all my respondents without which Voice of Consumers & Power Utilities from the field of reality would not have become a narration on Indian Energy Sector.

And to all who have spent most of their busy hours untiringly helping me to strengthen this commentary. Without their sustained encouragement, and unstinted cooperation this thesis would not have progressed to the extent of its completion.

I cannot but express, by debt of gratitude for your tremendous contribution and I am personally enriched with the receiver of citizens' knowledge.

My heartfelt thanks are due to everybody who have been associated with this assignment for the welfare of society.

I, feel deeply grateful to all concerned government departments, power utilities, authorities, ministries, for sharing their feedback in supporting this analytical approach study. The book is certainly going to assist in learning the supply chain of energy in India.

I am much beholden to, the patience, time and suggestions of respondents, whose understanding and co-operation made it possible for me to complete my thesis as smoothly as possible.

I am indebted to my country for the opportunity to carry out this study. I believe India is surely going to be blessed with efficient optimal energy models sooner before the entire energy is drained.

I am thankful to everyone who assisted me during my field work in counseling, educating, interpreting, organizing, collecting and analyzing data from various segments of respondents.

I, shall be failing in my duty if I miss to record my heartfelt thanks to the respondents of Power Utilities, Industrial, Domestic and Commercial Consumers of Visakhapatnam, East Godavari, West Godavari and Krishna Districts who extended all cooperation in supplying the needy information.

I also salute the exhaustive list of periodicals, journals, literature, reports, white papers, articles detailed out in the bibliography of this book.

I honour the earlier works by various researchers, individuals, institutions, organisations and committees which have been very much instrumental in shaping the Electricity in India.

More and more energy models are being designed to power the world. Global Energy challenges and opportunities are transforming nations towards healthy living.

Finally my respect, regard and thanks to all.

Dr SHREE RAMAN DUBEY
B.E. MBA. Ph.D

Prayer

Evolution of Power

Darkness to Lightness

Energy is Life

**"Humans have journeyed from darkness
to lightness with great sacrifices."**

With prayer to all inventors, discoverers, scientists and researchers who made known to the World about the magic of electrical power. Let us understand the evolution of power and importance of electricity in the entire energy profile of the earth.

Humans of today are indebted to electrical energy for transforming their lives from "Darkness to Lightness" in the century which has just passed into history giving modern cities, living comforts, health, wealth, happiness, knowledge, wisdom and so on.

Man could make wonders with electrical energy. Now can we imagine living without electricity? You all may agree with me that it may become another wonder to live without the usage of electricity.

Energy Vs Power, one form to another, the exploration continues to transform the world with series of progressive transitions in the energy sector.

Electrical Energy is the lifeline of the World.

Power Generation Vs Natural Energy Resources, speaks of the universal constrains, barriers, opportunities and challenges every nation faces in providing power to their citizens.

Energy is Life. Let us say the other way Life is Energy. One cannot exist without the other. The quest for survival and betterment across the Globe by all civilizations at any point of time was a great opportunity to explore the self.

Every generation has passed on something to the next for further analysis and findings. During this process there have been inventions and discoveries influencing our lives gradually and regularly. Right from the producing of spark due to heat generated on account of friction developed by rubbing of stones, from burning of coal, combustion of fossil fuel oils and gas to generating of electricity had been a series of attempts to discover the most economical and reliable form of Energy.

Of all, Electricity is indelible. This new form of energy opened many avenues for man to redefine Life. Gradually over the years it evolved itself into Electric Power to transform the whole world.

The result of which is transforming our lives from living in Dark Days with oil lantern to illuminating nights with electric bulb, journey by bullock carts to speeding supersonic trains, landing on moon and recent home in Space to exploration of Life on Mars.

Electric Power still continues to be the prime energy for growth and development in the world. Fortunate are the ones who have access to electricity and are reaping the fruits of modernized infrastructure in life. Life is a bane to the deprived ones. There are regions in the world where inhabitants might wonder on the achievements as said above.

Yes, they are still living in the Stone Age. The geographic barriers have confined us to share Energy across Continents and Nations. The restrictions and difficulty of shifting resources from places of abundance to scare is another major factor not helping the Global initiative of mutual cooperation and growth.

Earth Vs Energy, is a natural way to explore and discover our resources. All forms of energy is with the mother Earth.

Everyone today might be aware of the World Environment Day. It is celebrated on 5th June every year throughout the world to remind us against our roles and responsibility towards protecting environment, nature and life.

Energy is available on Earth in various forms and sources as primary, fossil fuels like coal, gasoline, natural gas & liquefied petroleum gas, nuclear fuels, tidal energy, geothermal, solar power, wind energy, bio-fuels, biomass & vegetable oil and secondary energy based on the type of conversion as needed from the main resources.

Each form has its own advantages and disadvantages. Today, the whole world is very much concerned about sustainable energy. The Energy development programme requires special attention by developed and developing nations to alleviate the Global Energy Crisis.

Developed Vs Under Developed Nations, gives us a comparative analysis on the outlook of development, needs, necessities, essentialities, supply demand, growth, strategies, policies, from country to country.

The great challenge is to balance human comfort with reasonable energy consumption levels. Gradually over the years reserve of fossil fuels will decline and become exhausted as they are non-renewable. Extraction of fossil fuels results in extensive environmental degradation and is becoming expensive.

Complete dependence on fossil fuels is a matter of serious concern. Biomass is renewable and is available in abundance, but the present technology is yet to explore its usefulness in replacing the gasoline or alternate fuel. There is no primary waste or pollution in hydro-electric power production. The fight for becoming giant in nuclear power, globally among leading nations cannot be denied at this point of time considering its economics. The available reserves of coal, crude oil, gas, lignite, and uranium are very limited and the rate of consumption is increasing every year.

As these natural resources cannot be recovered, renewable and non-depleting sources of energy is being explored throughout the world. Hydro and Wind based power plants are already making their way. It is very difficult to conclude today the configuration of next generation power plants 50 years down the line.

Over 2000 years ago, in the 6th Century BC, the Greeks, Thales observed that rubbing fur on amber caused attraction between the two, which is now known as Static Electricity, a beginning in the history of Electricity.

The works of Girolamo Cardano, Italian physician, in De Subtilitate (1550), William Gilbert, the English Scientist, in De Magnete (1600), Sir Thomas Browne in Pseudodoxia Epidemica (1646), were the earlier contributions into research of Electricity. Further work was conducted by Otto Von Guericke, Robert Boyle, Stephen Gray, Benjamin Franklin (1752), Luigi Galuani (1791), Alessandro Volta (1800), Andre-Marie Ampere (1820), Michael Faraday (1821) and George Ohm (1827). The great progress in this area had been in the early 19th century through Nikola Tesla, Thomas Edison, George Westinghouse, Ernst Werner Von Siemens, Alexander Graham Bell and Lord Kelvin.

The well known axiom **"Like-charged objects repel and opposite-charged objects attract"** was the phenomena investigated by Charles-Augustin-de-Coulomb in the late eighteenth century.

From the extensive works of research in electricity by Benjamin Franklin positive and negative charges were introduced, respectively for proton and electron. Charge originates in the atom. Electric charge is a property of sub-atomic particles. The movement of electric charge is known as an electric current, intensity being measured in amperes. An electric arc provides an energetic demonstration of electric current.

The concept of the electric field was introduced by Michael Faraday. Electric potential is closely linked to electric field measured in volts. James Clerk Maxwell (1831-1879), who was elected to the Royal Society, formulated the Maxwell's equations which described the behavior of both electric and magnetic fields, and for the first time expressed the basic laws of electricity & magnetism in an unified fashion.

An electric circuit is an interconnection of electric components, usually to perform some useful task. The components in an electric circuit can include elements as resistors, capacitors, switches, transformers, inductors, etc as per the design requirements. Electronic devices make use of the transistor, perhaps one of the most important inventions of the twentieth century, and a fundamental building block of all modern circuitry. A modern integrated circuit may contain several billion miniaturized transistors in a region only a few centimeters square.

Electricity is by no means a purely human invention, and may be observed in several forms in nature, a prominent manifestation of which is lightning.

Electricity is an extremely flexible form of energy and it may be adapted to a huge and growing number of uses. Energy can neither be created nor destroyed; it can be transformed from one form to another.

All primitive means could not produce energy from natural resources continuously. Producing energy steadily is a challenge even today with latest advance Technology. Electrical energy is more uniform.

The next important milestone will be the Storage of Energy. Here is the problem; the whole world is eagerly waiting to solve it. Whatever is generated requires immediate transmission and distribution. There is no intermediate system to act as permanent buffer between generation and transmission of power.

I admit to say that, "Electricity has been the greatest breakthrough in the field of science and technology for the welfare of mankind, growth and over all development of society in all walks of life". The curiosity kept on inspiring the researchers to push us in the Electronic Age, offspring of the beloved mother Electricity.

Man is being replaced by Machines and controlled by Computers. The Silicon Valley revolution is not the last this age has witnessed; it is again a beginning for a new finding.

Power Generation Plants are generally near to available resources and far from the end consumers. 100% generated power is never supplied. The shortage is due to operational performance, transmission losses and inefficient distribution system.

It is very difficult to design an overall integrated power system. For large electrical demands electrical energy must be generated and transmitted in bulk since electrical energy cannot easily be stored in quantities large enough to meet demands on a national scale, at all times exactly as much must be produced as is required.

Electricity is generated here in Thermal Power Plants. Thermal energy is derived from Boilers by burning Coal and the steam produced in Boilers is led to rotate Steam Turbines, which in turn act as the prime movers of Alternators for generating Electrical Power.

In a Boiler or Steam Generator, water is heated until it turns to Steam at temperature above 350 degree Centigrade, depending on the pressure of the Boiler. Then it is further superheated to temperature above 500 degree Centigrade. When water is boiled into steam, its volume increases about 1600 times, producing heat energy, the force used to turn the turbine rotor that generates electricity. In all Steam Generating Stations, the water used to create steam must be highly purified. This is important because the steam is forced against the row of blades that rotate the shaft. The steam constantly hits these metal parts, so even the tiniest impurities will erode the metal blades. The water is softened, filtered and de-mineralized until it is as pure as distilled water. Each Generating Station has a chemical Lab. Where water purifying process is regularly monitored. As the Steam releases heat energy to turn the turbine, its temperature drops. To reuse water used in Generating Power, the Steam is condensed back into water. To condense the steam, it is discharged into a vacuum and passed over cooling water in tubes.

For my readers to have an easy understanding of electricity Below is the basic process to produce Electricity.

Thermal Energy $\rightarrow$ Mechanical Energy $\rightarrow$ Electrical Energy (Electricity)

Even today the prime source for thermal energy is coal.

All the search is to find out best energy model which optimizes the issues governing its supply chain. Production of power from coal so far has remained the legacy of the World.

Will Renewable Power dominate over Coal Power?

INTRODUCTION

India in the new millennium

Wings & Dreams

If wings are not directed towards dreams where will India land?

India is marching ahead in the new millennium. The foremost challenge is of energy. Modernization needs infrastructural support, growth and development. Energy is the prime mover of Indian economy to maintain the momentum of globalization.

Old India Vs Modern India Vs Global India, the era of transition, transformation, reforms, restructuring, modernization is changing the dynamics of growth and development. India is globally emerging out with new wings and dreams.

India is global today. India is trying to glow and shine rapidly bringing in healthiness, happiness and harmony to one and all.

Will the new Millennium change the outlook of India? Will India become Smarter India? Is it not the responsibility of the citizens to think and work religiously for this national mandate?

Country's expectations are far beyond the aims of national policies. India wants to participate globally. India is becoming bigger, greater and smarter in all walks of life.

Did the world learn anything from the 1973 Oil Crisis? Is 1991 a great turning point in the history of Indian Economics? Did India learn anything from the national black out in 2012? Why Private participation in Energy? Is Private more capable than Public in India?

India is in crisis. The World is also in crisis. A thorough insight is only possible through the understanding of ground realities in the field. Without assessing the right sufferer any hypothesis is incomplete.

Citizens are always accessible to anyone provided a well defined approach is made to reach them regularly.

Citizens can only change the course of the country. Nation's aim should be the only aim of citizens.

Service providers all over the world should cultivate the habit of after sales service. This is not being emphasized in the electricity services in India.

My hearty intension of pouring down valuable time to this project was to come out with a template as to how mappings can be made between parameters in electricity services to the attributes of satisfaction among the consumers.

What should be a right template? India should follow whom? Can we sustain the global competition in energy, power and economy?

I could have written more elaborately but time had been knocking my door to compile it as early as possible for its release to the readers. This presentation had to cover many specific and non-specific areas in particular hence it took more than a year to finally reach its present shape summarizing all the findings, recommendations, suggestions, observations derived from this analytical study.

With great trust and sweat it has been crafted and forged to meet the educational, industrial, managerial, functional and social needs of the energy and power sector.

"How an integrated solution can be worked out to resolve the power crisis in India?", probably is the prime hypothesis attempted by the author stands right in the perspective of emerging energy models in India after the initiation of economic and electricity reforms in the last two decades.

The existing depth covered by the author is adequate for any beginner to understand the causes, reasons, parameters, issues and concerns of the energy and power sector in India. I am of the faithful opinion that this commentary shall certainly enrich your ability to analyze the issues of the energy sector.

Trend Analysis is the tool of the consultants like Morgan Stanley, Credit Suisse, Goldman Sachs, KPMG, and so on to advise on partnership in the power industry, acquisitions, divestitures and mergers of power companies & assets.

Analysis of equity/debt offerings, private equity, venture capital, partnership transactions and joint ventures is now becoming part and parcel of the emerging energy mix. Very next moment you do not know who is the Owner and Promoter of the Power Utility.

Mergers & Acquisitions may not be a right perspective if it is changing series of ownerships in short intervals of time. Though this is predominant in the private sector it is not an encouraging trend for the overall stability of the energy and power sector in India.

In practice there is hardly any control mechanism seen in India in the energy and power sector. In this fragile environment how to interpret Business Propensity Indicator (BPI)? To what extent selling and buying of power utilities for immediate turnaround can be tolerated without real results in the power sector.

I believe every conscious reader more or less is now and then pouring down his valuable time in reading the reports of newspapers, documentaries on television channels, magazines, annual reports, articles on energy security to update themselves on the issues like tariff hike, subsidy, incentives, cess, penalties, rewards, promotions grievances, suggestions, recommendations, policy initiatives, closures of thermal plants, concerns of environment & pollution, deregulation, de-licensing, reforms & restructuring, additional capacity envisaged, renewable is future power, storage discoveries, smart grid implementations, solar power campaigns, and many more political interventions and governments shortcomings related to energy crisis all over the world.

In continuation to the spirit of awareness in understanding the overall supply chain mechanism of energy in India this book will find its place a representation of an Indian Case Study for having an insight into the interfacing issues among the emerging prospective stakeholders in the energy sector.

Does liberalization means away from rationalization? Why there is no clear cut clarity in the fundamental principles of energy and power services in India?

Post reforms and restructuring has only marginally left its traces in revamping the sector. The experiments of liberalization are more bitter than the pains of imperialism.

What nationalization has to do with public or private? Are Public & Private, both not national issues?

Centre Vs State, though power is a concurrent responsibility, execution is largely state's responsibility. It is very much visible on understanding the analysis that the transmission sector is stuck in the concurrent centre state relationship.

State Transmission Utility (STU) ensures intra-state transmission. Central Transmission Utility (CTU) is responsible for the wheeling of power generated by the central generating units and inter-state independent power producers (IPPs).

Around 150 transmission projects are delayed due to developers inability to acquire land and timely clearances.

Why the share of private is not increasing in transmission?

Can Direct Benefit Transfer (DBT) be a success story? Where is the transparency in policy? A large section of subsidized customers are unaware of the support provided by the Government of India.

What should be an optimal subsidy mechanism? Any subsidy mechanism typically has inherent risk.

With almost 469 GW of power generation capacity expected by the end of 13th Central Plan, the Central Electricity Authority (CEA) has estimated a need for almost 1,26,650 MW of inter-regional transmission capacity during the same period.

Power Generation Vs Power Evacuation, is another area on critical path in widening the supply and demand gap. Many commissioned power plants are not operating because of power evacuation infrastructure. The status of evacuation network is unappreciable from the facts derived from the analysis of the power sector.

Power evacuation in India today poses a bigger challenge than power generation. The investment in transmission is not even one fourth of the total in power generation sector. If it was taken care of earlier than this grim situation would not have occurred today.

The Government of India is expected to flood this area with huge investments this year. There are many power transmission schemes worth Rs 1,00,000 crore notified for execution. The question is who will burn their fingers with uncertain policies of the power sector in India.

A 20 year plan shall require an investment outlay of Rs 2,60,000 crore. CEA has identified a need for almost 1,30,000 MW of inter-regional transmission capacity during the 13th Five Year Plan period.

Though the journey of electricity in India is more than 100 years it has not been running on rightly defined tracks of exact destination.

Case studies are reflections of realities to improve decision making skills and a learning process towards betterment in optimizing resources, utilization and efficiency in performance of the sector.

With this support I submit my sample model based on analytical approach to my readers for enriching their knowhow on the energy crisis in India.

With this trust, once the readers are through with this book I am sure you will be motivated and inspired to further probe into the intricacies of the energy sector. Are the hearings between government and citizens transparent in India? Are we not making electricity services a merchandizing business?

What I am trying to emphasize is that every citizen can economically make a difference to the energy crisis in India? It is no challenge to make the learned aware and take control of the situation. Real challenge is to organize the unorganized. Real competition is to not let the difficulties become impossibilities.

It is real challenge to man the team of unlearned in the energy sector. In this context the failure of state run energy utilities in India should not surprise anybody.

Why India is not doing good in the service sector? And electricity services is not at all an exception. Is it really necessary to link tariff with project cost of the power plant? It appears recovery of capital invested is the main objective rather than the service of the citizen.

Indian Energy Sector has been passively hearing the consumers for long. The loss was equally shared by the centre and state.

Did the global investors shared the risk and pain? Somehow the policies are profit oriented but not service motivated.

Profit Vs Service, an endless battle.

Policy Vs Reality, again an endless struggle.

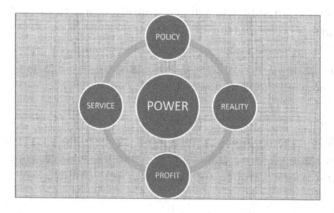

It is my earnest dream that every citizen who is a consumer and is being perceived as customer by the energy sector should be in a position to read the situation and do his best in contributing to reenergizing India. Every citizen should have that bit of patriotic principle to uplift India.

Action by every citizen is needed to drive this campaign of "Energy Crisis in India" for bringing in overall improvement in the country.

It is a national concern, a national issue, a national opportunity, a national challenge for all of us. Let us join with passion, zeal, determination, sincerity, enthusiasm, awareness, patriotism, to alleviate this crisis forever.

We have to correlate as to what extent the voices of consumers at the field matches with the gaps in the Acts of the electricity services in India.

The prime purpose for which this field research through survey was undertaken is to bring out the basic truths about the supply chain of energy and power in India.

And to be sincerely true to my efforts and commitments many such important findings have been surfaced here in the form of suggestions and recommendations from the consumers to transform the energy sector.

I am very much hopeful that the policy makers, regulators, legislators, implementers, administrators, as well as promoters, developers and generators will very much benefit by the comparative analysis and the views of the respondents from different segments of electricity consumers.

Will the Energy Sector in India ever recover the cost of capital invested and production of power?

Service and satisfaction should be the effective limbs for the ongoing growth and development of the energy and power sector. The philosophy of give and take needs to be honoured by all the stakeholders of the system. There are only few professionals with the knowhow of the entire system.

My submission of this researched literature is for all who are willing to understand the major areas of working, planning, serving, monitoring, marketing, consuming, selling, conserving, controlling and so on of the Indian Energy Sector.

You may by now have picked up the difficulties in designing such an effective energy model.

I have intentionally focused on electricity generation and end users of power.

Every home is an energy centre. Say if India has all the rooftops equipped with solar power generating stations, then every house in India is going to be a electricity generating, transmitting, distributing and supplying unit. Thus another transition in energy sector is leading to a future where consumer is also going to be the power generator.

The Indian Government is promoting consumers to become power developers. Will these power developers sustain the challenges which this new energy model is likely to bring in the energy sector? Does the existing solar power policy mean to make the other fuels redundant?

India is not only having a gloomy story to tell about the energy crisis. The whole world is passing through this opportunities and challenges. Why not we take up the responsibility to transform it into a glowing picture?

India in the last two decades has always been intermittently booming and shinning. Despite having a foreign policy on energy the foreign aids and alms were not constructively aligned in the sector.

Are we judiciously looking into such critical issues of the sector? Are we prepared for the emerging opportunities and challenges?

An insight into this report which you are anxiously waiting to read is certainly going to wider your vision and wisdom on energy issues in India.

I am hopefully considering that once your awareness improves, it automatically incites you to fight the challenges. Citizens should add value to growth and development.

With great belief and hope I submit this book, "Energy Crisis in India" as a valued referential documentary on the power issues in India. The summary are the voices of the citizens of India. I can say without hesitation that it shall be instrumental in bringing in improvement in the ailing sector.

During fighting the challenges, you definitely come across creating so many possible opportunities. Thus every stakeholder is swimming to reach the shore of energy security. All that is happening with indefinite permutations and combinations is to bring in betterment in the life cycle of energy management in India.

I appeal to my potential readers to rise to the occasion and let us contribute in alleviating energy crisis in India.

It is only possible to achieve the success in energy transition in India, when the entire nation is united for one vision, one mission, one objective, one goal, one aim, one responsibility, one cause and above all one attitude.

The Energy Transition in India can be very well understood by going through this commentary which has picked up painful confessions of the citizens of India related to energy services.

Education by imposing penalty to recover may not be always in the true spirit of the relationship between service utilities and the consumer.

Why the consumer defaults? A thorough analysis on this critical dimension is to be done in all the segments of consumers.

Why the service providers delay prompt services? Overall maintenance of the Indian Power System is another lacuna in the poor efficiency of the system.

Policies on renovation & modernization may not help if attitude of delivery is not being cultivated.

A matter of coincidence had befallen its grace on this Indian case study.

I begin with the fact that the period of research and study on the subject being analyzed started way back in the end of 2005 year which was just witnessing the implementation of the newly enacted Electricity Act 2003. The implementation was at its innocence at the very nascent stage. As the years rolled by it became very vibrant during the period 2007 to 2010.

My readers may not be surprised to note that by the time it reached 2012 to give "Power to all by 2012" as per the government's vision the energy as well as the power sector started swings of unattainable equilibrium.

Today we are hearing the agitations and anti people campaign for holding the amendments in the proposed Electricity Act (2014). Is this being done to change the beneficiary in the energy sector? A series of merry go round policies, strategies, reforms, restructuring and amendments are helpless in eliminating the energy crisis in India.

I have spent many years in research in the Power Sector. I have worked with people from the bottom of the pyramid in the energy sector. I am fortunate to be part of the various project teams which executed valuable projects in Oil & Gas sector, refinery, petrochemicals, city gas distribution, CNG stations, LPG, cross country pipeline projects, combined gas cycle plants, thermal power plants and projects in renewable.

I sincerely felt that the field survey undertaken to evaluate the energy crisis in India must be shared with the citizens of India to make them aware of the complexity involved in the entire cycle of electricity generation to consumption.

The role of the power consultants, energy researchers, evaluators, quantity surveyors, estimators, technology specialists, professionals, financial analysts, are increasing day by day. It is becoming difficult to select the type of energy model in India.

Energy Mix, Power Mix, Market Mix, Customer Mix, Service Provider Mix, Bankers Mix, Investors Mix, Regulators Mix, Promoters Mix, Project Developers Mix, Technology Mix, Collaborators Mix, are all emerging with new dimensions to the dynamics of reenergizing India.

Mixing Vs Fixing, is causing revisions, amendments, rectifications, corrections, overhauling the entire system again and again. This is another area bringing in instability in the power supply chain in India.

Competition because of deregulation, liberalization, privatization, globalization, corporatization is opening up new ideologies, philosophies, strategies, and ways to perform business and services.

Just by developing a habit of switching off lights, fans, AC, heaters, HVAC, TV, mobile chargers, etc in every house India can save around 20 to 25 % of electrical energy annually which is unnecessarily consumed without purpose.

New Connection, Metering, Billing and Collection of revenue is always a green area for criticism in electricity services in India.

Everyone should agree with the limitations this type of analytical field study accompanies with it. However it has its importance to establish an initial meaningful benchmark. Every question is an important issue of the sector.

I had nearly drafted out more than five hundred questions including critical and non-critical issues of the energy and power sector prior to the one you are reading today. Disliking the constrains I had no other way but to shorten the questionnaires for the respondents. However, I had introspected more than hundred times the content of the study so that in totality nothing is missed out as things resemble in the sector actually.

And you will see that the voices of the respondents discussed here are of paramount importance to the entire approach of the study presented for the benefit of all.

I am sure this case study will bring valuable inputs to all the concerned fraternities who wish to pursue similar research in formulating, evaluating and implementing optimal energy models.

"Energy Crisis in India", An Analytical Approach, Indian Case Study is an attempt in designing an optimal energy model for India.

Power Management in India has just taken off. This type of pure field research supplements the skills of power professionals. Indian Human Capital Management in Energy & Power is to become at par with global potential.

How to remove the grievances of customers permanently? Let us know from the hearts of the citizens what they are experiencing about the emerging electricity services in India. Are the power utilities dominating the consumers? To get a feel of these queries and opinions more and more field study is being recommended by me to the ones who really wish to reenergize the Indian Energy Sector.

Bring in awareness in the masses. Touch the hearts of common man. Unless the citizens are educated no policy on energy conservation, renewable implementation, environmental protection, heat recovery, smart cities is going to bring in the intended energy transition India is willing to set.

Through this narration I have tried to reproduce the views, opinions, comments, suggestions, ideas, findings, recommendations, philosophies, perceptions, sufferings, satisfactions, including critics, wisdom and analysis of the citizens of India from various segments of society.

It includes people from different services, organizations, self-employed, commercial businesses, small scale industries, heavy industries, governments both at state and centre, industrialists, residents, domestic consumers, academicians, reformers, etc and so on.

This book through the analytical approach has scientifically probed into the supply chain of energy in India. I have reviewed thousands of literature pertaining to the subject and browsed thousands of websites only for the theoretical thirst before I could virtually map the gap by actually quenching it through interrogating the sector. Series of pilot tests were conducted in many parts of India.

I understand that it is not only India troubled with the turbulence in the energy sector. The World nations developed or under development are having transition in their energy sector. It is matter of intensity only. Less or more every country is striving for self-sufficiency in energy security.

I am thankful to all associated with me for their valuable guidance and mentorship. My inclination towards finding the reality against policy perhaps could not stop me from reaching to all the stakeholders of the energy sector.

There are many issues pertaining to technology, administration, regulation, management and implementation everywhere in the country. Though our standards are not at par with global benchmark but we are not inferior too. Had India benefited from certainty in energy and power policy then today we would have been in the rankings of developed nations.

I believe that intellect is not to defend the default policies. A good wisdom is to correct it if it is not giving the intended results well within the time of recovery. Not wait till the catastrophic disaster has damaged the possibility of reconciliation totally. This requires a regular measuring mechanism to know whether the sector is performing above or below the average desired set parameters value or rating.

Unless the trend is known when is the alarm bell going to ring. Tough but not impossible to devise such standards if India wishes to compete in the race of globalization. Many MNCs' and TNCs' have beaten the performance levels of indigenous organizations in India. How are they excelling in Indian land of complexities? How are they performing in India's political environment?

Only adopting a mask of Global Culture is deterrent to the whole process of Mixed Economy. Only for pooling foreign resources India should not open markets keeping in view the potentials of national policies.

Why national policies are backed up with global commitments? Why Global Policies are backed up with national commitments? When both are exclusively considered while framing the National and Global policies in any country?

I always took things in the positive perception towards resolving the energy crisis as any department, organization, consultant or government would do. I had been throwing questions to the citizens to arrive at a betterment of the findings. As you all will agree that there is no end to perfection, it is here I thought to study a limited area which almost covers the hypotheses India wants to test in the energy sector.

Today, every home needs an energy manager irrespective of literacy and illetaracy in the world. In India the role of energy manager is becoming essential day by day. All houses are energy consumption centres. These are cost centres which requires minimization and continual controls for optimal utilization.

I could hardly find any such study which was questioning the energy utilities, policy makers, regulators, financers, promoters, consultants, technocrats, businessmen, contractors, developers, operators, logistics providers, investors, suppliers, service providers, collaborators, citizens, consumers, government, generators, distributors, administrators, legislation, customs, taxation, planning department, and other stakeholders of energy sector.

It is a mammoth task to include all under one study to understand the entire linkage of operating India's Energy System.

Meeting people is a great experience. Reaching their hearts to know the facts about a situation brings more interaction to learn and share the causes and solutions of the issues being attempted to be resolved.

What are the major fuels to produce electricity in India? And till when it can be done? Is our reserves and resources sufficient? Have we explored all possibilities?

Why did the public private partnership (PPP) model of infrastructure, energy and power development failed in India?

Do you think the existing framework of sharing risks between project developer and the government is not working at all? What should be the optimal risk sharing mechanism?

When will the power deficit in India dip to an all time low? Why bankrupt State Electricity Boards are shunning supply to consumers? There are studies working to create a new model which combines the best of solar power, wind power, tidal energy, bio-energy, geothermal energy, etc.

What is the success story of the ambitious LED bulb scheme in India? When will the highest ever addition in electricity generation capacity in one year touch 25,000 MW?

Renewable is not even 1% of the total installed capacity of 270 GW in India. Will energy storage by batteries make any difference in the overall savings? Why India is experiencing energy shortfalls? It is great challenge for us to reenergize it. Is it because of under utilization of our resources? Or. Is it due to poor performance of our power systems?

How to fight the current power crisis? Will the storage devices stabilize the grid? Is India thinking on Integration of Renewable Energy? The world has to work on introducing renewable energy storage solution.

Can solar power increase the self-sufficiency of commercial businesses in India? Will energy costs become predictable?

How to solve power crisis in India? Can all the wishes of consumers become the fundamental rights of citizens?

I like to share a very basic old wisdom which holds good in any situation and at any point of time. The mantra is, "A problem well defined is half solved." Despite that the secret is disclosed to all the crisis continues to prevail for years together.

I fear that the future is going to be more challenging in respect to crisis management in the energy sector than today.

India is unable to identify the crux of the crisis. Unless the area is identified the right diagnosis cannot be done to the underperforming system.

I unhappily put forward to say that, bad financial health, bad politics, bad policies, bad customer services, bad power supply, bad maintenance, bad performance, bad utilization are all disintegrating the efforts of reviving and reenergizing the ailing sector.

There are equally people like you and me who are worried with the poor trends in the sector. In fact the true sense of penning down this commentary with complexities, confrontations, criticisms, apprehensions, debates, narrations, speeches, discourses, from the field is to understand the vastness of the subject pertaining to the sector.

I am speaking on the challenges of an increasingly electrified world. Will electricity be the future life line only? Is it necessary to retire ongoing power plants immediately because of the de-carbonization movement?

War between energy and environment is rising day by day. Why India is still not able to establish well functioning electricity markets?

How many times a single act needs amendment after enactment? If the interpretations, meanings, purpose were not clear then why it was tabled and bill was declared fit for bringing in reforms.

A Bill needs the minimum attention for considering the feasibility of clauses in reality when they are actually implemented. And Bills related to the energy services requires a pilot test at any level either state or centre in addition to the constitutional guidelines of presentation, acceptance and enactment.

It is going to be a mystery in anticipating the number of amendments which will keep following in the electricity sector.

Will it bring relief to this category of retail consumers? Now the services are being split with respect to time of the day. Presently, this type of peak and non-peak hour tariff is only applicable for industrial users.

Union government at present is facing so many challenges to approve the proposed amendments in the Power Tariff Policy.

Will this help in flattening the peak and implementing various energy conservation measures?

I feel deeply grateful to say that, "Energy Crisis in India", An Analytical Approach, is also a brief intellectual summary on shared thoughts on India's Power Sector by citizens of India who are also the consumer of power.

I am thankful to all the respondents who have taken pain to understand the critical issues and given their valuable inputs to further enrich the field study with their findings, suggestions, recommendations and opinions.

I will always remain indebted to each one of you. Without your unconditional contribution this commentary would not have reached the fortunate readers.

I wish to place on record that the help received by all in bringing it to society will surely improve the citizen's literacy on India's Power System.

This will no doubt be a indelible reference energy model for understanding the overall mechanism of the energy system in India.

A good and truthful finding from this book that, "Electricity should not be used in unlawful manner by the citizen of India", is a lesson to all of us.

The world has experienced two great **Green and Industrial revolutions** which have transformed the thought process of human beings inspiring them to further explore their abilities and improve the standards of livings beyond the basic needs for survival. Today, in some parts of the world Earth Hour and Earth Day are being celebrated by saving energy, an initiation towards Energy Revolution.

Global Energy Crisis is emerging to be the common prime agenda for discussion on National and International levels.

Environment Vs Economy, a balance is essential. Environmental issues become secondary when the survival is at stake. There are issues of energy return on energy investment (EROI), CARBON TAX, problems of green house gas, formation of ozone (smog), toxic volatile organic compounds, and emissions of carbon dioxide, sulphur dioxide, global warning, air pollution, acid rain, nuclear safety, radioactive contamination and waste heat disposals. In addition to above storage and transportation of energy has been always a major constraint influencing the evolution of distribution technology. All these factors are important in selecting the type of energy generation and distribution.

Energy has been universally recognized as one of the most important inputs for economic growth and human development. There is a strong two-way relationship between economic development and energy consumption.

On one hand, growth of an economy, with its global competitiveness, hinges on the availability of cost-effective and environmentally benign energy sources, and on the other hand, the level of economic development has been observed to be reliant on the energy demand. Energy Intensity is an indicator to show how efficiently energy is used in the economy.

The energy intensity of India is over twice that of the matured economies, which are represented by the OECD (Organization of Economic Co-operation and Development) member countries. India's energy intensity is also much higher than the emerging economies, the Asian countries, which include the ASEAN member countries as well as China.

However, since 1999, India's energy intensity has been decreasing and is expected to continue to decrease. The indicator of energy–GDP (gross domestic product) elasticity, that is, the ratio of growth rate of energy to the growth rate GDP, captures both the structure of the economy as well as the efficiency. The energy–GDP elasticity during 1953–2001 has been above unity.

However, the elasticity for primary commercial energy consumption for 1991–2000 was less than unity. This could be attributed to several factors, some of them being demographic shifts from rural to urban areas, structural economic changes towards lesser energy industry, impressive growth of services, improvement in efficiency of energy use, and inter-fuel substitution. The energy sector in India has been receiving high priority in the planning process. The total outlay on energy in the Tenth Five-year Plan was projected to be 4.03 trillion rupees, which is 26.7% of the total outlay which is an increase of 84.2% over the Ninth Five-year Plan in terms of the total plan outlay on energy sector.

The Government of India in the mid-term review of the Tenth Plan recognized the fact that under-performance of the energy sector can be a major constraint in delivering a growth rate of 8% GDP during the plan period. It had, therefore, called for acceleration of the reforms process and adoption of an integrated energy policy.

What do you understand by Integrated Energy Policy? Will it bring energy independence to India?

In the recent years, the government has rightly recognized the energy security concerns of the nation and more importance is being placed on energy independence. In 2005, India emphasized that energy independence has to be the nation's first and highest priority, and India must be determined to achieve this within the next 25 years.

Energy and Economy are wheels of the nation. A proper alignment and balance is must for smooth movement. The rate of growth is mutually dependent on critical factors in formulating national policies. Economy of any Nation today cannot stand and prosper without this strong backbone. The West has been ahead in development of the Energy Sector because of the proper planning and utilization of available resources.

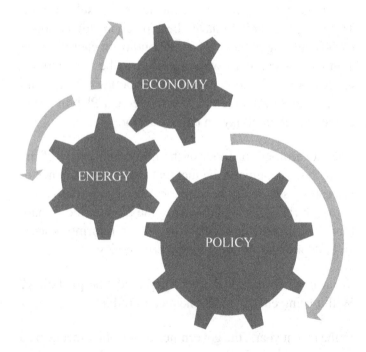

Policy drives both energy and economy of any country. Where do India stands in Energy Policy at National and Global levels? Is Indian Policy on Energy Trade at

International level performing to the expectations of the citizens?

South Asian Nations have a possibility for Energy Trade. India is importing LNG as it is experiencing shortage of indigenous gas. Bangladesh has substantial reserves and additional undiscovered reserves which would last for nearly 50 years even at a growth rate of 6%.

Will synergy of nations come out with optimal energy models feasibility and reliability?

Nepal and Bhutan have huge potential of hydro resources and exporting electricity to India may not be a wrong idea leading to earning of foreign exchange relieving us from the power crisis. The technology is changing exponentially. It has its own limitations.

India is the sixth largest consumer of energy in the world. The consumption rate was likely to be doubled by 2012. The Economic Reforms, 1991 was outcome of the Global pressure on Indian Economy. The nation would have collapsed and survival was a threat. India was fortunate to escape the misery but the rapid economic activities after liberalization appears again to be at stake considering the exponentially rising demand for energy.

Can the Indian Economy grow at a steady rate of 9-10%? The answer to it is only with Indian Power Sector. With enactment of the historic Electricity Act-2003 and series of reforms and restructuring in the sector, will it sustain the electricity rate of growth to support the GDP? The challenges of the future are in making the emerging sector viable and sustainable.

Load shedding is the rule of the day in India. How to create a Sustainable Energy Sector? India had been depending on technology from developed Nations till it started to be self-reliant. A good Integrated Power System is essential to produce and supply electricity economically. The overall development is only possible with effective operation of the new Power Mix.

Considering the size of its economy, India is poorly endowed with energy resources. It has only modest reserves of oil and gas which will only last for a few decades unless major oil or gas deposits are discovered.

India has, however, coal resources that are sufficiently large to meet the bulk of its energy needs for the next 250 years. To meet part of its energy needs through imports would require large investments in transport infrastructure. Since these investments are unlikely to materialize over the short and medium term, indigenous coal will remain the least cost source of energy for most uses.

Currently, more than two-thirds of India's energy needs are met by coal in one form or another. About 70% of India's coal production is converted into electric power, the remaining 30% is used for a large number of industrial purposes. About 70% of India's coal comes from large, highly mechanized opencast operations. These operations require little labor, can be implemented quickly and involve considerably lower production costs than underground mines. Productivity in opencast mines is generally high.

As a result of a budget crisis in 1991, the Government began to phase out its financial support to Coal India

Ltd. Faced with a serious financial crisis, Coal India's management decided to restructure the company's operations by phasing out loss-making mines, reducing surplus labor and tightening its financial management.

In the short term, Coal India's main objective is to remain financially viable while implementing its investment program without further budgetary support. In 1992, the company requested the Bank's assistance in these efforts. Coal India and the Bank agreed that the most effective way to assist Coal India would be for the Bank to contribute to the drafting of a reform program for the coal industry and to finance a time-slice of Coal India's investments (Coal Sector Rehabilitation Project).

Resources Vs Consumption, is with opportunities and challenges to fulfill the gaps between energy supply and demand.

Why India's energy consumption is lagging behind the World average energy consumption? Energy markets should have combined crisis recovery and strong industry dynamism. Energy consumption in the world is soaring day by day.

Is there any difference between industrialized countries and agriculture based economy nations? Oil, gas, coal, and electricity markets are operating everywhere in the world.

"Waste to Energy", conversion is being considered across the world. According to the Ministry of Urban Development, urban India alone generates around 70 million tones of municipal solid waste each year.

Wastes worth more than the value of gold are being simple dumped in land and water. In India landfills account for an overwhelming 95% of garbage disposal.

Growth of Biomass Power installed capacity can certainly become a boon to rural electrification. Why waste to energy conversion is not given exemptions on par with other renewable?

"Cash Vs Trash", it is likely going to be the new mandate in the future. It can have valued weight age to be one of the main agendas of the party contesting the political elections in times to come.

Who would not like to create Cash from Trash? That is what waste to energy conversion can bring. Though this area has mammoth potential yet it is unexplored.

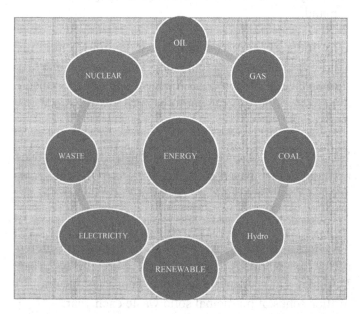

What is the best Renewable Mix for India?

China and India, have shown no signs of slowing down in demand for all forms of energy. Energy consumption decreases with financial weakness, recession and economic crisis.

China became the world's largest energy consumer in 2009. Oil remained the largest energy source (33%) despite the fact that its share has been decreasing over time. Coal posted a growing role in the world's energy consumption: in 2009, it accounted for 27% of the total.

Coal fueled the industrial revolution in the 18th and 19th century. Oil became the next leader. With the advent of the automobile, airplanes and the spreading use of electricity, oil became the dominant fuel during the twentieth century. The growth of oil as the largest fossil fuel was further enabled by steadily dropping prices from 1920 until 1973.

After the oil shocks of 1973 and 1979, during which the price of oil increased from 5 to 45 US dollars per barrel, there was a shift away from oil.

Coal and nuclear became the fuels of choice for electricity generation and conservation measures increased energy efficiency.

Japan, who bore the brunt of the oil shocks, made spectacular improvements and now has the highest energy efficiency in the world.

1991, has set the benchmark for reforms in India and initiated the change. Since then we have been changing. But at what cost, price and time.

Indian Economy is still stumbling. The tunes of energy security is unpleasant in hearing. The legacy of uncertainty is not leaving the arena of energy crisis in India.

Why everybody is continuously voicing for change? Keep changing is the mantra of the sector. Think the damage it will do without a proper vision.

Learned energy economists are required to turn around the sector with concrete roadmap for future. The issue of energy crisis is critical and very sensitive. It cannot be everybody's cup of tea.

1991, 2003, 2012 years are historic milestone years in the history of India's Energy Sector. People who have witnessed these periods can never erase it from their memories as citizens of India.

Will The Electricity Act-2003, Amendment Bill (2014) is going to make a fresh beginning in2015 year?

After the unexpected failure of "Power to All by 2012", the question is what will happen in 2017, 2022, 2025, 2032? As the focus is shifting towards renewable, will solar power become the dominant energy.

It is nearly 25 years the Economic Reforms in India were very rigorously initiated through the LPG Policy but all to the ultimate dismay. Why our GDP did not reach 10%

growth rate? Before this reform also we were sailing in the limits of 4 to 6%.

Is it not a matter of disappointment to India? The saddest part of the story is why our initiatives are derailing before reaching the desired destinations. India is remaining behind in its goals.

Reenergizing India is a big challenge today. Who will do it? How to do it? When it will be done? India's target is to achieve 100 GW of grid-connected solar power capacity by 2022.

Power and Public Protests are not surprising debates in India. Every energy project has to have hundreds and thousands of hearings before the concept becomes a reality. Politics, self interests and egos are permanent hindrances in timely completion of even fast track projects monitored by the PMO in India.

Land acquisition is never completed without conflicts. You may not be surprised to know that there are instances and cases where the designed operational life of the power plant is nearing completion but the land losers grievances have not been resolved and is being pursued by the next generation.

Railway linkages failure and untimely delivery of rakes have made many thermal power plants operate at under rated capacity. The statistics of India shows very good shinning figures of total installed capacity but in reality the country is performing at 60 to 70% of the installed capacity.

Thus I would like my readers to start from here. This type of categorized under rated performance because of poor utilization factor and logistics constrains creates very severe gaps at the beginning only.

In addition many power plants could not operate at full capacity because of inadequate evacuation capacity of power and linkages to transmission and distribution networks. The problem started with policy which never opened the transmission and distribution sector till recent past.

Revenue suffered because of poor metering, billing and collection. Penalties are only in theory. The population of unregistered consumers is increasing day by day. Unauthorized networks operate in retail supply chain of energy. An energy market without legislation and regulation is a stream sucking out the sector mercilessly despite progressive reforms, restructuring and amendments happening now and then.

How far these federations, communities, committees, societies, groups, associations can make their way in the real sense in the policy making of energy in India?

All India Power Engineers Federation (AIPEF) has decided to oppose the amendments proposed in Electricity (Amendment) bill 2014 which has been approved by union cabinet.

To quote from the daily news, AIPEF has claimed that amending the Electricity Act 2003 which governs power sector structure and policy, is a crucial exercise with far reaching long term implications.

It is a useful opportunity to change the course of the policy direction to address critical issues faced by the sector. Therefore while undertaking such a process it becomes extremely important to assess the immediate as well as long term challenges before the sector which cannot be completed without knowing the views of power engineers.

Let us look at the major seven concerns regarding proposed Electricity (Amendment) Bill 2014. First is translating "Power to all" objective into implementable action plan which ensures access to quality affordable supply for poor and newly electrified households.

Second is mitigating the possibility of cherry picking of high paying consumers by new supply licensees.

Third is protecting interests of small consumers by ensuring that they alone do not bear the burden arising out of these changes and are not subject to sudden tariff shocks.

Fourth is the incumbent supply licensee being vested with universal supply obligation will become the default supplier for agriculture and rural low tension consumers. As such it will be financially impacted most on account of migration of high paying consumers to new supply licensees and open access.

Fifth is Promoting energy efficiency along with renewable energy. Sixth is ensuring institutional autonomy of regulatory commissions. Seventh is avoiding needless complexity and thus reducing scope for misinterpretation and unnecessary litigation.

This is the most recent update to share with public of India. Will the series of amendments bring any appreciable and justifiable changes in the electricity sector?

I feel more and more innovative methods are required for improving customer amenities. India has to balance theoretical vigor with intensive field research in remote villages, hamlets, villages, small towns, small cities, and so on keeping in view the broad base of consumers.

The supply side issues can be untangled only by augmenting coal supply and boosting transmission and evacuation of power linkages network rapidly.

Nuclear Energy and Atomic Energy are yet blocked into the sensitivity aspects, security angle and budget concerns in India.

Agitated residents frequently protest against the ongoing power cuts. The situation is more pathetic in summer in India.

Power demand soars up to maximum at this time in the year. Consumers face power outages for hours together.

The levy of Cess Vs grant of Incentives is battling to decorate the new models of energy in India.

Consumers are being burdened. What should be the optimal generating mix? Private sector power plants are run on the sole motive of profit which is at the cost of the consumer.

Electricity Distribution System works with wider base of consumers and caters to various categories of customers.

The power distribution system is basically the retail distribution of power to streets, households, offices, establishments, shops, schools, markets, government offices, public places, and so on. There are more number of electric cables than number of streets, lanes, sub-lanes in any city and town. Maintenance is one of the major areas which very badly affects the overall performance of the power system.

Emerging India's Power Sector challenges are demand for power is likely to soar from around 120 GW at present to 335 GW by 2017, will need huge investments of about US $ 600 Billion, pace of capacity addition must increase fivefold to tenfold, necessary to create 35GW per year capacity for power equipment manufacturing and supply chain, prepare and bid over 150 power project sites, train and develop 800,000 skilled and semiskilled workers, construct and commission power plants, develop national integrated transmission network and distribute electricity supply to all villages, free power to farmers, secure fuel supplies, accelerate captive mine development and ready infrastructure for coal imports, promote renewable and alternate energy, conserve and save energy, reduce electricity consumption by demand side management, develop power markets, manage inherent risks and so on many in the chain and finally strengthen governance for overall reforms and development of the ailing power sector.

SECTION-A

PART I

NATIONALIZATION VS GLOBALIZATION

CHAPTER I

REENERGIZE INDIA'S ENERGY

Supply Vs Demand

India still lives with lanterns though electricity generation started at par with New York and London in 1882. Load shedding is the rule of the day despite the government's recent mandate of "Power to All by 2012".

Even after 100 years of service 100% demand of power could not be supplied. The rate of growth of the energy sector is far behind the asking rate.

More than 300 million people are still left without access to electricity. In supplying power to rural areas distribution company loses almost Rs 3-Rs4 per unit of sale. There are instances of intentional discriminating practices in administering load shedding. This may not be right strategy or policy in managing the shortcoming issues of the system.

I am trying to bring out an observation which probably opens our mind to understand the truth of energy, power, economy, infrastructure, GDP, inflation, food security, which keep struggling between the group interval from 5 to9 % in India.

When will all these go beyond the 10% mark forever? Will this dream of 10% turn into reality? The question is what really is holding us to consistently live in between 5 to 9% end limits. Are the increments and decrements getting neutralized?

Above is a subject of elaborate research in India. If you try to summarize with an overview of the entire process, in fact we are not at all performing. If population rise is a burden then on the other hand it is a resource to turnaround the GDP of India.

Youths are holding the nation. Old population might have done their best but as per economics they are redundant resources in the main stream of productivity.

My readers may be surprised to note that the total financial losses of distribution sector presently are around Rs 2,00,000 crore which is more than 2% of the country's GDP. Have you ever imagined what capacity addition India could have done with this huge investment?

Who is to be blamed for this huge drain? This is where we have to integrate our skills, knowhow, expertise, competencies, strengths, resources, reserves, potentials, capabilities, intellects, smartness, wisdom, learning, services, and so on to ultimately bring in the transformation and transition in the sector.

My concern to all is that there are several leaks, gaps, discontinuities, broken links, trying to help in draining of the useful resources in the entire system. Do not you feel that such performance calls for a periodic review of the implementation programs introduced by the reform Act

2003 in the electricity sector? Though at times periodic reviews were carried out but lacked sincere follow-ups and action plans for rectification and correction.

Suggestions and findings were just like the policies. Never got converted into rectifications and corrections. A policy initiated by one government is not at all a concern for the subsequent government in charge of the governance and performance.

I was in doubt only till the acceptance of the hypotheses by the large group of respondents as consumers of energy and customers of electricity.

The achievements in promoting and enabling competition are far below the expectations of citizens of India. The environment is filled with litigations and post-facto revisions.

Open access and distribution franchises models have not taken off and been mired in controversies.

There is need for strengthening institutional capacity and accountability mechanisms. Both justice and compensation have been denied to the consumers. The interest of the public could not be safeguarded with the reforms Act.

The recent shortages in coal and gas have resulted in uncertainty as well as increase in electricity prices.

Is not the ever increasing financial crisis a testimony to the poor performance by the power utilities in India? Can we purely blame the power utilities for the crisis? Can we purely blame the policy makers of the power sector?

Why capacity addition is not being backed up with land, capital, water, fuels and forests? Has the government ever realized that they were encouraging unwanted such excessive capacity addition without an integrated road map for the country?

If policies were worthy of winning why did it fail? All the above influences the energy sector.

What is being experienced? The energy sector is undergoing serious structural, legal and policy changes. Why the design of the legislation is not meeting the practical and realistic issues of the energy sector?

The citizens need not worry to know that there are many proposed changes which do not fall in public domain.

Will the proposed Electricity Act (2014) amendment provide more choice to consumers? Power can be purchased as a commodity. Will it have commercial retail outlets? Are we not again giving scope for decentralization of electricity services?

Can India control the future fragmentation of the sector? A new power market is emerging with choice of suppliers to a larger category of consumers.

The main objectives are carriage and content separation, rationalization of tariff determination, promotion of renewable energy, maintenance of grid security and functioning of regulatory commissions.

Is it not that the universal supply obligation concept is an initiation toward again nationalizing the electricity services?

One of the outcome of this analytical study on energy crisis is the different phases India's Electricity Services has witnessed and experienced during the cycle of 100 years of service to the nation.

Electricity Services In India

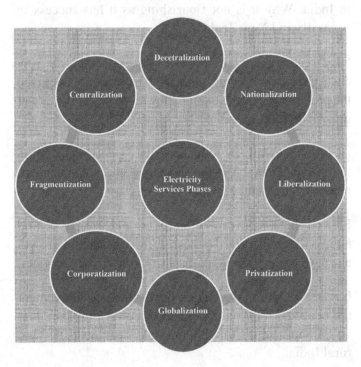

Population rise is a misnomer in the entire gamble. We are lacing in our basics of the system. I think the way fundamentals are built here requires an immediate correction. The process of rectification is to be expedited if India is to reenergized in short span of time.

Power holidays are supporting slow industrial economic growth. Free power to farmers is a distant dream battling between government and politics. Crippling irrigation system is dwindling down agricultural yields.

Is irrigation not the backbone of India's Economy? Till today the farming is not hundred per cent mechanized in India. Why it is not flourishing as it has success in Australia and New Zealand?

Food security is again a major concern seeing the way energy security is being addressed. Farmers are not given the professional status though they make up for the rate of growth directly or indirectly.

A nation healthy in food security is definitely going to have a firm base for development, advancement, modernization and growth.

Electrifying few metropolitan cities and leaving behind many villages deprived of basic infrastructure for growth and development speaks of disparity in electricity services.

Uncertain National policies have failed to implement the expected reforms. Independent power providers fear investment and are unwilling to take risk in electrifying rural India.

Rising population is undermining the minor attempts undertaken to transform the electricity services in underdeveloped regions of the country.

People below the poverty line are cursing their destiny. When will lantern to electric lamp become a reality? Solar lamps are replacing kerosene lanterns. Rural India is dwelling in the dusk.

The World is manifestation of energy in numerous forms. All the happenings is result of change of energy from one form to another.

Imagine life without energy? Humans have been struggling to discover the entire earth for easier and cheaper forms of energy. The rising population is invariably creating global energy demand. Are the nations prepared to sacrifice their share of the energy reserves?

Energy security is being sandwiched between the foreign policy and national policy. Global Policy and National Policy are the two facets of the same coin of energy crisis. Why national policy will 100% align with the Global Policy?

Air is abundant in nature. Thanks to mother Earth for sustaining the living organisms. No one ever might have explored and tried to reach the source of air. Probably the necessity has not arisen. But the way humans are polluting it this may one day again become scarce as other essential requirements for living. In near future man has to set up huge air purifying stations all over the world.

Water is another vital requirement sourced from the mother Earth's crust. The demographics have the water tables higher or lower from case to case, region to region governed by the profile of the land. The scarcity has forced us to convert sea water through the process of desalination to potable water. Many such sweet water plants have started breeding over the globe.

Today we are purchasing mineral water for drinking packaged in bottles. At last water has also been included in the list of commodity for trading. It is a commercial product now across the world. The next world war will be focused on the terrorism of water. Water crisis is going to be the bane for generations to invade this earth. Humans of the past somehow neglected to work on the mass balance of the water system in the world.

I put a sincere question to my readers and citizens of India, "Do India really require bottled mineral water? Or Are we victim of the Global Cultural Changes the world is experiencing today?

The world is speaking of Bio-Energy today. It was and is not uncommon in India the usage of cow-dung being utilized for cooking has been the prime energy since ages. A little bit of new –technology addition here and there to redefine the basic means of generating energy.

The quest for survival discovered the fossil fuels. Just prior to modernization the limited consumption was tending to shift aggressively towards alarming levels of demand. Fossil fuels are again a boon to the regional places where it is available. This is true in the case of crude oil. Only establishing of refineries and petroleum plants will not enhance the capacity additions in energy.

The crux of the energy issues somehow are not being interfaced with the integrated ideology by the national planning in India. India has suffered very badly in the issue of natural gas exploration.

Coal and kerosene are the respective primary energy fuels for cooking and lighting in millions of villages in India even in the era of dynamic energy mix. The policy somehow is passive on the exact quota of unsubsidized supplies to below poverty line domestic consumers. How to monitor the spillage and daily manipulations taking place in the retail sector?

Let us look at India's huge population base. The regional disparities cannot be eliminated in a day. But this does not mean that new models will not be tested. The energy sector is the most vibrant and dynamic in nature.

When China is ahead why India cannot make it? China is building India's power plants. China has become a major player in supplying power equipments to India. Many of the recent power plants constructed during the period 2005 to 2015 are 70 to 80% having the supplies from China.

Is power equipments supply from China was India's Power Policy? Or The China's marketing strategy to take advantage of the shortage of power equipments in India? Finally China has been successful in creating permanent business units in India.

Any deviation in foreign policy or international trade will surely impact the overall economics of generating power in India. This is not new to the energy providers and consumers in India at all.

China is now a global energy player. China not only grabbed the Indian Electricity Market but has deprived India from creating a huge manufacturing hub for power equipments. This setback is supplemented with the loss of employment opportunity to many Indians. China has gained by the global policy philosophy.

China and India are the competitors in Asia. China's growth despite its rising population is a lesson to all the learned people of the world. China is effective in utilizing resources and capitalizing opportunities. However at the end both the nations are striving to meet their energy demands.

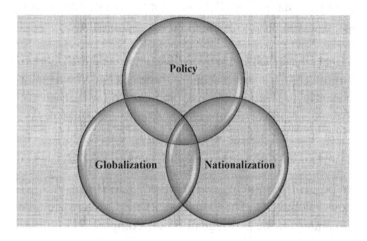

Can the nations demand be fulfilled only by globalization? Let us review the all India statistics for India supplying energy to the global markets. In fact the figures are as good as invisible in the exhaustive list of global contributors.

Only by becoming a member of the Global Summit on Energy, India cannot become free from the burden of energy crisis. What should be the optimal energy portfolio?

Is global competition for India within the overlapping spheres of Asia, America and Europe?

How to differentiate between Synergy and Competition? How to differentiate between Administration and Management? How to differentiate between collaboration and commercialization of services? The question of good governance and poor performance is prevalent everywhere in the world.

Will the policy in Asia work in America, Europe and Russia? The modernization of the nations is another factor for the perception of the policy. Sometimes the impacts of wrong policies are detrimental to the whole process of evolution and reformation. Who is responsible for the unbeneficial policies in the critical sector?

Just in the recent past India had a glimpse of unwanted black out through the country. Are our policies good enough to take the risk of unpredictability? How reliable is India's integrated energy system?

Criticism invariably opens new avenues. Hopefully it appears India is experiencing the same transition phase in energy. India is anxiously waiting for a success story in the energy sector.

How to win the crisis? Can crisis be eliminated forever? Or Nations have to survive by mitigation? No one wishes to kiss risk. If all the stakeholders in energy business are playing with safer strategies to protect themselves from being exposed to pros and cons of the emerging power market then who will give the service to the citizens of India?

Is deregulation a mechanism to protect the government from blames of failures? Is liberalization to shelve the responsibility of service? Exactly what the new policies flooding the energy sector meaning to common man?

Citizens are fighting out inflation day and night. Moreover the recent pain of progressive tariff hikes is adding to the chaos in society. A vast area of unmetered consumers always sucks the health of the sector.

I personally have a relevant observation that our statistics on quantum of energy injected, consumed, metered, billed, lost, stolen, spilled, unauthorized usage, doesn't give us the real figures to position ourselves accurately.

India is facing energy crisis as well as economic crisis. It does not mean that our pockets are empty but the alarm is that pocket is inadequate. Policy for self sufficiency is scarce in India. The people's real feedback is somehow not becoming the agenda points for formulating the effective frameworks in the country.

Voice of citizens is the voice of customers of energy. Without direct field investigations the realities are not making stream into the policy making. The awareness on the subject is another concern here in India. The protection of consumer rights should be redefined with orientation in valued customer based services.

Only not meeting peak power demand is not energy crisis. It should be visional with the global perspectives of energy.

Energy Utilities and Energy Consumers are the end providers and users respectively. The middle men are meddling the sector to their tune.

Are regulators really looking into implementing feasible energy models in India? The analytical approach should come into practice now. A thorough evaluation of any proposal should be examined sincerely before it is enforced by law.

More and more pilot tests in fields are required. A continual field survey and in-depth research should be part of the central planning in India. An exclusive monitoring cell should be set up across the country to prevent from derailment of the energy sector.

A political initiation should be comprehended scientifically and sincerely supported to translate into reality for the citizens of India. More and more energy economists are needed in the country rather than the journalists blowing out the shortcomings of misunderstandings creating rivalry in competition.

"Time is an essence of any mandate", somehow is not in the ethics of policy makers. Resolving issues after the total dissolution of opportunities is unjustifiable in the whole process of reformation of the energy sector.

Does Global Energy Crisis have any policy for the world? One thing is crystal clear that directly or indirectly more or less every nation is affected by the imports and exports of energy.

Countries with ports are advancing into the through puts of energy. Port is an essential infrastructure for the logistics of fuel. It improves the accessibility to fuel linkages. Good and reliable fuel linkages should be the prime area of focus for the policy makers.

My readers may not be surprised to note that the Energy Policy always spoke of enhancing capacity either by conventional generation or by renewable but never came out with any concrete policy on developing the manufacturing sector for power equipments.

The simple basic, "How to construct power projects without power equipments?" was not considered by the Indian Policy makers' right at the beginning of energy sector reforms. The gap still hampers the progress of power projects.

Untimely completion of projects and indefinite delay in commercial operation of power plants further widens the power supply and demand gap. Dishonoring the fuel supply agreements is widening the gaps in supply and demand of coal.

One remarkable point of focus is that Wind and Solar power have the major advantage of no cost in transporting the primary fuel. This renewable sector is blessed with zero logistic cost of primary energy. This is an area of research and development to make it a regular power replacing the generation by coal. Though the present rate of electricity by Solar PV has fallen it has miles to go.

Any new method of generating power is a point of experiment. How long India will experiment with new energy mix?

India's infrastructure is very good to promote manufacturing sector for the energy sector. All the equipment needs of the energy sector can be met by indigenous manufacturing. Lot was spoken in the political arena to just remain as policy.

Reality cannot be ascertained without in-depth insight into the India's Power System. The question is who will carry out this assignment.

Today energy is the fundamental right of any citizen in the world. A citizen without access to energy is living a compromised life. Every Nation is facing the Global Challenges of Energy. Energy has transformed itself to a commodity of international trade. Energy is struggling to survive in the global competition.

The gain of one nation is loss of another nation. Leveraging is the rule of the global energy markets. Surplus nations are dictating scarcity. The naturally enriched nations with abundance are the market leaders.

Are we not speaking of Global Development? Are we not brainstorming on Global Sustenance? Nations with the limited provisions are having nightmare to bridge the gap between supply and demand.

India is no exception to the Global Energy Crisis. Is there balance between exports and imports of energy?

The global prices of Oil have been controlling the global economy. At what rate the GDP should grow?

The rate of economic growth influences the statistics of demand and supply in energy. The policy on subsidy in energy sector never had the freedom from the political tangles of Indian system of governance.

No single party can be blamed for energy crisis in India. In a democratic setup though citizens voice their dissatisfaction issues keep floating between the banks of policy and reality. The same is also true in the energy sector. A nation with poor economy has worse challenges of providing fundamental amenities to the citizens. The citizen needs are to be justifiably addressed by the country.

Why the national policy is not having a unanimous vision? It is reflection of the citizens. The learned fraternities are falling behind in formulating and implementing national goals and objectives. The quality of human resources shouldering the responsibility needs to have new dimensions for improving the overall scenario.

Energy for food, shelter and health is the basic priority of any nation. Though the LPG fuel became the leader in cooking food yet there are appreciable percentage of Indian population banking on the conventional coal, wood and other natural sources of fire energy. There is wider scope in supply chain improvement to cater to the remotest of remote inhabitant places in India.

Parallel is the burden of national growth, development and sustenance. The major share is consumed by industrialization, modernization, transportation and infrastructure programs being implemented.

The electrification of the railways might have reduced the consumption of coal and diesel but this has equally generated a huge demand of power. The liberalized financing of vehicles by the bankers and the financial institutions have flooded the levels of demand in petrol and diesel exponentially surmounting the oil import demands.

Moreover the model of industrial diesel power in recent times has added to the appreciable unauthorized consumption of diesel. Even small diesel generator sets have become big market leaders. Where is the regulation in this area?

It is Power by diesel at what price? Has anyone thought of it? How much diesel is consumed in this unorganized and unauthorized alternate way of generating power? The Electricity Supply or Reform Acts has literally no say in it. There are several unidentifiable producers of power by this model in the country. They are having their own policy and regulation.

Irrigation is a big leak in the sector irreparable till date due to the unresolved subsidy liability being faced by the Indian policy makers. Who pays for the subsidy? Will the private sector do the funding as the State has been doing for decades together in India?

Indian farmers have remained poor still when the country boasts of giant NRI's commanding the Global Business in the world. The disparity of growth is going unaccountable.

This puts a question to the future of India's energy security in times to come ahead. The Indian Power Market has no reminiscences of the nationalization philosophy anymore. Welfare concept is being transformed into the professionalism in services. The orientation of the energy sector is being greased with the rate of return concept.

The evolution of the cyber cities has exponentially raised the demand of power. Is India really placed to create smart cities? Just by illuminating few cities we cannot claim to have accomplished our vision of development.

The IT sector in reality is more like the dormant account being widely managed by the younger generations with the visions of developed nations. Unaccountable electricity is being drained in information and communication sector in India. No doubt it is essential in building overall infrastructure of the country.

All this is happening under the banner of reforms and restructuring. But the question is at what cost? What risk?

Ultimately power is whose responsibility? All the states in India are not at par with the average national statistics of natural energy resources. The first point of energy crisis starts with this inequality among the states within the country. Similar is the scenario at a global level too looking into the comparative references while analyzing the root causes of energy crisis.

How to scientifically study this energy crisis in India? How to arrive at a conclusion related to the issues of power crisis in India? Who are the best respondents to these queries? Where to get the exactness of the gaps? Who can confess the reality of the energy crisis in India?

I too as a promising citizen of India have been anxiously waiting to explore the above queries. Prior to the assignment I had the awareness that this is only possible through a field analysis. That is to say, it is essential to bring out the comparisons between the views, opinions, perceptions, awareness, grievances, and satisfaction of the power utilities providing the services and the electricity consumers availing the services. By doing this the gaps between the power utilities and consumers can come to surface.

This book, "Energy Crisis in India", is a short narration of the battle field where the war of energy crisis is being fought between the Indian Power Utilities and Electricity Consumers. It is like the bow and arrow. The arrows are the issues being generated at the seat of the sector. The question is who is holding the bow?

It may not be a professional encyclopedia but is not less than a brief meaningful summary for any beginner willing to analyze the energy sector in India. This can be a platform to become productive from the day you have completed reading this thesis crafted with sincere dedication and thorough study on the subject.

My sole purpose for publishing this field survey is for the benefit of society. I always thought to own the responsibility to bring awareness about the energy crisis in India to the victimized citizens of this country struggling to light the lamps of modernization.

As a learned nation blame game should not be our cup of tea. I believe the states should come forward interestedly with perception of integration to resolve the issues affecting the core sector. I primarily feel our art of negotiation is not to converge and comprise.

One of my intricate findings of this voluminous case study is, that attitude overrules any system, contract, guidelines, documents, Acts, orders, judgments, stipulations, limits, memos, agreements, memorandums, articles, postulates, and so on.

We simply hang on to trivial issues to convert it into intolerable complexity. Is not painful to all of us?

Everyone wishes to win by argument rather than attitude. All stakeholders need to cultivate the attitude of business, society, service, economics, performance, governance, certainty, reliability, commitments, time frame, and so on.

Energy Crisis in India is not a subject of gossip but is a serious national issue of concern for all of us. Everyone can look into resolving it at their respective levels and potentials.

Politics should not play with the potentials, abilities, capabilities and initiatives of the energy sector.

The rules of the battle are governed by the uncertain policies, ineffective reforms, unproductive restructuring, emerging energy and power mix, the nascent power markets, the political duality, the unbundling of State Electricity Boards, improper functioning of the public enterprises, the inefficiency of the productivity management, the diagnostic perils of the electricity sector, instability of the government, the foreign policy, the impacts of international trade and economy, and so on, the list is infinite.

For any individual or organization to study all the issues once through by any single survey or research is not feasible and impractical to the findings arrived for implementation. It is sad but true to acknowledge that most of the reports and workshops conducted never went to the root of the ailing sector.

How to price these electricity services? Who should benefit, the Power Utilities or the Electricity Consumers? Who will gain bulk purchasers or the retail consumers?

How one can expect to correct a system which had been derailing since its inception? Moreover power was considered to be a service rather than commodity for trading. The philosophy of operating the Indian Energy Sector has completely changed today.

Every citizen is now a prospective profit centre for the industry. What is the option left to the poor citizens? Though the policy reforms have brought the choice of selecting your electricity service provider but where is the capacity to purchase the power gradually getting escalated under the blanket of tariff regulation.

Do you think the IPPs, CPPs, MPPs, UMPPs could really make the difference in the energy scenario? Creating an opportunity to the private sector was to share the responsibility to eliminate the energy crisis.

How far this policy stands in reality today?

The summary to be inferred is that the energy consumption rate is increasing without the equality in rate of production. Fossil fuels are produced by nature. Man cannot generate them in a day or two. Man in fact is mining it out at a more rapid rate. The reserves in India are limited. Additional resources are not being explored rapidly.

The majority of it is consumed by the manufacturing sector. An energy policy of industry is to be in line with the policy of the energy sector. How to draft an integrated plan at the global level?

The heavy industries are crowned to be bulk consumers of electricity. At the same time the commercial consumers cannot be neglected equally. Though this is not that well organized but forms the major area of revenue collection in India. The management of the domestic consumers is as good as managing the entire population of the country.

Every citizen is a customer. Every citizen is an electricity consumer? How to satisfy every consumer with their energy demands? Once the power supply is accessible the reliability of availability, power quality and safety are other distribution challenges of the electricity service providers.

Is power not the sole responsibility of State? Power is whose responsibility? What can be a good energy mix? How to have an energy balance? Is Corporate not a pendulum between service and business perspectives?

Do you think Private can completely replace Public Utilities? Is the competition between Private and Public the mantra of the Regulators in India?

Who will win the war of revolution in Indian Energy Sector? Is Power the dominating factor in energy policy?

Coal is a pollutant fuel is known to all since ages of Industrialization? Why did we begin with coal? We would have started with the renewable in the beginning itself? Why today hue and cry on making renewable the king of primary energy?

Is India equipped to operate the emerging models of energy mix? Where is the single umbrella to hold the energy and electricity sectors together in India?

The autonomy of Department of Energy has its own limitations in policy making. Is not the dependency on foreign investments a perennial matter of debate for the country? How can we expect investors without their share of the gain?

When will the sun shine on Indian Energy Sector?

Who will take the responsibility of addressing the concerns of consumers? Is there any Ministry of Consumers (MoC) constituted as administrative machinery for the responsibility and accountability?

How can the departments with profit motives do the business of service? Never the public utilities crossed the breakeven point to earn profits over expenditure.

Don't you think there is difference between Management and Responsibility? Authorities have drained valuable time in managing the issues rather than shouldering the responsibility of resolving the issues at all levels.

Why no one questioned the system of governance in the energy sector early to reforms? Does it take so long to reconcile after everything is lost? When the defaulters and penalizers are from the same community the complexity of the issue is bound to overrule the benefits of the deregulation in the power sector.

Micro and Macro approaches of study have their own limitations and suitability. Analytical studies in India needs vigorous encouragement to rapidly understand the interfacing issues in complex sectors like energy and power industry. This is perhaps the only way of learning and taming ourselves in the global environment where computations in competition is changing randomly and exponentially in all dimensions.

Research has its own significance and contribution if carried out with outmost vision, mission and national objective. It should not be just to establish some data and for statistical reports presentation.

Will the shortfall in the government's recent mandate, "Power to ALL by 2012" be realized in the successive Visions 2017, 2020, 2025, as it is being envisaged with respective energy policies from day to day?

Let us think of the stakeholders of the energy sector in India. A very interesting finding of this analytical approach need not perplex you to understand that how can only de-licensing the generation sector can bring in equal development in transmission and distribution sectors of the integrated Indian Power System.

Is not the policy to strengthen the electricity sector by disintegration a subject of concern today as far as India is concerned? The functional, administration, management, performance, efficiency, reforms, restructuring, unbundling, financial, economical, implementation, consumption, conservation, earnings, receivables, outstanding, reserves, surplus, payments, subsidies, and so on are key indicators of the power sector. There is an exhaustive list very much evident from the analytical chapters to follow here on the discussion of energy crisis in India.

It is not that India is the only country in fray? The tussle is equally alive in the developed nations. The threat of energy security has engulfed everybody today. The greenhouse effect is seen everywhere in the world. The imports of coal from Indonesia and Australia in India have increased tremendously to supplement the poor mining targets by Coal India Limited and its subsidiaries collieries. The tussle in the sector never seems to end.

India is going to focus heavily on the latest financing developments for renewable energy in areas like capital markets, project securitization, funds, green bonds and investment strategies. It will also focus on government policy and the role of the financial community in supporting renewable energy.

Given the strong innovations that the financial communities are showing in the renewable energy space, we expect this to be a very exciting decade for renewable energy revolution in India. Think about electrifying the entire country with renewable based power.

Will Green Power meet the future electricity demands in India? Is India well equipped with the technology in renewable? Renewable based power has long journey to go before any one conclude about its feasibility in replacing the entire infrastructure of present power system dependent on conventional fuels.

Conventional Vs Non-Conventional fuels fight will never die. A blend is essential in the total energy mix. Only one category cannot lead. Natural geographic of any area has its limitations with the availability of all type of resources.

The forum will bring together leading project developers in renewable energy sectors, fund sponsors, financiers, advisors, utility representatives, lenders, institutional investors, equipment suppliers and other key industry players to share their perspectives on the latest innovations and developments in the renewable project finance and investment market.

What should be the social business models to serve the vast numbers of consumers at risk of poverty in India? How to reach the poorest consumers? Will they remain deprived of the benefits which are being enjoyed by the reserved beneficiaries of reforms?

One of the remarkable findings which I wish to share with my readers is that there is gradual unending widening of gap in genuine conversation among the power utilities, regulators, government, consumers and other stake holders of the energy sector. The outer world is being presented with the slogan of deregulation in the sector but the truth has its own pros and cons both for the power utilities and the consumers. It is like one arrow and two birds hit at the same time.

At this point of time it is very difficult to conclude who is the leader? Will the public utilities let the crown of dominance go to the private utilities in the energy sector? The turbulence is rightly seen from concept, exploration, commissioning, and distribution to consumption of the energy in India.

Has not the deregulation created more number of internal customers? The splitting of functional responsibility in case of the electricity services do not 100% justifies the policy on the issue of realigning the sector.

It appears that departments are being created as per the issues sprouting in the sector. An area policy maker has to justify their worthiness.

The gaps, irregularities, uncertainties, scams, defaults, delays, shortfalls, disagreements, withdrawals, hearings, decisions, disputes, obligations, violations of norms, unclear policies, and stumbling strategies and so on are impediments to the overall development of the energy sector.

The Indian Energy Sector continually is being influenced by the policies of capitalization, exploitation, utilization, nationalization, privatization, liberalization, corporatization and globalization. What is next in fate? It is likely to be revealed but it is matter of time. Will the sector again become nationalized?

How to make the conversations productive in India? The awareness levels of Indian consumers are nil.

How to achieve best practices in Corporate Governance? The rules are entirely different in Private Enterprises. India is rapidly developing young entrepreneurs in the energy sector. India is transforming its business culture. It is becoming global.

The World is now the Market. The proposal of initiating plans for 1, 00,000 MW Solar Power is an overall boost to the entire energy sector in the world. India is welcoming International Power Utilities to do business in the energy sector.

The definition of Private Utilities hopefully encompasses domestic and foreign enterprises ready to participate in resolving the energy crisis.

Energy Crisis has changed the dimensions of the electricity sector in India. The strength of Capital is dictating the policy in the sector. More often than not, policy decisions rests in the hands of these Giant Corporate.

What to do about this energy crisis? Can you reason out the causes responsible for the situation India is facing? Will India continue to sail as the snail rather than fight it out as a lion?

The issues of governance, execution, strategies, managing organizations, professional services, performance parameters, overcoming structural barriers, business cultures, service philosophy, consumer psychology, synthesis, synergy, collaboration, decision making, revenue opportunity, penalties, funding, financial closures, agreements, licenses, clearances, obligations, implementations, subsidies, technology, operational services, renovations, innovations, certifications, compliances, and so on are other key areas which needs a regular review, rethinking, reorientation, reorganization, realignment on continual basis to let the initiated reforms reach its redefined goals.

The roles of the CEO, CFO, COO, and CMO have become more dynamic with global perspectives.

People Management Mix Vs Emerging Energy Mix is a concern for effective productivity in the sector. Present day the rate of collabration and synergies in the Indian Electricity Sector is bringing in various cultural philosophies of working styles. The styles of management from all over the world is influencing our service and business concepts.

How many revenue models India has to experiment in the energy sector before it reaches optimization of the resources and perfection in operational efficiency?

Energy Models demand is very dynamic in nature today seeing the importance of energy mix. Viability of energy models is not meeting the turbulence of the sector. How can all the stake holders become the beneficiary of the policies at a time?

If you can take a tour to many of the underperforming and even the outperforming states in India, you will certainly observe that many feeders are unmetered. The government has been voicing about the default customers at the floor of parliament leveraging it to their best possible line of defense.

The unmetered consumers are invariably a revenue drain in the electricity services. India has been slow on the utilization of technology for surveillance and monitoring of the power system. The application of reliable technology too is not good.

Will a strong bill on metering, billing and collection change the scenario of the electricity sector? How the healthy position is to be attained? There is lot of imbalance in vesting responsibilities and powers.

Do we really need to differentiate between a supply licensee and distribution licensee? Is supply being recognized as an independent identity of function like generation, transmission and distribution?

The next reform is Supply of Power. Opportunity is in business of retail power. Distribution will focus on bulk supply of power. Further household connections, commercial connections, small scale industries, agriculture connections, and so on will become the segment of retail consumers of power.

How to increase accountability of licensees? When will clarity come in tariff determination? How to decide tariff for retail sale of electricity by a supply licensee?

Why National Tariff Policy is unable to define clearly the overall direction for implementation?

Incentives by governments are as good as the drains of subsidy. There are many terms in the Acts which are not specifically defined.

Why cannot we improve public participation in tariff and grant of license? What is the accountability of the regulators to consumers? Why commissions on regular basis cannot have representatives of consumers to represent their cases, findings, suggestions, opinions, views, thoughts for betterment of the energy sector?

What should be the bottom line for plant operators?

Bottom Line Vs Bottleneck, where is the thin demarcation in the sector related to performance evaluation of the power industry.

CHAPTER II

LICENSE VS LIBERALIZATION

Opportunities & Challenges

Where is the "Wheel of Prgoress" in India? It engages and dis-engages now and then, here and there, limping towards the final goal.

What do you understand by liberation in energy sector? Has the rules of the game changed entirely?

Does liberalization means de-licensing? If liberalization is an opportunity then de-licensing is a great challenge. India's deregulated power sector is facing stiff challenges to sustain itself in the era of liberalization.

Politics and Policy are the wheels of the bicycle of the government. Without politics the power position is unachievable and without politicization of the policy where is the question of sustaining the energy sector in India.

Power is sandwiched between politics and policy. I feel at times that the mandates of departments should be free from the clutches of party influences. National agenda in energy and power should not be a voice of any one ruling party.

Political party in power does not mean that all the discretion in power policy is to be governed by the perception of the single philosophy. Energy is a national issue at any point of time just like the security of the country. The rules of commodity manufacturing and marketing should not be encouraged in the energy sector.

Politics looks for any opportunity to take advantage but not the responsibility and accountability of challenges all over the world. This is as per the inbuilt nature of politics. The problem to be addressed is that opportunities feasibility should not be beyond realistic challenges. Any transformation takes time to bring in desired changes. But before one change is implemented 100% another policy of change should not be an interruption or hindrance to the previous policy which is likely to become a reality.

3 P's

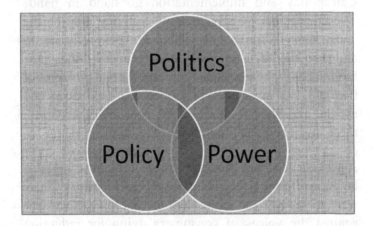

Business and Service are two different visions under one mission is a challenge to any policy maker in the world. Defining service as a commercial commodity is new dimension in this era of emerging energy business models.

I take the responsibility on behalf of the citizens of India to represent their voice on the Indian Electricity Sector. India being a democratic country welcomes openness in speech to the consumers of energy. The point of discussion is to consider their views, opinions, comparisons, analyses, debates, arguments, perceptions, awareness, understandings, contributions, arising on issues critical and non-critical to the energy sector.

Public services to what extent can be rendered? Any volume, any space, anytime, anywhere, to anybody are always confusing, conflicting and incomprehensible while brainstorming either in policy making or in implementing body.

Can policy and implementation go hand in hand? The constraints in implementing a policy may be the constraints of the policy. There are primarily issues and then the need for resolving secondary issues. The hindrances of the implementation are the real problems of the field. The grievances in services are field views and are the important feedback of the consumers. Feedback mechanism helps in timely correction of the system.

A periodic feedback process from society can be valuable inputs in reforming the Indian Power Sector. Power Utilities want to recover the entire cost of supplying electricity against the voices of consumers dying for reduction in tariff hikes. To avoid conflicting circumstances the government at times maintains a distant to the worries of consumers.

The policy on pricing and billing of energy is the core of all the discussions and debate. Why consumers cannot have a direct say in the pricing of energy? Who actually benefits from the pricing policy?

How to strike a balance between tariff and service? Where are cleaner policies for cleaner technology? Do you know what amount of capital assets invested in energy projects in India have become nonperforming assets?

Midway closure of power projects is becoming a culture in India. It is like murdering the visions and dreams of millions and millions of Indians. Everybody is just murmuring what to do. Do you agree with the present statistics of success?

Public or Private it is India's drain. I am trying to make quadrants of defense and offence. I am trying to convey to all concerned that energy is to be conserved by everybody. Energy is to be shared by everybody.

Over consumption of energy is to be stopped by everybody. If citizens are not concerned with the economics of energy then the nation is bound to suffer on account of misleading consumption trends.

What is our energy utilization efficiency? Is it not a national concern?

My readers should consider my views as a narration and lecture on "Energy Crisis in India". It is not solely to collect a gathering of audience but to find contributors in reforming the society. My voice is the voice of citizens of India. My respondents of this case study are valuable resources of the field being analyzed.

The questionnaires to them are the personifications of the issues the energy sector is struggling to resolve. It is a tool to do the analytical study of the energy crisis in India. Readers can as well consider it to be a commentary on the predicament of the ailing sector.

Every citizen has the right to know about the bill he pays for electrical units consumed daily. Cost Vs Price needs transparency. The entire nation is stakeholder in building India. Subsidy is citizen's money.

I believe that awareness programs should become mandatory to the policy makers, power utilities and consumers. Knowledge on interfacing issues among stakeholders in operating the power system no doubt will help in eliminating unnecessary and unwarranted gaps in the energy sector.

Awareness prepares you to face opportunities and challenges. Issues without action plan to resolve it will never be closed. Action plan is effective only if you are reasonably knowing the cause of the problem. A solution without understanding the cause is impracticable. Many of the recent policies have become unworkable in the sector.

The power sector in the name of opportunities is being burdened with unfeasible policies. Public Sector concept of challenge is entirely unmatchable with the Private Sector. Private defines challenges as risk and concerns of mitigation in the sector.

Each question is an indispensable issue of the sector. To bring out the comparative hindrances a thorough study of the sector had been done by the author prior to formulation of the questions reflecting the unique problem.

Learning by questioning is the best method I believe in. When we make decisions we are bound to do mistakes. Thus it is practical approach that we make mistakes by making decisions. This confirms that at least you are acting on the issues. Most of our issues do not receive any action from the concerned. Under these circumstances I put to my learned readers, "What is the useful way to make decisions?"

Why people criticize national services? Are private service providers making any difference? Are the public enterprises able to fulfill the social goals?

Social and economic problem often reflect an imbalance of power. With the explosion of digital technologies power utilities are sweeping up vast quantities of data about consumers. The same policy makers are supporting encouragement in consumption and conservation of energy. Thermal power generation licenses is being sanctioned without hesitation of environmental concerns and at the same time a turnaround is also being voiced in the power sector.

Now how to conserve and consume energy at the same time? This will no doubt have criticisms and applauses accordingly aligned with the performance and perfection in relation to the responsibility shouldered by the concerned stakeholders. The analysis is elaborately debated within the limitations of the possibilities of mathematical understanding by the various segments of the readership in India.

I believe the analysis on the feedback of the respondents clearly reflects the truth of the citizens who are equally the customers and consumers of electricity in India.

Let us understand the sensitivity of information from the people who are daily living, facing, experimenting and witnessing the power utilities services, government's policies, authorities' implementation, and the performance of the power system.

The respondents opinions, suggestions, criticisms, grievances are valuable inputs for the betterment of the energy sector. This field survey brings out indelible findings and recommendations to correct the derailing sector. The ground realities can only be known through actual interrogation of the consumers. And at the same time essentiality of investigating power utilities cannot be turned down.

This is an explorative study bringing out the problems and issues of the power sector for open discussion and opinions to the public of India. I have attempted to organize their opinions in a structured way by utilizing a comprehensive questionnaire as an examining tool.

I am thankful to the respondents for their unconditional contribution in this analytical study to probe and arrive at various schools of thoughts, ideas, views, clarifications, queries, apprehensions, about the Indian Electricity Sector.

Electricity has been preferred over other energy because it is the basic life line of living today across the world. Modernization is slave to equipments, appliances, electrical & electronic devices, automation & controls, computers and so on all running on electrical energy.

My research skills took me nearly to the core of the problem. I could incite the citizens to voice their unsatisfied areas of services. Their unhappiness speaks of the unsatisfactory services provided by the power utilities. Every single stakeholder of the Indian Power System should be held guilty for the overall chaos.

Reliability of good quality power is a matter of concern in all parts of India. Moreover the energy profile integration is pending for decades and decades. We do not know when the golden dawn will befall on the power sector.

What strategy is to be adopted to leverage from the synthesis in the ideologies of public service providers and private service providers?

Is there any difference in providing service to public with license and without license? Does license bring accountability and responsibility? When the norms of the regulations have not changed what benefit is attained by de-licensing in the power sector?

Liberalization in power generation without freedom and autonomy in determining and fixing tariff of power solely generated by self owned power station is a matter of regular debate in the power industry.

Can "SERVICE" and "BUSINESS" go together hands in hands? Cost Vs Profits, Supply Vs Demand, Public Vs Private, Policy Vs Reality, Conventional Vs Unconventional, Fossil fuels Vs Renewable, Bulk Power Vs Retail Power, Regulation Vs Reforms, Administration Vs Management, Consumption Vs Conservation, Services Vs Satisfaction, Nationalization Vs Globalization, License Vs Liberalization, Enterprises Vs Corporatization, are daily living and dying between opportunities and challenges.

Regulation too is not clear on the definition of service and business as two different identities any where either at the State or at the Central level.

How Public Energy Utilities are different than Private Energy Utilities? Is the policy impartial to both?

How to strike balance between company profitability and higher customer satisfaction? Is the Indian Energy Sector lacking innovation? Is our employee pool really engaged in rebuilding the power sector? There are appreciable doubts about the efficiency of employee management.

Who will finance to serve the poor consumers in emerging power markets? Sympathy cannot be mantra any more in the foreground of severe competition in the energy sector. Are the opportunities going to be the real possibilities in the energy sector?

I somehow have a feeling that our approach towards the emerging energy sector is lacking creativity of change. We still prefer to ride the old corroded bicycle by pushing and pulling the chains of reforms and restructuring in the energy sector.

How long you can grease it? How long you can crawl de-chaining it? Are not we junking the momentum of energy as well as economy of the country?

The Indian Electricity Sector is starving for real good ideas, encouragement, motivation, innovation, creativity to manage the change. Novelties should dictate energy models of future. It requires a mix of growth, development, sustenance, renovation, modernization, research, optimization, dynamism, stimulation, business dimension, service inclination philosophies, customer oriented ideologies, value addition, to formulate successful electricity models in the sector.

The transition of the Power Sector is to be guided accordingly. The question is till when we can keep learning on the subject. When will we actually start laboring on it to make the policies into reality?

How to develop leaders with desired skills in the energy sector? Who can meet the expectations of millions and millions of consumers? The perception of citizens as customers is a dual policy conflict at any level of governance, administration, regulation and management. Why employees are not satisfied with their senior management?

I have been sincerely thinking that rather than just creating few "Smart Cities" the country should focus on creating "Smart Leaders". The energy sector lacks leadership trainings in leading an engaged workforce with responsibility and accountability. It is now time to reinvent performance management system to increase the efficiency of human resources in India.

This is a study to probe into the reality of the energy policies with especial focus on the power sector being the leader in energy industry.

Land sanctions keep hitting the energy projects. Land shortage slows down finalization of new power projects. Expansions of power projects are also being affected. Subsidies, tariff and taxations are key areas of discussions and debate for the policy makers. Why Indian Government is unable to fix it forever?

Power is the supreme of all energy. Electricity dominates the energy mix. Now the question is to go for which power. Power by coal, oil, gas, solar, wind, geothermal, bio-gas, nuclear, tidal, and hydro, any alternate fuel, and the choice is competitive and challenging.

There are markets for power, market for coal, market for oil & gas, almost all. How to map the market of thermal power to coal? How to improve the domestic coal supply? Nearly 80,000 MW to 1,00,000 MW of new capacities are to be supplied coal.

Was the monopolistic approach in coal sector for more than a century not the prime cause for the present energy crisis? Power projects are not meeting the goal of COD (Commercial Operation Date) commitments because of various parameters.

Can we change the way the world uses energy? The goal is complete transformation of the entire energy infrastructure of the world.

Load-shifting is new concept and a remedy for regulating power using the theory of storage. Battery's capable of load-shifting are going to be the future of energy industry. The balance is to be made between charging and discharging accordingly to availability, demand and prices of electricity. It can also store solar power generated during daytime and release it at night and serve as back up during outages.

Load-shedding is the unbearable cry of citizens. Who is hearing the Voice of consumers? Small scale industrial entrepreneurs are facing pathetic time in many power shortage states of India. Big industries have switched over to DG –Power or are relying on their captive power generation. The survival of the industries is at stake in many of the states unable to support industrial growth.

Is it not that there is justifiable gap between Industrial Policy, Energy Policy and Power Policy?

Electricity Storage is going to be the new era. The point of discussion welcomes the brainstorming on consumption at day and night. Which is more? How to meet the demand in day? How to manage a cloudy day when we are speaking of solar power in sunny day? How to battle the erotic winds?

I believe, "We should bake as many types of bread we can when the dough is moist." There is no fun once your resources are hardened and the plasticity is lost. Any policy should not yield beyond the limits of elasticity of economics of generation.

Why government should think of Corporate Wellness? Why business should think of social service? Is there difference between energy market and energy sales? How to analyze it? Are the stakeholders not thinking on commercial, financial, intellectual, technological, strategic, emotional, openness, satisfaction, team development, project completion, leadership styles, growth orientation, authenticity, integrity, loyalty, viability and analytical aspects of the Indian Energy Sector?

Everyone wants to take advantage of energy and from energy. Who is the real owner of it? The end consumer has to consume it as per his power purchase capacity. How to bring about rationalization in prices of energy?

What is the trusted brand of power in India? Which power utility is highly transparent to the electricity consumers? Why citizens are not having direct voting in determining tariff?

The case study which is being narrated here to the readers is to bring in awareness in all the different categories of consumers and various power utilities providing the services. I believe this manuscript is going to bring valuable insight to the readers who equally are trying to learn and labor the issues of the ailing sector.

"Energy Crisis in India" is a sincere attempt to evaluate the root causes which are responsible in creating the gaps leading to unwanted crisis. The case study elaborated and illustrated here represents a model to address the business, social, national, global and service concept of Indian Energy Sector.

The case study focuses with its limitations attention on the requirement of an ideal model in the Indian Electricity Sector. Are not the policy makers committing preventable mistakes year by year?

Who is the real sufferer? Is it The Government of India or the Citizens of India? Government and Citizens are the wheels of the gradually cycling Indian Economy. When will we leave the legacy of underperformance in the energy sector?

Another prominent lacking area is rigorously testing the proposed idea and its functional success. A simulation test on the policies is not a bad recommendation by majority of the learned fraternity in this industry.

What is the probability of flawed reasoning in the decision-making process in the energy sector in India?

Energy Industry in India is booming. Opportunity to serve is infinite. The question is service in time. Who will take the challenge? Why we are unable to see the roots of disorganization of the energy sector? Are again the fragmentations going to distort the entire sector?

The gap in theory and practice always creates confusion in interpreting the exact problems of the sector. Is that India is yet in the shoes of conventional wisdom? Is not the role of entrepreneurship driving change and innovation in the energy sector?

Is Business in Energy for service to Society? Is service for society the business of the power utilities?

Who is the interface between business and market? Never review the past which distorts reality. Is the energy sector learning from mistakes?

It is tough to understand the emerging leadership across cultures to operate global energy business in India.

Sphere of Energy

If you can look at the sphere of energy it becomes imperative of the issues concerned to the relationship with energy in India. Every stakeholder in the energy sector is doing best within the limited reasoning abilities is the feedback from the respondents of the sector.

Trust and Transparency in the energy sector needs to be established at all levels. Why we are not testing our thinking? A pilot test in field reality prior to implementation of a policy may not be a bad idea anywhere in the world. Unless you test the theory of reformation empirical evidence cannot be established.

Financing of Renewable Energy Projects by Indian Renewable Energy Development Agency (IREDA) is being untimely granted. Rooftop solar poses several hurdles for the individual investor.

Now after making the citizens promising power consumers the government is trying to make them prospective investors. Will the citizens support this solar power mission model by becoming entrepreneurs of solar power? Scaling rooftop generation will have technological and infrastructural challenges. How safe will be the reliability of grid power connected with millions and millions of independent solar power generators in India?

Electric Power is indispensable today anywhere in the world. It is prime requisite for the transformed and modernly equipped infrastructure living. The modernization has made us dependent on energy more than earlier times.

It is difficult to analyze how the humans faced summer and winter without mechanized cooling and heating respectively before falling prey to these parasites. The consumption pattern is uncontrollable. The ratio of dependability is alarming in all walks of life.

How to define spend analysis? Consumer is at wish and will to use electricity as he likes. How to justify his consumption? Wastage by consumer is going unaccountable? Where to book this loss?

Is it not that such cumulative power loss by consumers is accumulating at the national level as energy crisis in India? Power utilities are unable to bring out the performance in energy management in India. Thus the problem of enterprises management is being unnecessarily supplemented by the inefficiency of consumer management.

Consumer Management is a national challenge. There may be roughly hardly 100 to 200 power utilities, energy providers, other service and miscellaneous institutions and departments to be supervised, administered, controlled and monitored in the energy sector in India. What about one billion consumers?

Are Power Market and Consumer Market one and the same? Which should be considered as a benchmark for analysis? What domestic electricity consumers have to do with trading of electricity? Why they should bother with the background of determining tariffs? What they need is cheaper electricity by any means irrespective of the identification and status of the power utility?

An overview infers that the subject is not as simple as it looks. Can the electricity consumer's preferences be same as the preferences of the power utilities? Have the power utilities formally predicted what the consumers want?

Did the energy sector failed to leverage the power of people? Overstaffing of State Electricity Boards ultimately ended up into unbundling of the mammoth department during the reform regime. Why Public Enterprises are inefficient in managing people?

The World Bankers had different motives. They were eying this unhealthy system to collapse. "Energy crisis in India" was a situation they were waiting to capitalize. Their SWOT Analysis further strengthened their investments in India by the open door policy.

The Government of India wanted to create an atmosphere of win-win situation for all the stakeholders of this sector. Unfortunately the expectations were marginally met. The method of investments by incentives did not bring any magical changes in the sector.

Now the question to all is, "Till when will the power sector keep on reforming and restructuring?" Has the Indian government ever thought on the Energy Intensity Index?

Will the patch work system of approach by regulators help to revamp the power sector? There is a deeply rooted feeling in the consumers that the policy makers are providing interim relief like the cobbler stitching now and then on the worn out sole of the shoe.

The instability of the government at the centre adds to the crisis its own colors of interpretation. The story further continues with the blame game finally living with the bitterness of issues rather than the sweetness of solutions.

Do the policy makers want to make profits without prosperity? There is definitely difference between prosperity of a citizen and prosperity of a consumer?

My finding from the analytical approach is, "Every citizen is a consumer of energy in India". Is the basic truth of the challenge? Where to locate the energy crisis? How to address it? Who will resolve it? When will the promising dawn grace the country?

Is it not humans are questioning their own advancement? Humans want energy to sustain life. This is a universal truth. No doubt but today it is electric power from which source. Which is cheaper among this thermal, hydro, nuclear and renewable?

How to develop charismatic leaders with ethical skills? The literacy in the sector is below the minimum level of awareness. The policy does not square with reality. The energy sector is missing opportunities to connect with the customer's inner and outer world satisfactory senses.

It is like daily watching the football game between power providers and power consumers. Players are the different categories of stakeholders in the Indian Energy System. The policy is being kicked by all to finally reach the goal of reality. The game of implementation is having its own limitations and strategies.

Evaluation of strategies and policies was not that familiar in India in earlier days of Independence. The Economic

Reforms of 1991 brought the outlook of India with global perspectives. India was now being considered as a partner of change. The role of regulation was looking beyond the concept of nationalization.

Power Providers Vs Electricity Consumers is a daily saga of the energy industry. Electricity services is managed by a huge network of generating units, transmission network, distribution system, billing and collection centers, consumer complaints and grievances cell and fault restoration departments.

The promptness in attending the faults and tripping and readiness to restore the system within a timeframe is an ongoing work without interruption and holidays. Consumers may not be interested in the real problems faced by the service providers. Consumers evaluate their performance on daily basis.

Load shedding either planned or unplanned is not willingly accepted by the consumers. The government is not new to the agitations by the citizens. Today the educated society approaches with analysis and facts.

The same analysis and facts are presented and miss-presented in the sector. The awareness of retail consumers is lagging behind and inappreciably below a desired minimum level. The condition of the rural consumers which constitutes a wide base in India requires revolutionary and reformatory changes to address the issues of disparities.

The minimum power cut duration of one area is the actual period of availability in many areas throughout the day in India. Despite the human capital potential the unavailability of power is the prime impediment for infrastructural development and growth. In addition to it the delay in implementation of fast track projects for rural development is handicapping the dreams of villagers all over India. The schemes for people below the poverty line are marginally progressing with regrets and grievances.

Forget about the promises of the policies assuring to do miracles in every five year plans. On average the opinion polls of the consumers on this is not satisfactory to the expectations of the power utilities and government departments.

Why it is continuously following the same trend even after 60 years of electricity services in India? Every consumer is perplexed with this query. Not even once could our revenue recover the cost of power generation in India? Subsidy had been the life line of the sector. Why did government both at State and Centre kept pouring in when they knew leaks were untreatable in Indian Electricity Sector? This is a subject of study for all right from the government to citizen of the country.

Who has not read and heard about farmer's suicide in India? If you go through the statistics you will be ashamed to support your own philosophy of living.

Irrigation is the life line in India. Energizing pumps through rural electrification could not be resolved till today. Internet Café and mobile centers have come up in villages but not the sub-stations and transformers which were indented in 1980 to 1990 year. Trust me you may not be able to trace out the requisition file today. The initiating bench of officers might have retired without closing the issue.

The supplies of power equipments always are major shortcomings in developing the integrated supply chain of electricity especially in rural areas. The per capita consumption in urban and rural areas has extreme figures of high and low reflecting the widest gap in availability. Despite power purchasing capacity and affordability in rural areas the consumption requirement is not fed by the power suppliers.

Rural India appears to be second in priority. Is it the vision of the policy makers? Why FDI is not invested right at the root of villages? Why NRIs are not making their destinations villages? Who will transform India's Villages?

Voice of Villagers right from energy for cooking to healthy living is being not given the emphasis it deserves in the true sense. How can you make Villages equal To Smart Cities without electricity? Who will build the linkages? Only few schemes with snail's pace are as good as unimplemented and unattended issues. The rapidness in policy changes should match the infrastructural support strengthening factors of energy sector development.

I put to my readers to analyze what we did with our electricity sector. Blame, blame and only blame game till when.

Why the planning departments are unable to bring out perfectly tailored sustainable growth plan for the energy sector?

Is it not that Coal's future can decide Energy's Future in India? Coal is the major key decision maker in India. Coal is the core for electricity in India. Any policy without its consideration is calling for fuel risk mitigation.

Coal for cooking and coal for power generation have very different price mechanism, competition, concerns and challenges. Similarly oil for lighting, transportation, industry and oil for power generation have altogether different plans, allocation, pricing and strategy.

A subsidy for lighting and cooking may not match with subsidy for industry. What is the priority, Industry or Domestic consumers of electricity? Why sick Industries are not subsidized? Why there cannot be a balance between the profit making and sick industry?

Does India have different policy for sick industries? Is closure the only way? Why disinvestments from healthy industries?

Energy Utilities and other energy businesses can only firmly reconnect with bulk and retail customers if the politics is stable in India. Utilities have to learn to cooperate with their customers and expand their perception of services.

The role of Customer Relationship Manager is being redefined in energy services so that innovation will emerge as newcomers force the pace; existing companies may either pull out or reshape their business.

My readers should without hesitations never think a company should ever underestimate the importance of a large, satisfied and happy customer base. The truth is that established utilities have lost a lot of confidence and trust, and they haven't been as vigorous as they could've been in thinking how to strengthen and develop their relationship with customers. The question of customer's integrity and loyalty in India somehow appears to be a different subject of education.

If citizen's of India start saving electricity three fourth of the energy crisis is manageable without any risk to energy security. The philosophy of "Saving Energy" is to be cultivated in our daily living from dawn to dusk. Each individual human on this earth can create energy by optimizing usage of energy in living and thus by doing so the contribution of society and nation can make a tremendous savings in millions and millions all over the world.

Utilities and Customers are for each other. Both have to survive. This is the true justice. Production of Power and Market of Power are to be equally managed with the economics of power.

How to have service without paying the price for its production? The nearest approach is to at least reach the breakeven point of cost of production of power. All opportunities may not be engineering possibilities. The politics should not intervene beyond its limitations to exploit the concepts of production management, financial management and energy management.

The Energy Transition in India is very imperatively being witnessed with the recent changes seen in energy sector, electricity sector, infrastructure sector, oil & gas sector, logistics sector, railways, ports, irrigation & agriculture sector, small & heavy industrial sector, renovation & modernization of villages and cities, creation of cyber & smart cities, etc; so on and on. There is technology revolution everywhere in India.

India is being integrated within the country and to the world. The outlook of Global India is much based on the success story of energy sector.

Energy & Economy have to go hand in hand to meet the dreams of millions and billions Indians. Citizens also have a major role to play in facilitating the implementation of policies and schemes being enacted by the regulators.

India generates huge waste daily. I am not a specialist on converting electricity from waste but my observation and deep thinking on the subject promisingly shows me future for powering India. Just imagine the volume of waste India produces annually? Can be utilized to generate power meeting the crisis we are facing. This is one area of substantial research and development in India. India should rapidly pick up before we waste the available waste energy resources.

Waste management to Energy management should be the new vision. Every heavy industry like refinery, petrochemical, steel, chemicals, and many more generate waste gases amounting to tonnes and million tonnes every year.

Let us benefit by recovering the heat which is lost as valuable energy. Energy Loss by Heat Loss accounts for major loss in production and process industries.

India has only finger tips numbered agencies to really make any huge difference in the national statistics of energy conservation.

Every citizen is a centre of consumption and conservation. A disciplined approach and right habit is what is necessary to make a realistic revolution in all walks of life. How to improve the functioning and accountability of regulating bodies and commissions? How to differentiate between a supply and distribution licensee?

Is there any difference between electricity theft and unauthorized use of electricity? How many cases of offence are booked by the electricity Inspectors? How many consumers are sincerely penalized daily for violating the procedures to be followed strictly as per the prescribed electricity services standards in paying the bills?

Voice of consumers reveals that the cases of harassment have increased in the background of unclear definitions related to guilty of theft.

Energy Conservation in India in the true sense is a failed commitment. The question is to what extent it can be conserved, say 10%, 15% or 20%. I would like to bring your attention to the energy drain our markets are doing with unproductive illumination on the hoarding boards.

Do you think it is justifiable to drain millions of energy units being unnecessarily consumed by signboards? Unaccountable wastage without the needs and necessities all over the World. I confess to say that the Global Vision should be to discourage excessive electrical energy consumption by this means.

The country drains huge electrical energy units by so many unacceptable ways of consumption. An awareness drive among the citizens is very much essential to understand the importance of availability of energy.

PART II

POLICY
VS
REALITY

CHAPTER-III

DESTINY OF ELECTRIFYING INDIA

AN UNFULFILLED DREAM – "LANTERN TO ELECTRIC LAMP"

Today, at the dawn of 21st century India's deregulating power sector is characterized with uncertainty of regulatory reforms, disparity in electricity services, widening gaps in power supply chain, de-licensed power generation, unbundling of SEBs, underdeveloped power market, infancy in power trading, emerging power & energy mix, fuel supply insecurity, load shedding, power holidays & blackouts, immature energy conservation, unethical wastage of electrical energy, government's unsupported visions and un-conducive competition in the sector.

The power sector over the 100 years since under British Rule to the recently enacted historic Electricity Act-2003 has experienced and journeyed through decentralization, nationalization, privatization, liberalization, deregulation and corporatization of electricity services in India.

Who will switch on India's Power future? How can India balance power supply and demand? Can the Government of India do justice to the Power Utilities and Electricity Consumers? Is the Role of Regulation fading away? Will there be solution to Energy Crisis by 2012? All the above is running in the minds of Indian citizens. India is deeply concerned about the future of energy.

The Indian Electricity Sector is passing through a very bad period despite the implementation of recent new policies initiated from time to time, as and when required addressing the unresolved issues which have now become chronic in nature.

All efforts to deregulate the sector also have paid no dividends. The never ending parallel trends in rising demands of energy for growth and falling short in its availability achievement against targeted levels because of the consistent inefficient energy sector is a mystery awaiting solutions in no man's land.

Unfortunately, the results of this decade reforms seem to have fallen well below the expectations. The Central and State government are short of solutions. Is it too early to judge the final outcome of the change?

Do the Power Utilities in Private Sector have equal opportunities in the deregulated power sector and liberalizing power market?

According to International Energy Agency (IEA) (2009), Worldwide 1.456 billion does not have access to electricity, of which 83 per cent live in Rural Areas. India is no exception to it, as per the 15th Census of India (2011), the Rural –Urban population distribution is 833.1 million (68.84 %) is as to 377.1 million (31.16%).

Agriculture, an activity that is the primary source of livelihood in rural areas, accounts for nearly 75 per cent of India's population. It is surprising to note that the eastern region which is home for nearly 45 per cent of the population is equipped with only 25-30 per cent of the households electrified and 60 per cent of the villages electrified.

Corporatizing- Electricity Services in India

The deregulation of the power sector had been initiated to corporatize the electricity services in India to resolve the energy crisis. The public utilities in the state sector were unable to perform despite reforms and restructuring of the electricity sector. The smaller entities born from unbundled SEBs are also not rising to the expectations as anticipated prior to implementation of state reforms Act.

The purpose of providing adequate power with consistent supply, quality and reliability kept on bringing in deregulation in the sector completely changing its operation philosophy today. Nationalization of the power sector to Corporatization of electricity services in India has its own saga of pros and cons.

The Independent Power Producers (IPPs), Captive Power Producers (CPPs), Merchant Power Producers (MPPs), Public Private Partnership (PPPs), Central Power Utilities, State Sector Utilities and MNCs Utilities are all players of the emerging power sector trying to capitalize the Indian Electricity Market with competitive electricity prices to the consumers.

Is the Indian Electricity Market really liberalized? How to design a successful liberalized power market dynamic model operating in a huge democratic country like India to have better price for both the buyers and sellers of electricity with all sorts of diversities in the emerging power mix? The protection of electricity consumers and power utilities in liberalized power market is an unending question of debate in the sector.

How will the private utilities form a consortium or committee to parallely run their government in addressing their issues at par with central and state sector utilities? The power exchanges have been created as per the mandates of the National Electricity Policy to eliminate the disparity in electricity services by bridging the gap between surpluses and shortages in power supply. The market is in very nascent stage without clear rules of the game and prospective anxious players are lobbying to develop a self regulated market mechanism to capitalize the trading of electricity in India.

The rural electrification schemes like Minimum Needs Program (MNP), Accelerated Rural Electrification Programme (AREP), Rural Supply Technology Mission (REST), Rajeev Gandhi Grameen Vidyutikaran Yojna (RGGVY) were all rushed in the first decade of this promising century to translate the destiny of rural India.

The Central outlays through Rural Electrification Corporation have always been inadequate to finance such a huge task. Flow of FDI is very marginal through the prospective renewable energy route.

Unproductive NGO's are banking on the issues of environment and pollution impeding the ray of hope of millions of villagers to at least light their homes with electric lamps. Moreover the issue of subsidies on kerosene and diesel are creating a threat to afford even the lanterns, the lamp of the poor.

Why India is not able to light all the lamps of the poor citizens?

Electricity is not only essential for lighting and household purposes but it allows for mechanization of many farming operations (threshing, milling and hoisting grain for storage) apart from energizing irrigation pumps. Besides farming aquaculture, horticulture, textile, cottage, mining, sugar factory, rubber factory, medicinal herbs, rice mills, jute mills, paper factory, wood mills, oil mills, bio-fertilizer, orchids, farm houses, dairy products etc are many other activities being the source of livelihood in rural areas. The cold storage units, mills, factories, processing units, stores etc all require proper availability of power supply to facilitate the above means of earnings.

Rural Areas with high potential of contribution in India's growth are not being facilitated with electricity over the years. The country has failed to support many such harvest houses. Moreover it has also not utilized available renewable energy sources. The rising demand of power in rural areas cannot be neglected anymore.

Today electricity is being demanded as a fundamental right by the people of India. The domestic segment constitutes the big base of electricity consumers under different slabs of consumption and categories. The consumers locality speaks about the availability, accessibility, affordability and reliability of power supplied to them. The power supply services in rural areas are not at par with the urban areas.

Making electricity available to consumers at their door steps from the place of power generating plants through series of complex supply chain requires great management control to effectively operate the complete integrated power system. The State utilities were born with the vision to achieve the commanding heights but to the dismay lost its mission ending up in organizational restructuring for survival. Despite empowering public enterprises to face the competition in the energy sector impacted by series of reforms initiated by the government of India over the last two decades the performance of the state owned power utilities is unappreciable.

Load shedding is the rule of the day for domestic consumers. Industrial consumers are suffering from power holidays. Energy crisis is bringing in migrating of small and big industries across the country.

The impact of power shortage on GDP of India is mounting day by day. The impact of power cuts is very seriously affecting the total yields as irrigation is not being backed up by substantial power supply availability and accessibility.

The irrigation system is not 100 per cent energized and much depends upon the diesel pump sets being used by the farmers. Rural electrification needs more attention to uplift the standards of living in villages.

Electricity is an essential basic infrastructure for developing and growing the economy. Without this prime energy the overall development of society, nation and world cannot be thought of. Electric power is the core energy on which undoubtly our modern life depends.

Living standards of citizens of rural areas are inferior to the population residing in cities or towns as they are having access to internet, communication systems, transport systems, household electrical powered appliances, better medical care, illuminated buildings, hygienic town and environment, living comforts etc. The rural areas development is paralyzed without electricity.

Cities and towns have evolved from villages. The government's primary focus was only on areas where the capital cost could be realized very fast giving service to more people in less time. The long term perspectives of developing villages connected to cities were somehow given second priority.

Government had been banking on the geographical constraints and political interference were invariably welcomed inappreciably to aggravate the situation more from time to time. It was regularly failing to meet the committed targets in electrifying villages thus widening the gap in disparity of electricity services. The rural population in search of lively hood is densely populating the cities and towns resulting in complete disorder of the supply and demand.

Electrical energy reaches to about 50 per cent of India's population and only 50 per cent is billed. Thinking existence of a Rural Power Market is like catching fish in the desert. Indian Electricity Sector could not develop an organized market even till today. It is ridiculous to think of a power market in the states with regions where electricity hardly has any traces. Though unintentional the Rural Power Policies are unreasonably crafted to ultimately dwell in the dusk.

Tariff Policy in the Indian Electricity Sector has been always a debatable issue since its inception. As per the Electricity Act 2003, passed by the parliament, the Central government is required to formulate the National Electricity Policy and Tariff Policy. The Electricity Act uses policy, methodology and determination three distinct terms related to establishing tariffs. Determination of Tariff by two levels (Central and State) of independent regulators is without scope for ambiguities.

The price of electricity is much cheaper from captive power plants for usage by owner but is sold to the purchaser at market price. The merchant power plants are bringing great turbulence in determining electricity prices.

Energy deficit and electricity pricing without economics of scale is being advantageously manipulated to capitalize the liberalized power market by big Corporate for their profit motives rather than on rationalization of electricity pricing in India. Subsidies and cross-subsidies were the chapters of state utilities and regulators prior to reforms and restructuring.

More than any other factor, the way electricity prices are determined has inhibited India's power market development. Under pricing and political interference in price determination have worsened the financial situation of the main electricity producers, wholesale buyers and suppliers: the SEBs. This increases the risk for private players who wish to enter the electricity market.

The SEBs' end-use electricity tariffs vary widely according to customer category. The major categories are households, agriculture, commercial activities, industry and railways.

The power sector was among the first sectors to be opened up for private sector investment during the early 1990s. Though the initial impetus was on investment for power generation projects, the government subsequently allowed private investment in distribution and transmission projects also.

The present India's Power System operates under reformed policies, restructured SEBs and deregulated & liberalized power market. Both policy and performance are equally responsible in creating gaps in the electricity supply chain. The capacity to generate is not consummate with the capabilities of transporting power through the current infrastructure in the transmission system. The numbers of agencies participating in the generation segment are very high as compared to transmission and distribution segment.

Power supply chain management in India lacks professionalism. An integrated power supply chain management at national level including all the states is to be developed. Deregulation in generation was not complemented with de-licensing in T & D, power trading and exchanges.

The franchisee model experimentation was full of frustration derailing the participation of the private players. Rural India is not a prospective area of electricity business as the rate of return envisaged is always at risk. Corporate do not want to forgo profits and deliver services. Allocation and availability of power is poor even in many suburban areas of the country. Government is limping to answer the power demands of the rural citizens.

Small group of entrepreneurs with diesel power generation are evolving envisaging the opportunity for capitalizing the unorganized fragmented retail market of electricity supply in the neglected rural areas starving of energy both for domestic and irrigation purpose. At places they have started supporting the commercial consumers challenging the State power utilities inefficiency.

Performance - Rural Electricity Distribution System

Urban Vs Rural, are policies different. Why this discrimination in services of electricity? Why urban is given more priority in distribution of power supply?

What will happen when "SMART CITIES" will come up in India?

Rural Electrification Policy (2006) mandating electrifying all villages and households was introduced very late. There were wide gaps in implementing government policies and plans, shortfalls in accomplishing targets, late amendments due to delayed corrections on failure and unsuccessful programmes, untimely linkages & clearances had impacts on completion and commissioning of power projects affecting COD (commercial operation date), (fuel supply agreements) FSAs & PPAs closures are still holding full fledged operation of power stations.

Problem of primary energy distribution and allocation to power stations still remains an area of threat to power producers especially depending on gas based power generation. The completion of the national gas network corridor through interconnecting regions has severely affected the power projects commissioning and loss of generation.

Power and fuel are mutually interdependent in deciding the feasibility and success of the power projects being envisaged and implemented to address the issues of power crisis in the electricity sector.

The rate of fuel consumption is directly proportional to rate of power generation but the brighter side of power generation is overshadowing the bitter side of depletion of primary energy being rapidly consumed to generate electricity. Hence one unit of electricity generated consumes substantial units of primary fuel.

Policy makers need to strike a balance to maintain equilibrium in choice of fuel to generate power. Power generation is as good as energy consumption, so energy conservation and renewable energy sources exploration are focal areas for bridging the created gaps in energy.

Electrifying couple of metropolitan cities like Bangalore, Chennai, Mumbai, Delhi and Kolkata cannot be a benchmark for accessibility of electricity by all in the country. The dark areas have been untouched by the power utilities and are awaiting light at the mercy of the government. There are major regions in the States like Bihar, Jharkhand, Uttar Pradesh, Orissa, Chhattisgarh, Northeastern States and many remote areas of even developed States which have not seen the electric bulb glow.

Decades after decades the coal rich states have been supporting the generation of power throughout the country only to remain itself in the shadow of energy. A significant proportion of consumption reported as being in the agriculture sector is actually consumed by other sectors but not properly metered. Actual farm consumption could be only 10% of overall consumption.

A part of the population could afford a costlier electricity service, but available supply cannot satisfy their demand. A large majority of the population is rural. Officially, close to 70% of the villages are electrified. However, only half the Indian population does in fact have electricity. Since a large portion of the population lives below the poverty line, they cannot afford electricity at current costs; this is particularly true in rural areas.

Free power to farmers for the agricultural sector is not only a financial drain on the State Electricity Boards (SEBs) and the government but also a national energy drain. With no cost to themselves farmer do not seem to be much concerned about energy conservation measures, they have no incentive to install energy efficient motors, or energy saving devices, do not even bother to switch of motors, wasting energy.

The SEBs incurs further losses due to the low power factor of the rural grid in addition to the huge cost it has to incur on capital expenditure to lay long lines in remote areas. The Board is bloated with huge staff and reducing of employees without union resistance and political interference is a big challenge for public enterprises management. The system of employing contract workers and a constant demand to regularize their service have added to the staff cost considerably in the past. Unions are resisting reforms and successive managements have not been able to convince them and bring about sharp reduction in employee cost.

Uncertainty of Regulatory Reforms

The Role of Regulation in the power sector is being repeatedly reviewed and prospectively redefined over the last 100 years. Even today there is no unique standard charter for providing and guiding electricity services in India. It is difficult to ascertain whether the regulatory mechanism is getting deregulated or the controls are being liberalized.

The Central and State government's power utilities are accountable to the government where as the private sector power utilities accountability is yet to be clearly demarcated and defined.

The government's diplomacy in completely abolishing the License Raj is being partially administered through the MoUs, agreements and clearances. The government's main objective is to make power available and affordable to all. The main texts currently governing the electricity industry and the power market in India still are the Indian Electricity Act (1910), the Electricity (Supply) Act (1948) and the Electricity Act-2003.

The designing, implementing and monitoring a power policy by the government of India for utilities, consumers, market, investors, power builders, regulators for all the agencies operating in the power sector without partiality is always a huge task both at the centre and state within a time frame.

In democratic India every power policy will become reality cannot be assured and ensured by the government which operates under influential political conflicts ever since independence. The dynamics of the sector over the last two decades (1991 to 2012 years) has changed so drastically that even the series of reforms and subsequent improvised policy amendments and revisions failed to control the sector from becoming sick and energy deficit.

Policy to reality has many hurdles and milestones. Welfare and business both cannot be under one umbrella of policy. Though policy has brought privatization and competition, nationalization philosophy cannot be completely comprised and sacrificed in the Indian electricity sector.

Policy, Regulation and Reforms are the roots of the massive trunk India's Power Sector balancing the tender branches constituting the State, Central and Private Sector to be facilitated, guided and monitored for yielding better ripen fruits to the power hungry citizens of India.

These roots are to be carefully nurtured by the government to make the promising tree healthier in delivering desired electricity services at economical prices to the vast category of consumers satisfying their energy needs battling all the problems of the ailing sector.

The roots are so deep that simply truncating them with the sword of deregulation may not be the right answer for the security and future of electricity services in India. Government speaks of Energy Conservation and Earth Hour programmes in rural areas which are starving for energy. The policy on tapping renewable energy resources is very diplomatically experimenting its success in these backward areas.

The government shamelessly edifies it to be its concern for conservation of energy where as people instead are dying of hunger and unhygienic standards of living due to inaccessibility of electricity.

Policy Vs Reality gaps are very wide in rural areas. Moreover the unclean and dual policies are ineffective in battling out the perennial issues of power shortages and upliftment of standards of living in rural areas.

A review of the historic reform period 2001 to 2012 in the history of India's Energy Sector, brings to the surface that the rate of enacting new policies was in the range of 3 to 5 every year averagely, equaling nearly more than 35 policies or Acts or amendments introduced in the last decade.

Though the fire was ignited by 1991 Economic Reforms the flames could not be sustained despite enactment of Electricity Act-2003. Every new policy or Act is made with the lessons learnt from the past but it fails to meet its desired objective and purpose. But all goes to dismay. Where is the truth?

CHAPTER IV

ENERGY CRISIS IN INDIA

Problem Vs Solution

I begin with the theme of re-energizing India's Energy Sector. Who will provide energy solutions to India? What is the sanctity of a collaborative approach to such national issues? What should be the realistic rate at which energy sector has to grow?

How to push up India's GDP? How to rationalize the per capita income of citizen in India?

Energy Vs Growth no doubt is mutually related at any level of living.

Poverty Vs Rich, the war is endless in any society in the World. Development invariably meant to bring equality in all respects.

Optimism is only being assured but not realized completely in practicality. Can India have flawless system? Some of the provisions of the Acts in light of fast paced changes taking place in energy sector may bring in uneconomical business models. Many of the clauses /section needs further clarity from case to case. The important one being there is lot of confusion on procurement of renewable energy.

The regulators have totally failed in ensuring prudence in power procurement. The multiplicity of buy and sell makes it harder for any type of services sector. It is like series of compartments of bulk and retail consumers in and out in the same train of electricity sector.

What is to be at the sole discretion of commission? Many citizens feel that discretion to the commission is unwarranted and imprudent in many of the sections and clauses of the Act.

Purity in Policy should be the vision of any nation. Uninfluenced by the egos of ruling party in a democratic set up of governance. Why India's implementation of energy policies is non-performing again and again? Are we driving the aircraft of energy dreams without a cockpit?

Such bold pilots skilled with charismatic leadership are not seen flying with the vision of millions and millions of Indians. Country requires more and more energy professionals today. The outlay on research and development is marginal in the sector knowing the turbulence it faces from dawn to dusk.

The government should allocate appreciable percentage every year.

Every year the government of India voices to turnaround the ailing sector. This has been the mandate of all the political parties either at centre or state. How the momentum of growth is to be maintained? Nothing truly seems to happen consistently in the energy sector.

It appears the intrinsic nature of energy not to be in equilibrium perhaps has got induced into the sector right from concept to operation of the services. There should be equal opportunity to look for establishing research and development in the sector along with the road map to re-energize the sector.

Why customers are less satisfied with the energy utilities in India? Especially with the services of power utilities the issues are escalating day by day. Many such type of facts are prevailing in the economic development of India.

Criticism and Journalism are not analytical voices of the sector. Anything on logic is protected by the umbrella of perception. Indian citizens are more victims of the political slogans. This is perhaps because of the illiteracy. It adds to the below poverty line disparities and grievances.

Is it not that the energy is going to the developed segment of the nation only? It is reaching the markets to make huge revenues only. Energy is being drained to create models benefiting the few in the sector. Needy are yet thirsty.

What is the pyramid of beneficiaries from the overall development and growth of the energy sector in recent times?

Pyramid of Beneficiaries

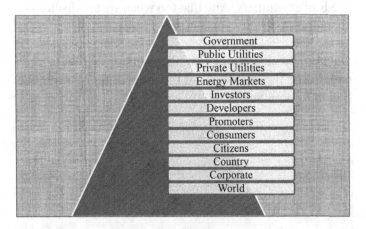

Government
Public Utilities
Private Utilities
Energy Markets
Investors
Developers
Promoters
Consumers
Citizens
Country
Corporate
World

Development and Sustenance are parallel requirements of any nation. Have the policy makers demarcated the quantum of energy is consumed in the respective areas in India's growth?

Growth, Development and Sustenance are the core issues for any economist. How are the energy economists contributing to the statistics of energy in India? Are they able to make any difference?

Power supply chain of generation, transmission, distribution, supply, connection and collection is not limited to few stakeholders. It requires nodal studies to understand the entire vibration of the power system network. Right from people efficiency to power utilities performance.

It is difficult to read the minds of unsatisfied consumers. What are the key factors affecting customer's satisfaction? How do we come to know unless it is asked to them? This is one of the first steps in understanding the behavioral needs of consumers. And that too when we are discussing about the electricity consumers in India.

An analytical approach to the subject is required to understand the intricacies of the interfacing issues in the Indian Energy Sector.

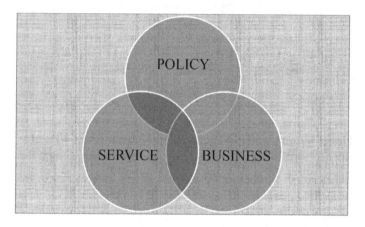

I wish not to begin emphasizing my points with the statistical figures reported in the annual reports, journals, and consultant's analysis from India and World because this is already available with all of you at the websites, libraries, periodicals, summary reports etc and so on.

Before I can proceed to my readers in presenting this complete analytical case study the above brief synopsis in the introductory chapter should be retained in mind as a background to gain from the other chapters of this book. Now it will be based on the understanding capacity of the readers on this critical subject. The issues are like the cobweb of the spider in reality.

Power is to be generated by the energy of primary fuel. Power plants are being owned by public and private. The Power Utilities are operating under the policy guidelines from the regulator at centre and state as the case may be.

Don't you think the political system of India greatly impacts the implementation programs at respective state levels? The ruling party at the Centre is invariably inclined in favoring and facilitating the states being governed by them. The bureaucracy functions irrespective of the ruling party but is always preying to the dancing tunes of the governance.

The areas of Governance and Administration have always been a matter of debate right from the years of formulation of the system. The introductions of principles of management in recent times have marginally been successful through the process of restructuring and accountability in the system.

Does it not astonish that being a power producer you do not enjoy the rights of pricing electricity? How far it can hold in the new era of corporatizing electricity services in India?

What should be the pyramid of energy? How to prioritize primary energy in relation to secondary energy?

Is not electricity the secondary energy dominating the world? It is available by generation only. The greatest bane to human and limiting factor for natural resources.

Had electricity been in mines like coal the story of global energy would have been totally different?

Dr Shree Raman Dubey

Pyramid of Energy

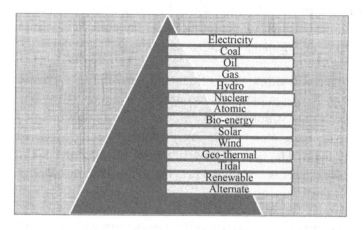

Who will power India's future? How to renew opportunities of excellence in the sector? How to energize growth?

Under performance of power utilities and dissatisfaction of electrical energy consumers are the two inseparable facets of the deregulating power sector. The deregulation is continually destabilizing the opportunity to revitalize and revamp the sector. Energy crisis and energy trading are the two wheels of the mounted deregulating power sector invariably running with policy misalignment probably against the anticipation to derail the liberalizing power sector.

The point of analysis is that nearly all possible style of governing in the power sector has been implemented but the key performance indicators more or less statically remain unresponsive to the desired change.

In the last two decades from 1991 Economic reforms, enactment of Electricity reforms in 2003, subsequent

National Power Policy (2005), National Tariff Policy (2006), Rural Electrification Policy (2006), Integrated Energy Policy (2006), Power Exchanges in India (2007), Point of Connection (2010) to many more small or big new policies or notified amendments the power sector has been flooded to sustain and restore the healthiness of the sector.

The indelible Core Sector even after 50 years of service to the nation is energy deficit. In reality National Planning & Policies, Commissions and the Public Enterprises constituted for economic development failed to shoulder the States responsibility effectively and could not deliver "WELFARE and BUSINESS" together, thus branding the Power Sector ineffective. Neither the opportunities are completely dying nor are the challenges ending in the Indian Electricity Sector.

However the Indian Power Industry is one of the largest and most important industries in India as it fulfills the energy requirements of various other industries. It is one of the most critical components of infrastructure that affects economic growth and the well-being of India.

India has the world's 5th largest electricity generation capacity and it is the 6th largest energy consumer accounting for 3.4% of global energy consumption. Due to the fast-paced growth of the Indian economy, the country's energy demand has grown at an average of 3.6 per cent per annum over the past 30 years.

India has stepped its development agenda and power is an inevitable element of economic growth and development. Growth in the power sector is related to India's GDP growth rate and hence, in order to sustain the growth of 8-9% in GDP, India needs to continuously add power generation capacity to commensurate with this pace.

Although, the Indian power sector is one of the fastest growing sectors in the world and energy availability has increased by around 36% in the past 5 years, the demand for power outstrips its supply.

Nearly 60 crore Indians do not have access to electricity. The energy and peaking deficits have been hovering around double digits for the past two years and the condition might worsen in the coming years considering the huge demand of power from India's rising population and rapid industrialization and urbanization. Hence, there is no slowing down of demand for the Power Sector, thus offering ample scope for rapid capacity expansion. The Government has been investing in this industry through various development schemes like Rajeev Gandhi Rural Electrification Program, "Power for all by 2012" and Accelerated Power Development and Reform Programme (ARDRP), Ultra Mega Power Projects etc.

India has also been encouraging participation of private players in this Sector. Renewable energy sources are also being encouraged considering the growing environmental concerns. The future prospects of nuclear power, hydro power and power from renewable energy sources only paints a rosy picture to the investors.

Who will switch on India's Power future? How can India balance power supply and demand? Can the Government of India do justice to the Power Utilities and Electricity Consumers?

Is the Role of Regulation fading away?

The expectation, "Will there be solution to Energy Crisis by 2012?", has also not met the National objectives. All the above is running in the minds of Indian citizens. India is deeply concerned about the future of energy.

From 1900-1950 under the British Rule electricity was a luxury, 1950-1990 era was the monopoly of the State Electricity Boards and 1975-2010 the central sector power utilities accounted for the majority of power capacity created. Will the private sector now establish their command over the public utilities?

India's economy continues to be under inflation and people starve for power. The policy of UMPP to rapidly enhance capacity addition in generation is at the verge of failing. The citizen's last hopes of cherishing their dreams through UMPP's have been nipped in the bud.

Does liberalization means Nationalization to Corporatization? The power market is being liberalized to attract huge investments by the Corporate to establish the electricity trading business in India.

The transition from Independent Power Producers (IPPs) with regulated tariffs to recently emerging Merchant Power Producers (MPPs) with deregulation in setting up off tariffs speaks of liberalizing the power market.

The question arises as to how many of the power producers will be the key traders of electricity. The present regulation does not believe in converting all the power utilities into electricity traders. The undefined domain and functional demarcation between bulk electricity traders and retail electricity traders to operate in the market is going to bring in turbulence as the consequences of liberalization.

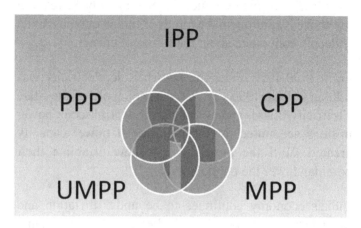

Again its restriction to perform all the functions of generation, transmission, distribution, supply and trading of electricity by any single entity or utility in the Central, State and Private sector reflects half hearted approach and commitment of the policy makers in liberalizing the Indian Electricity Market.

The concept of treating electricity services as a commodity for trading cannot be advocated right now in the present scenario of emerging power mix and market in India. PPPs, IPPs, CPPs and MPPs are the newly born baby utilities without administrative and legal domain recognitions, either they are under the regulation as per Central Utilities or State Utilities is not clearly defined independently as Private Utilities.

The Private Power Utilities are operating in the sector as Ancillary Power Utilities based on either grant of license or without licenses as per the stipulation defined by the regulations. The question is of equal status quo to Private Power Utilities in the emerging power sector as they are the drivers of the Indian Economy.

Service Vs Trade, the philosophy can never converge with national ideologies in India.

It appears that the whole exercise of electricity reforms in the sector over the two decades (1991 Economic Reforms-Power to all by 2012 year) was inclined to introduce trading of electricity rather than servicing of electricity to the people of India.

Today, Global Energy Crisis is concern of everyone. World's dependencies on Electric Power is again questioning the sustainability of modern, better and clean living. Developed nations are redefining the choices in power generation. India is struggling to craft a complete power supply chain. Will the emerging Indian Power Sector transform the Destiny of Energy?

Citizens fundamental need of electricity are now to be purchased paying the unregulated price of production and service.

ELECTRICITY IN INDIA

Electricity in India is over a century old. India was not far behind; New York was electrified in 1882 and followed by London in 1888. Who is the pioneer in the history of generating electricity in India? It is very difficult to rank any single company or power utility, as many of them were operating more or less in the same period. Electricity generation in India began under the British Rule with a demonstration of electric lighting in Calcutta in 1879.

The Government of Bengal granted an exclusive 21 year license for electricity to illuminate and power the area of Calcutta to the Calcutta Electric Supply Corporation Limited, which was registered in London. CESC commissioned the first power station in 1899 and sold power at one rupee per kWh, the tariff set at parity with electricity in London at that time (CESC Limited 2001). In Calcutta (now Kolkata), CESC Limited started power generating and distribution in 1899.

The British Electric Traction Company was a company in Bombay (now Mumbai) which used to generate electricity since 1882. The company was bought over by the Bombay Electric Supply & Tramways Company Limited, and was known as BEST (Bombay Electricity Supply and Transport, now as Brihanmumbai Electricity Supply and Transport). In 1979 the company was converted into an Indian company as The Calcutta Electric Supply Corporation (India) Limited.

In 1902, the world's then longest transmission line was erected from Shivasamudram to the Kolar Gold Fields in Karnataka. In 1910, Tata Hydro-Electric Power Supply Company, (now Tata Power Limited) was set up, and soon a number of private companies built urban power supply systems across pre-independent India under franchises that allowed for reasonable rates of return and included regulatory oversight to prevent monopolistic abuse.

India's Power Sector during the period 1900-1950, under the British rule was very small, fragmented and was being handled through licensees and private suppliers catering to the preferred customers who could afford this luxury.

A handful of these companies still continue today as private electricity suppliers for several major cities including Kolkata in Eastern India, Mumbai and Ahmadabad in Western India. However, the vast majority of the private entities were amalgamated after independence into state-owned enterprises by The 1948 Electricity Supply Act, modeled on a similar British Law from 1926.

100 Years of Electricity in India

I have categorized 100 years of electricity in India into five valuable periods for easy understanding of my readers.

1900 -1950, Under British Rule, it was completely decentralized. 1950 – 1975, Under SEBs monopoly, it was following the philosophy of nationalization. 1975-1991, Under Central Sector Power Utilities, commanding heights.

1991- 2003, Under Economic Reforms, LPG Policy the power sector was experiencing liberalization, privatization and globalization.

2003- 2012, Under Electricity Reforms Act-2003, the power sector was introduced to deregulation, unbundling of SEBs and corporatization of electricity services.

Even after 100 years of beginning load shedding is the rule of the day in India. Power Sector's failure is evidently hampering India's growth enabling to compete, contribute and command the global market.

India's population continues to rise and could reach 1.5 billion by the middle of this century. India's GDP has been growing at an annual average fluctuating growth rate of 6-9% in the last two decades.

The Indian Electricity Sector during the entire period from the time of political independence in the year 1947, the liberalized economy in 1991, the historic reformative Electricity Act-2003 to the Government's mandate of power to all by 2012 has experienced an annual average growth rate of 6-9%. Over the last two decades though both the Indian economy and electricity were growing more or less neck to neck then why the Indian Power Sector today is characterized with an average electricity shortage of 10-15%, peak power demand shortage of 15-20%, AT&C losses of 20-25%. The national monopoly in electricity generation and supply has been rejected over the last two decades. The economies of scale in transmission system still limit the scope for competition. Industrial consumers being the backbone of the Indian economy are suffering from power holidays.

Earth hour programs are being implemented to bring in awareness among the consumers to conserve and save energy. Many villages are in darkness, living with lamps waiting to see the electric bulbs glow in their homes.

Today, electricity is being demanded as a fundamental right by the people of India. How many years will India take to make it available to all the citizens of India?

Private Sector was always reluctant to undertake socio-economic development as their prime motive was profit, and social service was not an essential commitment. But there were Private Companies like CESC, BSES, TATA POWER providing electricity.

Before Independence, purchasing electricity might have been a luxury and the group would have been limited. It was only after the end of British Rule, the need for extending it to all was felt. The continuous repeated failures and regular slippages by the States and the Centre in timely enhancing additional capacity generation decelerated the targeted power development as outlaid in the progressive Five Year Plans since independence, forcing us to face the Energy Crisis today.

The Economic Growth which is propelled by the development of Power Sector faces stiff challenges to sustain the envisaged rate of growth. The major responsibility had been collectively shouldered by the respective SEB's independently till the reforms and restructuring were initiated and implemented.

The exponential pace of industrialization and infrastructure development after the 1991 Economic Reforms created the greatest need for consumption of electricity ever in the history of India. To increase the capacity of generation new Green Field Power Projects were to be executed under the then prevailing Laws & Acts which were not conducive to the development of Electricity in India.

In addition to above allocation of Power as per PPAs (Power Purchase Agreements), un-proportionate distribution, politicization of tariff, theft & metering, poor maintenance, equipment failures, transmission & distribution losses, under capacity utilization, high levels of debt, huge amount of subsidy, default in payment, inconsistent operational and commercial performance are the chronic problems remaining over the decades waiting for a graceful fortune rain to be washed out for ever.

These vertically integrated, inefficient, bankrupt and dwindling SEB's (State Electricity Boards) were functionally disintegrated into Generation, Transmission and Distribution entities for better management and increasing overall performance.

In spite of the unfolding of SEB's, States failed to meet the objectives and the last ray of hope from the Private Sector was nipped in the bud. Implementation of New Regulations, Acts, reforms and restructuring took place from time to time with very marginal improvements. This provided interim betterments but energy deficit kept on mounting day by day. The cold war between the domestic and industrial users is boiling up.

The central role of agriculture and rural electrification in the society keeps on politically dictating cheaper electricity burdening the Indian power system.

Rural electrification in India has not been a success story in the past. There is no manifesto without promise of uninterrupted power supply to citizens of India. It is the trump card for political parties to bank the votes. Governments are having restless time in optimizing the sector.

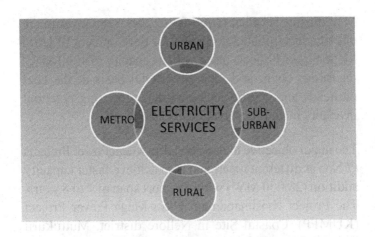

Where are the profits in providing electricity services to consumers? Why profits cannot be made in Rural India? Why our policy is to develop metro and smart cities when millions of villages are yet in dark?

Many States are behind the dark cloud and some are only at the mercy of grace waiting eagerly to see the sunshine. The present rate of electricity consumption in India is far behind the overall supply of Energy. There is hardly any State in India with surplus power and energy to share.

Indian Power Planners are continuously striving to overcome this power deficit problem. There is fear that the power generation by diesel generating sets, captive and merchant power plants from the unorganized and unaccountable providers may cause instability in developing the electricity market.

In line with the target of Power to All by 2012 an additional generating capacity of 100,000 MW was envisaged by the Government of India. It was to be achieved, 40,000 MW during 10th Plan (2001-02 to 2006-07) and 61,000

MW during 11th Plan (2006-07 to 2011-12). Government of India has initiated a scheme for development of Ultra Mega Power Projects (each with a capacity of 4000 MW) on Build, Own, and Operate (BOO) basis at the coal pit heads and coastal locations thus attracting potential investors including private participants.

The major objective to develop Ultra Mega Power Projects (7 Nos at different locations) is to achieve faster capacity addition (28,000 MW) within a short span of 7 to 8 years. The Project Krishnapatnam Ultra Mega Power Project (KUMPP), Coastal Site in Nellore district, Muttukuru Mandal of Andhra Pradesh is being planned with the aim of sharing power. The proposed beneficiary states were Maharasthra (800MW), Tamil Nadu (800MW), Karnataka (800MW) and Andhra Pradesh(1600MW). The UMPP did not take off till the end of 2011 year.

Hinduja Group could not set up 1000 MW power project under Mega Power Policy even after two decades through an initial joint venture with National Power, United Kingdom (presently National Power has withdrawn support). This project was originally envisaged by Andhra Pradesh State Electricity Board (APSEB) in 1989-90.

Indian government is failing to protect the commitments of NRIs. The patriotism of these giant entrepreneurs is not being religiously honoured by the government in the power sector.

One of the important outcomes of this emerging power mix should be to immediately remove the unwanted regional disparities existing in availability of electricity by focusing on pooling of power, optimizing share of allocation, control in drawings from grids and promoting intra & interstate energy trading across the nation.

The leading power utilities in liberalized India have been frequently reconciling, introspecting, discussing, debating, exploring and redefining the challenges of regulation, sustainability, demand planning, strategic sourcing, commercial structure of emerging markets, global integration, risk associated with huge investments in new power projects and measures for improvement against impeding factors to meet the long waiting expectations of all, but the journey never seems to end.

India's power sector is leaking. Is energy crisis due to this leaks? Why India is unable to arrest it? Without the logical thinking persistently the shortage of power is being emphasized and exaggerated estimates of future demands for power is the cry. Do India has answers for energy crisis? The continuous struggle between Policy and Reality continues to test the endurance limit of power sector.

TRANSITION-
India's Electricity Sector

The domination of the SEBs resulted in their monopoly in the State sector, the contribution of the central power utilities was at commanding heights in the Central sector, the Private sector was instrumental in initiating capitalization of the power sector and corporatization of the power sector is being influenced by the emerging power mix are the transition phases of electricity in India.

The power industry in India was in the private sector at the time of independence and the total commissioned capacity of the power generation in the country was about 1350 MW. There was no power industry in the rural India which was employing 70% of the people in agrarian sector.

In 1948, very next year of the independence, the Electricity Supply Act 1948 came into existence with the aim and object to bring the power industry in the public sector. The question of the development of the economy was before the nation and without expansion of the power industry no economy can expect to develop. The agrarian sector must develop. But without electricity no intensive farming is possible, so no development. Therefore the power industry was brought into the public sector under the Electricity Supply Act 1948.

The State Electricity Boards were constituted in all the bigger state of the country and generation plants, transmission network with Grid substation and Transmission lines were erected. The system of rural electrification for power distribution was developed with the construction of distribution substations and its supply lines. The villages were electrified and for it, the Rural Electrification Corporation (REC) was formed to finance the work of rural electrification.

During the last 60 years, the power sector of the country developed tremendously. Our Commissioned capacity of power generation increased from 1350MW in 1947 to 200 000 MW now.

It is about 100 times increases in our commission capacity of power generation. Our power transmission system expanded widely with the erection of substations, super grid substation and allied transmission lines throughout the country. For the development of proper power distribution system, supply areas, circles, divisions, subdivision and sections were created in all the state electricity boards of the different state of the country. As per the statistics available, about more than half a million villages have been electrified, more than 14 million of the irrigation motors pump sets were energized.

The world capitalist system has always been passing through crisis, one after another. Earlier also the world capitalist system has faced the crisis of depression. India is one of those countries which adopted the market economy at the pressure of the world capitalist power.

The philosophy of the self reliant and making the nation, a country of mixed economy by constituting the public sector enterprises, etc was forgotten, and just a reverse policy to that of the self reliance was accepted in the middle of 1991. It is just U turn of the economy policy.

Our power policy also changed in just the rear direction leading to dismantling of about 13 State Electricity Boards, privatization of the power direction in the state of Orissa and Delhi. In the dismantled state electricity, board attempt is on to privatize the power distribution and revenue collection by franchises. The works of the power sector are being done by outsourcing.

The new economy policy at the pressure of the imperialist power and dictated by the World Bank and the International Monetary Fund was adopted in 1991. The power sector becomes the first victim in 1996 when the Orissa State

Electricity Board and the Haryana State Electricity board were also dismantled by their own state Reform Acts.

Up till now about 13 state electricity board have been dismantled. In addition to Orissa and Haryana, they are Andhra Pradesh, Karnatka, Gujrat, Uttar Pradesh, Uttranchal, Rajasthan, Madhya Pradesh, Delhi, Assam, Maharastra and West Bengal. The State Electricity Board which are still existing are Bihar, Jharkhand, Meghalaya, Chhatisgarh, Tamilnadu, Kerla, Himachal Pradesh & Punjab. Among the dismantled State Electricity Board all except Assam and Maharastra have been dismantled by enacting state Act, for dismantling.

A central Electricity Act was enacted in 2003. This Act is the clear manifestation of what the Government of the India intends to do in the power sector.

The electricity Act 2003 has provided for a state alone system for the entire rural India. The rural will detach from the grid system and will be asked to generate power of their own for its requirement preferable from the non – conventional source of energy i. e. solar panels, wind mills, sea tides etc with the help of their gram panchayat, cooperatives, franchises etc. This is not possible for the present consumption of power for the entire rural India exceeding 56% of its total generation. About 140 lakh irrigation motor pumps are being run by electricity. This huge requirement of the rural India cannot be fulfilled by the stand alone system of the Act.

State Sector

The breaking of large entity SEBs overall functions into small entities GENCO, TRANSCO, DISCOMs and TRADECO to carry out independent functions of generation, transmission, distribution and trading speaks of rearranging the organizational structure rather than any novelty which can be justified in true sense to be the reforms to revolutionize the sector.

A large entity has been restructured with a view that the smaller entities would be easy to manage by providing them autonomy and also to work as a responsible corporate structure.

The Public Enterprises Management of SEBs are large public enterprises needing professional competencies to deliver satisfactory services with the economics of scale and substantial profits margin. Splitting up of large entities into small enterprises to resolve the power crisis problem speaks of the organizational responsibilities restructuring rather than implementing brainstormed scientific measures to revamp the sector.

The government at large was trying to address the functional issues. Either a large entity or small entity as Board or State public undertaking is under the State government and State sector. What gross differences it would have made had the unbundling of SEBs, was not thought of?

Will the unbundling of SEBs revamp the power sector?

In 1950 about 63% of the installed capacity was in the private sector and about 37% was in the public sector. The Industrial Policy Resolution of 1956 envisaged the generation, transmission and distribution of power almost exclusively in the public sector. As a result of this Resolution and facilitated by the Electricity (Supply) Act, 1948, the electricity industry developed rapidly in the State Sector.

In the Constitution of India "Electricity" is a subject that falls within the concurrent jurisdiction of the Centre and the States. The Electricity (Supply) Act, 1948, provides an elaborate institutional frame work and financing norms of the performance of the electricity industry in the country.

The Act envisaged creation of State Electricity Boards (SEBs) for planning and implementing the power development programmes in their respective States. The Act also provided for creation of central generation companies for setting up and operating generating facilities in the Central Sector.

The Central Electricity Authority constituted under the Act is responsible for power planning at the national level. In addition the Electricity (Supply) Act also allowed from the beginning the private licensees to distribute and/or generate electricity in the specified areas designated by the concerned State Government/SEB.

The Electricity Boards in the states were created with enactment of the Electricity (Supply) Act, 1948. The electricity boards were given full responsibility for development of the power sector in their respective states including setting up of power generation plants, transmission lines and distribution systems.

Legally, the SEBs were now autonomous bodies and free to set their own tariffs. Apart from the SEBs, there were a few entities like the Bhakra Beas Management Board and the Damodar Valley Corporation and private players such as BSES and CESC operating in the power sector at that time.

India's electricity supply has long been dominated by the public sector. Public ownership and public management of the main elements of the supply industry have been the rule since independence. At that time, most existing electric utilities were integrated into 19 SEBs (see Electric Supply Act of 1948) and eight electricity departments. These boards were part of state governments.

Both the central and state Indian governments enjoy legislative rights on the subject of electricity. Electricity distribution, however, is the exclusive domain of the state governments.

Prior to 1991, the electricity business in the states was in the form of vertically integrated State Electricity Board (SEBs). SEBs were owned and operated by the states and were responsible for generation, transmission and distribution services within the state. SEBs operated under the proviso of the Electricity Supply Act of 1948, and were supplemented in their efforts by the Central Public Sector Utilities (CPSUs) like the NTPC (National Thermal Power Corporation), the NHPC (National Hydro-electric Power Corporation), and the PGCIL (Power Grid Corporation of India).

The 1st Plan emphasized that support for projects that ensure irrigation potential is met. At this point, only 1 in 200 villages were connected to grid supply across the country. The 2nd plan named rural electrification as an area of special interest, and proposed to cover all towns with a population of 10,000 or more. Only 350 out of a total of 856 were eventually electrified. The 3rd plan for the 1st time raised the issue of efficiency in the sector. The REC (Rural Electrification Corporation) was created in 1969 with renewed focus on poverty alleviation. The target based pump set energization and guidelines for village grid connectivity for all villages with a population of at least 5000.

The early 80's saw major changes in conjunction with the creation the Commission for Additional sources of Energy (CASE) in 1981, which evolved into a full-fledged Ministry for Non-Conventional Energy Sources (MNES) in 1992.

The 6th and 7th Plan periods witnessed the launch of innovative rural energy programs like the National Program on Improved Chulha (NPIC) in 1983, The National Project on Biogas Development (1981-82), Special Program Agriculture (SAP) and integrated energy programs like IRPE (Integrated Rural Energy Planning) and Urjagram.

With the institutionalization of the MNES in the early 90s, rural energy provision now largely rests with the RECs and MNES. Covering a wide range of technology and fuel options including renewable sources, national efforts at rural energy provision offer a variety of programs to address the range of energy requirements of rural populations.

Growth in the period from 1947 until reforms were instated in 1991 was impressive in increasing capacity generation from 1362 MW in 1947 to nearly 74 699 MW by 1991-92. Despite a per capita power consumption increase from 15.55Kwh to 252.7 Kwh, SEBs were financially weak.

The 4th Plan and the findings of the Venkatraman Committee report created to examine the financial working of the SEBs, concurred that SEBs should at the very least aim at revenues sufficient to cover operational and maintenance charges, depreciation of reserves and interest charges on the capital base.

The performance of SEBs at the national level was never impressive since their inception, they were making an overall negative rate of return, the recovery percentage has been between 60-80%, the gross subsidy per unit distributed has remained constant at 34% of the cost of delivery, and on average realizations from a subsidized sector like agriculture make up only 10% of the cost of supply.

Despite repeated warnings by the Planning Commission and subsequent committees examining the power sector such as the Committee on Power (Rajadhyaksna Committee) and the Planning Commission Work Group on Energy Policy (1979), the crucial issue of rational pricing of electricity was left un-addressed. Increasing SEB losses, pressure on scarce public resources and the reforms of 1991 ultimately forced the opening of the hitherto monopolistic SEBs to private participation.

Even as the 50 year period saw nearly 80% of the country connected to grid supply, up from the few urban pockets of electricity supplied at the time of independence, the SEBs cumulatively were being given an annual gross subsidy of Rs 7,450 crores by 1991-92, losing about Rs 4021 crores a year showing an average rate of return (without subsidy) of about -12.5%. By March 31,2001 the gross subsidy had shot up to Rs 38,000 crores a year with total SEB outstanding to CPSU and others at Rs 27,760 crores.

The SEBs incorporated under the Electricity Supply Act-1948 were government owned. While electricity was perceived as a public good, there was lack of clarity as to who should pay for it. The lack of transparent and well defined subsidies that would be paid from the exchequer to the SEBs to implement specific government policies led to tariffs that were not sustainable.

Despite the recommendations of the Venkataraman Committee (1964), which suggested that SEBs should aim at an overall return of 11 percent, and the 6th Plan's calling for an energy pricing policy, the commercial principles underlying tariff revision more often than not were superseded by political considerations.

Is there any end to number of tariff revisions against strict stipulations? Power generating utilities are inclined towards matching their costs again and again by banking on tariff revisions. It is sensibly difficult to justify from case to case.

The share of the electricity sector in the Five Year Plans has been in the range of 15-20%. However, investment has gone into generation rather than transmission and distribution. In terms of actual investments 70% has gone towards generation, 20% towards transmission and only 10% toward distribution.

The Government of India consequently launched the APDRP (Accelerated Power Development and Reform Program), to ensure matching investments in Transmission & Distribution (T&D). By 1991-92 year, T&D Losses stood at over 20% officially and 30% unofficially, taking into account the inaccuracy of non-metered consumption and losses sometimes disguised as agricultural consumption.

The Distribution Policy Committee Report in 2002 paints a similar picture, with actual losses ranging between 40-50%, including technical losses of about 15-20% and commercial losses of about 25-30%. Thus for every two units of energy consumed, one unit was lost due to T & D losses.

The Government of India, in accordance with its Liberalization, Privatization & Globalization policy opened the sector for private participation in early 1992 with amendments to the Electricity Supply Act of 1948. But private participation was encouraged only in generation, protecting SEBs from competition.

This change necessitated a comprehensive new set of regulations covering generation, transmission, distribution and trading. The culmination of a decade of piecemeal efforts at reforming the power sector finally passed in Parliament as the Electricity Act-2003.

State Electricity Boards have been the main components of the electricity services in India for the last 50 years rendering a commendable service in electrification of the country. As recently as 1998, the responsibility of fixing the tariff for power was handed over to an independent commission.

The consumption of power was never considered either as a service to community, or a commodity. The financial mess in the power sector is largely due to the concept of running the utility companies as government departments and not as a business.

The SERCs have recorded in the tariff notifications that there is inefficiency in energy metering, billing and revenue collection by SEBs. Most of the State Electricity Boards are losing almost half of the energy sold due to improper measurement through metering, faulty billing and non-efficient means of revenue collection.

Accordingly, in the complete commercial cycle the company is losing half of the revenue due to commercial and technical losses. This loss is especially prominent in far –flung rural areas. All that which was so carefully crafted with great expectations had to be unbundled on part of the unaccountable carelessness in the overall Indian Power System.

Central Sector

The extensive efforts put in by the SEBs and other utilities to meet the power requirements of the country were inadequate in the face of rapidly growing demand. It became imperative that large investments came into this capital intensive sector along with new players.

1960-1975, was a period of increased nationalization and the central government sought to augment their role by establishing a number of publicly owned companies that generated and transmitted power to more than one state, these were created under the initiative of then Prime Minister Indira Gandhi.

From, the Fifth Plan onwards i.e. 1974-79, the Government of India got itself involved in a big way in the generation and bulk transmission of power to supplement the efforts at the State level and took upon itself the responsibility of setting up large power projects to develop the coal and hydroelectric resources in the country as a supplementary effort in meeting the country's power requirements.

The National thermal Power Corporation (NTPC) and National Hydro-electric Power Corporation (NHPC) were set up for these purposes in 1975. North-Eastern Electric Power Corporation (NEEPCO) was set up in 1976 to implement the regional power projects in the North-East. Subsequently two more power generation corporations were set up in 1988 viz. Tehri Hydro Development Corporation (THDC) and Nathpa Jhakri Power Corporation (NJPC). These agencies were initially entrusted the responsibility of constructing and operating large size thermal and hydroelectric power plants respectively, to supply power to the State Power Utilities.

To construct, operate and maintain the inter-State and interregional transmission systems the National Power Transmission Corporation (NPTC) was set up in 1989. The corporation was renamed as POWER GRID in 1992.

Damodar Valley Corporation, the first major multi-purpose integrated river valley project of the country conceived in line with Tennessee Valley Authority (TVA) came into existence on July 7, 1948 by an Act of Central Legislature.

In keeping with industrialization in DVC commend area, power generation, transmission and distribution gained priority for providing electricity to the core industries like Steel, Coal, Railways and other industries/consumers to respective State Electricity Boards.

Bhakra Management Board (BMB) was constituted under Section 79 of the Punjab Re-Organisation Act,1966 for the administration, maintenance and operation of Bhakra Nangal Project w.e.f. 1st October, 1967. BBMB is statutory body under the supervision of Government of India.

However, Government of India does not have any financial stake in this Body. BBMB also provides Engineering and related technical and consultancy services in various fields of Hydro Electric Power and Irrigation Projects.

NTPC was set up in 1975 as a Central Sector generating company for the development of thermal power. The Corporation has grown rapidly to become the largest thermal generating company in India.

However, in addition to attaining large size, the operations of the company have also become diverse and are now not limited to thermal power only. Company has diversified into hydro power, power trading, coal mining etc. In order to embody its diverse operations the company has been rechristened as NTPC Limited.

Power Grid Corporation of India Limited (POWERGRID) was incorporated as a Government of India enterprise on 23rd October, 1989 under the Companies Act, 1956.

POWERGRID, the Central Transmission Utility (CTU) of the country and one of the largest transmission utilities in the world, is playing a strategic role in the Indian Power Sector and is considered as the nerve center of Power Sector.

Today, POWERGRID is operating about 64,800 Ckt km of transmission lines and 110 Sub-stations having transformation capacity of about 66,600 MVA. The current inter regional transmission capacity of PGCIL is 17,000 MW. The transmission system availability is maintained consistently more than 99% by deploying best Operation and Maintenance (O&M) practices at par with international utilities.

National Hydro-electric Power Corporation (NHPC) was incorporated in 1975 under Companies Act 1956. NHPC is a Schedule "A" Enterprise of the Government of India. NHPC has now become the largest organization for hydro power development in India, with capabilities to undertake all the activities from conceptualization to commissioning of hydro projects.

The main objects of NHPC include, planning, promoting and organizing an integrated and efficient development of hydroelectric, wind, tidal, geothermal and gas power in all aspects, and transmission, distribution and sale of power generation at power stations. The total installed capacity of NHPC as on 31.12.2012 including that of NHDC is 4665 MW. The Corporation is presently engaged in construction of 12 projects with the installed capacity of 5132 MW.

North Eastern Electric Corporation Ltd. (NEEPCO) was constituted in 1976 under the Indian Companies Act, 1956 with the objective of developing the power potential of the North Eastern Region of the country through planned development of power generation projects, which in turn would effectively promote the development of the North Eastern Region. Since then NEEPCO has grown into one of the pioneer Public Sector Undertaking under the Ministry of Power, Govt. of India. NEEPCO is having an installed capacity of 1,130 MW (755 MW hydro & 375 MW thermal) as on 31.12.2012, which meets more than 60% of the energy requirements of the North Eastern (N.E.) Region.

Rural Electrification Corporation Limited (REC) was incorporated in the year 1969 to facilitate the development of power infrastructure in the rural India. The main objectives of the Corporation are to promote and finance projects aimed at Integrated System Improvement, power generation, promotion of decentralized & non-conventional energy sources, energy conservation, renovation & maintenance, power distribution with focus on pump sets energization, rural households electrification and other related works in rural & urban areas. REC, is the nodal agency for implementation of RGGVY programme, has 17 nos. of Project Offices spread all over the country.

Power Finance Corporation Limited (PFC) was set-up in July 1986, under the Companies Act to serve the Power Sector exclusively, under the administrative control of the Ministry of Power. PFC was registered as a Non-Banking

Finance Company (NBFC) with the Reserve Bank of
India in February 1998. PFC is also notified as a Public
Financial Institution (PFI) under Section-4(A) of the
Companies Act 1956. Apart from extending financial
assistance/ guarantees to power utilities, the Corporation is
also playing a crucial role in the institutional development
of its borrowers. PFC is facilitating development of Ultra
Mega Power Projects by setting up SPV companies.

THDC, a Joint Venture Corporation of the Govt. of India
and Govt. of U.P., was incorporated as a Limited Company
under the Companies Act,1956, in July'88 to develop,
operate and maintain the Tehri Hydro Power Complex and
other Hydro Projects. THDC is presently responsible for
the implementation of the Tehri Hydro Power Complex
(2400 MW), VishnuGad Pipalkoti Project (444 MW) and
six other new Hydro Electric Projects, with total installed
capacity of 695 MW. The cost of the Tehri Hydro Power
Complex being shared in the ratio of 75:25 (equity portion)
by Govt. of India & Govt. of U.P. for power component,
while the irrigation component(20% of cost of Tehri Dam
& HPP) is being entirely funded by the Govt. of U.P. The
current installed capacity of THDC is 1000 MW.

The Satluj Jal Vidyut Nigam Limited – SJVN (formerly
Nathpa Jhakri Power Corporation Limited – NJPC)
was incorporated on May 24, 1988 as a joint venture of
the Government of India (GOI) and the Government of
Himachal Pradesh (GOHP) to plan, investigate, organize,
execute, operate and maintain Hydro-electric power
projects in the river Satluj basin in the state of Himachal
Pradesh. The debt equity ratio for the Nathpa Jhakri
Hydro-Electric Project (NJHEP) is 1:1 and the equity-
sharing ratio of GOI and GOHP is 3:1 respectively.

In addition to the financial assistance from the World Bank, SJVN has also been financed loan by a Consortium of European Banks and the Power Finance Corporation (PFC). Nathpa Jhakri Hydro Electric Power Project, the largest underground hydroelectric project was commissioned on 18.05.2004 and has generated already 15,795.255 MU up to January 11, 2007. Currently SJVNL is executing Rampur HEP (412 MW) in the State of Himachal Pradesh with World Bank assistance.

Private Sector

During the post independence period, the various States played a predominant role in the power development. Most of the States have established State Electricity Boards. In some of these States separate corporations have also been established to install and operate generation facilities. In the rest of the smaller States and Union Territories power systems were managed and operated by the respective electricity departments. In a few States private licensees were also operating in certain urban areas.

The policy of liberalization the Government of India announced in 1991 and consequent amendments in Electricity (Supply) Act have opened new vistas to involve private efforts and investments in electricity industry. Considerable emphasis has been placed on attracting private investment and the major policy changes have been announced by the Government in this regard.

The first ever economic liberalization in the early 1990 was announced by the Ministry of Power that India would open its state owned electricity sector to foreign investment. In 1991, the federal parliament passed amendments to the

Electricity Supply Act, 1948, to allow 100 per cent foreign private ownership of generating plants.

The 1991 Amendments adopted a cost-plus approach to India's newly created Independent Power Producer (IPP) program, providing for a guaranteed return on equity of at least 16%, a five-year tax exemptions and other attractive investment incentives.

As per National IPP Strategy, between 1991 and 2003, 22 projects of more than 50 MW were commissioned alongside nine small independent generators bringing the total capacity addition to nearly 6000MW.

India failed by a long shot to achieve the aggressive capacity expansion objectives laid out in the central government's original IPP policy. Although thousands of MOUs were signed with foreign and domestic project developers, only a miniscule fraction eventually broke ground for construction and reached commercial operations.

Apart from high project mortality in the development stage, the controversy surrounding the Dabhol project (Rs 100 Billion) abandoned by the Enron Corporation was taken over by two of the government's largest companies NTPC Ltd and GAIL and the Tamil Nadu IPPs has raised strong cautionary signals to potential investors.

Most foreign investors including the major players such as Electric de France, PowerGen and Mirant, have withdrawn from India, for time being and continue to wait and watch for new favorable legislation to be enacted with fresh amendments promising them to navigate the emerging Indian Electricity Market.

The renegotiation and cancellation of PPAs in India reflected these failures of reform and with the retreat of global energy investors and power builders well established domestic electricity and infrastructure companies such as Tata and Reliance have partially filled the gap.

The Dabhol Power Company became India's first and largest fast-track IPP, prior to the first renegotiation in 1996, where Enron Corporation was holding the major stake. The 216 MW GVK natural gas fired power plant was developed as one of the original fast track projects in India, under the IPP reform program. The plant sells its entire output to the Andhra Pradesh Transmission Corporation (AP TRANSCO) under an eighteen year PPA, the state owned utility and off taker in Andhra Pradesh, that derived from the unbundling of the Andhra Pradesh State Electricity Board.

The 368 MW Lanco Kondapalli power plant is the third major tariff-bid IPP in Andhra Pradesh. It sells all of its capacity via a 15 year PPA with AP TRANSCO. The 515 MW, Essar Power IPP under Essar Power Limited is a partially captive power plant that sells its output to an adjacent Essar Steel Plant and to the Gujarat Electricity Board, though Gujarat at that time was not a leader in reform efforts. The Paguthan power plant is a 655MW natural gas fired IPP in the state of Gujarat, selling all its capacity to the Gujarat Electricity Boards under a 20 year PPA. In contrast to both Gujarat and Andhra Pradesh, Tamil Nadu was a late reformer. The IPP experience in Tamil Nadu was not a success story.

Tata Power finds its origins in the early 20th century as a Bombay (now Mumbai) generation licensee. Tata Power

Limited is one of India's largest energy utilities, started as the Tata Hydroelectric Power Supply Company in 1911 a pioneer in the Indian Power Sector. Tata Power Limited provides services in power generation, transmission and distribution. It has also undertaken projects in power plant /utility operations and management in Saudi Arabia, Liberia, Iran, Sierra, Leone and Algeria. It is setting up independent power plants (IPPs) and captive power plants (CPPs).

Reliance Group has rapidly grown its new energy division bought out from shareholders of Bombay Suburban Electric Supply (BSES). In the energy sector, the newly created Reliance Energy Limited has proclaimed its ambition to dominate the energy market from "well-head to wall- socket." In addition to its position as the largest electricity distribution company in Mumbai, Reliance Energy has now become the dominant electricity player in New Delhi, following the unbundling and privatization of the New Delhi electricity board.

Reliance has made clear its intention to move directly to consumer markets in the newly deregulated electricity market. Reliance Energy's control of large distribution franchises, its intention to continue expansion of its generation and distribution capabilities, its access to gas fields and existing infrastructure make it a potentially fierce domestic competitor in the IPP market. Reliance plans to build 10,000MW by 2012.

Sasan Power Limited was incorporated on February 10, 2006 as a wholly owned subsidiary of Power Finance Corporation Limited in order to build, own, operate and maintain the Sasan Ultra Mega Power Project

(SUMPP-6x660 MW) at Sasan, Madhya Pradesh. It was transferred to Reliance Power Limited under the provisions of a share purchase agreement dated August 7, 2007 and is now a fully owned subsidiary of Reliance Power.

The Sasan project was awarded following an international competitive bidding (ICB) process at a levelized tariff of Rs 1.196 /kWh. Power Purchase Agreement had been executed with 14 procurers comprising 7 States and their off take would be as Madhya Pradesh (Lead Procurer) will be entitled for 37.50% share, followed by Punjab (15%), Uttar Pradesh (12.5%), Delhi (11.25%), Haryana (11.25%), Rajasthan (10%) and Uttarakand (2.5%). The Sasan project is scheduled to be on stream by December 2013, when the first 660 MW comes on line and fully commissioned by 2016 at an estimated cost of Rs 18,342 crore.

Coastal Andhra Power Limited was incorporated on August 24, 2006 as a wholly owned subsidiary of PFC in order to build, own, operate and maintain the Krisnapatnam Ultra Mega Power Project (KUMPP) at Nellore district in Andhra Pradesh. It was transferred to Reliance Power Limited on January 29, 2008 through ICB route at a levelized tariff of Rs 2.33 /kWh. Power Purchase Agreement has been executed with 11 procurers comprising 4 States i.e. Andhra Pradesh will have 40 % share of power from the project and the other states 20 % each Tamil Nadu, Karnataka and Maharashtra. The project was expected to be on stream in September 2013 and fully commissioned in October 2015.

Rosa Power Supply Company Limited (RPSCL) was incorporated on September 1, 1994. It was a subsidiary of Aditya Birla Power Company Limited (ABPCL) was transferred to Reliance Power on November 1,2006 and is now a fully owned subsidiary of Reliance Power. Rosa Phase I & II coal fired project with combined generating capacity of 1200 MW has been commissioned in 2010.

Tato Hydro Power Private Limited (4x 175 MW), Siyom Hydro Power Private Limited (4x 250 MW), Urthing Sobla Hydro Power Private Limited (4 x 100 MW)and Kalai Power Private Limited (8 x 150 MW) were all incorporated in the year 2007 to set up hydro electric power project in the state of Arunachal Pradesh by Reliance Power Limited clearly shows their interest in renewable energy.

The country's first UMPP has taken off with the recent commissioning of (Unit 1-800MW supercritical) of TATA Power's Mundra UMPP. However, the project is facing challenges owing to the unprecedented rise in fuel costs. The other awarded UMPPs are also finding the going tough. Work at Reliance Power Limited's KUMPP has been stalled since June 2011.

In March 2012, the distribution utilities of Andhra Pradesh, Tamil Nadu, Karnataka and Maharashtra had collectively issued a notice to Reliance Power, imposing a penalty of Rs 4 billion for delays in project execution. According to a recent CEA report, the first 660 MW unit of the 3,960 MW Sasan UMPP is scheduled to be commissioned by January 2013.

Tilaiya UMPP is at a preliminary stage of development. Reliance Power's Sasan and Tilaiya UMPP's are mired in controversy as the CAG's draft report states that Reliance Power would accrue "undue gains" by diverting surplus coal from the blocks allocated for the UMPP's to other power projects.

The 4,000 MW Bedabahal UMPP in Odisha has procured environmental clearances for its captive coal mines but the requests for proposal are yet to be invited from the selected bidders. The MoP expects to initiate the UMPP's final bidding round after receiving the Attorney General's opinion on the issue of surplus coal diversion from associated mines to other plants. The 4,000 MW Surguja UMPP has not made any progress due to pending environmental clearances for associated captive coal blocks located in the Hasdeo Arand coalfields.

The union government is in the process of identifying sites for setting up new UMPPs. In Odisha, an imported coal based UMPP is proposed to come up at Bhadrak. The CEA is soon likely to identify a site for a third UMPP, also in Odisha. Meanwhile, Lodhva village in Junagadh district of Gujarat has been identified as another potential site. The Gujarat government has agreed to allocate 500 hectares of land for the proposed project. With regard to the 4,000 MW Cheyyur UMPP in Tamil Nadu, initial bids are likely to be invited in September 2012.

In my opinion finally to sum up, private participation in the bidding process of future UMPPs would depend largely on the government's ability to resolve issues related to the Indonesian coal price hike, provide clarity on surplus coal diversion and expedite environmental clearances. Unless these issues are resolved, the objective of the UMPP programme, to facilitate faster capacity addition, will remain unfulfilled.

GE Energy has a presence across the energy value chain in India. It has significantly expanded its energy sector portfolio over the years. The company provides equipment and technology solutions for segments such as thermal power, nuclear energy, renewable energy, transmission and distribution and grid modernization. GE has the most experienced and reliable gas turbine and steam turbine technology fleet in India.

In 2011, GE introduced the Flex-Efficiency 50 technology, a global product engineered to meet the environmental and grid conditions of all major markets including India. The recent focus on using higher efficiency thermal products in India has seen the introduction of GE's latest 660 MW and 800MW supercritical steam turbine technology in this market.

Recent examples of GE's turbine technology deployments include the provision of 9FA gas turbine technology for the 2,400 MW expansion of the Samalkot power plant in Andhra Pradesh, which is expected to be the largest gas turbine combined cycle project in India.

GE is also providing 6FA flexible gas turbine technology to Sravanthi Energy to generate about 450 MW of electricity in two combined cycle blocks. The GE Triveni (GET) joint venture offers a portfolio of steam turbine products (30-100 MW) for the industrial power generation market.

GE has a long standing partnership with BHEL. BHEL-GE Gas Turbine Services Private Limited serves power generation plants with a typical life cycle of over 20 years. GE has also set up local assembly unit for wind business and invested in local supply chain.

ADB plans to lend $ 1.3 billion to the Indian Power Sector over the next three years. Adani Power Limited has a vision to create 20,000 MW by 2020. Hinduja Energy of Hinduja Group is planning 10,000 MW over a decade. KSK Energy has committed to commission 2000 MW by 2015.

Deregulated-
Indian Power Sector

The deregulation of the power sector had been initiated to corporatize the electricity services in India to resolve the energy crisis. The public utilities in the state sector were unable to perform despite reforms and restructuring of the electricity sector. The smaller entities born from unbundled SEBs are also not rising to the expectations as anticipated prior to implementation of state reforms act.

The purpose of providing adequate power with consistent supply, quality and reliability kept on bringing in deregulation in the sector completely changing its operation philosophy today.

Nationalization of the power sector to Corporatization of electricity services in India has its own saga of pros and cons. Electricity to the Indian citizens is in transition from a service to commodity concept.

The management philosophy of Public Enterprises is being replaced with the style of Corporate Management practices. More and more emphasis is on Business Administration rather than on only administrating the public enterprises. Administration and Management are the ends of the fulcrum between which the power sector has been swinging desperately under the merry go round of the restructuring process.

There are nearly more than 50 major policies implemented from 1877 to 2015 year in India. It is difficult to detail out all those policies and its respective focus areas in this book.

What I wish to convey is that an insight into these policies outlined and the facts from ground realities understanding can bring greater awareness on the subject.

I have tried to summarize the major policies by way of commentary and comparative statements so that the readers can better understand the argument on Policy Vs Reality.

Today, India's power sector should be integrated and consolidated. For this "SMART GRID" is the way ahead along with the aggressive push through renewable. Are we smartening our grids? The present pace is marginal.

Conventional Technology Vs Clean Technology, there should be clear policy. The Change Management is facing all challenges of transition in the energy sector in India.

Did "Green Power" concern emerge from the focus on pollution and environment primarily? Did it evolve to conserve the fossil reserves? Both the hypothesis is being tested for acceptance and rejection equally.

How to pool up the additional resources and funds in this pathetic ground reality of power sector in India?

Will the competition in "Renewable Energy Market" in Asia-Pacific make changes in the Global Energy Scenario?

Where is India standing today? As a citizen it is responsibility of all to safeguard India from drain of energy.

Consumption Vs Conservation of energy is reflecting our unawareness of the energy seriousness in the country. It is a subject of national interest and global commitments considering the exports and imports balances of energy.

National Vs Global policies, the central idea is to minimize energy drain all over the world. How to arrest the drain of energy in India?

There are many factors linked to the drain of energy daily. This needs to be regularly analyzed both at micro and macro levels. Now the question is who is ringing the bell of emergency. I believe the entire nation has to integrate in stopping the drain of energy. It is leaking drop by drop to strengthen the energy crisis.

A planned approach is must to address this sensitive issue in India. Why India cannot improve as China and Japan? May not be a role model to imitate hundred percent but a beginning can be initiated without losing further time in designing concrete strategy to revamp the power sector.

Cost Vs Schedule of power projects is a very important guiding factor to determine the power tariff in the end. Government is under pressure to bring in revisions in power tariff determination philosophies day by day.

Who is monitoring it? Who is controlling it? Is Government responsible for cost overruns of power projects implemented by private players?

How the budget can be efficiently organized so that all the departments of electricity supply chain, i.e., generation, transmission and distribution grow proportionally meeting the supply and demand gaps in India?

Budget Vs Politics impacts and influences are part and parcel of the Indian Power System. Is the CAPEX outlay to State owned enterprises in the power sector administered without partiality?

Many of the power utilities companies in the private sector could not have the targeted income from revenues, expenditures beyond anticipated budgets, falling operating profits, rising interest amount on project finances and in addition to it the depreciation hardly leaves any profit after tax (PAT) to increase the EPS (earning per share).

Investments Vs Returns, who will bell the cat. Will "Mitigation of Risk" remain a subject of debate forever in the sector?

Why private players are not willing to burn their hands in the emerging power distribution business in India?

Despite the initiatives by the government to push the domestic production of coal it is found that import of thermal coal is increasing day by day.

Will Indian power sector see the light of the day?

Electrical equipments growth never matched the requirement of power projects in India. This is an unpardonable policy gap which is one of the major prime reasons for delay of many power projects being constructed in India in the deregulated regime.

Why "Manufacturing of Power Equipments" never became a serious agenda point for the central policy planners in India? It appears India was comfortably sailing with the philosophy of imports.

Manufacturing Vs Construction the gap is evident from the project delays seen in the power sector. Delivery of power equipments to project sites in time is always a critical factor in India despite latest project management tools and better logistics infrastructure.

Purchase of Power Vs Selling of Power the battlefield has many stakeholders to play their games within the laws of limitations in the power sector. Do you think there is transparency in Power Trading in India?

Power Service Vs Power Trading, Will the two different philosophies ever converge in India?

Despite Coal India Limited being the single largest coal producing company in the World with reserves of nearly 65 billion ton, accounting for 80% of India's overall coal production and commanding 74% of the Indian Coal Market is unable to meet the fuel supply agreements (FSA).

How to improve the productivity of coal mining in India? Will commercial mining bring in competition in the coal sector?

How to arrive at an ideal generation mix of coal, hydro, solar, wind and other renewable energy sources to achieve most cost efficient power with reliability?

How to supply power for minimum cost? Whom the policy makers are going to favour?

Power Utilities Vs Consumers, Who is the real beneficiary? Who will solve India's Energy Woes?

Even after deregulation and liberalization the capacity addition during the 13th Five Year Plan is going to be driven by Public Sector Enterprises (PSEs).

PSEs Vs Private has the competition faded away. Is it that Private Enterprises are quitting the arena of electricity services?

How far service of electricity will remain with the state enterprises? Why only SEBs are being blamed?

Cost of Power Vs Quality of Power, is continually testing the performance of India's Power System. What should be the best strategy for purchase of power? Are the Discoms optimizing power procurement to derive least cost option?

Long Term Power Procurement Vs Short Term Power Procurement, Where is the Break-Even Point? Can it really bring in optimization? Is there an established energy model?

Power Producers Vs Electricity Consumers the push and pull is an essential factor to bring the betterment in the overall system.

I wish to communicate to my readers through this commentary the critical issues which are deeply embedded and integrated so strongly in India's Energy Crisis.

After reading through the above lines one should now become at least familiar with the issues floating in the sector. The awareness of the sector perhaps shall certainly make the differences in understanding the causes of the energy crisis in India.

The readers shall agree with me as to "How one can expect results overnight?"

Today's "Energy Crisis in India" is the outcome of cumulative gaps in policies, Acts, regulations, visions, missions, goals, objectives, services, and many more parameters over the years.

Capability Vs Competency is repeatedly being questioned in the Indian Energy Sector? I think competition without capabilities is like the pen without ink.

Talent Pool in Energy & Power Sector needs to be developed rapidly and consistently to effectively operate the Indian Power System.

To share my views with you let me confess that Power Sector is an area where long gestation periods are to be accommodated before any promising results are seen at the end.

Time Vs Results needs patience and perseverance. How much endurance? What is the ideal time frame?

Cheap Power Vs Quality of Power, what exactly we are focusing on. How to increase the revenues of power utilities?

Will "SMART GRID" implementation in India ensure reliable power? Who is responsible for the gaps in transmission sector?

Is it because of the rate of return that private players are not investing in the transmission sector? Is it because of the national power policy that transmission is not at par with generation sector? Will the new tariff policy do justice to the schemes mandated by the government of India?

How to make transmission projects more financially viable? How to strengthen the "National Grid"? Why India is lagging behind in implementing better technology in the T&D System? Is the distribution franchise model really successful in India?

Power evacuation and efficient distribution are posing a much bigger hurdle than the power generation.

Installed Capacity Vs Power Evacuation gap is getting wider day by day. The pace of transmission projects needs momentum and is to be increased to bridge the gap.

Will India focus on new technologies for higher transmission voltages of 1200 KV for bulk power transmission? The development of high capacity power transmission corridors (HCPTCs) is to be seriously expedited.

And above all the prime factor is attitude towards resolving the energy crisis in India.

Do the citizens of India are aware of the ground reality of the power sector? A small consumer should also understand the pricing mechanism of the electricity services.

Big Consumer Vs Small Consumer the factor of subsidy is discriminating the services.

Bulk Power Vs Retail Power the issues are full of ambiguities and governed by different yardsticks.

How many long years it will take to see the results in the power sector initiated through the reforms, restructuring, Acts etc? No doubt the government initiatives have started changing the concepts of electricity services but the hundred percent realities is still hanging as dream.

The non-performing assets (NPA) in the power sector are a subject of worry and major concern in India. Huge investments have been blocked without fruitful results. It is a difficult time for promising promoters and investors.

Investment Vs Insurance, who will come forward to mitigate the risk,? The professionalism is not to create conflict in ownership and management.

Will we emerge out from power crisis?

Public sector institute continue to play the dominant role in the generation and supply of electricity in India, primarily state-level government owned utilities, called state electricity board ("SEB") and central utilities such as the National Thermal Power Corporation ("NTPC") and the Nuclear Power Sector Corporation of India Limited ("NPCIL").

The central government, through public companies, owns and operates one-third of total generation capacity and interstate transmission lines. At the state level, SEBs own and operates most of the remaining two-third of the generation capacity, as well as the majority of intrastate transmission and distribution system.

Although the central government institutions, particularly after corporatization, have fared better, the SEBs increasingly faced the threat of bankruptcy during the development of India's IPP program in the 1990s. At a time when new generation capacity and distribution infrastructure was desperately needed, the near insolvency of the SEBs created a serious impediment to private investment in the electricity sector. Public fund had also contracted. Without fund to invest the development of the electricity sector, economic growth far outstripped electricity consumption growth during the 1990s.

Despite the opening of generation to IPPs in 1991, the private sector provided less than 10,000 MW of total generation capacity through the 1990s.

Through 2003, IPPs account for little more than 5000MW of new capacity since the introduction of private participation more than a decade earlier. The public private partnership was thought will operate with a synergy of both school of concepts towards revamping the sector.

Power sector is witnessing a critical phase. State Electricity Boards (SEBs) are responsible for providing electricity to the people. Most of the SEBs are cash strapped. They are not even able to earn a minimum Rate of Return (RoR) of 3% on their net fixed assets in service after providing for depreciation and interest charges in accordance with Section 59of the Electricity (Supply) Act, 1948.

The power sector in the country has accumulated a huge deficit, and dues to Central Power Generating Companies because of the deteriorating financial performance. To turn around the financial health of the power sector, the Government has taken up reforms in the power sector for gradual elimination of losses. There reform process in power sector in India was initiated in 1991. The sole objective in launching of their forms was to mobilize private sector resources for power generating capacity addition.

The Government of India has amended Electricity Supply Act, 1948 and the Indian Electricity Act, 1910 to facilitate the private sector participation.

We all know that Electricity Act 2003 has been enacted. How many of us understand that the objective is to introduce competition, protect consumer's interests and provide power for all.?

Let us understand that the Act provides for National Electricity Policy, Rural Electrification, Open access in transmission phased open access in distribution, mandatory SERCs, license free generation and distribution, power trading, mandatory metering and stringent penalties for theft of electricity.

It is a comprehensive legislation replacing Electricity Act 1910, Electricity Supply Act 1948 and Electricity Regulatory Commission Act 1998.

The Act is aiming to push the sector onto a trajectory of sound commercial growth and to enable the States and the Centre to move in harmony and coordination with the national plans and policies.

To meet the challenges posed by growing demand for power in the long term the Government of India announced the Mega Power Policy in 1998, envisioning the development of large, multi-state generation project. Those project were to supply power to multiple states and this usually lead to difficulties in reaching agreement on risk sharing as well as on payment security mechanism, and risk reducing the credit-worthiness of the project. Therefore, the need for a single credit-enhancing agency, which could buy power from these private power stations and sell to the state utilities and other buyers, was felt.

Power Trading Corporation (PTC) was incorporated in 1999 to manage the risks effectively and act as an entity which could undertake trading of power to achieve economic efficiency and security of supply including the neighboring countries. Although in recent time new public and private players have entered the power trading market. PTC has the first mover advantage over these new entrants in terms of access to sellers and market penetration etc.

Most of the electricity-supply industry in India remains in the public sector. The central government, through public companies, owns and operates one-third of the power generation and interstate exchanges. At the state level, SEBs own and operate most of the remaining two-thirds of the generation capacity, as well as single-state transmission and distribution systems. States define their own tariff structures. State-wide electricity systems are relatively small, in line with the low country per capita electricity consumption.

The sector would benefit from further national integration and the economies of scale that would accompany it. Although the central government is politically committed to reforming the regulatory framework to facilitate the development of a power market, implementation of the reform policies has been slow.

Power-sector policies are designed and implemented by the Ministry of Power at the national level and by ministries in charge of power or energy at the state level.

Political intervention in electricity matters is common at the national level. Fuel-supply issues for power generation projects may also need clearance from the Ministry of Coal (and the Ministry of Railways) or the Ministry of

Petroleum and Natural Gas, whose opinions often differ from those of the Ministry of Power.

Political intervention motivated by social concerns is frequently exerted and can frustrate efforts to rationalize electricity prices.

I would like to bring awareness to my readers that most of the problems of the Indian power sector arise from the present distribution and retail pricing system and from the fact that too little of it is actually paid for.

As per the general national statistics out of total electricity generated, only 55% is billed by the power utilities and 41% is regularly paid by the electricity consumers.

Electricity is either stolen, not billed, or electricity bills are not paid has become an unwanted culture in India which amounts to a mass of implicit subsidy. Finally the financial burden thus created undermines the economic efficiency and viability of the electricity supply chain and is not in the long-term interests of consumers.

My readers should kow that retail tariffs as well as bulk tariffs are based on a cost-plus mechanism established at the time of India's independence in 1948.

Why electricity prices are subsidized? You need not be surprised to note that current retail prices of electricity represent less than 75% of real average costs.

Why the cost plus approach is followed? The energy economists should work on it. Does it meet the economics of scale?

Subsidy leakage is worse than the physical power crisis. There is also a large amount of cross-subsidization between consumer categories. The agriculture and household sectors are cross-subsidized by above-cost tariffs for commercial and industrial customers and railways.

In fact till today our policy makers find it difficult to justify the process of subsidization. Why some category are preferred over the other?

It really needs to be probed scientifically, administratively, managerially, intuitionally, financially, socially and nationally keeping in view the equal rights to the citizens of India.

Who is the most favored consumer?

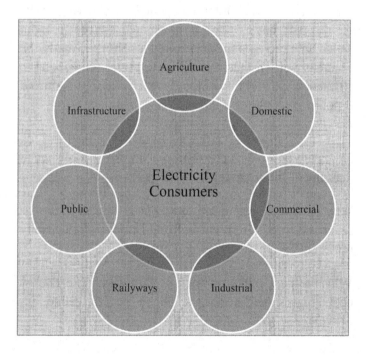

It appears that the Indian policies in the energy sector are getting more inclined towards the perception of consumers rather than the concept of services to the citizens.

The situation worsened in the 1990s. Official data demonstrate that subsidies to households trebled to 80.8 billion rupees over the period 1992-1993 to 1999-2000. Subsidies to agriculture more than tripled to 227 billion rupees over the same period.

The government sought to justify these subsidies on social grounds but it clearly failed to achieve its social goal, as higher-income groups in fact appropriate most of the benefits since the subsidy is applied to the price of electricity within a given consumer-category, indifferently to the individual level of income.

Policies to achieve market pricing have been introduced in India. Central and state electricity regulatory commissions are slowly being established. They will issue tariff orders, and should eventually implement them.

Policies to implement a minimum price have been pursued since 1996. The goal is a minimum price of 50 paise/kWh (1.1 US cents/kWh) for agriculture. But, delays in implementing such reforms have prevented even this simple goal from being met. Inflation (8% in 2000) has outpaced the growth in price per kilowatt hour.

Policies in place also call for all end-use sectors ultimately to be charged at least 50% of the average cost of supply. This target was intended to be met in three years, but it has not yet been achieved in any of the states. The poor cost-recovery rate, the very low price and the widespread non-payment of electricity are all deterrents to private investors.

Investors cannot be assured that their applications for tariff increases to recover costs will be met, even by theoretically independent regulatory commissions. The side effects of this way of subsidizing energy consumption are significant. Overpricing of industrial electricity hampers competitiveness. In other sectors, under pricing of electricity is a direct incentive to waste power.

Emerging Power Mix

Today, the impact of Energy Crisis is equally felt by the Power Utilities and Electricity Consumers. Indian Power Sector is a conglomeration of various agencies like Power Utilities from State, Central and Private sectors, Regulators at Centre and State, foreign and domestic investors, foreign main power equipment suppliers and technology collaborations, primary fuel energy suppliers, power traders, service providers etc trying to meet the power demand of various categories of consumers like public, agriculture, industrial, railways, domestic and commercial in the country which are causing interfacing issues that are taking complex dimensions day by day.

The Independent Power Producers (IPPs), Captive Power Producers (CPPs), Merchant Power Producers (MPPs), Public Private Partnership (PPPs), Central Power Utilities, State Sector Utilities and MNCs Utilities are all players of the emerging power sector trying to capitalize the Indian Electricity Market with competitive electricity prices to the consumers.

The primary governing factor in determining cost of electricity generation is based on what forms of energy like coal, oil, natural gas, nuclear, hydro, waste, geothermal, wind, solar, bio-fuels others are being used at power stations. The next valuable parameter is the cost of exporting power through the transmission network to the nearest load dispatch centers followed by available distribution and supply power system.

The economic reforms were also intended to improve the business environment in the electricity industry and the tax system has also undergone tremendous reforms in the last two decades. The tax laws have been simplified for better compliances. The provisions under the direct taxes have been relaxed with creating of incentives for benefiting the participants in the power market.

The Corporate rate taxes, Dividend Distribution Tax (DDT), Capital gains/Transfer of capital assets, Minimum Alternate Tax (MAT), Tax holiday against corporate profits, depreciation, Fringe Benefit Tax (FBT), Transfer pricing regulation, special provisions in Special Economic Zone (SEZs), Foreign Direct Investment (FDI) etc; were all brought in with additions and deletions to suit the promotion of huge investments and development of the power market.

The power sector in India is considered to be a part of the core infrastructure and thus has been granted several incentives both at the Central and State level. The indirect tax implications on setting up of a power project and day to day operations were taken care to provide benefits to power builders/suppliers in custom duty, deemed export benefits under The Foreign Trade Policy (FTP), 2004, by the policy of the Ministry of Commerce and Industry in the Government of India, deemed exports provided ICB procedures have been followed at Engineering and Procurement Contract (EPC) stage, service tax, sales tax/VAT, Electricity Duty etc.

In-spite of sustained efforts, the power sector has not attracted the magnitude of private sector investments envisaged by the sector planners. There are several important concerns that need to be addressed and mitigated. Identifying certain mitigants puts again the question of its feasibility in resolving the policy issues.

In order to improve investments into the power sector, especially from private players, the government has undertaken a number of policy initiatives. Some of the major initiatives include: Private players both domestic and foreign are allowed to set up power generation facilities (with the exception of nuclear fuel) without restriction on capacities.

Private participation has been permitted both in transmission and distribution (Tata, BSES, AES, RPG, AEC, and SEC). Private players can construct, operate and maintain transmission lines. However, the lines need to be under the supervision and control of the central or state transmission utility.

Private transmission facilities may either take the form of an independent power transmission company or a joint venture with the state-owned transmission utilities. There are no ceilings on foreign direct investment limits in either power generation, transmission or distribution projects.

The government is seeking significant reforms in this sector and has introduced a new electricity bill in the parliament. Government intervention has been minimized and an independent central regulatory authority has been set up to review the electricity tariff and other related issues. Several states have also set up electricity regulators.

Measures to stop theft of power and to reduce transmission and distribution losses are being planned to improve the revenue generation of the state electricity boards (SEBs), which are the main suppliers of power to consumers. Reforms have been initiated to allow for state level tariff rationalization.

The government has adopted a new programme, the Accelerated Power Development Programme (APDP) through which it will provide funds to state electricity boards for renovation and modernization of older power plants. The government has allocated US$ 150 million for this purpose. Many states have formulated Captive Power Policy in order to support their domestic industries.

Every Indian is currently aware of the low per capita consumption of power and the current capacity is not adequate to meet the demand. There are significant investment opportunities existing in all segments within the power sector.

During my survey the respondents confessed that the government expects an enhanced role from private players and the private sector is likely to contribute almost one-fifth of the additional generation capacity.

It is seen that some of the power distribution activities in some states have already been privatized and many are in the process of adopting this structure.

Many were happy to share the success of privatization of power distribution in Delhi. The state governments of Andhra Pradesh and Karnataka have started drawing up a road map for privatization of power distribution in their respective states.

What can be an ideal road map for India?

There are opportunities also existing in introducing energy audit and efficiency concepts, development of renewable sources of energy generation – mini hydro, wind mills, solar, bio-gas and introduction of clean coal technology for power generation.

FDI up to 100% is allowed under automatic approval route in respect of projects relating to electricity generation, transmission and distribution, other than atomic reactor power plants. No limit on the project cost and quantum of FDI. The category which would qualify for such approval were Hydroelectric power plants, Coal / Lignite based thermal power plants, Oil /Gas based thermal power plants.

Under revised mega power policy, the main objective is to set up mega power projects to generate power at the lowest possible tariff by utilizing economies of scale and setting up of such plants at pithead or coastal areas so that it can act as catalyst for the reforms in the beneficiary states.

Power Trading Corporation (PTC) incorporated for buying power from mega power projects in private sector and selling it to the beneficiary states. Certain fiscal concessions given to mega power projects to make the tariff cheaper, like duty free import of capital goods, deemed export benefit and Income Tax holiday for 10 years.

Liquid Fuel Policy aims at setting up of short gestation power projects based on liquid fuels viz; Naptha, HPS, LSHS, HFO, FO, Refinery Residue and Petroleum Coke. The policy guidelines for the private sector participation in Renovation and Modernization, details out various options like Lease, Rehabilitate, Operate and Transfer (LROT), sale of plant and joint venture between SEBs and private companies. Import of Naphtha by actual user Power Project without any import restriction allowed. Fuel policy encouraging use of other alternative fuels announced.

Electric Power is a round the clock basic necessity across the globe. India is no exception, and supply position in many of our rural and semi-urban areas needs substantial improvement.

People might manage with scarcity but that is no indicator of true demand for electricity which goes grossly unmet. At present, the country faces 7.3 per cent energy deficit amounting to nearly 45 billion units (BU) and 10.6 per cent peak power deficit which is 13.5 Giga Watts (GW).

The Indian Emerging Power Mix is the greatest boon of the Electricity Reforms in India endowed with unending challenges ahead to translate the dreams of citizens of India into reality.

CHAPTER-V

POWER MANAGEMENT IN INDIA

Ownership Vs Management

Is India not mastering Leadership Behaviour? Does management means Ownership? Simply by talking ownership can anyone become a successful manager.

Ownership Vs Management is an interesting area for study especially in the Indian Energy Sector. Can social values be obtained through private ownership? Determination of prices by the government for products of social values is to be introspected again and again for better alignment with Global Energy Markets.

Is Owner not the Manager? Can the Manager take the responsibility and risk of the Owner? There are emerging school of thoughts in the management of public and private enterprises in India. Though in recent times many Indian Companies have been operating Global Businesses in the energy sector yet the principles of global markets are new to them. It has always been a challenge to increase domestic production by attracting foreign investments.

Domestic Vs Foreign, the policy in the power sector keeps swinging without concentric goals.

Indian Policies are to be in line with the Global Practices if India wants to be in race and pace with Global Markets. India is poor on the utilization of Data Management System (DMS). The country's comprehensive energy outlook is only possible when data, management and system are integrated throughout the width and breadth.

The Energy Management is a new concept and lot of work is to be done in this area. Citizens have to take accountable responsibility in properly utilizing and conserving energy.

Who is the OWNER? & Who is the MANAGER?

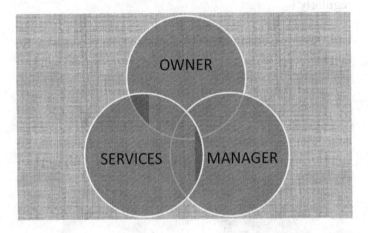

There is a always a conflict between the Owner and the Manager anywhere in the world. Roles and responsibilities of governance, administration, planning, functioning, controlling, monitoring and servicing is not always very much professionally defined.

The Manager works diligently under the power of attorney to discharge the responsibilities and functions on behalf of the owner. This might be simple when one to one relationship is established and the quantum of transactions are less. But when we speak of hundreds of stakeholders in the sector conflict is bound to prevail.

Will "BOSS" deliver with the philosophy of "MOS" (Manager, Owner and Services)?

The Conflict Management is an emerging art to address the Human Capital Management issues. The quality of human resources is gaining importance in energy sector in India. It may not be new for my readers who follow the literature on Corporate Governance and Management regularly.

Utilities Vs Consumers, Are the rules clearly and well defned?

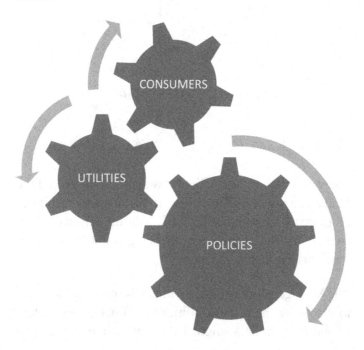

Efficiency of Power Utilities and Loyalty of Consumers are the wheels of the Indian Electricity Sector. Operational and Commercial losses have become legacy of the sector and hence has been truly branded ineffective. It is remolding itself gradually towards betterment with the lessons learnt from the past experiences.

The present evolving Power Industry is a mix of Central, State and Private sectors breeding a new culture in the service and business of electrical energy. The impact of reforms and restructuring has paved way for new opportunities and competition in the vibrant Power sector.

The continuous demand of energy due to rapid growth in Industrialization, Infrastructure development, urbanization and rural electrification has changed the dynamics of the sector. The sector was continuously striving to resolve the critical issues of autonomy, management of Public Enterprises and developing a liberalized market by the process of reforms after the political independence, and still it is struggling to define new rules to make the present ailing Power Sector more viable and sustainable.

The life cycle of electricity from generation to supply takes place under an environment which is very complex in nature without a single line of uniform command. Developing an effective and suitable Power System for India being a huge nation with wide base of consumers requires in depth study and research at national level.

Rationalization of electricity prices in India where political intervention keeps dominating the National Policies is a perennial problem and remains unheard even at the floor of Parliament. Though the Power Market has been liberalized, consumers are not satisfied with the quality of power and reliability in supply.

PERFORMANCE – INDIA'S POWER SYSTEM

Who is monitoring it? Who is accounting it? Who is leading it? Why it is lagging not leading?

Leading Vs Lagging has so many issues and bottlenecks in the power sector.

Performance of electric utilities is essential for the reform of the electricity sector in India. It is very difficult to arrive at the reasons for the present energy crisis in India. However with all the facts through annual reports, publications, daily news, discussion papers, periodicals, summits, review of literature the insight summarizes that without monitoring performance of the power sector the government's objectives and goals cannot be realized.

Deregulating the policy, plans, Acts, rules, licenses, administrative and legal controls, operating standards, investment and expenditures, interests and loans, revenue and subsidies, taxation and duties, etc by the regulators to revamp the sector can ultimately be coined as reforms and restructuring.

Moreover it was dreamt that opening foreign investments would bring in latest technology through MNCs power builders in having modern power stations minimizing auxiliary power consumption and system losses but the sector is surviving on domestic power builders.

The power revolution has started to identify key performance indices reflecting major elements of utility day to day operations, including technical, operational and financial.

It is nearly over two decades the power sector has been sailing in deregulated regime but the rewards of the reforms are far away from realizations. The ailing sector is crippling the Indian economy. Deregulation was brought in to support the private sector in turning around the electricity industry but to dismay the expectations have been brutally murdered.

Monitoring Performance Of The Power Sector

(Key Indicators Matrix)

Regulator	Power Utilities	Power Suppliers	Consumers
Policies & Acts	Operational	Quality & Reliability	Service Satisfaction
Plan implementation	Technical	Service Restoration	Supply Quality
Licenses	Commercial	Metering & Billing	Billing & Payments
Clearances	Capacity Utilization	Power Connections	Access to electricity
Processing	Renovation&modernization	Customer Centers	Availability
Overall Coordination	Operation & Maintenance	Repairs & Replacements	Load shedding
Interfacing & Resolving	Productivity & Pricing	Penalty & Security	Power Holidays
Energy Conservation	Plant Load Factor	Consumer Awareness	Blackouts
Pricing & Trading	Power System Losses	Consumer Participation	Overdrawing
Power Market Development	Equipment Failures	Load dispatch centers	Outages
Per capita consumption	Utility Management	Wheeling of Power	Conservation
Population Demand	Training & Development	Exchanges Operation	Saving & Loyalty
Promoting Competition	Capacity factor	State Utilities	Wastage
Investment & Outlays	Plant Load factor	Central Utilities	Theft of power
Electricity Infrastructure	Operating factor	Private Utilities	Unethical usage

Research & Development	Inventory Management	Export & Import	Complaints
Consumer Grievances	Environment & Pollution	Bulk & Retail	Consumption
Power projects & Fuel Linkages	Grid Discipline and Load Dispatch Connectivity	Overall Interfacing Issues	Business Losses
Gaps in Energy Reforms	National Network	Producers & Electricity Consumers	Protection & Safety

I have worked out the above table which brings out the complex matrix of key indicators responsible and accountable for performance of India's Power System. Monitoring of these indicators is very much essential to know the skewness of the sector.

Uncertainty of Regulatory Reforms

Regulation Vs Reforms, Where is the ultimate break even point?

The Role of Regulation in the power sector is being repeatedly reviewed and prospectively redefined over the last 100 years. Even today there is no unique standard charter for providing and guiding electricity services in India. It is difficult to ascertain whether the regulatory mechanism is getting deregulated or the controls are being liberalized.

The Central and State government's power utilities are accountable to the government where as the private sector power utilities accountability is yet to be clearly demarcated and defined.

The government's diplomacy in completely abolishing the License Raj is being partially administered through the MoUs, agreements and clearances. The government's main objective is to make power available and affordable to all. The main texts currently governing the electricity industry and the power market in India still are the Indian Electricity Act (1910), the Electricity (Supply) Act (1948) and the Electricity Act-2003.

The State Electricity Boards were established under section 5 of the Electricity Supply Act, 1948. The period of establishment from the first state to the last was from 1950 to 1975. The States, Andhra Pradesh, Karnataka, Kerala and Tamil Nadu were constituted during 1950-57 in Southern Region, followed by West Bengal, Bihar and Orissa in Eastern Region, supported by Madhya Pradesh, Maharashtra and Gujarat in Western Region during 1956-61.

It is surprising to note that the States in Northern Region and North Eastern Region started establishing their respective electricity boards late during the period 1957 to 1975. By the time State Electricity Board in Meghalaya came into existence, the newly established State Electricity Board in Andhra Pradesh had a service period of 25 years since its inception in 1950.

The delayed establishments of the boards were the beginning of disparity in electricity services in India as simultaneous development of electricity infrastructure in all the States could not be taken in line with the national policy envisaged in 1948.

Further insight into these legal documents and their amendments, as well the Electricity Regulatory Commissions Act (1998), other policy statements, additional resolutions and new regulations brings to the surface the dual policy of the government which may not have been intentionally drafted over the years but intends to reflect the gloomy picture of its dwindling values and national responsibility in hundred per cent electrifying India.

The government knowingly or unknowingly elapsed 25 years from 1950-1975 in progressively establishing the SEBs in States and again drained nearly 20 years from 1991 to 2010-11 in gradually restructuring and unbundling the SEBs.

The overall process of unsteady formation and slow unbundling consumed valuable 45 years which was nothing more than only playing permutations and combinations in establishing, reorganizing, restructuring and revamping the state owned utilities fitting them into new organizational models edifying their potential for providing efficient electricity services.

Before the power sector could reap the benefits from one policy there was new policy to be implemented overruling the existing one, thus the central government kept on redesigning policies and plans with untrue rolling commitments without any time frame for one reason or the other.

Will liberalization sacrifice the roots of nationalization and rationalization?

Liberalized market is an opportunity for prospective traders in electricity but the regulatory uncertainty brings in huge risks impeding the flourishment of the power market which was envisaged by policy makers to revive the power sector.

The Indian Electricity Sector is still exploring a suitable market design to battle the energy market manipulation. How to achieve performance at least to the satisfactory levels?

I think India needs more and more dedicated and sincere engineers to turnaround the power sector. Despite Ownership, Management, Leadership and good Administration things are not changing to the desired expectations.

The 1991 Economic Reforms provided for creation of private generating companies but the Electricity Regulatory Act was promulgated in 1998 after a gap of nearly one decade. Gaps in regulatory reforms, non-alignment of subsequent amendments, uncertainty and its inefficiency in implementation were helping the derailment of the sector from attaining integrated development.

Unequal government's policy initiatives in the three segments of generation, distribution and transmission were lagging behind by considerable time gap in years contributing to the under capitalization of the prime intention of reforming the sector. Why the government failed to compute the right proportions?

The dual policy of the government to unbundle the SEBs in the States and at the same time sustaining them by allocating reserved power to the State utilities from pooled power market enabling it to sell to the consumers directly reflects their unwillingness to completely liberalize the electricity trading in the Indian power sector.

Buying power from private utilities to sell it to the SEBs and again reselling it to the consumers by the State utilities may not be an optimal feasible solution in developing a fair market. Is this power model justifiable keeping in view the business philosophies of public and private utilities?

The regulatory reforms are translating SEBs from seller of electricity to the buyer of power from private utilities, thus itself becoming a major consumer of power.

Providing electricity was considered to be a service to the consumers which is now being reoriented into a new concept as commodity to customers eliminating the after sells effect. This is being viewed as the intention of the government to privatize generation of power keeping the distribution supply and trading of electricity solely in their domain.

Policy to emphasize on energy trading in the States which are starving for energy with power hungry consumers speaks of the uncertainty regulatory reforms.

Many States have delayed restructuring the SEBs, not complying with the directives within the disputed unspecified time frame. Some of the unsuccessful States have badly experienced the taste of reforms and restructuring putting a check on the ones tending to be restructured.

Energy deficiency and energy trading are the two unavoidable faces of the same coin being irrelatively tossed in the political arena of the Indian power sector undergoing reforms and restructuring without known beneficiaries among the public utilities, private sector utilities, policy makers, regulators, investors, promoters and consumers.

Fuel Supply Agreements (FSAs), Power Purchase Agreements (PPAs), land acquisitions, financial closures, rate of return, pollution and environmental clearances, railway linkages, tariff determination and electricity pricing, power market development, constituting power exchanges, coal reforms, exploring renewable energy, promoting solar energy, brainstorming on nuclear energy, experimenting new energy models, energy conservation, utilizing coastal port facilities for imports and domestic shipment, other logistics advantages, import duties exemption, tax holidays, mega and ultra mega power projects status are the essential major factors for policy makers to tune it with release of one or more policy changes or amendments in the electricity Acts without proper correlation and partial comprehensiveness.

India's foreign policy to gain market knowledge, compete and to create value in today's dynamic and increasingly interconnected global energy markets had unappreciable impacts in resolving the domestic energy crisis.

Global firms, financial institutions, MNC Power builders, bankers and energy consultants retrenched themselves from Indian energy markets as they could not operate effectively in the environment power sector was sailing fearing liquidity risk under the influence of reformed policies since 1991.

The power sector unexpectedly remained with very marginal foreign investments and had to enormously depend upon domestic sources for financing the power projects with permutations and combinations in redefining the investment policies suiting to the immediate survival needs of the National Power Policy.

India's liberalized power market was meticulously capitalized with a predetermined disguised market strategy as a destination for exporting manufactured power equipments by the foreign companies averting totally the risk of huge investments in project construction, operation and maintenance.

Recovery of interest on debt, return on equity investment, depreciation, fixed operational & maintenance expenses, fuel consumed for generation (variable part is nonexistent in hydroelectricity as compared to thermal generation) and other miscellaneous expenditures is done through tariffs bifurcating them into either fixed costs or variable costs to determine the price per unit. There is uncertainty that the trading in electricity is based on the capacity charges or energy charges as the underlying principles.

The first legal framework governing the decentralized electricity sector in India was passed in 1877 when it was dominated by distribution licensees (private enterprises) facing lack of cooperation and coordination among themselves.

This Act was later repealed and replaced by the Indian Electricity Act, 1903. The first comprehensive basic legal framework for the power supply industry in pre independent India with considerable authority to the provincial governments was The Indian Electricity Act, 1910 which regulates the granting of licenses to market operators, producers, transmitters and distributors of electricity. It defines who controls the distribution and consumption of energy. It regulates licensees' accounts, the installation of electricity-supply lines and other works.

Finally, it determines who controls the supply, transmission and use of energy by non-licensees. The Act calls for fair treatment of customers and to do so, the Act requires that tariffs are defined through policy. There was no concept of State owned utilities prior to independence. The sector was dominated by private companies and the responsibility of developing the sector in providing electricity services to the nation was not imperatively felt necessary under the British Rule.

The Electricity (Supply) Act, 1948 which was modeled along the lines of the existing Electricity (Supply) Act, 1926, United Kingdom, mandated establishing the SEBs. SEBs does not have to comply with the financial and accounting rules of the Indian Company Act.

They are vertically integrated utilities with a commitment to enlarge the customer base from urban areas to rural areas. The Act defines the power and duties of the SEBs and generating companies. It defines the approval process for the establishment, acquisition and replacement of power stations. The Sixth Schedule of the 1948 Act established financial principles for determining licensees' tariffs, stipulating that profit should not exceed a 16% internal rate of return. The Sixth Schedule uses a cost-plus methodology in determining those returns. The Central Electricity Authority (CEA) was also created to develop a national power policy across India.

With the enactment of the Indian Constitution in 1950, electricity was placed in the concurrent jurisdiction of the Central and State governments. Though Post Independence, electricity supply was treated as a core industry and was given strategic importance keeping in mind its impact on industrial development and social obligations, today the industrial growth is being paralyzed because of acute power shortages.

The Industrial Policy Resolution of 1956 reserved generation and distribution of electricity exclusively in the domain of the states, while letting existing private licensees to continue. This led to the domination of the electricity sector by government enterprises over time.

Amendments in 1976 enabled generation companies to be set up by Central as well as state governments and resulted in the establishment of several central utilities, namely National Thermal Power Corporation, National Hydro Power Corporation, North Eastern Electric Power Corporation etc.

Amendments in 1991 resulted in the formation of Regional Load Dispatch Centers to operate the power systems in the region. Generation was opened to private investment and foreign investment was encouraged.

In 1998 the transmission sector was opened to private investment subject to the approval of the Central Transmission Utility.

Under the policy on Private Participation in the Power Sector, 1991 private sector entrepreneurs may set up companies, either as licensees or as generating companies. Up to 100% foreign equity participation is allowed.

The policy, in this regard has widened the scope of private investment in the electricity sector, and has introduced modifications in the financial, administrative and legal environment, for the private enterprises in the electricity sector towards making investments in the sector by private units attractive.

Based on this policy, a scheme has been framed to encourage private enterprises 'participation in power generation, supply and distribution," Electricity Laws (Amendment) Act, 1991 this amendment of the Indian Electricity Act reinforced the integration of the grid in India by giving more authority to the regional load dispatch centers (RLDC).

Again in 1995 the introduction of Mega Power Policy, its subsequent revision in 1998 covered both the public and private sector and the policy on UMPPs.

Electricity Regulatory Commission Act 1998, facilitated the establishment of a regulatory commission at the center called the Central Electricity Regulatory Commission (CERC) and one regulatory commission in each state, called as the State Electricity Regulatory Commission (SERC). All most all states have so created SERC either under the Central Act or under their own Reform Act.

On January 6, 2006, the Central government notified the National Tariff Policy for the power sector in compliance with Section 3 of the Electricity Act 2003 and in continuation of the National Electricity Policy passed on February 12,2005.

Future determination of tariff to be based on Multi Year Tariff (MYT) principles. Availability Based Tariff (ABT) to be introduced at State level by April 2006 and the cross-subsidy surcharge to be brought down progressively by 20 per cent by 2012 were the salient features of the policy.

Disparity in Electricity Services

Disparity in electricity services is booming with discrimination day by day. Will there be an end?

Today electricity is being demanded as a fundamental right by the people of India. The domestic segment constitutes the big base of electricity consumers under different slabs of consumption and categories. The consumers locality speaks about the availability, accessibility, affordability and reliability of power supplied to them. The power supply services in rural areas are not at par with the urban areas.

Making electricity available to consumers at their door steps from the place of power generating plants through series of complex supply chain requires great management control to effectively operate the complete integrated power system.

The State utilities were born with the vision to achieve the commanding heights but to the dismay lost its mission ending up in organizational restructuring for survival. Despite empowering public enterprises to face the competition in the energy sector impacted by series of reforms initiated by the government of India over the last two decades the performance of the state owned power utilities is unappreciable.

Load shedding is the rule of the day for domestic consumers. Industrial consumers are suffering from power holidays. Energy crisis is bringing in migrating of small and big industries across the country.

The impact of power shortage on GDP of India is mounting day by day. The impact of power cuts is very seriously affecting the total yields as irrigation is not being backed up by substantial power supply availability and accessibility.

Is irrigation in the concurrent list in India? Whose responsibility is to facilitate energy and power issues in irrigation? Can we strengthen the agriculture sector without reenergizing the irrigation in India? The irrigation system is not 100 per cent energized and much depends upon the diesel pump sets being used by the farmers.

Rural electrification needs more attention to uplift the standards of living in villages. Why they are being deprived from the facilities and amenities? Is sustaining "METRO CITY" is the only motto of the government in India?

Rural Citizens are unfortunate in availing the benefits of modernization. Is "Silence is the best response to a foolish question", the policy adopted by the government on many non-addressable issues in the sector?

Electricity is an essential basic infrastructure for developing and growing the economy. Without this prime energy the overall development of society, nation and world cannot be thought of. Electric power is the core energy on which undoubtedly our modern life depends. Undeniably the renewable cannot immediately take up the mainstream market of power in India. Indisputably my readers, consumers, customers and citizens should agree with me.

Tariff Policy in the Indian Electricity Sector has been always a debatable issue since its inception. As per the Electricity Act 2003, passed by the parliament, the Central government is required to formulate the National Electricity Policy and Tariff Policy. The Electricity Act uses policy, methodology and determination three distinct terms related to establishing tariffs. Determination of Tariff by two levels (Central and State) of independent regulators is without scope for ambiguities.

The price of electricity is much cheaper from captive power plants for usage by owner but is sold to the purchaser at market price. The merchant power plants are bringing great turbulence in determining electricity prices.

Energy deficit and electricity pricing without economics of scale is being advantageously manipulated to capitalize the liberalized power market by big Corporate for their profit motives rather than on rationalization of electricity pricing in India. Subsidies and cross-subsidies were the chapters of state utilities and regulators prior to reforms and restructuring.

More than any other factor, the way electricity prices are determined has inhibited India's power market development. Under pricing and political interference in price determination have worsened the financial situation of the main electricity producers, wholesale buyers and suppliers: the SEBs.

This increases the risk for private players who wish to enter the electricity market. The SEBs' end-use electricity tariffs vary widely according to customer category. The major categories are households, agriculture, commercial activities, industry and railways.

There are large cross-subsidies between customer categories in India, tariffs for households and agriculture are generally well below actual supply costs, while tariffs to other customer categories are usually above the utilities' reported average cost of supply.

In 1999-2000, the average price of electricity sold amounted to 208 paise/kWh – 26% below the average cost of supply. The total under-recovery of costs – the difference between total costs and total revenues – amounted to 272 billion rupees in 1999-2000, an increase of 190% since 1992-93.

Most of this subsidy is reported to be for the agricultural sector. The double effect of under pricing, that has resulted in growing wastage of electricity over the past decades, and the development of auto-production largely explains why India has a higher electricity intensity of its GDP than the rest of Asia.

Central government and state budgets are burdened by subsidies, which account for a large share of current expenditures, at the expense of investments in the electricity sector or other sectors such as education and health.

Demarcation between household connection and agriculture connection to rightly categorize as subsidized consumer is an ongoing issue in India. In the name of irrigation and agriculture India is helpless to streamline the shortcomings in the system supporting huge units of energy drain.

Many customers, from agriculture but also households in urban areas, do not pay but continue to receive service. These customers effectively enjoy a 100% subsidy. This non-payment problem could far outweigh the official subsidies issue. Since SEBs are managed like government, it is difficult to operate the power sector on the basis of economic criteria.

Metering, billing and collecting revenues have been neglected. Decision-making remains highly centralized. Lower level employees have little decision-making authority. Issues of integrity, loyalty and comprising on implementation of penalties are supporting the default consumers. The quality of humans affects both the power utilities and consumers. Finally the overall system in India.

Subsidy reform, to the extent that it increases the SEBs' financial viability, would boost their capacity to invest and, therefore, increase sales to customers who currently lack access to electricity.

In the long run, a reduction in subsidies could lead to an increase in electricity consumption by end-users not currently served or whose supply is severely curtailed, by blackouts, brownouts or time-limited service. Indeed, this is the implicit goal of electricity sector reforms, including subsidy reduction.

The 1996 Common Minimum National Action Plan for Power sought to promote auto-generation by calling on SEBs to provide access to their grid to transmit power that is surplus to a company's own needs to other end-users.

Gaps- Power Supply Chain

Why the power sector continues to lag behind despite the implementation of the progressive measures at the Centre and State? Majority of the countrymen believe that the recent power policies were never realistic with all the doubts of its feasibility and success in times to unfold.

There has been very marginal improvements in the performance of the utilities after restructuring but the shortage situation and per capita consumption of electricity are yet open critical issues being invariably addressed by the policy makers for overall sustainability.

Though there is gradual improvement in introducing and implementing SCADA, AMR, GIS, DT metering, e-meters, energy audits, recent performance and achievements by some Electricity Distribution Utility after the adoption of the PPP Model an example of success of the reform process the energy supply is lagging far behind the rapidly growing demand in spite of the sea changes in regulations and tariff structures.

Public Private Partnership (PPP) & Independent Power Producers (IPP's) may be the future life line for this corroding Power System which is so severely submerged under issues and challenges to be very evidently branded as the most Inefficient Sector.

The power sector was among the first sectors to be opened up for private sector investment during the early 1990s. Though the initial impetus was on investment for power generation projects, the government subsequently allowed private investment in distribution and transmission projects also.

The present India's Power System operates under reformed policies, restructured SEBs and deregulated & liberalized power market. Both policy and performance are equally responsible in creating gaps in the electricity supply chain.

The capacity to generate is not consummate with the capabilities of transporting power through the current infrastructure in the transmission system. The numbers of agencies participating in the generation segment are very high as compared to transmission and distribution segment.

Power supply chain management in India lacks professionalism. An integrated power supply chain management at national level including all the states is to be developed.

Deregulation in generation was not complemented with de-licensing in T & D, power trading and exchanges. Rural Electrification Policy (2006) mandating electrifying all villages and households was introduced very late.

There were wide gaps in implementing government policies and plans, shortfalls in accomplishing targets, late amendments due to delayed corrections on failure and unsuccessful programmes, untimely linkages & clearances had impacts on completion and commissioning of power projects affecting COD (commercial operation date), FSAs & PPAs closures are still holding fully fledged operation of power stations.

Problem of primary energy distribution and allocation to power stations still remains an area of threat to power producers especially depending on gas based power generation. The completion of the national gas network corridor through interconnecting regions has severely affected the power projects commissioning and loss of generation.

Power and fuel are mutually interdependent in deciding the feasibility and success of the power projects being envisaged and implemented to address the issues of power crisis in the electricity sector. The rate of fuel consumption is directly proportional to rate of power generation but the brighter side of power generation is overshadowing the bitter side of depletion of primary energy being rapidly consumed to generate electricity. Hence one unit of electricity generated consumes substantial units of primary fuel.

Policy makers need to strike a balance to maintain equilibrium in choice of fuel to generate power. Power generation is as good as energy consumption, so energy conservation and renewable energy sources exploration are focal areas for bridging the created gaps in energy.

India ranked eighth in the world in total electricity generated in 1998 between France and the United Kingdom with about 494 TWh. But because of India's large population, consumption of electricity per capita was only 460 kWh/year among the lowest in the world.

The world average is 2,252 kWh per capita. India currently has around 200 000 MW of installed power generating capacity as on March 2012. Thermal power plants comprise almost 80 per cent of this capacity, hydroelectric plant about 16 per cent, while the remaining is from nuclear plants. A relatively smaller percentage is contributed by the non-conventional energy sources. A large number of private power projects are in the pipeline.

The Indian Power System is divided into five regions for the purpose of planning and operation: Northern, Northeastern, Eastern, Southern and Western. Each region is directed by operating personnel using load dispatch and communication facilities located at regional and state load dispatch centers.

Power development has been the key to the economic development since 1950.

The Power Sector has been getting a good share of 18-20% of the total Public Sector outlay in initial plan periods.

It is true that remarkable growth and progress have led to extensive use of electricity in all the sectors of economy in the successive five years plans. However, the energy crisis is persisting despite all measures of the government taken from time to time.

In the field of Rural Electrification and pump set energization, country still needs to do more.

Ministry of Power has confirmed a target of 88 000 MW of extra generation capacity in the next five years, as part of the country's new 12th Five-Year Plan (2012-2017).

India's current generating capacity is 200 000MW, but still suffers from a peak shortfall of 10 per cent.

During the post independence period, the various States played a predominant role in the power development. Most of the States have established State Electricity Boards. In some of these States separate corporations have also been established to install and operate generation facilities.

In the rest of the smaller States and UTs the power systems are managed and operated by the respective electricity departments. In a few States private licensees are also operating in certain urban areas. The market for generation in India is comprised largely of state-owned power plants, developed and managed by SEBs or unbundled state generation companies or central sector utilities.

In 1999-2000, India had a total generation capacity of 113 GW. A decade after the market opened for private generators, IIPs constituted less than ten percent of this total capacity. 15 GW of the total capacity came from captive power plants.

The fuel mix of the balance consisted of 61 per cent coal, 24 per cent hydro, 10 per cent gas, 3 per cent nuclear and 2 per cent oil. Coal and hydroelectric power will likely provide the majority of future incremental capacity.

Coal power plant efficiency and availability in the 1990s was low by international standards, and many plant used poor quality unwashed coal, with low heat and high ash content. The predominance of coal in the generation market of the 1990s also skewed generation toward base capacity, with resulting shortfall in peak period supply, which has continued to be problem with the overall electricity generation market in India.

Considering the size of its economy, India is poorly endowed with energy resources. It has only modest reserves of oil and gas which will only last for a few decades unless major oil or gas deposits are discovered. India has, however, coal resources that are sufficiently large to meet the bulk of its energy needs for the next 250 years.

To meet part of its energy needs through imports would require large investments in transport infrastructure. Since these investments are unlikely to materialize over the short and medium term, indigenous coal will remain the least cost source of energy for most uses.

Currently, more than two-thirds of India's energy needs are met by coal in one form or another. About 70% of India's coal production is converted into electric power; the remaining 30% is used for a large number of industrial purposes. About 70% of India's coal comes from large, highly mechanized opencast operations. Transmission within states and most local distribution were in the hands of the SEBs. Until recently, all generation, transmission and distribution of power belonged to the public sector except for some licensees such as Bombay Suburban Electricity Supply (BSES), Tata Electric Corporation (TEC), or Calcutta Electricity Supply Corporation (CESC). Private utilities and independent producers represent only a marginal share of electricity supply. Since 1991, the sector has been open to private investors, initially for generation and later for transmission and distribution

Final consumption of electricity has increased by an average of 7% per year since 1947. This sustained growth is the result of economic development and the increase in electrical appliances. It has been accompanied by a gradual shift from noncommercial sources of energy, such as biomass, in the household and commercial sector as well as the reduction in the use of coal for process heat in industry and kerosene for household lighting.

Of total final sales of 332 TWh in 1999-20001, industry accounted for just over one third, agriculture for 30% and the household sector for 18%. But for many years, electricity supply has fallen short of demand and the sustainability of this trend is very uncertain.

Though the overall demand-supply gap decreased from an estimated 8.1% in 1997-98 to 5.9% in 1998-99, it rebounded to 6.2% in 1999-2000. Peak power shortages fell from 18% in 1996-97 to 12% in 1999-2000.

In spite of sustained growth, electricity consumption per capita was only 416 kWh per annum (in 1998), far below the world average of 2,252 kWh. The International Energy Agency's World Energy Outlook 2000 projects electricity demand in India to increase by 5.4% per year from 1997 to 2020, faster than the assumed GDP growth rate of 4.9%. The duration and number of blackouts and brownouts are beyond acceptable limits, leading to shortfalls of up to 15% of demand.

It seems that the seasonal variation in the load between summer and winter is limited, and changes during the day are not high either as compared to other countries. Inadequate power transmission and distribution result in shortages which in turn affect consumption patterns and induce commercial users and the most affluent domestic customers to rely on standby/in-house investments in auto-production capacity.

A significant proportion of consumption reported as being in the agriculture sector is actually consumed by other sectors but not properly metered. Actual farm consumption could be only 10% of overall consumption. A part of the population could afford a costlier electricity service, but available supply cannot satisfy their demand.

A large majority of the population is rural. Officially, close to 90% of the villages are electrified. However, only half the Indian population does in fact have electricity. Since a large portion of the population lives below the poverty line, they cannot afford electricity at current costs, this is particularly true in rural areas.

Challenges of Power Tariff- Cost Vs Profit

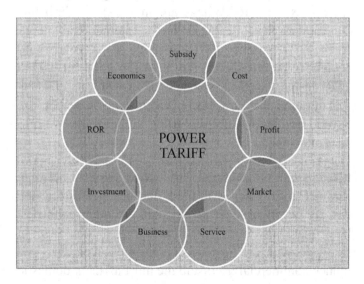

India's electricity supply is mainly based on coal burnt in boilers feeding steam turbines, an adequate technology for base load power generation and to a lesser extent for intermediate-load generation. Hydroelectricity capacity and the shares of hydro in generation have been decreasing over the years, reducing the availability of peak-load power.

The Indian system is biased toward the production of base load power, while the supply-demand gap is mainly in peak-load electricity.

India's Ministry of Power is planning to conduct independent audits of the country's electricity transmission system following the crippling blackout that affected half of the population at the end of July 2012. As well as the decision to conduct independent third party audits of the grid protection system, it was also agreed to establish an effective plan to ensure the integrated operations of the national and regional grids in adherence with the Indian Electricity Grid Code.

It was also decided that all utilities must adopt best operation and maintenance practices, and would be subject to random checks by regional power committees. India has suffered its worst blackout in over ten years on July 30 & 31 following a grid failure that left more than 300 million people without power in New Delhi and much of the north of the country.

The grid failure was caused by overdrawing by states as they tried to satisfy the high power demand of their citizens as temperatures soared. The outage forced the shutdown of hydro plants and thermal power stations in

Punjab and Haryana. Gas is gaining an increasing role. Nuclear accounts for a marginal share of capacity and is not expected to be a major source of power in the immediate future.

IMPACT OF REFORMS AND RESTRUCTURING

Unbundling of SEBs

Empowering Public Enterprises through unbundling of SEBs may not be the right answers for resolving energy crisis in India. The financial autonomy and accountability of PEs occupy an important place in a democratic country like India. The underlying philosophy of empowering public enterprises is that their performance will improve if they are granted more autonomy and are liberated from the stranglehold of bureaucracy. The proponents of the autonomy package derive strength for their argument from the experience of superior performance of public enterprises during the 1990s reform period.

How to improve the performance of ailing PEs in India? It is now like catching fish in the desert. Public Enterprises totally differ in their background, cause of genesis, history of development, nature of goods manufactured and services offered. They operate in an environment for which they were never trained and the basic concept of design is no more prevailing.

They are like the butter between the sand witched breads of Nationalization and Globalization. So it is imperatively not possible to measure their performance with the same yardstick. However, there are common areas which need to be considered to improve performance including profitability of the Public Sector Enterprises. Public Enterprises have social goals and are not commercial enterprises believing in the philosophy of generating employment, raising living standards of people, achieving self sufficiency, and overall economic independence.

SEBs- Performance in India

National level.

SEBs Performance Parameters	ALL India Average
Commercial Losses	20-40%
Technical Losses	15-30%
AT&C	45-50%
Subsidies	30-50%
Rate of Return	Negative, -5 to 3%
Collection Efficiency	60-75%
Billing Efficiency	70-80%
Average Cost of Supply	2.5-5.5 Rs/kWh
Average Revenue Realized	2.0-3.5 Rs/kWh, 50% gap
Power Theft	20-30%
Load Shedding Power Stations (Above 100 MW each unit)	2000 MW to 5000 MW annually per power station
Feeder Metering Balance	20-30%
Consumer Metering Balance	15-25%
Plant Load Factor	55-80%
Peak Load Shortage (MW)	7 to 20%
Energy Shortage (MU)	7to 30%
Power Transformer failure rate	5-15 %
Distribution Transformer failure rate	5-25%
Disruption due to Grid failure	Once a year to two times

Transmission & Distribution Losses	25-40%
Trading of Electricity	0-3%
Efficiency of Implementing Schemes	0-50%
Success of State Reforms Acts	0-50%
Impact of Reforms and Restructuring	0-60%
Overall functioning of the Integrated Power System	40-65%
Loans and debts	15-50%
Financial Performance (Outlay Vs Expenditure Gap)	25-50%

One of the important aspect of this study was to understand the parameters which affected the performance of the state power utilities. The major indicators have been tabulated to be easily understood by the learning readers on this subject. These indicators have become perennial in the Indian Electricity Sector.

My research is also oriented around these critical indicators. It begins with the quest for causes of this situation in which the power sector is sailing.

As mentioned above, every State Electricity Board (SEB) in India is either unprofitable or bankrupt. Just as the generation of IPPs began to come online in 1995-96, nine of the nineteen SEBs were already in the red. By 2000-2001, the problem had worsened.

Every SEB in India was incurring substantial losses and became an increasingly unable to pay electricity purchased from central public-sector power companies such as NTPC or from IPPs. Contributing to this budget crisis, cumulative electricity transmission and distribution losses amounted to 260 billion rupees per year, due technical line loss, commercial line loss (electricity theft) and the cross-subsidy tariff structure that heavily subsidizes agriculture at the expense of commercial and industrial consumer, who must pay at rates above the average cost of service. Only slightly more than half of electricity in India is billed, and less than half of electricity consumed is paid for regularly.

An entrenched system of cross-subsidization encouraged by political interference and buttressed by concern with equity for rural farmer worsened the financial situation of SEBs. Retail electricity tariff vary widely according to customer commercial, industry and railways. Tariffs for households and agriculture are generally far below the cost service, while tariffs to other customer categories, particular industry, are typically much higher than the SEBs' average cost of supply.

As a result, the average price of electricity sold in 1999 to 2000 was 26% below the average cost of supply, resulting in large losses incurred by the SEBs. Financial constraints on SEBs resulting from uneconomic tariff structure and poor collection became the most serious challenge, sometime insurmountable, faced by IPPs in India.

The few private companies then operating under British Rule were nationalized immediately after political independence. The formation of State Electricity Boards and introducing of Central Sector in generation and transmission systems were the early initiatives in developing the Power Sector.

Why did the monopoly of Public Enterprises ended in Indian Power Sector? The period from 1950 to 1991, was dominated by the Public Enterprises. Because of such a long period and no competition within the states the overall performance suffered with no chance for recovery.

The Industrial Policy Resolution of 1948, The Industries (Development & Regulation)Act, 1951 (IDRA), Industry Policy Resolution, 1956, The Monopolies & Restrictive Trade Practices Act, 1969 (MRTPA), The Foreign Exchange Regulation Act, 1973 (FERA) were all constituted to protect the Core Sector as per the National Policy and a time had come to surrender initiating the Economic Reforms,1991.

Plant load factor have been performing at in between 70-73 for the state sector, 84-87 for the central sector and 83- 91 for the private sector. The state sector that has the highest installed capacity is the least efficient. The private sector utilities have clocked good efficiency rates and the central utilities have managed to achieve competent efficiency rates. Going forward, with private players being encouraged to enter the Power Sector, the state utilities will be required to work on improving their efficiency.

Do you think simply downsizing organization will bring better controls and performance?

Liberalizing- India's Power Market

India is the third largest producer of electricity in Asia. The concept of trading may seem odd in power deficit India. One of the greatest impacts of reforms and restructuring has been the attempt to develop a open power market.

Power trading is recognized by Electricity Act-2003 as a separate licensed activity. The opportunity for trading is to address the issue of diversity in demand created now and then from various states and regions of the country according to surpluses and shortages in power. Will the liberalizing of power market benefit the power sector? There is increasing competition in power trading business.

How effective will be the long term PPAs entered by the power trader with power utilities? The success of PSAs with electricity consumers especially the unhealthy SEBs will be unfolded in times to come. The power sale for the transfer of power from a surplus utility to a deficit utility under short term trading mechanism yet needs to be evolved with proper perennial solutions. The implementation of demand side management (DSM) has its own philosophy and ambiguities.

Is the Indian Electricity Market really liberalized? How to design a successful liberalized power market dynamic model operating in a huge democratic country like India to have better price for both the buyers and sellers of electricity with all sorts of diversities in the emerging power mix? The protection of electricity consumers and power utilities in liberalized power market is an unending question of debate in the sector.

How will the private utilities form a consortium or committee to parallely run their government in addressing their issues at par with central and state sector utilities? The power exchanges have been created as per the mandates of the National Electricity Policy to eliminate the disparity in electricity services by bridging the gap between surpluses and shortages in power supply.

The market is in very nascent stage without clear rules of the game and prospective anxious players are lobbying to develop a self regulated market mechanism to capitalize the trading of electricity in India. The recent imposition of trading margin by CERC affecting the revenues of trading companies has not been honoured.

The regulation at the same time in order to establish its moral responsibility and sincere commitment wishes to reduce the cost of power for consumers. The distribution utilities who are the bulk buyers of power are benefiting with the apprehension of probable threat to the generating utilities likely to suffer by selling at lower prices to power traders.

The policy that the State governments and the distribution licensees can undertake trading without obtaining a separate license where as the transmission utility cannot take up trading and a trading licensee cannot have transmission business is a regulatory restriction in impeding competition in completely liberalizing the power market, is the perception of the market players.

Major foreign investors in the Indian power sector include CMS Energy, Unocal, Woodside Petroleum, Siemens, ABB, AES Transpower, Powergen, CLP, PSEG, Tractabel, Alstom, General Electric, Hitachi, Steag, Mitsubishi, Shanghai Electric, Torrent, etc.

The policy of liberalization the Government of India announced in 1991 and consequent amendments in Electricity (Supply) Act have opened new vistas to involve private efforts and investments in electricity industry. Considerable emphasis had been placed on attracting private investment and the major policy changes had been announced by the Government in this regard.

The Electricity (Supply) Act, 1948 was amended in 1991 to provide for creation of private generating companies for setting up power generating facilities and selling the power in bulk to the grid or other persons. Financial Environment for private sector units modified to allow liberal capital structuring and an attractive return on investment. Up to hundred percent (100%) foreign equity participation can be permitted for projects set up by foreign private investors in the Indian Electricity Sector. Administrative & Legal environment modified to simplify the procedures for clearances of the projects.

Policy guidelines for private sector participation in the renovation & modernization of power plants issued in 1995. In 1995, the policy for Mega power projects of capacity 1000 MW or more and supplying power to more than one state introduced. The Mega projects to be set up in the regions having coal and hydel potential or in the coastal regions based on imported fuel.

Power Trading Corporation (PTC) has been incorporated recently to promote and monitor the Mega Power Projects. PTC would purchase power from the Mega Private Projects and sell it to the identified SEBs. Is this a justifiable policy?

In 1995 Government of India came out with liquid fuel policy permitting liquid fuel based power plants to achieve the quick capacity addition so as to avert a severe power crisis. Liquid fuel linkages (Naphtha) were approved for about 12000 MW Power plant capacity. The non-traditional fuels like condensate and orimulsion have also been permitted for power generation.

SECTION-B

PART I
ENERGY & ECONOMY

CHAPTER-I

LIGHTING POWER SECTOR

Energy Vs Economy, the pull & push is must for growth and development of India. Who will light India's Power Sector? When will India have sound economy? How will India's Energy Sector become healhy?

India is not an exception to the global energy crisis. Energy crisis in India's Power Sector solely cannot be attributable to any single parameter however based on the thorough review and comprehensive background of the ailing sector the probable factors may be inefficient national power policies, uncertainty of regulatory reforms, unaccountability of public power utilities enterprises management, crippling performance of India's Power System, under developed power markets, regional disparity in electrifying rural and urban areas, lacking synergy in integrating and utilizing the resources, slow pace in exploring renewable and alternate primary energy to generate electricity, allocating and pooling power in states, delay in constructing, connecting and operating national power grid, unexpected failure of IPPs, inadequate power plants and untimely commissioning of power generating projects under the reform regime, unsuccessful implementation of the government's targeted programmes, insecurity of gas and coal supply agreements, neglecting renovation and modernization of old power stations, underrated generation, power market exploitation by captive and merchant power producers, not the last but the least politicization of the power sector.

Power consumer's partial awareness on electricity supply Acts, undedicated energy conservation practices, unethical usage, theft, pilferage and wastage of electricity are all unaccountable losses of power adding to the prevailing energy crisis.

Energy Crisis in India's Power System regularly undergoing series of appreciable reforms and restructuring over the last 20 years is still a burning national problem facing unlimited challenges and unending Governments mandate, the recent one being Power to all by 2012. The question of addressing all of them at a time is a distant dream in the present scenario.

The Role of the State had been invariably restricting its philosophy to visualize "Citizens as Customers", much under the obsessed impression of orthodox belief as custodian of national welfare and social economic development though in recent times transforming India proudly speaks of active participation in Global Energy Markets.

Have you ever wondered why your power bills keep rising even when electricity consumption doesn't? What could be the reason? An interesting finding from this analytical research is that your utility may be supplying costlier power even when there's enough cheap electricity in the grid.

"Costly Electricity Vs Cheaper Power", the debate is going to never end. How can the cost of generation of electricity remain lower than the supply of power to consumers? Are the enterprises applying the Cost –Volume Profit Analysis (CVP) to improve their financial health? The Break Even Analysis is the most widely known form of the CVP Analysis.

Why citizens should be in the dark when there's enough electricity in the country? An interesting outcome of the analytical approach to investigate the energy crisis in India is that despite the huge sales volume of the product electricity the control on cost of production and services could not be optimized.

The Public Enterprises providing power utility services have no control on the process of capital structure and financial decision is again questionable with the background history of its prolonged sickness in recent times.

Why actions were delayed on the financial aspects and investment analysis of the energy sector? A careful insight into cash and funds flow analysis reveals that the policy makers were waiting to take action till the enterprises become completely sick and unproductive. It speaks of the helplessness of the managers and administrators of the system in India.

What can be an ideal mix of public and private policy makers? Will there be a common platform for both public and private in the energy sector?

The cost on fuel logistics is another area of importance in deciding the final price of electricity generation and distribution?

Are we having a pure competition in the sector? Are the power utilities maintaining quality of their product and services?

Social businesses will have social goals. How to translate strategy into results? How to be efficient in effectively executing the strategies?

What to do about this energy crisis? Will India still sail like the snail?

Is there really any boom for establishing projects on the "BOOM" model? The interpretation of BOOM, follows Built, Own, Operate and Maintain. What is the difference between these models "BOO", "BOOT" and "BOOM" actually? Why these models with huge gestation periods?

I bring to my readers an important notable point that the problem in this model is of "Transfer" and "Maintain". The question is of "Ownership" and "Management".

The Power providers are reluctant to follow the "BOOT" model as it has no meaning to transfer the complete establishment after running the plant for so long years as per the contract. This is really ridiculous to understand as what remains after the technically specified life of the plant.

Did the government mean that again the Renovation & Modernization (R&M) will be their baby to be taken care of? An example of unclear policy for longer visions in the sector.

India got to develop more thinkers on the subject of people strategy because some people are owners, some are managers, some people are leaders, and some are followers. And again all the worry about authenticity, leadership, integrity, loyalty, virtues, ethics, in implementation, functioning, controlling and guiding.

How to measure character? Its sadly unsurprising that unethical practices are persisting for no gain. Does business performance has to do anything with the strength of character? What should be the moral principle of an employee?

This is a study to probe into the reality of energy policies with the especial focus on the power sector being the leader in energy industry.

Power is the supreme of all energy. Electricity dominates the energy mix. Now the question is to go for which power. Power by coal, oil, gas, solar, wind, geothermal, bio-energy, nuclear, tidal, hydro, or any other renewable or alternate energy.

The fossil fuels and water is locked in lands so the question is of ownership and sharing. What about the wind and solar energy?

Coal for cooking and coal for power generation have very different price mechanisms, competition, challenges & concerns, and similarly oil for lighting, oil for transportation, oil for industry and oil for power generation have altogether different plans, allocation, pricing strategy and so on.

A subsidy for lighting and cooking may not match with subsidy for industry. The various application areas cannot be generalized and measured by the same yard stick.

How to design a pyramid of subsidies? How to rank them in order of preference and necessity? Are we not creating disparities in electricity services by showing preference to the consumers eligible for the subsidy grant?

Have you ever interrogated, investigated and witnessed the manipulation and corruption India is facing in providing electricity to the below poverty line consumers? How power utilities can meet the economics of scale in this scenario?

Pyramid of Subsidies

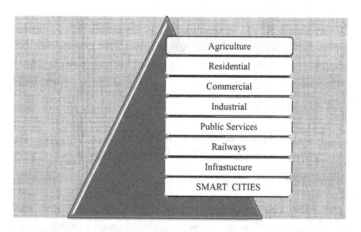

And finally all the happenings at the end for maximizing profit. Do you think the disguised incentives can make the system healthy? Is there a clear crafted framework of governance? Who are the participants in shaping the Corporate Strategy?

Cost Vs Profit, all are brainstorming from dawn to dusk. Is the energy sector lacking mentors with rich background of selective Leadership traits in India? It is time for resulting advices rather than pouring down valuable time on studying the history of failure of the sector.

I strongly believe that technology cannot break the living culture. India might have implemented the latest technology based power systems for efficiency and reliability.

Is India's excellence in public administration is diminishing. Why government should be regularly criticized for power tariff hike? Did deregulation of the power sector meant keep hiking the power tariff for the electricity consumers?

Can the financial losses the electricity departments have been suffering be just treated by increasing the tariff?

The sorry state of affairs in the functioning of the State's Public Sector Undertakings is very much imperative where huge losses are being caused to the state exchequer due to poor management and lack of financial discipline.

When will the energy sector have a congenial atmosphere? One side the policy speaks of liberating and other side it imposes penalties on non-compliance of Renewable Energy Certificates (REC) and Renewable Purchase

Obligations (RPO). Do you think the National Action Plan is effective?

One major question is why promote private investments through fiscal incentives, tax holidays, depreciation allowance and remunerative returns for power fed into the grid.

Are rural areas banes to the service providers? Is energy management in India at par with the developed nations? Is energy crisis in India due to poor policies or inefficiency in governance of the complete energy supply chain right from the reserves to the end users?

Was India misguided in concept of reserves and resources of energy? The energy sector has been swinging between business and society.

Can a Constitutional Act of any country compromise with the rights of the citizens?

Is India able to satisfy the respective needs, necessities and essentialities of consumer, customer and citizen in the power sector?

These 3C's certainly changes the entire outlook of the system.

3C's

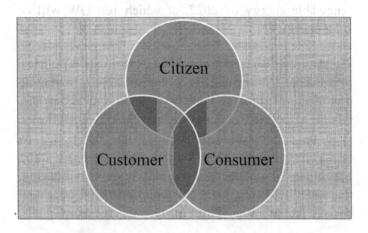

The importance of ports and cost of logistics in exports and imports of oil & gas always has a say into the pricing of energy. The efficiency in Logistics Management of fuels is a prime factor in determining the price of energy after the cost of exploration and mining.

There is a very important point of awareness which the changing society should try to understand related to the perception of consumer, customer and citizens in regard to the business, service, welfare, and society in India.

Will Solar Power be the next big industry break through? Is renewable energy becoming a key component?

In today's business environment innovation, communication, collaboration, strategy, leadership, change management and managing people are the essentials for making not only smart decisions but effective decisions.

The government of India has set a target of 175 GW of renewable energy by 2022, of which 100 GW will be solar energy.

The national issues of governance, performance, policies, reforms, restructuring, executing strategies, managing organizations, professional services, structural barriers, business culture, consumer psychology, synthesis, synergy, collaboration, technology up gradation, new energy models, decision making and so on are other key areas which needs a regular review, rethinking, reorientation, reorganization, realignment on continual basis to let the initiated reforms reach its redefined goals.

Is the Indian Energy Sector lacking innovation? Is our employee pool really engaged in rebuilding the power sector?

Employee Vs Management, Owner Vs Management, Policies Vs Goals, Ownership Vs Social Values, Business Vs Services, like that the quadrant game never stops. Are the public enterprises satisfactorily fulfilling the social goals in India?

The Global companies are very social friendly nowadays. Why this shift is needed? Can Indian Companies in Energy, Power & Infrastructure transform their objectives accordingly?

The Unionism in India is rising now and then. India loses huge production in the energy sector every year because of labour issues related to welfare and compensation.

India is weak and sensitivity of the issue paralyses its annual targets of production. I am sharing with you all that we have to improve much on Labour Management and employee welfare.

Skills are not rated as per the risk involved. A very green area for research and development in the mining sector.

Social and Economic problem often reflect an imbalance of power.

What is the core difference between Public, Private and Foreign, when we are operating in the Global Environment?

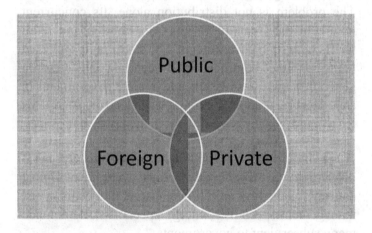

Private is Indian, Foreign and Global. When should the policy favour Private investments, Public investments and Foreign investments?

Who will provide financial security to the investors?

I sight from a recent political and ministerial environment the changes India has been witnessing in Power, Energy and Coal. The UPA had a junior minister for power, a retired non-performer for renewable energy and a coal minister who resigned under a cloud. The NDA put its bright ministers in charge of three related ministries—power, renewable energy and coal. There is a holistic approach to the issues but nuclear power must be included, and close coordination with petroleum and gas ministry must be ensured.

India's energy problems are due to the lack of an integrated holistic vision of the sector, poor attention to detail, and poor planning by governments at central and state levels. The problem is not distribution alone. Its concurrent nature in the Constitution puts distribution and retail tariffs with state governments. The statist philosophy led to the continued dominance of the central public sector in generation and transmission, and by state governments in state-level generation, distribution and load dispatch. This led to pandering by governments to their own enterprises.

When independent regulatory commissions for tariff determination were created, they were also almost entirely manned by retired bureaucrats (not economists, management specialists, energy specialists). This made many subservient to governments.

The government allowed high debt (up to 80%) in electricity investments and asked nationalized banks to lend the funds. Today, over R3 lakh crore of bank assets are non-performing. Utilities, especially electricity, are funded elsewhere from long-term savings in pension funds, etc. In India, banks lend for these long-term investments from short-term deposits, and interest costs are high, reflected in power tariffs.

Crony capitalism and non-supply of gas and coal has led to stranded generation capacities. Coal India has reneged on supply commitments of coal, many times of poor quality, with expensive damage to turbines. Open access, freedom to buy from any supplier in India, was disallowed by many state governments, leading to substantial quantities of cheap power left unused.

To quote from the power news there are many power distribution licences which are being revoked. Government has prepared a short-term action plan for streamlining operations and improving efficiency of these companies.

The action plan aims at achieving some stipulated targets by this year, focusing on rudimentary aspects of distribution like billing, collection, new connections and disconnections as well as installation of new meters.

India is targeting at 100 per cent billing of all consumers. Plans are afoot to install 300,000 new electric meters. Taking up new connection drives and going for disconnection of defaulting consumers both are equally important.

Why introducing middle man in power distribution? What should be the optimal model fr distribution of electricity in India?

India is in midst of a major shift in power distribution operation where the Electricity (Amendment) Bill 2014 seeks to segregate the distribution network from the electricity supply business leading to introduction of middle man.

Government have been projecting the segregation of electricity distribution and supply as a move that will enable consumers to choose suppliers similar to mobile phone service providers The logic is tempting, but over simplistic.

The electricity (amendment) bill is basically anti people and does not look at root cause of power sector ailments but only treat the symptoms of problems.

Can retail supply dictate electricity markets in India? Distribution and retail supply is the most critical link.

As all of know that the UPA government had promised power to all by 2012 and now NDA Government has extended the time bar to 2019. Why the timeline is not being considered as an important parameter in the whole process?

My readers to update you even today there are 34 crore households which are yet to get power connection.

Does the Global Energy Models suit India? Why Global Energy Policy fails in India? Is backwardness, poverty, underdevelopment, inadequate infrastructure some of the major areas making the overall effort unsuccessful.

Under these prevailing circumstances how to relight the power sector.

Citizens are under severe exploitation. Under such circumstance how to assure round the clock supply to all consumers.

Why to discriminate electricity consumers? Did thecategorizationn of "1MW Consumers" make any difference to the Power Sector? Till when will the rural consumers suffer in ndia? Still there are more than 80 million households to be electrified.

MNRE has announced state wise allocation of Rs 4750 Cr. to states and UTs for target capacity of setting up over 9500MW grid connected Solar PV power projects. The ministry has considered the disbursement of grant based upon the RPO target of 2015-16. Subsidy to be provided to unemployed youths and farmers for the project size of 0.5MW to 5 MW.

Coal India will invest Rs 5,000 crore in the Railways to procure wagons for speedy transportation of coal.

Railways is currently facing a shortage of wagons for carrying coal, causing strain on its ambitious target of transporting 1.18 billion tonnes of freight this year.

One of the state governments is planning to get 1,500 MW of stranded capacity on track by reviving private projects shut down due to lack of power purchase agreements (PPAs). This non-inking of PPAs has left these projects with no buyers for their electricity, which has forced them to stop generation.

The proposal will enable consumers to get power at cheaper costs and revive the idle assets of these independent power producers. The government is planning a policy to revive around 1,500 MW of shut down private power projects by private-public partnerships (PPP) model.

Neyveli Lignite Corporation plans to achieve a total generation capacity of 12,221 MW by the end of the 13th five year plan in 2022, against 2,990 MW at present. The corporation expects to achieve a lignite mining capacity of 49 million tonnes per annum (MTPA) by that year, compared to 30.60 MTPA in the lignite mines of Tamil Nadu/ Rajasthan at present.

CHAPTER-II

GREEN POWER IN INDIA

Fossil Vs Renewable

Will India go "Green" by 2017, or 2022, or 2025 or 2032?

How to achieve Net Zero Emissions? Is it practically feasible? Does India has efficient Solar PPA model to be implemented in the sector? Why electric utility industry are creating their own pollution permits?

Can rural electrification utilizing renewable energy be achieved in India? What will be the time frame?

The rivalry between fossil and renewable is maintaining and inciting the metabolism of the energy sector.

Who is the leader in Asia? Do China and Japan have different energy policies than India? Why the China Energy Model is not working out in India?

Why America is rapidly cosing down coal based power plants? Do you think they do not need power by conventional methods?

Why the philosophy of electricity from Nuclear Energy is always trapped into National Security issues of any country? Are we not constructive in our minds?

Let us examine the spheres of 3S's.

3S's

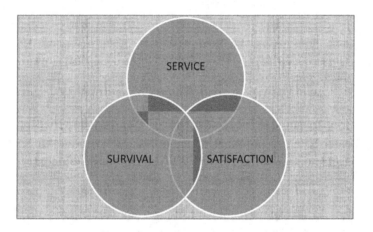

Electricity services for survival to satisfaction of consumers has its own saga of story every day. Services model should be such that it brings in equilibrium between survival needs and levels of consumer satisfaction.

Now the question is to Indian Electricity Consumers? What they want? Survival based services or satisfaction based services. An analytical debate in this area is not without ambiguities.

Quest for clean survival despite Global Energy Crisis, Economic Recession and merry go-round Liberalized Energy Policies are opening prospective avenues for Green Power across Asian Continent.

Can the least developed countries invariably battling with energy and poverty develop the clean energy industry and sustained renewable energy markets?

Increasing share of renewable in countries with energy mix least diversified due to resources, geographical constraints and other national factors are the challenges ahead.

Moreover the ice of National commitments for alleviating poverty with Global objectives of electrifying all villages is never melting down bridging the gap between abundant potential utilization and undercapitalized renewable resources.

Unfortunately all the reforms implemented to improve accessibility of electricity in rural areas are dwindling between the philosophy of business and service.

Will Renewable Energy translate the Destiny of Rural Asia?

Before I speak on the green power a brief insight into the historic fuels is essential to know the transition in fuel today.

Let us understand, how Coal formation began during the Carboniferous Period - known as the first coal age - which spanned 360 million to 290 million years ago.

Coal is a fossil fuel and is the altered remains of prehistoric vegetation that originally accumulated in swamps and peat bogs.

The energy we get from coal today comes from the energy that plants absorbed from the sun millions of years ago. All living plants store solar energy through a process known as photosynthesis.

When plants die, this energy is usually released as the plants decay. Under conditions favourable to coal formation, the decaying process is interrupted, preventing the release of the stored solar energy. The energy is locked into the coal.

Lignite is the lowest rank of coal. Will Brown Coal also compete with Black Coal in near future? Will we run out of fossil fuels?

What India is doing for Energy Sustainability? Coal takes million and million years to be created. We should be thankful to nature, earth and our ancestors for leaving it for us to benefit from this natural energy for living.

Million and million years of efforts brings a package of energy reserve to us which can only last for 100 to 150 or to the most 250 years taking into account all the permutations & combinations and corrections.

That means from today onwards if you travel similar number of million and million years towards future time you will create the required energy for replenishment in nature back. Does not it sound mysterious?

You have to wait million years to get a reserve of coal energy for 100 years. This is perhaps a strong reminder to all concerned with energy on this Earth. This is something which can be classified as stored energy in form of coal usable after mining.

In case of renewable like solar, wind, and tidal, if today's opportunity of tapping solar rays, intersecting winds, encountering tides is lost this energy is lost forever.

Every day is a store house of abundant renewable energy on this Earth. We must be fooling ourselves if we are not becoming green in our minds. It is an opportunity with greater prospects for the technologically advanced nations today.

"Technology Vs Renewable", is the magic stick for faster transition in the energy sector. Advanced technology is always boon to boost the betterment of power systems performance in the sector.

Efficiency is ultimately linked to the price of electricity. Modern Power Systems are replacing the obsolete technologies for up gradation to minimize technical losses in the supply chain of electricity.

The modern face of India is very rapidly changing with the introduction of high rise buildings, malls, multiplexes, big commercial complexes, all are excessively illuminated, equipped with escalators, HVAC system, fire detection systems, hoardings, entertainments, advertisements etc related to consumption of electrical energy.

Technology is changing whatever is possible in the built environment. Smart buildings are making ways rapidly in residential areas today.

Now days green buildings are the innovations to conserve energy. Modern buildings are equipped with integrated design concept where infrastructure is associated with facility system, communication system, business systems, security systems, safety systems, entertainment systems, centralized HVAC systems, all adding to the consumption of electricity.

Yes, let us take this seriously. We as humans on earth do have prime responsibility to conserve energy for future life to live and sustain.

"Fossil Vs Green", to what extent? What will happen if green power is inadequate? Can Green Power independently sustain the entire load of the national grid in India? How to tap maximum green power?

"Present Vs Future", needs of energy. Where does India stand today? What sacrifices the world can make today to save the future world?

"Domestic Vs International", issues are cropping up in the sector. Either it is technology collaboration, or equipment manufacturing & supplies, maintenance spares, automation technology, efficiency improvements, renovation & modernization, or emerging fuel mix opens new challenges of technology competencies and compatibilities, investing security, fund mobilization, allocation of coal blocks, renewable obligations, debt-equity portfolios, and so on, the policies are not crystal clear.

Can India integrate all renewable energy available across the country? When can India give up all green house gas emissions?

"Industrial Pollution Vs Green Environment", what type of policy suits India?

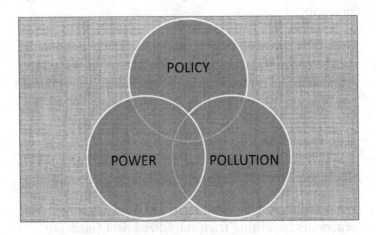

Is China going to become the King of Renewable? Why India cannot compete?

Is Japan the next boom Market for the Geothermal Energy Industry? How many geothermal wells India has to drill to capture the earth's natural heat for homes, offices, industries, agriculture, markets, etc?

Driven by rapid expansion in developing countries, renewable are becoming a significant source of the world's power. According to the recent United Nations Environmental Programme investment in developing countries is around 45% to 50%.

Scientists Vs Economists, where is the successful energy model to vote for. Is clean energy cheaper than coal? India at present without any hesitation should immediately start funding research into renewable, power storage and smart grid technologies.

Is India following the foot prints of the United States which is experiencing the significant shift in its energy landscape.

Green Vs Brown, that is racing towards enhancing solar, wind, tidal, geothermal, bio-energy based power production and revamping the old inefficient conventional power stations by renovation & modernization (R&M).

Will the R&M theory benefit the Indian Power Sector? It is perhaps going to be an unjustifiable budgetary burden and financial drain by the government of India?

What is the cost of renovating 1MW of capacity? Are generators benefiting from subsidized debt financing?

Is Indian Power Utilities benefiting from the R&M objectives? Is India analyzing the options in the sector?

Shutdowns Vs Shortfalls in generation always are linked to the outages of power supply. What should be the suitable running time to consider power plants for R&M? Current R&M is not keeping pace with the government mandates.

Residual Life Assessment (RLA) reports the healthiness of the power stations. There are essential parameters like load factor, fuel consumption, gross station heat rate, operating efficiency, thermal efficiency, power factor, auxiliary energy consumption to be monitored periodically for understanding the trends.

Analysis of constrains and barriers should be done regularly to find the gaps. How to increase the life of the Indian Power Generating units?

Life extension studies should be pro-actively undertaken. India lags behind in studies related to LE schemes, RLA and R&M.

India must pursue technologies that maximize energy efficiency, demand side management and energy conservation.

Energy efficiency & conservation is being considered as the most important virtual energy supply sources.

Consumers actions are also important to make the healthiness of the power utilities providing electricity services in India.

Every Consumer's recommendations should sincerely be considered by all the stake holders of the energy sector.

Acceleration of Renewable should not be just for the sake of initiating policy in the country. India is experiencing a significant shift in its energy landscape.

Are we learning the lessons like Japan and China? Over the last forty years, the use of fossil fuels has continued to grow and their share of the energy supply has increased. In the end of the last decade search for alternate energy has increased many folds all over the world.

Fusion Power is the process driving our sun and other stars. It generates large quantities of heat by fusing the nuclei of hydrogen isotopes. The heat can theoretically be harnessed to generate electricity. The temperatures and pressures needed to sustain fusion make it a very difficult process to control and doing so is an unsolved technical challenge.

The tantalizing potential of fusion is its theoretical ability to supply vast quantities of energy, with relatively little pollution. Both the United States and the European Union are supporting a moderate level of, along with other countries.

Is Fusion Power 100% free of pollution? Where to place Nuclear –based power in the category of energy list?

India is very poor in waste management? The utilization of waste for energy generation is not being sincerely thought of by the policy makers in India. The quantum of waste which India generates if utilized scientifically can light the whole World.

A great resource is going undercapitalized. This would have indirectly helped towards cleaner and greener India. The disposal of waste and its impacts and influences on environment has wider scope in India for studying and analyzing the total ecological system of the country.

Renewable resources are available each year, unlike non-renewable resources which are eventually depleted. A simple comparison is a coal mine and a forest. While the forest could be depleted, if it is managed properly it represents a continuous supply of energy, vs the coal mine which once it has been exhausted is gone. Most of earth's available energy resources are renewable resources.

Just imagine if one person on average generates one kg of waste daily then the total waste daily generated by humans on this earth is nearly 9 billion kg. The above analysis should be an eye opener to all of us in line with the discussion on energy crisis in the world.

Renewable resources account for more than 93 percent of total U.S. energy reserves. Annual renewable resources were multiplied times thirty years for comparison with non-renewable resources. In other words, if all non-renewable resources were uniformly exhausted in 30 years, they would only account for 7 percent of available resources each year, if all available renewable resources were developed.

Renewable energy sources are even larger than the traditional fossil fuels and in theory can easily supply the world's energy needs. 89 PW of solar power fall on the planet's surface. While it is not possible to capture all, or even most, of this energy, capturing less than 0.02% would be enough to meet the current energy needs.

Also, solar generation does not produce electricity at night, which is a particular problem in high northern and southern latitude countries; energy demand is highest in winter, while availability of solar energy is lowest.

The available wind energy estimates range from 300 TW to 370 TW. Using the lower estimate, just 5% of the available wind energy would supply the current worldwide energy needs. Most of this wind energy is available over the open ocean.

Waves are derived from wind, which is in turn derived from solar energy, and at each conversion there is a drop of about two orders of magnitude in available energy. The energy of waves that wash against our shores add up to 3 TW.

Production of biomass and bio-fuels are growing industries as interest in sustainable fuel sources is growing.

CHAPTER III

INDIA'S POWER REVOLUTION

Will the Xth and XIth Five Year Plans mark the beginning of Electricity Revolution in India? The journey of Indian Power Sector from political economy to liberalized electricity markets is a saga of pros and cons in building the nation.

The Indian Electricity Sector operates under the visionless policies and directionless redefining regulations, underperforming power Utilities, unsatisfied electricity consumers, underdeveloped power markets and emerging power mix being steered by the series of ineffective reforms and restructuring aimlessly challenging its overall sustainability.

In the light of the above it becomes imperative to review and study the major factors influencing the power sector becoming ineffective. The gaps between the policy & reality and implementation & impacts are necessary to analyze the success and failure of the ailing sector.

Electricity is critical to national economic development. India's Power Sector over the 50 years has passed through many needy changes and is still under customization to become the Ideal Sector. India requires Large Capacity Power Projects to meet the target. Supply of Electricity is a long journey from generation to end consumers. It operates under various bodies.

It appears that the year 2012 will make history in the electricity services in India. There are many mandates like power to all, formation of national grid, raising of inter regional transmission capacity to 37,150 MW, to generate 10 per cent of its power from renewable energy, 20,000 MW of nuclear power, extending services to 97 million un-electrified households, etc; of the Government of India to be achieved by the end of 2012.

Would it be a magical year for the National Power Policy makers to liquidate all the issues of the sector by 2012?

All the recent reforms Acts, policies, rules, regulations, plans, targets, recommendations, advises, suggestions, deadlines and many more in the pipeline thought of either resolving or dissolving the sufferings by 2012 in the power sector.

The year 2012 will make a new beginning in the power sector. After nearly two decades from initiation in 1991.

The XIIth Plan and onwards may not face the turbulence of sea changes in almost all the sections of the power sector throughout India. It is very much evident from the summary of key policy initiatives by the government of India as shown in the table above.

Why competition is needed in India's Energy Sector? The growth of India's is mutually dependent on the likelihood of benefits from the electricity sector, oil & gas sector and coal sector. These core infrastructures are the prime movers of economy in developing India.

Energy crisis in India is the result of primary undercapitalization of the available oil, gas and coal resources. At present potentially estimated reserves are not limited and would promisely last for 75 to 100 years with the present rate of exploration and consumption. The issues in exploration, production, transportation, marketing and services in oil, gas and coal sector continues and carrying out proper assessment of competition in India's Energy Sector could not be done so far.

The Electricity sector dominates the oil, gas and coal. The risk in competitions are very different in each sectors. The Energy sector has numerous interfacing at the Central and State levels. Unless there are substantial reforms in oil, gas and coal it is difficult to develop the electricity sector.

In recent times the dishonoring of the fuel supply agreements has resulted in closure of many power stations. The fuel security is a matter of serious concern for the Independent Power Producers (IPPs). The national network of oil, gas, coal and electricity is imperatively essential for overall development to alleviate regional disparities in energy.

It is high time India needs to address inadequate implementation of policies, regulatory sections, legal framework, natural monopoly characteristics of key segments, lack of political will, incumbency benefits of existing public monoliths, clearances and approvals required for projects, existence of distribution controls linkages, high sunk costs barriers to competition.

The absence of independent regulator, dominance of public sector monopoly, presence of stiff legislation concerning land acquisition, rehabilitation and environmental management, constraints of port capacity & infrastructure, acute shortage of coking and non-coking coal supplies and deterioration of quality are the major factors impeding competition in coal sector.

Reasons for limited private participation in captive mining are lack of transparency in block allocation, restrictions on disposal of surpluses, release of blocks with low prospects, lack of developed infrastructure, cost and unavailability of quality geological information.

Coal Vision 2025 completely silent on the issue of competition. Private participation to be equally opened up for exploration, monopoly structure of the coal industry to be restructured similar to the unbundling of SEBs and lifting of license in generation of power. The reforms in the India's Coal Sector are to be at par with the reforms in the India's Power Sector to sustain the survival, growth and development in the sector.

The main barriers to competition are availing timely clearances for pollution, forest, water, land and fuel linkages from government departments. Six states are yet to electrify more than 75 per cent of rural households Bihar, Jharkhand, Assam, Orissa, Uttar Pradesh and West Bengal. Public Private Partnership in rural electrification projects in States through government initiatives such as the Rajiv Gandhi Grameen Vidyutikaran Yojna (RGGVY).

Rural Electrification Policy notified by GOI on August 23,2006. Elimination of transmission congestion and high levels of cross subsidy surcharge to make Open Access Policy effective and boost trading volumes. Presently 3% of total power is the quantum of electricity traded. Competition in India's electricity sector is intended to bring power industry in the overall interests of consumers.

Free power to farmers for the agricultural sector is not only a financial drain on the SEBs and the government but also a national energy drain. With no cost to themselves farmer do not seem to be much concerned about energy conservation measures, they have no incentive to install energy efficient motors, or energy saving devices, do not even bother to switch of motors, wasting energy. The SEBs incurs further losses due to the low power factor of the rural grid in addition to the huge cost it has to incur on capital expenditure to lay long lines in remote areas.

The Board is bloated with huge staff and reducing of employees without union resistance and political interference is a big challenge for public enterprises management. The system of employing contract workers and a constant demand to regularize their service have added to the staff cost considerably in the past. Unions are resisting reforms and successive managements have not been able to convince them and bring about sharp reduction in employee cost.

Competition In Electricity Sector

Why is energy crisis engulfing liberalized India? Is India unable to design, implement and manage an integrated regulatory frame work to effectively mitigate the energy risk at national and global levels?

The designing, implementing and monitoring a power policy by the government of India for utilities, consumers, market, investors, power builders, regulators all the agencies operating in the power sector without partiality is always a huge task both at the centre and state within a time frame.

In democratic India every power policy will become reality cannot be assured and ensured by the government which operates under influential political conflicts ever since independence.

The dynamics of the sector over the last two decades (1991 to 2012 years) has changed so drastically that even the series of reforms and subsequent improvised policy amendments and revisions failed to control the sector from becoming sick and energy deficit.

Policy to reality has many hurdles and milestones. Welfare and business both cannot be under one umbrella of policy. Though policy has brought privatization & competition, nationalization philosophy cannot be completely comprised and sacrificed in the Indian electricity sector.

The initiation of the Liberalization, Privatization & Globalization (LPG-Policy) in 1991year was the prime attempt towards deregulating the Indian Power Sector. Deregulation never meant there would be relaxation in the performance of the Indian Electricity Utilities.

Liberalization was brought in to supplement both the State and Central sector utilities in all the three segments generation, transmission and distribution equally to transform and face the infrastructure growth at national as well as global level.

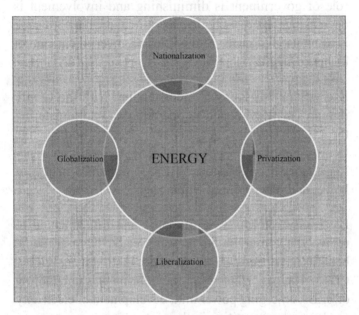

India's Energy should adopt which model? I would like my readers to perform the exercise on it. This helps us to improve our analytical wisdom on the subject of energy management and energy revolution in India.

Policy on Energy Model in India should be a subject of interest to all the stakeholders of the system.

Over the last two decades since 1991 economic reforms the electricity sector in India also experienced major reforms and its impacts are eventually being seen transforming the sector. The major concern being the role of government as an operator, policy maker, felicitator and controller fluctuating like a pendulum without equilibrium.

The misconception in India's power sector is that the role of government is diminishing and involvement is decreasing. It is difficult to ascertain and what yard stick is to be used to measure the roles of government cannot be generalized.

Every State has its own understanding with the Centre in many matters related to operating and administering the State Utilities despite the central bodies like Central Electricity Authority (CEA), Central Electricity Regulatory Commissions (CERC) under Ministry of Power and other Central Ministries.

Electricity reforms were initiated and implemented to revive the ailing Indian Power Sector. Though some benefits have been derived the sector is still facing Energy Crisis. The major impact of the reforms was unbundling of SEBs, emerging power mix, development of electricity market and competition in the sector.

In India trading of electricity will be an opportunity for business no one might have ever thought of it too early. The reforms opened avenues for many prospective power builders but they were left with promises only.

The State utilities were constituted to shoulder the responsibility of developing India through its contribution in manufacturing sector, energizing pumps for enhancing irrigation yields, improving standard of living in urban &

villages by electrifying households, infrastructure growth and finally per capita consumption of electricity.

Despite their considerable contributions for over 50 years India still is facing Energy Crisis. The State utilities have marginally benefited from reforms in autonomy of operation, return on investment, capitalization of market, funds mobilization and overall enterprise efficiency. Despite the global World & Asian bank support inefficiency continues to rot the Indian Power System.

It appears that the recent national power policies were designed to shift the risk from public enterprises to corporate without real benefits in the true sense because technical, financial, organizational, institutional and socio-political factors are still the vibrant influencing reasons for instability of the sector. It may be too early to conclude the success of power sector reforms; however it has brought in competition in the sector.

The cumulative apparent unproductive efforts with incompetency in transformation of energy, undefined basics of traded markets, irrationalized price formation in energy, difficulty in developing energy chains and derivatives, market illiquidity and mastering energy risk management is impeding the country's potential to capitalize the present abundant reserves to alleviate energy crisis.

Are India's energy policy makers short of techniques to meet energy risks in the complex markets of oil, coal, gas and electricity? Despite awareness that levels of volatility are very high due to the extreme market conditions and additional risks that are unique to energy the Indian Electricity Sector is paralyzed.

The global perspective that energy markets differ significantly from other traded commodities is equally true in India. Why and how risks in energy sector, particularly gas and electricity are more acute has been an ongoing issue without resolution despite demanding reforms of the Indian Power Sector.

Modern infrastructure, particularly electricity, is critical to economic development. Deficits cause shortages that constrain total output, magnifying the return to their elimination. India, faced with inefficient and bankrupt state-owned vertically integrated electricity supply industries, was under strong pressure to reform.

An imperfect diagnosis encouraged private investment in generation to address shortages, with IPPs selling power under long-term contracts to the largely unreformed state electricity boards (SEBs). Buying IPP Power at prices above retail tariffs when the SEBs could not even cover the cost of under-priced electricity from state-owned generators exacerbated financial distress and was a recipe for conflict.

Reforming the SEBs, though unbundling, full metering, effective accounting and management structures creating commercial discipline, under multi-annual regulation insulated from client list political pressures, is an essential first step.

Privatization of the distribution companies once they are properly enterprised should then follow to sustain reform. Liberalization has brought out competitiveness and effectiveness through various reforms and strategic thinking in government enterprises.

This recognized emergence paved way to disinvestment, expected to enhance the financial performance and profitability of public sector enterprises. Profit test is a conventional test to access the economic efficiency and rate of return (ROR), which is widely accepted measure to determine profitability.

Electricity generation in India is over a century old developed broadly under the three indelible regimes beginning with generation by private companies prior to independence, followed by concept of nationalization leading to monopoly of SEBs during the period 1950 to 1975, then supplemented by central utilities till 1991 and again liberalizing by opening the doors to private participation after enactment of the Electricity Act-2003.

The addition of 100,000 MW in power generation by 2012 is envisaged by the government of India through its successive IXth, Xth and XIth five year plans.

The funding of ultra mega and mega power generating projects both at centre and state levels is a great challenge in the emerging power sector. Nearly seventy per cent of the power generated is based on primary fuel coal. Many power generating projects could not be commissioned in schedule losing deemed generation because of poor FSAs and PPAs.

Moreover the poor quality of coal, underrated performance, lower efficiency and ash disposal to avoid environmental pollution are the perennial problems of thermal power generating stations. The percentage share of potential hydro and nuclear power is not rising in generation.

Power is being generated from small capacity solar, wind and bio-gas units contributing very marginally at national level. APGENCO the state sector utility continues to dominate the generating capacity in Andhra Pradesh.

T&D system plays a vital role in exporting electricity from power generating stations to the various categories of consumers living in plain lands, on mountain terrains, at bank of rivers, desserts and forests covering all spread across the width and breadth of the country.

The overall performance of the Indian Power System is based on consistent stability of the power grid operated by the state and central utilities. Load dispatch centers at the national, regional and state level need to improve their coordination to control mismatch, overdraw, grid discipline and peak demand being the essential factors causing grid instability.

Distribution of electricity to consumers was a service provided by the state utilities without the prime motive of profit till the SEBs went bankrupt leading to its unbundling for survival.

Even after the progressive reforms metering, electricity pricing, billing, rate of return and risk in distribution business are the issues completely unresolved. Government initiatives to electrify all households and villages have not achieved the desired results.

Private participation model in this segment has paid no appreciable dividends in transforming rural India. The central utilities are reluctant and inactive to take up the responsibility of electrifying villages. Despite criticism the state utilities are still the backbone of the distribution system.

The greatest impact of reforms and restructuring of the power sector is the evolving power mix in Indian power sector. The power utilities from the State, Central and Private sectors though operate in the same environment but are functionally and administratively being controlled at different levels by respective independent authorities.

Independent utilities from time to time came into existence to manage the generation, transmission and distribution segments respectively either by the impact of reforms as seen in case of SEBs which were unbundled or public private partnership models as initial step towards privatization of the sector.

Moreover the constitution of Commissions at State and Centre to regulate tariffs and protecting it from private power suppliers to capitalize the market somewhere appears to be the loop hole in the development of the power market.

India has always been a power-deficient country. The demand for power is huge in India. The supply of power in India has not been able to meet its demand.

Under the Government's "Power for all by 2012" plan, it has targeted per capita consumption of 1000 kWh by the end of the 11th Five Year Plan (2007-2012) as compared to levels of 734 kWh in 2008-09.

In order to provide per capita availability of over 1000 kWh of electricity by year 2012, it was estimated that capacity addition of more than 100,000 MW would be required. This shows that huge capacity additions are required at good efficiency rates, indicating that the opportunities available in this sector are huge.

The role of the Government in the development of Indian power industry has been very crucial. Government's policies aim at protecting consumer interests and making the sector commercially viable. Government regulates this industry in various ways (Tariff control, Subsidies, environment norms, etc.) due to its linkages to various industries and to the growth of the economy.

As far as regulation is concerned, Electricity Act, 2003 is a very important Act as it allowed private sector participation in the generation of power, thus creating competition. It also allowed 100% FDI participation in the power generation, transmission and distribution, thus inducing investments in the power sector.

The Government was investing in this industry through various development schemes like, the Rural Electrification Program was an effort to lighten up villages which have faced acute shortage of Power over the years, 'Power for All by 2012' plan aimed at a per capita consumption of 1000kWh by the end of the 11th Five Year Plan (2007-12), the Accelerated Power Development and Reform Programme (APDRP) was being implemented so that the desired level of 15 per cent AT&C (Aggregate Technical and Commercial) loss can be achieved by the end of 11th plan. (Currently it is 30%).

The Government of India had planned nine Ultra Mega Power Projects (UMPP) of 4 GW each with an estimated individual investment of US$ 4 billion (Rs. 192 billion). Four of these projects are expected to be commissioned between 2011 and 2017. The UMPP is an initiative by the government to collaborate with power generation companies to set up 4,000 MW projects to ease the country's power deficit situation.

In India, 100% FDI is allowed in the Generation, Transmission and Distribution segments of the Power Sector. The FDI inflow in the Power Sector has been on the rise in the last 5 years. This trend is expected to continue in the coming years considering the huge opportunities available in the sector.

FDI inflow is important for the power sector because it brings in money and India's power sector is in huge need of investments. More importantly, FDI also brings in advanced technology making the sector more efficient. Hence, this proves to be a major growth driver for the power sector.

With the thermal power generation segment facing the issue of shortages of coal (major raw material), other power generation sources like nuclear, hydro and renewable energy sources will get attention in the coming years.

Nuclear power projects account for 2.75% of India's total installed capacity which is about 4.77 GW.

The Planning Commission's expert committee on an Integrated Energy Policy has suggested in its report that there is a possibility of reaching a nuclear power capacity of 21-29 GW by 2020 and 48-63 GW by 2030.

The hydro power segment offers investment opportunities as India is considered to have hydro power generation potential worth 1,50,000 MW; of which only 25% has been harnessed till date. Using renewable sources to generate electricity has several advantages like a perennial energy source, potential for lower reliance on imported fossil fuels and lower CO_2 emissions.

However, at present the major hurdle facing rapid expansion of renewable power is high initial cost as compared to the competing fuels. But taking in to consideration the environmental concerns, this segment receives encouragement from the Government.

Its share in the country's total generation capacity has increased from 1.1% in 2001-02 to 10.63% as on 31st March, 2011 and is expected to increase in the future. These three non-thermal sources of power also offer good investment opportunities. Companies are diversifying their power portfolios to take advantage of opportunities available in hydro power and renewable energy sources.

Power Sector is a highly capital-intensive industry with long gestation periods, before the commencement of revenue generation. Since most of projects have a long time frame (4-5 years of construction period and operating period of over 25 years), there are some inherent risks which this sector faces.

Coal is the mainstay of the power production in India and is expected to remain so in the future. India has limited coal reserves, plus, availability of domestic coal is a challenge on account of various bottlenecks such as capacity expansion of Coal India Limited (the largest coal producing company in the world, coal blocks allocation, tribal land acquisition, environmental and forest clearances, etc.

Transportation of coal is a big concern in itself. Within the country, coal is transported by Indian Railways and in case of imports; coal is to be unloaded at ports. In both cases, India currently faces capacity shortage. Hence, a project developer has to account for and manage its logistics chain in a manner that ensures regular fuel supply which is a big challenge.

The power sector is heavily dependent on main equipment suppliers. In fact, equipment shortages have been a significant reason for India missing its capacity addition targets for the 10th five year plan. While the shortage has been primarily in the core components of boilers, turbines and generators, there has been lack of adequate supply of Balance of Plant (BOP) equipment as well. These include coal handling, ash-handling plants, etc. Apart from these, there is shortage of construction equipment as well. Hence, inadequate supply of equipments is a cause of concern for the power companies.

The Aggregate Technical and Commercial Loss (AT&C) is defined as the power lost due to inefficient transmission and distribution infrastructure. India's AT&C losses are as high as 30% compared with 5-10% in the developed markets which means out of every 100 units produced, 30 are lost during transmission and distribution.

Technical losses are due to inadequate investments over the years for system improvement works. Commercial losses are mainly due to low metering efficiency, pilferage and theft of power. This is a huge problem for the power sector.

The power sector has other concerns like shortage of skilled manpower for construction and commissioning of projects, contractual disputes between project authorities, contractors and their sub-vendors, delay in readiness of balance of plants by the executing agencies.

Difficulties have been experienced by developers in land acquisition, rehabilitation, environmental and forest – related issues, inter-state issues, geological surprises (particularly for Hydro projects) and contractual issues. These issues continue to pose challenges to maintain the pace of development of power projects.

In India, major proportion of power is generated from thermal sources where the main raw material used is coal. Around 83% of thermal power is generated using coal as a raw material whereas 16% of thermal power is generated with the help of Gas and 1% of thermal power is generated with the help of Oil.

Hydroelectric power or hydroelectricity is electrical power which is generated through the energy of falling water. India has hydro power generation potential worth 150,000 MW, of which only 25 % has been harnessed till date.

The energy obtained from renewable sources like sun, wind, biomass can be converted into power. Renewable energy sources have great potential to contribute to improving energy security of India and reducing greenhouse gas emissions. India is among the five largest wind power generators in the world.

Energy to the People

India is starving. How to feed it with sufficient energy? What is the economics of scale? Who will address the voice of people?

Did the power utilities and electricity consumers benefit from the recent reforms in the Indian Electricity Sector.? Consumers demand and utilities supply. In other words it would be more appropriate to define utilities & consumers gap (service perception) rather than demand and supply gap (commodity concept).

Despite reforms the power utilities and electrical energy consumers gap is increasing day by day at the rate of nearly 15 per cent annually. Utilities prejudiced in meeting the demands of big consumers. Small consumers like to be preferred equally without discrimination.

Electricity pricing is not rational. Tariff determination is debatable at the State and Central level equally. Regulators are redefining concept of service as business. Thus the question is who will interface the issues between utilities and consumers in the emerging power mix.

Domestic and Commercial category is the major consumer of electricity in India. Making electricity available right from remote villages, small towns, sub-urban, urban areas to big metropolitan cities is always a great challenge to the power utilities and electricity suppliers.

Moreover when the power sector is energy deficit the fulfillment of responsibility is below expectations of the consumers. The power system faces regular power cuts due to shutdown, burnout & tripping of transformers, voltage problems and grid failure. Inefficiency of the power system is affecting the customers.

The power supply service to electricity consumers is not satisfactory. Consumers have started depending on alternate sources of power supply by DG (diesel generating) sets, invertors and home-ups. The diesel power generation in the country is growing at an alarming rate of 4 to 6 per cent.

The power supply quality & reliability is a chronic problem in the power system. The reforms could bring changes in managerial and administrative controls of the state owned organizations delivering electricity services but failed to improve the shortages in power supply, efficiency in operation, quality of power, operation & maintenance, metering and billing system.

Consumers both in the domestic as well as commercial are suffering from poor quality of power supply damaging their home appliances and electrical equipments.

Commercial consumers lose potential business hours daily due to power cuts and voltage problems. Consumer grievances related to loss of damages and electrical safety both at residential and commercial establishments needs immediate attention by the authorities.

In India every year huge business turnover is being lost due to poor quality of power supply. Moreover consumers dissatisfaction over the voltage variation and damage of electrical equipments cannot be deferred.

The policy makers are enforcing regular energy audits to improve the overall quality and reliability of the power system for industrial consumers.

Independent regulatory commissions were set up to optimize the tariff for industrial consumers but the prevailing situation is worsening. The rate of closing for small scale industries is increasing day by day as the government's actions are bearing no fruits. Sick industries are pleading for extra subsidies to sustain and survive.

The reforms initiated hundred per cent metering system to improve the billing and receivables from consumers. At national level nearly 50 per cent of the energy consumed is not billed. Power utilities need to increase the service centers and consumers have to be loyal in paying their bills. The financial health of the utilities directly depends upon rate of return.

Power Utilities are unable to recover the cost of electricity generation and in addition to it subsidies & cross-subsidies are worsening the situation of state owned service providers. Though default consumers are being penalized government should design mechanism to completely curb these practices.

Reforms were initiated to improve the power system performance in India because its impact was severely felt on the industrial and infrastructure growth over the last two decades. Many small and big industries are closing down due to poor electricity infrastructure. Industries are migrating to electrically developed regions.

Power system performance and efficiency is directly based on the power maintenance of power lines, equipments and sub-stations. Industrial output losses due to repairs, replacements, shutdowns, breakdowns and failure of power equipments are serious concerns of the industrial consumers. The reformation process is very slow making the maintenance department unhealthier day by day.

Power utilities are falling far behind the expectations in maintaining the power system. Consumers are deprived of power supply for long time due to maintenance works. The installed power equipments are not being periodically maintained and frequency of failures are very high.

One of the prime reasons is inadequate manpower and material resources with the utilities. The incoming power supply lines are loosely connected to the line poles overcrowded with many connections making it very difficult for the respective consumer to identify their own connections. There are areas the system maintenance is a big question.

The energy crisis in India has opened other avenues in diesel power generation, captive power and merchant power for industrial consumers. Unexpectedly the open access policy did not succeed to cheer the industrial consumers.

The reforms went undercapitalized bearing no considerable thrust on satisfying the needy industrial consumers. The services rendered by power utilities are not an easy task. More power markets are needed in India.

The energy flows across the country needs to be optimized if the energy starved areas are to benefit from the pooling and exporting of power from surplus areas. The global alliance model did not take off in revamping India's power sector. The only motive of business somewhere clouds the real service moral of company's operating utilities who commit promising agendas to bring satisfaction to the electricity consumers.

The IPPs experience in India since its inception till date is not a success story. Industrial consumers are hoping to benefit from the emerging power mix, developing market and new electricity infrastructure.

Moreover many of the States in India have enforced power holidays to manage the power shortage problems. Industrial consumers are burdened with unsubsidized tariffs. The performance of the industrial sector over the last six years has drastically fallen. In addition to the load shedding, power holidays and elimination of metering and billing system there is disparity of electricity services being provided to consumers from different localities in the state as well as country.

The removal of regional disparities in accessibility of electricity when the power sector is energy deficit is a major problem to be addressed on continual basis. The electricity industry and services to the consumers operate under many reformed /amended policies and Acts. The awareness level among the consumers is not appreciable.

Understanding know how and practice of conserving energy, minimizing wastage of electrical energy, ethical usage of power, sincerity in paying electricity bills, discouraging theft of power, reducing power losses at offices, residences, public places etc can help the sector to compensate the rising demands.

The State and Private sectors so far have not entered the nuclear power generation and only the Central Sector has been burdened by the policy makers. In regard to the Renewable Energy Sources (RES) the contribution of Central Sector is nil.

The Power Policy makers need to optimize the power generation allocations equally to all sectors keeping in view the type of primary energy being used. Without which the concentration in one sector will off balance the other sectors creating further gaps rather than bridging it to resolve the energy crisis the power sector is presently witnessing.

The power output from electricity industry has become a convenient form of energy for use by agriculturists, industrialists, business and domestic consumers is equally true with respect to the meeting of future electricity demand in India.

PART II

BUSINESS
VS
SERVICES

CHAPTER-IV

INDIAN POWER UTILITIES

GENERANTION, TRANSMISSION AND DISTRIBUTION

(Power Utilities- State, Central and Private Sectors)

This chapter discusses A. Generation, B. Transmission and C. Distribution of power utilities of state, central and private sectors.

A. GENERATION

Electricity generation in India is over a century old developed broadly under the three indelible regimes beginning with generation by private companies prior to independence, followed by concept of nationalization leading to monopoly of SEBs during the period 1950 to 1975, then supplemented by central utilities till 1991 and again liberalizing by opening the doors to private participation after enactment of the Electricity Act-2003.

The addition of 100,000 MW in power generation by 2012 is envisaged by the government of India through its successive IXth, Xth and XIth five year plans. The funding of ultra mega and mega power generating projects both at centre and state levels is a great challenge in the emerging power sector. Nearly seventy per cent of the power generated is based on primary fuel coal. Many power generating projects could not be commissioned in schedule losing deemed generation because of poor fuel supply agreements (FSAs) and power purchase agreements (PPAs). Moreover the poor quality of coal, underrated performance, lower efficiency and ash disposal to avoid environmental pollution are the perennial problems of thermal power generating stations. The percentage share of potential hydro and nuclear power is not rising in generation. Power is being generated from small capacity solar, wind and bio-gas units contributing very marginally at national level. APGENCO the state sector utility continues to dominate the generating capacity in Andhra Pradesh.

Thermal power segment, which has the largest capacity generation share in the Indian power industry, is dependent on inputs like coal, oil and gas for the generation of power. Coal shortages and the low thermal quality of coal supplies cause disruptions in power generation and result in lower plant load factors. When domestic supply of coal is insufficient, coal is imported. This is unfavorable for power companies as it leads to rise in costs. With these problems associated with thermal power, the Power Companies enter into Long Term Agreements (LTA) with coal suppliers or acquire coal mines to ensure regular supply of coal. Besides, currently coal players in India are adopting aggressive strategies by acquiring Coal mines outside India. Domestically, a good number of coal mines have received environmental clearances. Such actions will be beneficial for thermal power players. Gas-based power plant face problems because of shortages in gas supply. The discoveries in the Krishna-Godavari Basin are expected to improve gas availability in India which is a big positive for India's gas-based plants.

1. Sectors contribution in generating electricity.

Table no:4.1 Sectors contribution in generating electricity in India.

Sr. No	Sectors contribution in generation	Major	Moderate	Minor	No opinion
1	Central Sector	90.5	9.5		
2	State Sector	90.5	9.5		
3	Private Sector		66.7	33.3	
4	Public Private Partnership		9.5	85.7	4.8
5	Others		4.8	76.2	19

Sectors contribution in generating electricity is depicted in table no. 4.1. It is observed from the table that the major players are central and state with equal per cent of 90.5, private sector is a moderate player 66.7 per cent and public private partnership is minor player with 85.7 per cent. The above table concludes that central and state sectors are playing major role in generating electricity in India. Recently private sector is also contributing in generating electricity.

The above conclusion is very much evident from the present existence of companies like TATA Power, Reliance Power Limited, Adani Power Limited, Lanco Power, GMR Energy, GVK Power and many more in the private sector contributing in generating electricity in India.

2. Biggest power generator in the state.

Table no:4.2 The biggest power generator in the state.

		Who is the biggest power generator in the State.		Total
		APSEB/ APGENCO	NTPC	
Sector	State	7	0	7
		100.0%	.0%	100.0%
	Central Public	5	2	7
		71.4%	28.6%	100.0%
	Private	7	0	7
		100.0%	.0%	100.0%
Total		19	2	21
		90.5%	9.5%	100.0%

Table no. 4.2 reveals about the biggest power generator in the state. The question posed several power utilities like APSEB/APGENCO, NTPC, Lanco Power, GVK Power, GMR Energy, Reliance Power and others, but the respondents most of all 19 respondents central, state and private opined that APGENCO is the biggest power generator in the state, 2 respondents opined for the central power utility NTPC. The table concludes that even though they have number of power generators in the state, APGENCO which was constituted after unbundling of SEBs in Andhra Pradesh is dominating all the power generators and stood as the biggest power generator in the state.

3. Capacity addition of 100,000 MW in power generation by 2012.

Table no: 4.3 Opinion on capacity addition of 100,000 MW in power generation by 2012.

		Opinion on capacity addition of 1,00,000 MW in power generation by 2012		Total
		Not achieved	No opinion	Total
Sector	State	6	1	7
		85.7%	14.3%	100.0%
	Central Public	7	0	7
		100.0	.0%	100.0%
	Private	5	2	7
		71.4%	28.6%	100.0%
Total		18	3	21
		85.7%	14.3%	100.0%

Sr. No	Five Year Plans	Achieved	Not achieved	No opinion
1	IXth		100	
2	Xth		100	
3	XIth		85.7	14.3

Table no. 4.3 discloses the opinion of respondents on capacity addition of 1,00,000 MW in power generation by 2012. 18 respondents (85.7%) out of the total sample respondents 21 opined not achieved and only 3 respondents (14.3%) told no opinion. The category was analysis reveals that cent per cent central, 85.7 per cent state and 71.4 per cent private utilities opined not achieved the addition capacity.

It is also evident from the table that IXth & Xth five year plans 100 per cent each not achieved and XIth plan 85.7 per cent not achieved. It can be summarized that capacity addition of 1,00,000 MW in power generation by 2012 year in progressive phases through IXth, Xth and XIth five year plans has not met the national target planned. The XIIth five year plan target is 88000 MW.

4. Sources of financial investment in enhancing the generating capacity.

Table no:4.4 Various sources of financial investment in enhancing the generating capacity.

Sr. No	Financial Sources	Major	Moderate	Minor	No opinion
1	Annual Budget	57.1	9.5	33.3	
2	Financial Institutions	66.7	19	4.8	9.5
3	Company's IPO/ Public Finance	28.6	38.1	19	14.3
4	Foreign Direct Investment (FDI)	9.5	14.3	38.1	38.1
5	Private Investments	38.1	28.6	23.8	9.5

Financial Sources	N	Mean	S.D	F-value	P-value	Decision
Private	7	2.0571	.69966	1.175	0.331	N.S
State Public	7	1.6000	.50332			
Central Public	7	1.9714	.55891			

Various sources of financial investment in enhancing the generating capacity is shown in table no 4.4. Financial institutions 66.7 per cent and annual budget 57.1 per cent are the major sources of investment in generation. The other sources like private investments, company's public issue and FDIs are playing moderate and minor roles. By seeing the above analysis it can be suggested that

FDIs should be improved by deregulating the policies and procedures to attract more and more foreign investment.

The ANOVA Test F-value 1.175 and P-value 0.331 are found to be insignificant at 5 % level of significance. Hence the hypothesis is accepted and both the variables are independent to each other. There is no significant difference in the opinion of respondents of the three types of sectors in the aspect of financial sources. Further the average opinion score for the private sector is greater than the remaining two sectors followed by central public, which suggests that the financial sources in private sector is more precise then the remaining two sectors.

5. Major share of overall annual cost of electrical energy generated.

Table no:4.5 Major share of overall annual cost of electrical energy generated.

| | | Which accounts for the major share of overall annual cost of electrical energy generated | | | |
		Semi-fixed cost	Operating Cost	Semi-fixed cost & Operating Cost	Total
Sector	State	0 .0%	7 100.0%	0 .0%	7 100.0%
	Central Public	1 14.3%	6 85.7%	0 .0%	7 100.0%
	Private	0 .0%	6 85.7%	1 14.3%	7 100.0%
Total		1 4.8%	19 90.5%	1 4.8%	21 100.0%

Table no. 4.5 shows the major share of overall annual cost of electrical energy generated. Among 19 respondent's state sector respondents equaling to 100 per cent, central and private respondents about 85.7 per cent each out of the total sample 21 respondents opined operating cost to be the major share of overall annual cost of electrical energy generated. The table concludes that the overall operating cost is the major share of annual cost of electrical energy generated. A negligible per cent of 4.8 each for semi-fixed cost and semi fixed cost and operating cost opined by the total sample respondents.

6. Primary energy used for generating electricity.

Table no:4.6 Various sources of primary energy used for generating electricity by utilities in the state.

		Primary energy mostly used for generating electricity by utilities in the state.			
		Coal	Gas	Others	Total
Sector	State	2	5	0	7
		28.6%	71.4%	.0%	100.0%
	Central Public	5	1	1	7
		71.4%	14.3%	14.3%	100.0%
	Private	1	6	0	7
		14.3%	85.7%	.0%	100.0%
Total		8	12	1	21
		38.1%	57.1%	4.8%	100.0%

Primary energy sources for generating electricity are coal, hydro, nuclear, wind, gas, biogas and others, but the respondents gave response to coal, gas and others. Central sector utilities respondents 71.4 per cent revealed that coal is their major source while private 85.7 per cent and state 71.4 per cent revealed gas as their major source. The researcher observed that the majority of the state and private utilities are based in KG-Basin (Krishna-Godavari Basin) where availability of gas is more; hence the plants run on gas. Whereas NTPC, the central sector utility is based in Visakhapatnam depends on coal. It may be concluded that the usage of primary energy depends upon the locality and availability of sources of energy. (Table no 4.6)

7. Preference to import coal despite huge reserves in India.

Table no:4.7 Preference of utilities to import coal despite huge reserves in India.

Utilities Importing Coal	1	2	3	4	5	6	Weight Rank
Domestic coal quality not up to world standards	3 (6)	6 (30)	1 (12)	11 (3)	(0)	(0)	4 (51)
Delay in allocation of blocks	4 (24)	13 (65)	4 (16)				1 (105)
Delay in operation of allocated blocks	1 (6)	1 (5)	16 (64)	3 (9)			3 (84)
Shortages in Fuel Supply Agreements	12 (72)	1 (5)		5 (15)	3 (6)		2 (98)
Logistics constrains				2 (6)	17 (34)	2 (2)	5 (42)
Pricing of coal	1 (6)				1 (2)	19 (19)	6 (27)

Preference of utilities to import coal despite huge reserves in India is given in table no 4.7. Here the respondents are asked to rank the preference for import of coal. Respondents gave 1st rank to delay in allocation of blocks, 2nd rank to shortages in fuel supply agreements (FSAs), 3rd rank to delay in operation of allocated blocks, 4th rank to domestic coal quality is not up to world standards, 5th rank to logistics constraints and last rank to pricing of coal. It is concluded that the respondents are not caring for high price of coal but they need good quality and quantity of coal for generation of power.

8. Peak power demand occurred in a day.

Table no:4.8 Respondent's opinion on peak power demand occurred in a day.

		When does the requirement for maximum power demand occurs in a 24hours period.		
		6PM- 8PM	6PM- 8PM & 8PM-10PM	Total
Sector	State	4	3	7
		57.1%	42.9%	100.0%
	Central Public	3	4	7
		42.9%	57.1%	100.0%
	Private	4	3	7
		57.1%	42.9%	100.0%
Total		11	10	21
		52.4%	47.6%	100.0%

Respondents opinion on peak power demand occurred in a day is illustrated in table no.4.8.11 respondents i.e., 4 from private, 4 from state public and 3 from central public told that during the period 6 PM-8PM they experience maximum power demand. 10 respondents out of the total sample respondents 21 revealed maximum power demand during the period 6 PM-8PM and 8PM-10PM. Thus from the table it is evident that the maximum power demand is occurring during the period 6PM-10PM in a 24 hours period. The reasons might be that peak business hours, children education, watching TV, domestic works etc.

9. Overview performance of power plants after reforms.

Table no: 4.9 Respondent's perception on the performance of power plants after reforms in the state.

Sr. No	Power Plant's Performance	Very satisfied	Satisfied	Marginal	Unsatisfied	No opinion
1	Thermal efficiency	61.9	33.3	4.8		
2	Plant Load Factor (PLF)	61.9	38.1			
3	Plant Availability Factor(PAF)	57.1	38.1	4.8		
4	Plant Use Factor	57.1	33.3	9.5		
	Average Percentage	58.7	36.5	4.766667		

Power Plant's Performance	N	Mean	S.D	F-value	P-value	Decision
Private	7	2.4286	.53452	0.354	0.707	N.S
State Public	7	2.5357	.58503			
Central Public	7	2.6786	.55367			

Table no 4.9 present's respondent's perception on the performance of power plants after reforms in the state. It is very interesting to note that respondents are very satisfied with power plant performance indicators like thermal efficiency and plant load factor 61.9 per cent each and equal per cent of 57.1 each to plant availability factor and plant use factor. It may be concluded that operational efficiency of the power plants has marginally improved after reforms.

The above ANOVA table depicts that there is no significant difference in opinion of the respondents of the three types of sectors on the aspect of power plant's performance after the reforms. Hence the hypothesis is accepted. Further the average opinion score for the central public 2.6786 is greater than the remaining two sectors followed by state public 2.5357, which suggests that the Power Plant's Performance in central public is more accurate than the remaining two sectors. The present performance of the central utilities is matching with the table's conclusion.

10. Nuclear Power is not an area of interest for private generation.

Table no: 4.10 Nuclear Power is not an area of interest for private generation.

Private Nuclear Power Generation	1	2	3	4	5	6	Weight Rank
Area not opened for private	3 (18)	2 (10)	16 (64)				3 (92)
Is under control of centre	3 (18)	17 (85)	1 (4)				2 (107)
Policy to undergo change	14 (84)	2 (10)	2 (8)	3 (9)			1 (111)
Safety, security and environmental issues				17 (51)	4 (8)		4 (59)
Construction period is more for nuclear power plants			2 (8)		17 (34)	2 (2)	5 (44)
Limited radioactive sources	1 (6)			1 (3)		19 (19)	6 (28)

Respondents gave 1st rank to policy to undergo change, 2nd to nuclear power under control of centre, 3rd rank to area not opened for private, 4th rank to safety, security and environmental issues, 5th rank to construction period is more for nuclear power plants and last rank to limited radioactive resources. These are the factors which are contributing for nuclear power not being the area interested for private generation. The table concludes that the central government should immediately frame and enact policies to promote nuclear power generation at par by lifting of license which is already instrumental in thermal power generation initiated through Electricity Act-2003. (Table no 4.10)

B. TRANSMISSION

Transmission & Distribution system plays a vital role in exporting electricity from power generating stations to the various categories of consumers living in plain lands, on mountain terrains, at bank of rivers, desserts and forests covering all spread across the width and breadth of the country. The overall performance of the Indian Power System is based on consistent stability of the power grid operated by the state and central utilities. Load dispatch centers at the national, regional and state level need to improve their coordination to control mismatch, overdraw, grid discipline and peak demand being the essential factors causing grid instability.

During 12th Plan period, a total of about 109,000 circuit kilometers (ckm) of transmission lines, 270,000 MVA of AC transformation capacity and 13,000 MW of HVDC systems are estimated to be added. Highlights of this transmission expansion are addition of three new HVDC bipole systems of 13,000 MW capacity and quantum jump in 765 kV transmission systems. During 12th Plan about 27,000 ckm of 765kV lines and 149,000 MVA transformation capacity addition is expected. This huge increase in the 765kV system is due to a number of pooling and de-pooling 765/400kV stations that have been planned to evacuate power from cluster of generation projects mainly in pit-head and coastal areas and transfer their power through long distance transmission lines up to load centers in the country. In addition to above, 400kV lines of 38,000 ckm, 220kV lines of 35,000 ckm and transformation capacity of 45,000 MVA and 76,000 MVA, respectively is estimated to be added during 12th Plan period.

Considering 76 GW generation capacity addition for 12th Plan over and about 63 GW target (the Mid –term assessment for 11th Plan by Planning Commission) for 11th Plan, total fund requirement for development of transmission system is estimated to be of the order of Rs 180,000 crore (Rs 100,000 Cr in Central Sector, Rs 55,000 Cr in State Sector and Rs 25,000 Cr in Private Sector). The renewable generation capacity addition in the country, up to the end of 9th Plan i.e. 2001-02 was just 3,475 MW which, owing to conducive policies and programmes of central and state governments, has reached nearly 20,000 MW in just 9-10 years. Most of this renewable capacity is in the renewable potential rich states of Tamil Nadu, Maharashtra, Karnataka, Gujarat and Rajasthan. These five states contribute more than 80 per cent of total renewable capacity installation in the country. During the 12th Plan a tentative target for grid interactive renewable power addition of 18,500 MW (wind-11,000 MW, solar-3800 MW, small hydro-1600 MW and biomass/baggasse etc-2100 MW) has been estimated. In this estimated capacity addition the wind power concentration is more in Tamil Nadu, Gujarat and

Rajasthan. The solar power would be available mainly in the states of Rajasthan and Gujarat. Similarly small hydro would be available in Himachal Pradesh, Uttrakhand, Sikkim and Arunachal Pradesh. State wise estimate of above capacity addition is yet to be assessed.

T&D System is backbone of any integrated power system; hence the importance of National Grid cannot be foregone as this is the bridge to alleviate Energy Crisis in India matching and unifying the surplus and deficit power regions of the country to cater to all the citizens across the width and breadth of India.

11. T & D system equally not developed as power generation.

Table no:4.11 Transmission and Distribution (T&D) system equally did not develop as power generation in state.

		Why the transmission and distribution (T&D) system equally did not develop as power generation in state.		
		No clear cut policy between centre and state	All	Total
Sector	State	0	7	7
		.0%	100.0%	100.0%
	Central Public	2	5	7
		28.6%	71.4%	100.0%
	Private	0	7	7
		.0%	100.0%	100.0%
Total		2	19	21
		9.5%	90.5%	100.0%

Only two sample respondents 28.6 per cent central utilities opined that there is no clear cut policy between the centre and state, where as all the rest respondents equaling to 90.5 per cent distributed as seven samples each of private and state utilities, five from central utilities opined for all factors like T&D was restricted to state, opening to central sector very late, and no clear cut policy between centre and state regarding T&D system equally did not develop as power generation in the state. It is suggested to the government to open the transmission segment just like generation in order to equally develop the transmission and distribution system in India. (Table 4.11)

12. Percentage development in the Inter-State transmission system.

Table no:4.12 Percentage development in the Inter-State transmission system.

		The percentage development in the Inter-State transmission system.			
		26%-50%	51%-75%	Above 75%	Total
Sector	State	1	4	2	7
		14.3%	57.1%	28.6%	100.0%
	Central Public	1	3	3	7
		14.3%	42.9%	42.9%	100.0%
	Private	0	3	4	7
		.0%	42.9%	57.1%	100.0%
Total		2	10	9	21
		9.5%	47.6%	42.9%	100.0%

Percentage development in the Inter-State transmission system is presented in table no: 4.12. About 10 respondents equaling to 47.6 per cent of the total sample revealed 51-75 per cent, in this regard state sector is contributing to 57.1 per cent. About 9 respondents equaling to 42.9 per cent contributing to above 75 per cent, in this regard private sector is contributing to 57.1 per cent and 2 respondents for 26-50 per cent. By seeing the above data it can be concluded that the Inter-State transmission system is performing in between 51-75 per cent as per nearly 57 per cent of the respondents from the state utility which is very well in concurrence with the improvement required in developing the Inter-State transmission system by the State Transmission Utility (STU), which has been taking broader responsibility in providing Intra-State transmission services(within the state). The government has been expecting that the STU start supplementing the efforts of the Central Transmission Utility (CTU) in Inter-State transmission system. The analysis also reflects that equal number of respondents 42.9 per cent from the central utility expressed their views for Inter-State transmission system development to be in between 51-75 per cent and above 75 per cent both, which more or less coincides with present performance of central transmission utilities in India.

13. Perception on Intra-State network.

Table no:4.13 Respondent's perception on Intra-State network.

		Opinion on Intra-State network.			
		Excellent	Very Good	Good	Total
Sector	State	1	6	0	7
		14.3%	85.7%	.0%	100.0%
	Central Public	2	4	1	7
		28.6%	57.1%	14.3%	100.0%
	Private	2	5	0	7
		28.6%	71.4%	.0%	100.0%
Total		5	15	1	21
		23.8%	71.4%	4.8%	100.0%

Respondent's perception on Intra-State network is observed in table no. 4.13. About 15 respondents (71.4%) of the total sample revealed very good. Category wise analysis shows that about 85.7 per cent state, 71.4 per cent private and 57.1 per cent central respondents opined very good. 5 respondents told excellent, in this regard 2 each from centre and private and 1 from state sector. Only 1 central sector respondent revealed good. The Intra-State transmission network is equally good as Inter-State network. The researcher identified that state transmission utility is at par with the central transmission utility, but the enormous gap exists in generation.

14. Frequency of shut down of the unit because of transmission problems.

Table no:4.14 Frequency of shut down of the unit because of transmission problems in the year 2010.

| | | Frequency of shut down of the unit because of transmission problems in 2010. | | | |
		Not even once	1-2 times	Above 5 times	Total
Sector	State	2	4	1	7
		28.6%	57.1%	14.3	100.0%
	Central Public	4	3	0	7
		57.1%	42.9%	.0%	100.0%
	Private	4	2	1	7
		57.1%	28.6%	14.3	100.0%
Total		10	9	2	21
		47.6%	42.9%	9.5%	100.0%

Table no.4.14 brings out the frequency of shut downing of the unit because of transmission problem in year 2010. It is healthy sign to observe that a total sample of 10 respondents 4 each from private and centre, and 2 from state revealed that their unit is not shut down even once on account of transmission problems. About 9 respondents, 4 from state, 3 from central and 2 from private told that their units are shut downed for one to two times. And it is very interesting to note that only 2 respondents that is one each from private and state revealed that their unit was shut downed for above five times.

It can be concluded from the above analysis that the frequency of shutdown of units annually is very less due to transmission network problems, however the transmission system should consistently perform well.

15. Severity causes for unstable operation of the Power Grid.

Table no:4.15 Severity causes for unstable operation of the Power Grid.

Sr. No	Operation of Power Grid	Major	Moderate	Minor	No opinion
1	Mismatch in generation and demand	23.8	61.9	14.3	
2	Overdraw due to power shortages	42.9	52.4	4.8	
3	Lack of GRID discipline			95.2	4.8
4	Predominance of thermal/base load stations		42.9	52.4	4.8
5	Inadequate peaking capacity	23.8	47.6	28.6	
	Average Percentage	**18.09**	**40.94**	**39.04**	**1.92**

Operation of Power Grid	N	Mean	S.D	F-value	P-value	Decision
Private	7	1.8000	.36515	0.229	0.797	N.S
State Public	7	1.8000	.40000			
Central Public	7	1.6571	.57404			

Severity causes for unstable operation of the Power Grid are stated in table no.4.15. Mismatch in generation and demand 61.9 per cent and over draw due to power shortages 52.4 per cent are the moderate causes and lack of grid discipline 95.2 per cent is the minor cause for the instability of the power grid.

The ANOVA Test F-value 0.229 and P-value 0.797 signifies that there is no statistically significant difference in the opinion of the respondents on the causes for unstable operation of the Power Grid of the three types of sectors. Further the average opinion score for the private sector and state public sector are equal and high when compared with central public sector. But based on the low standard deviation for private sector it is evident that this sector has severity of causes for unstable operation of the Power Grid.

16. Which GRID network is performing with highest efficiency.

Table no:4.16 Performance of GRID network with highest efficiency.

		Which GRID network is performing with highest efficiency.			
		Western	Southern	No opinion	Total
Sector	State	3	4	0	7
		42.9%	57.1%	.0%	100.0%
	Central Public	2	4	1	7
		28.6%	57.1%	14.3%	100.0%
	Private	1	5	1	7
		14.3%	71.4%	14.3%	100.0%
Total		6	13	2	21
		28.6%	61.9%	9.5%	100.0%

Performance of GRID network with highest efficiency is portrayed in table no. 4.16. About 61.9 per cent of the total respondents opined that of all the GRIDs Southern GRID network is performing well. Next to it is Western GRID network with 28.6 per cent is performing with highest efficiency. It can be concluded from the above analysis that Northern, Northeastern and Eastern grids are not at par with the Western and Southern grids. The Northern, Northeastern and Eastern power transmission system needs immediate attention by the government and transmission utilities to strengthen the grid network for better efficiency and performance.

The survey data, above analysis, conclusion and recommendation during the research work subsequently matched with the very recent GRID disturbance in Northern, North-Eastern and Eastern region on 30th and 31th July 2012 bringing about complete blackout in the region, just before the final compilation of the study was being prepared by the Researcher.

An insight into the pruned down crisp summary of the subsequent events to understand the catastrophic collapsing of all the three grids due to multiple tripping attributed to the internal power swings, under frequency and over voltage at different places from the report further brings to the surface the objective with which the sample study related to energy crisis in India's Power System has been undertaken by the Researcher.

There was a major grid disturbance in Northern Region at 02.33 hrs on 30-07-2012. Northern Regional Grid load was about 36,000 MW at the time of disturbance. Subsequently, there was another grid disturbance at 13.00 hrs on 31-07-2012 resulting in collapse of Northern, Eastern and North-Eastern regional grids. The total load of about 48,000MW was affected in this black out. On both the days, few pockets survived from black out. Ministry of Power constituted an Enquiry Committee(members of Committee were CEA, POWER GRID, NTPC, NHPC, NRPC, WRPC,) to analyse the causes of these disturbances and to suggest measures to avoid recurrence of such disturbances in future.

The Committee analyzed the output of Disturbance Recorders (DR), Event Loggers (EL), PMUs, WAFMs, SCADA data and reports submitted by various SLDCs, RLDCs/NLDC, POWERGRID and generation utilities to arrive at the sequence of events leading to the blackouts on 30th July and 31st July 2012. Committee also interacted with POWERGRID and POSOCO on various aspects of these grid disturbances. Some teams also made field visits to sub-stations, generating stations, NRLDC, NLDC, UPSLDC and Haryana SLDC. The Committee has identified several factors, which led to the collapse of the power systems on both the days. Factors that led to the initiation of the grid disturbance are weak inter-regional corridors due to multiple outages, high loading on 400 kV Bina-Gwalior –Agra link due to overdrawal by some of the NR utilities, utilizing Unscheduled Interchange (UI), inadequate response by SLDCs to the instructions of RLDCs and load encroachment causing separation of the NR system from the WR system.

On 30th July,2012, after NR got separated from WR due to tripping of 400 kV Bina-Gwalior line, the NR loads were met through WR-ER-NR route, which caused power swing in the system. Since the center of swing was in the NR-ER interface, the corresponding tie lines tripped, isolating the NR system from rest of the NEW grid system. The NR grid system collapsed due to under frequency and further power swing within the region. On 31st July,2012, after NR got separated from the WR due to tripping of 400 kV Bina-Gwalior line, the NR loads were met through WR-ER-NR route, which caused power swing in the system. On this day the center of swing was in the ER, near ER-WR interface, and, hence, after tripping of lines in the ER itself, a small part of ER (Ranchi and Rourkela), along with WR, got isolated from the rest of the NEW grid. This caused power swing in the NR-ER interface and resulted in further separation of the NR from the ER+NER system. Subsequently all the three grids collapsed. The WR system, however, survived due to tripping of few generators in this region on high frequency on both the days. The Southern Region (SR), which was getting power from ER and WR, also survived on 31st July,2012 with part loads remained fed from the WR and the operation of few defense mechanism, such as AUFLS and HVDC power ramping.

The Committee was of the view that in an emergency system operating condition, such as on 30th and 31st July 2012, even some of the corrective measures like better coordinated planning of outages of state and regional networks, specifically under depleted condition of the inter-regional power transfer corridors, mandatory activation of primary frequency response of governors i.e. the generator's automatic response to adjust its output with variation in the frequency, under-frequency and df/dt based load shedding relief in the utilities' networks, dynamic security assessment and faster state estimation of the system at load dispatch centers for better visualization and planning of the corrective actions, adequate reactive power compensation, specifically Dynamic Compensation, better regulation to limit overdrawal/underdrawal under UI mechanism, specifically under insecure operation of the system, measures to avoid mal-operation of protective relays, such as the operation of distance protection under the load encroachment on both the days and deployment of adequate synchrophasor based Wide Area Monitoring System and System Protection Scheme might have saved the system from collapse.

The Committee recommended reviewing the protection system, frequency control, Total Transfer Capability (TTC) procedure, improving coordinated outage planning and ensuring special protection schemes implementation. The most important recommendation was the review of the Penal provisions of the Electricity Act 2003, to ensure better compliance of instructions of Load Dispatch Centres and direction of Central Commission.**(1)**

The Researcher also discovered the correlation of the Committee's Analysis of the GRID disturbance as discussed above with the conclusion of the table no.4.15 throwing light on severity of causes for unstable operation of the Power Grid.

{Report of the Enquiry Committee on GRID DISTURBANCE IN NORTHERN REGION ON 30th July 2012 AND IN NORTHERN, EASTERN & NORTH-EASTERN REGION ON 31st July 2012, published 16th August 2012, Ministry of Power, New Delhi}

17. When will the linkage of all power projects to the national grid be completed.

Table no: 4.17 Linkage of all power projects to the national grid will be completed.

		When will the linkage of all power projects to the national grid be completed.				Total
		By 2012	By 2020	By 2025	No opinion	
Sector	State	0	0	6	1	7
		.0%	.0%	85.7%	14.3%	100.0%
	Central Public	1	0	6	0	7
		14.3%	.0%	85.7%	.0%	100.0%
	Private	0	2	5	0	7
		.0%	28.6%	71.4%	.0%	100.0%
Total		1	2	17	1	21
		4.8%	9.5%	81.0%	4.8%	100.0%

By vision 2025 year, about 17 (81.0%) total sample respondents, 6 each from centre and state, and 5 from private sector revealed that linkage of all projects to the national grid will be completed. Because of the delay in linkage to the national grid the export and import of power from surplus and deficit states within the country will not be materialized. (Table no: 4.17)

India's Power System is divided into five regional grids namely Northern, Western, Southern, Eastern and North Eastern grids. Except for Southern grid, remaining four regional grid operate in synchronism. Southern grid is connected to Eastern and Western grids through asynchronous links. Northern grid has an installed generating capacity of about 56,058 MW as on 30.06.2012. Major generating stations are located in the eastern part of the NR grid. Due to such concentration of generation in the eastern part of the grid and major load centers in the central and western part of the grid there is bulk power transmission from eastern to western part over long distances. To handle this bulk transmission of power to other regions it has to be wheeled through the Eastern Regional grid.

The conclusion of the table is that linkage of all power projects to the national grid be completed by vision 2025 by majority of the power utility respondents is based on the above prevailing gaps due to geographical constrains, incomplete inter and intra regional power system connectivity, developing new linkages to the new and ongoing power projects in thermal, hydro and nuclear and technological standardization of the complete integrated national power network grid.

18. Exporting of power to energy deficit areas.

Table no:4.18 Exporting of power to energy deficit areas.

		Do you export power to energy deficit areas.			
		Yes	No	No opinion	Total
Sector	State	0	5	2	7
		.0%	71.4%	28.6%	100.0%
	Central Public	1	6	0	7
		14.3%	85.7%	.0%	100.0%
	Private	1	5	1	7
		14.3%	71.4%	14.3%	100.0%
Total		2	16	3	21
		9.5%	76.2%	14.3%	100.0%

Exporting of power to energy deficit areas is shown in the table no. 4.18. About 16 total sample respondents equaling to 76.2 per cent, in this regard 6 respondents (85.7%) from central and 5 each (71.4%) from private and state revealed that, they are not exporting power to energy deficit areas. As concluded in the table no: 4.17, due to delay in linkages to the national grid the export and import of power from surplus and deficit states within the country will not materialize which is also coinciding with the conclusion of table no: 4.18, as there were no export of power to energy deficit areas.

19. Power sector again become unviable because of transmission bottlenecks.

Table no:4.19 Whether power sector will again become unviable because of transmission bottlenecks.

		Will the power sector again become unviable because of transmission bottlenecks.			
		Yes	No	No opinion	Total
Sector	State	5	0	2	7
		71.4%	.0%	28.6%	100.0%
	Central Public	4	2	1	7
		57.1%	28.6%	14.3%	100.0%
	Private	4	0	3	7
		57.1%	.0%	42.9%	100.0%
Total		13	2	6	21
		61.9%	9.5%	28.6%	100.0%

The power sector will become unviable because of transmission bottlenecks are revealed in table no.4.19.13 (61.9%) out of the total sample respondents of 21, opined yes, 2 respondents (9.5%) told no and the remaining 6 respondents (28.6%) had no opinion. Based on the evidence from the above analysis that nearly 62 per cent of the total respondents said yes that the power sector will become unviable, the same can be concluded in line with the present gap existing in transmission system of the power sector.

It is suggested that though government had the vision of constructing national grid and connecting all regions for export and import of power from states within the country and outside, the achievement has been very marginal, hence protecting this segment from private participation may be deregulated as in generation of power. The transmission sector should now be given top priority to match the generating capacity. The disparity in electrical energy flow across the country should be eliminated to remove the unappreciable classification of surplus and deficit regions.

20. Provider for better transmission network services.

Table no: 4.20 Provider for better transmission network services.

		Who do you rate the overall development of T&D system in India.		Total
		State transmission utility	Both are equally good	
Sector	State	4	3	7
		57.1%	42.9%	100.0%
	Central	2	5	7
		28.6%	71.4%	100.0%
	Private	2	5	7
		28.6%	71.4%	100.0%
Total		8	13	21
		38.1%	61.9%	100.0%

Table no.4.20 depicts who provides better transmission network services. About 13 respondents of the total sample equaling to 61.9 per cent, 5 each from centre and private, and 3 from state revealed that, both i.e., centre and state are equally good providers for better transmission network services and 8 respondents from which 2 each are from centre and private, 4 from state revealed state transmission utility is a better network service. The state utility respondents 57.1 per cent supported the state transmission utility as provider for better transmission network services because they are good at intra transmission network (evidently as per the conclusion of table no.4.13), but are falling short in inter-state transmission services thus limiting themselves in their ability to draw power as the central transmission utility.

It is suggested to the STU that they start focusing more on the inter-state transmission network. The Central as well as State government need to support the STU in improving their Inter-State transmission network. Both the CTUs and STUs (from all the different States) need to develop better understanding in operating the power transmission system network across the country.

21. Rating the overall development of T&D system.

Table no:4.21 Respondent's opinion on rating the overall development of T&D system in India.

		Rating the overall development of T&D system in India.			
		Excellent	Very Good	Good	Total
Sector	State	0	7	0	7
		.0%	100.0%	.0%	100.0%
	Central Public	1	4	2	7
		14.3%	57.1%	28.6%	100.0%
	Private	0	4	3	7
		.0%	57.1%	42.9%	100.0%
Total		1	15	5	21
		4.8%	71.4%	23.8%	100.0%

Respondent's opinion on rating the overall development of T&D system is described in table no: 4.21. 15 respondents (71.4%) from the total sample, i.e. 7 (100.0 %) from state and 4 each (57.1%) from private and centre opined very good rating, and 5 respondents (23.8%) i.e. 3 from private and 2 from centre revealed good rating. Only one central respondent expressed excellent opinion. Overall the table concludes that the rating for development of T&D system in India is adequate.

However the present average rising demand in between 9-10 per cent of power at national level is to be matched by further enhancing the transmitting capacity of T&D system in India. Moreover various load dispatch centres, sub-stations and generating stations, which are to implement the restoration operations in the real time, upon receiving instructions from the apex load dispatch centres (LDC) are not adequately managed in terms of experienced manpower and also particularly during odd hours. Utilities therefore expressed that the qualified operating personnel having undergone orientation courses under certification programme should be posted there.

It is suggested to the government both at the Central as well as State level that the Power Utilities of all the central, state and private sectors in generation, CTUs and STUs start focusing on developing effective Human Resource Management (HRM) to train, groom and develop sound power professionals technologically, functionally, administratively and managerially with a proper blend at all levels to man the modern emerging India's Power System professionally.

22. Government emphasize on privatization of transmission to achieve backlog targets in XIIth five year plan (2012-2017).

Table no:4.22 Government emphasize on privatization of transmission to achieve backlog targets in XIIth five year plan (2012-2017).

		Will the Government emphasize on private participation in transmission segment to avhive its back-log targets in (2012-2017) five year plan			Total
		Yes	No	No opinion	
Sector	State	6	0	1	7
		85.7%	.0%	14.3%	100.0%
	Central Public	5	1	1	7
		71.4%	14.3%	14.3%	100.0%
	Private	6	0	1	7
		85.7%	.0%	14.3%	100.0%
Total		17	1	3	21
		81.0%	4.8%	14.3%	100.0%

Government emphasis on privatization of transmission to achieve backlog targets in 2012-2017 years XIIth (Five Year Plan) is depicted in table no .4.22. About seventeen respondents, six each from private and state, and five from centre are in favor of privatization. The table concludes that central, state and private sectors all are in favor of privatizing the transmission system. The enactment of Electricity Act-2003 brought in delicensing in generation of power to enhance generating capacity thus promoting competition in generation segment but whereas the transmission was protected and not opened to private sector. The capacity of the transmitting system also needs to be equally at par with the generation segment, hence the government should immediately take measures to open the transmission system to bridge the gap in supply chain of electricity services.

C. DISTRIBUTION

Distribution of electricity to consumers was a service provided by the state utilities without the prime motive of profit till the SEBs went bankrupt leading to its unbundling for survival. Even after the progressive reforms metering, electricity pricing, billing, rate of return and risk in distribution business are the issues completely unresolved. Government initiatives to electrify all households and villages have not achieved the desired results. Private participation model in this segment has paid no appreciable dividends in transforming rural India. The central utilities are reluctant and inactive to take up the responsibility of electrifying villages. Despite criticism the state utilities are still the backbone of the distribution system.

The recent growth of the country has led to rapid urbanization and the trend is likely to continue in the future. This has impacted the energy requirement of the country due to changes in lifestyle, consumption pattern and consumer base, resulting in requirement of additional capacity in the distribution network. To aggravate the situation, the cumulative book losses (accrual basis) of the state utilities are estimated as Rs 1, 06,247 Cr at the end of the year 2009-10. Therefore, the poor financial health of utilities has resulted in under –investment in the distribution network leading to poor upkeep and maintenance. Consequently, the quality of supply gets hampered leading to customer dissatisfaction and poor recovery. This in turn leads to further deterioration of financial health. This is a vicious cycle and needs to be arrested as per the recent report of The Working Group on Power for Twelfth Plan (2012-17).

Providing access to electricity and actual flow of electricity are both important. Although, access to electricity has been provided to 96 per cent of the villages, many villages are unable to get daily 6-8 hours of power supply. Therefore, it is important that steps may be taken towards providing improved power supply in such areas. Going forward, the 12th Plan should address the issues of both electrification and energization. Apart from continuation of the current scheme and extending its scope, it is also necessary to take initiatives such as inclusion of productive load, feeder separation and central subsidy for consumption of power by BPL consumers.

According to the Report under the 12th Plan about 75,000 MW capacity is proposed to be added which needs an investment of Rs 450,000 Cr (@Rs 6 Cr/MW). As a rule of thumb the proportion of fund requirement for Generation, Transmission and Distribution is in the ratio of 2:1:1. Therefore, the fund requirement for distribution may be about Rs 225,000 Cr to evacuate and distribute power to be generated from the added capacity. Out of this 225,000 Cr around 75,000 Cr is proposed to be funded through R-APDRP (Rs 40,000 Cr) and RGGVY (Rs 35,000 Cr).

Transmission of electricity is defined as the bulk transfer of power over a long distance at a high voltage. Transmission and Distribution is as important as generation. The capacity additions to meet India's growing power demand should be supplemented by adequate transmission infrastructure. Globally, every dollar invested in generation has an equal amount invested in transmission and distribution.

However, in India traditionally every dollar invested in generation has a corresponding half a dollar invested in transmission and distribution. Due to this, transmission capacity in India lags behind the generation capacity. Huge investments are required in Transmission and Distribution if India's power sector is to meet the rising power demand.

23. Distribution segment should be opened to the central transmission utilities.

Table no:4.23 Respondent's opinion on the distribution segment being opened to the central transmission utilities.

		Distribution segment should be opened to the central transmission utilities.		
		Strongly agree	Disagree	Total
Sector	State	7	0	7
		100.0%	.0%	100.0%
	Central Public	6	1	7
		85.7%	14.3%	100.0%
	Private	7	0	7
		100.0%	.0%	100.0%
Total		20	1	21
		95.2%	4.8%	100.0%

In table no .4.23 respondent's opinion on the distribution segment should be opened to central transmission utilities is presented. It is very interesting to note that a whopping majority of 20 respondents (95.2%) out of 21 sample respondents strongly agree for central participation in transmission. The table concludes that a vast majority of 95.2 per cent of the respondents from all sector i.e., central, state and private are in favor of novelty in changing the distribution from state to central utilities because to overcome the present drawbacks.

24. Percentage of electricity generated is actually metered at the consumers end.

Table no:4.24 Respondent's opinion on the percentage of electricity generated is actually metered at the consumers end.

		What % of electricity generated is actually metered at the consumer's end.				
		40-45%	46-50%	51-55%	56-60%	Total
Sector	State	0	2	5	0	7
		.0%	28.6%	71.4%	.0%	100.0%
	Central Public	1	0	5	1	7
		14.3%	.0%	71.4%	14.3%	100.0%
	Private	0	2	5	0	7
		.0%	28.6%	71.4%	.0%	100.0%
Total		1	4	15	1	21
		4.8%	19.0%	71.4%	4.8%	100.0%

Respondent's opinion on the percentage of electricity generated is actually metered at the consumers end is furnished in table no.4.24. About 15 respondents (71.4%) of the total sample i.e., 5 from each central, state and private sector respondents revealed the loss of metering is in between 51-55 per cent. On an average it can be concluded that only 50 per cent of the electricity generated is metered which coinciding with the marginal average is revealed by All India energy statistics. This might be the basic reason for the power sector to fall into losses. It is suggested that government should take appropriate steps to cover more percentage of consumers under metering to earn revenue and reduce losses.

25. Customers loyalty towards utilities in paying their electricity bills.

Table no: 4.25 Respondent's opinion on customers loyalty towards utilities in paying their electricity bills.

Sr. No	Locality	Major	Moderate	Minor	No opinion
1	Urban	33.3	66.7		
2	Sub-urban	4.8	66.7	28.6	
3	Village	4.8		90.5	4.8
4	Remote Village		4.8	66.7	28.6
5	Others				

Respondent's opinion on customers loyalty towards utilities in paying their electricity bills is illustrated in the table no.4.25. It is observed that urban and suburban 66.7 per cent each revealed moderate opinion on customer's loyalty. Village 90.5 per cent and remote village 66.7 per cent with minor opinion on customer's loyalty towards utilities in paying electricity bills. The analysis gave a true picture that the revenue collection from villages in India is very poor and it is proved in the present study.

The conclusion arrived and suggestion recommended by the Researcher on the consumer views related to reasons for not paying electricity bills within due dates as discussed in Chapter-VIII (Domestic & Commercial Electricity Consumers), Table no.8.18 is equally important while analyzing the consumers loyalty towards power utilities in paying their electricity bills because both utilities and consumers mutual loyalty in terms of service and revenue collection irrespective of localities can revamp the ailing power sector. Thus the Power Utilities and Consumers are synonymous to service and revenue being the inseparable faces of the power sector tossed again and again falling in no man's land despite all the exercise of reforms and restructuring.

26. Factors governing electricity distribution pricing.

Table no: 4.26 Factors governing electricity distribution pricing.

Sr. No	Electricity Pricing	Major	Moderate	Minor	No opinion
1	Operating Cost	14.3	71.4	14.3	
2	Maintenance Cost	4.8	85.7	9.5	
3	Administrative Cost	14.3	76.2	9.5	
4	Borrowings/Interest	85.7	14.3		
5	Taxes & Duties	66.7	19	14.3	
6	Provision for depreciation		66.7	33.3	
7	Reasonable rate of return	81	9.5	9.5	
	Average Percentage	**38.11**	**48.97**	**12.91**	

Electricity Pricing	N	Mean	S.D	F-value	P-value	Decision
Private	7	2.1837	.22908	0.488	0.622	N.S
State Public	7	2.3061	.20912			
Central Public	7	2.2653	.26635			

Table no.4.26 furnishes about factors governing electricity distribution pricing. Factors like borrowings/interest (85.7%), reasonable rate of return (81%) and taxes & duties (67.7%) are the major factors that govern electricity pricing. Though the operating cost (71.4%), maintenance cost (85.7%) and administrative cost (76.2%) are moderate but borrowings /interest and high taxes & duties made the utilities financially unhealthy. In order to sustain in the business they are forced to increase the price of electricity.

For the dimension factors governing electricity pricing it may be evident statistically that there is no significant difference in the opinion of the respondents belonging to the three types of sectors. F-value 0.488 and p-value 0.622 denotes insignificant association between the variables at 5% level of significance. Hence the hypothesis is accepted and both the variables are independent to each other. Further it clearly shows that the average score of the state public sector is greater than the private and central public sectors which suggest that state public sector has highest pricing than the remaining sectors.

27. Expected rate of return from the distribution business.

Table no:4.27 Respondent's opinion on rate of return from the distribution business.

		Rate of return do you expect from distribution business.					Total
		6-10%	11-15%	16-20%	21-25%	Others	
Sector	State	2	0	2	3	0	7
		28.6%	.0%	28.6%	42.9%	.0%	100.0%
	Central Public	0	0	1	5	1	7
		.0%	.0%	14.3%	71.4%	14.3%	100.0%
	Private	1	3	2	1	0	7
		14.3%	42.9%	28.6%	14.3%	.0%	100.0%
Total		3	3	5	9	1	21
		14.3%	14.3%	23.8%	42.9%	4.8%	100.0%

Respondent's opinion on rate of return on the distribution business is illustrated in table no: 4.27. It is to be noted that about 9 respondents (42.9 %) of the total sample, i.e., 5 from centre, 3 from state and 1 from private opined that their expectation rate of return is in between 21- 25 per cent. Next to this 5 respondents (23.8%) i.e.2 each from private and state, and one from centre expecting 16-20% rate of return. The table concludes that if they do not get the minimum desired expected rate of return they are unwilling to take up distribution business.

Rate of Return (ROR) was the prime reason for collapse of the great empire State Electricity Boards (SEBs) despite their autocratic monopolistic rule who were once at commanding heights battling between the philosophy of service and business in developing the India's Power Sector. All the praises and applauses the SEBs were acclaiming till their fall have today become subject of criticism and symbol of failure brand in the power sector. SEBs would have never thought that their destiny would be ungraceful disintegration in providing electricity services to the citizens of India over 50 years.

In addition to the above the Researcher explored that even today in spite of all policy changes, deregulation, liberalization, open access, emerging power mix and market, unbundling of SEBs into smaller and fragmented independent entities, series of government reform initiatives, FDI and domestic funding in the sector, etc, all which is being done with the prime objective to improve the ROR, it is not taking place even minutely. There is no question of comparing the central utilities in generation or transmission as they never operated in a risk intensive distribution segment of the sector. And it is out of understanding why there cannot be a provision for mandate for central utilities to take up distribution of electricity supply directly with consumers, when the Electricity Act-2003 can mandate unbundling of SEBs consequently creating a new entity DISCOMs to take up distribution services. Again to make the matter more complex the introduction of power trading and exchanges which are presently mobilizing themselves and with all the doubts of their success in rationalizing the electricity prices and ensuring ROR in between 15-20 per cent at national level.

28. 100 per cent rural household's electrification can be completed by.

Table no:4.28 Respondent's opinion on 100 per cent rural household's electrification can be completed by.

		100 % of rural households' electrification can be completed by.			
		By 2015	By 2020	By 2025	Total
Sector	State	1 14.3%	1 14.3%	5 71.4%	7 100.0%
	Central Public	1 14.3%	0 .0%	6 85.7%	7 100.0%
	Private	1 14.3%	2 28.6%	4 57.1%	7 100.0%
Total		3 14.3%	3 14.3%	15 71.4%	21 100.0%

Respondent's opinion on 100 per cent rural electrification can be completed by the vision 2025 as per 15 respondents (71.4%) of the total sample i.e., 6 from centre, 5 from state, and 4 from private sector.3 respondents each opined by 2015 and 2020 respectively. Due to the lack of facilities and poor infrastructure in the electricity sector they are unable to electrify all rural households as soon as possible. The table concludes that 100 per cent rural household electrification needs larger time for completion because the earlier definition of rural electrification was very narrow and therefore complete benefits of electricity were not reaching to all the people. Earlier a village was classified as electrified if the electricity is being used within its revenue area for any purpose whatsoever. As per the new definition which was introduced in the year 2004 it requires setting up of basic infrastructure such as distribution transformers and distribution lines in inhabited locality as well as Dalit Basti/Hamlets, electrification of at least 10 per cent rural households and access of electricity to public buildings like Schools, Dispensaries, Panchayat Bhawans etc. Further to it Government of India, in April 2005, launched Rajiv Gandhi Grameen Vidyutikaran Yojana (RGGVY) for providing access of electricity to all rural households. Rural Electrification Corporation Limited (REC) is the nodal agency for implementation of the scheme in the entire country. Free electricity connection to un-electrified Below Poverty Line (BPL) households as per norms of Kutir Jyoti Programe in all rural habitations is being implemented under the scheme Electrification of Below Poverty Line Households. (Table no.4.28)

29. Whether reforms minimized the risk in the distribution segment.

Table no:4.29 Respondent's opinion on whether reforms minimized the risk in the distribution segment.

		Have the reforms minimized the risk in distribution segment.				
		Yes	No	Risk is yet high	No opinion	Total
Sector	State	2	3	2	0	7
		28.6	42.9%	28.6%	.0%	100.0%
	Central Public	1	4	0	2	7
		14.3	57.1%	.0%	28.6	100.0%
	Private	1	3	3	0	7
		14.3	42.9%	42.9%	.0%	100.0%
Total		4	10	5	2	21
		19.0	47.6%	23.8%	9.5%	100.0%

Respondent's opinion on reforms minimizing the risk in distribution segment is portrayed in table no.4.29. About

15 respondents (47.6%) of the total sample are on negative side saying that reforms have not minimized the risk in distribution segment. It is suggested that changes in policy are necessary to minimize the risk.

The distribution system directly interacts with the small, big and bulk consumers of electricity on daily basis regarding adequate supply, quality and reliability of power. But the consumers are facing power shortages, poor quality damaging electrical equipments and power cuts due to maintenance or transmission & distribution power system failure and many more unfavorable grievances. The power distribution utilities even in the private sector are facing the risk of delivering uninterrupted services, despite the reforms and restructuring of the distribution system.

30. Recommendations to make the existing distribution system more conducive.

Table no:4.30 Recommendations to make the existing distribution system more conducive.

Conducive Distribution System	1	2	3	4	5	Weight Rank
Service providers to be consumer friendly	1 (5)	12 (48)	4 (12)	2 (4)	2 (2)	2 (71)
Consumers to be loyal in paying for the services	1 (5)	5 (20)	10 (30)	3 (8)	2 (2)	3 (65)
More autonomy to service providers	14 (70)	2 (8)	1 (3)	3 (6)	1 (1)	1 (88)
Less interference of regulators	2 (10)	2 (8)	3 (9)	13 (26)	1 (1)	4 (54)
Empowerment to resolve legal issues	3 (15)		3 (9)		15 (15)	5 (39)

Respondents gave 1st rank to more autonomy to service providers, 2nd rank to service providers to be consumer friendly, 3rd rank to consumers to be loyal in paying for the services, 4th rank to less interference of regulators and 5th rank to empowerment to resolve legal issues. These are the recommendations given by the respondents to make the existing distribution system more conducive. (Table no: 4.30)

It is suggested to the government to make the existing distribution system more conducive the distribution system should be consumer friendly and this is only possible when the distribution utilities/service providers operate under less interference by the regulators satisfying the basic needs of electricity services desired by the customers at economical prices without power interruption, better quality and reliability in power supply. Equally it is suggested to the consumers to religiously improve their loyalty by paying for the electricity services and energy consumed in time so that the financial health of the distribution utility is not paralyzed. Thus the Researcher attempted to express the importance of mutual dependency of distribution utility and consumers in making the distribution segment of the power sector healthy.

31. Opinion on implementation of Multi-Year Tariff (MYT) in the state.

Table no:4.31 Respondent's opinion on implementation of Multi-Year Tariff (MYT) in the state.

		Opinion on implementation of Multi-Year Tariff (MYT) in the state.				
		Excellent	Very Good	Good	Below average	Total
Sector	State	1	4	1	1	7
		14.3%	57.1%	14.3%	14.3%	100.0%
	Central	2	3	1	1	7
		28.6%	42.9%	14.3%	14.3%	100.0%
	Private	1	1	2	3	7
		14.3%	14.3%	28.6%	42.9%	100.0%
Total		4	8	4	5	21
		19.0%	38.1%	19.0%	23.8%	100.0%

Respondents opinion on implementation of Multi-Year-Tariff (MYT) in the state is given in table no.4.31. About16 total respondents, 4respondents opined excellent implementation of MYT, 8 respondents viewed it as very good and 4 respondents commented good on implementation of MYT in the state. 5 respondents were of the negative opinion regarding success of implementing MYT in the state.

The table concludes that a little more than three fourth of the respondents were in favor of MYT because it is very clearly seen that the present tariff is not appropriate to meet the cost of supply of electricity which invariably hinders the sustainability of distribution companies. It is suggested that adoption of MYT would reduce the effort and expenditure of distribution utility and accordingly there is need to determine rational tariff to reduce the gap between ARR & ACS immediately to improve the financial health of the power sector.

32. Performance of the state load dispatch centre (SLDC) in the state.

Table no: 4.32 Respondent's opinion on performance of the state load dispatch centre (SLDC) in the state.

Sr. No	SLDC's Performance	Very Satisfied	Satisfied	Marginal	Unsatisfied	No opinion
1	Optimum scheduling of power	95.2	4.8			
2	Dispatch of electricity	85.7	14.3			
3	Monitoring of power grid	81	19			
4	Coordination with national and regional load centre	76.2	23.8			

SLDC's Performance	N	Mean	S.D	F-value	P-value	Decision
Private	7	2.8214	.31339	0.112	0.895	N.S
State Public	7	2.8929	.28347			
Central Public	7	2.8214	.37401			

Respondents opinion on the performance of the load dispatch centre in the state is shown in table no: 4.32. It is interesting to note that the performance of SLDCs in the state is very satisfactory. SLDC's performance indicators like optimum scheduling of power (95.2%) very satisfied, dispatching of electricity (85.7%) very satisfied, monitoring of power grid (81%) very satisfied and coordination with regional load centre (76 %) very satisfied.

The Researcher identified that all utilities felt the need to strengthen and have a dedicated communication network between SLDCs and all power plants in the respective control areas, which does not adequately exist at present and the agencies depend mainly on mobile phone facility, which is not completely reliable for such purposes. Availability of reliable and efficient communication facilities at all active installations connected to the grid is essential to ensure faster restoration.

The ANOVA Test F-value 0.112 and p-value 0.895 signifies insignificant association between the variables at 5% level of significance. Hence the hypothesis is accepted and both the variables are independent to each other. The above table depicts that there is no significant average difference of opinion between the three types of sectors in the aspect of performance of the load dispatch centre (SLDC) in the state. Further the average opinion score (2.8929) for the state public sector is greater than the remaining two sectors, which shows a little over good performance than those two sectors.

CHAPTER-V

GOVERNANCE & PERFORMANCE

POLICY, REGULATIONS AND REFORMS

(Power Utilities- State, Central and Private Sectors)

An attempt has been made in this chapter to study about A. Policy, B. Regulations and C. Reforms being implemented for power utilities state, central and private sectors.

A. POLICY

The designing, implementing and monitoring a power policy by the government of India for utilities, consumers, market, investors, power builders, regulators for all the agencies operating in the power sector without partiality is always a huge task both at the centre and state within a time frame. In democratic India every power policy will become reality cannot be assured and ensured by the government which operates under influential political conflicts ever since independence. The dynamics of the sector over the last two decades (1991 to 2012 years) has changed so drastically that even the series of reforms and subsequent improvised policy amendments and revisions failed to control the sector from becoming sick and energy deficit. Policy to reality has many hurdles and milestones. Welfare and business both cannot be under one umbrella of policy.

Though policy has brought privatization and competition, nationalization philosophy cannot be completely comprised and sacrificed in the Indian electricity sector.

Policy, Regulation and Reforms are the roots of the massive trunk India's Power Sector balancing the tender branches constituting the State, Central and Private Sector to be facilitated, guided and monitored for yielding better ripen fruits to the power hungry citizens of India. These roots are to be carefully nurtured by the government to make the promising tree healthier in delivering desired electricity services at economical prices to the vast category of consumers satisfying their energy needs battling all the problems of the ailing sector. The roots are so deep that simply truncating them with the sword of deregulation may not be the right answer for the security and future of electricity services in India.

1. Prior to independence electricity supply in India was done by private companies.

Table no:5.1 Prior to independence electricity supply in India was done by private companies.

Electricity in India	1	2	3	4	Weight Rank
Need for nationalization was felt only after independence	1 (4)	17 (51)	0 (0)	3 (3)	2 (58)
As per constitution the role of state was to provide electricity	0 (0)	1 (3)	19 (38)	1 (1)	3 (42)
Formation of state electricity boards (SEBs)	1 (4)	3 (9)	2 (4)	15 (15)	4 (32)
Electricity was a luxury during British rule.	19 (76)			2 (1)	1 (77)

Table no.5.1 presents about prior to independence, electricity supply in India was done by private companies. For this the respondents gave 1st rank to electricity was a luxury during British Rule, 2nd rank to need for nationalization was felt only after independence, 3rd rank to as per constitution the role of the state was to provide electricity and the 4th rank to formation of State Electricity Boards (SEBs). The table clearly indicates that India was so poor and people could not afford to have electricity in their houses and only rich people could afford to have electricity and hence it was a luxury item prior to independence. The opinion of the respondents also coincided.

2. Success of joint ventures among central & state utilities and opening the doors to private power builders.

Table no:5.2 Respondent's opinion on success of joint ventures among central & state utilities and opening the doors to private power builders.

Success of Joint Ventures	1	2	3	4	5	6	Weight Rank
All state utilities are financially deficit	6 (36)	3 (15)		3 (12)	2 (4)	7 (7)	3 (74)
Operating such joint ventures is difficult		4 (20)	5 (20)	3 (9)	7 (14)	2 (2)	4 (65)
Government could not manage mega projects	11 (66)	4 (20)	4 (16)	1 (3)	1 (2)		1 (107)

Government did not have the proposal	2 (12)	10 (50)	2 (8)	4 (12)	2 (4)	1 (1)	2 (87)
Political interference		1 (5)	10 (40)	1 (3)	7 (14)	2 (2)	5 (64)
Huge project financing	1 (6)			9 (27)	2 (4)	9 (9)	6 (46)

Respondents opinions on joint ventures among centre and state utilities rather than opening the doors to private utilities by the government are provided in table no: 5.2. Here the respondents gave 1st rank to the factor government could not manage mega projects, 2nd rank to government did not had the proposal,3rd rank to all state utilities are financially deficit, 4th rank to operating such joint ventures is difficult, 5th rank to political interference and the last rank i.e., 6th is to huge project financing.

The above rank analysis reveals that primarily the government was not having capacity to manage mega projects and hence they had no concrete proposal. Further it can be concluded that the above statement was supported by the poor health of the financially deficit SEBs. The Researcher identified that there was wide gap in performance of power utilities in central sector and state sector, so synergy between central and state utilities was not seriously thought of equally by the central and state government.

It is suggested that the central and state government should look into possible joint ventures between the state and central utilities in areas where combined operations can help in revamping the sector and bringing in turnaround of the unbundled SEBs entities carrying the liabilities of the past legacy, in addition to the private power builders with huge potential of investment and political freedom being encouraged by the government in the sector.

3. Private sector entry into the electricity services.

Table no:5.3 Respondent's opinion on private sector entry into the electricity services.

Private Sector Entry	1	2	3	4	5	Weight Rank
Business opportunity		13 (52)	3 (9)	1 (2)	4 (4)	2 (67)
Service to the nation			8 (24)	11 (22)	2 (2)	4 (48)
Business & service	1 (5)		9 (27)	8 (16)	3 (3)	3 (51)
Threat to central & state utilities	1 (5)	7 (28)		1 (2)	12 (12)	5 (47)
Competition in the power sector	19 (95)	1 (4)	1 (3)			1 (102)

Table no.5.3 furnishes the details of respondent's opinion on private sector entry into the electricity services. The respondents were asked to rank their preferences. They gave 1st rank to competition in the power sector, 2nd rank to business opportunity, 3rd rank to business and service, 4th rank to service to the nation and 5th rank to threat to central and state utilities. The table concludes that government is unable to compete in the emerging power sector because of limited resources, unclear policies and lack of conducive reforms.

4. Capability of Central Utilities to build UMPP by BOOT basis.

Table no: 5.4 Respondent's opinion on capability of Central Utilities to build UMPP (Ultra Mega Power Project) on Build Own Operate Transfer (BOOT) basis.

		All the Ultra Mega Power Projects (UMPPs) have been awarded to private power builders on build own operate (BOOT) basis.			
		Yes	No	No opinion	Total
Sector	State	1	0	6	7
		14.3%	.0%	85.7%	100.0%
	Central Public	2	0	5	7
		28.6%	.0%	71.4%	100.0%
	Private	1	1	5	7
		14.3%	14.3%	71.4%	100.0%
Total		4	1	16	21
		19.0%	4.8%	76.2%	100.0%

Table no.5.4 speaks about respondent's opinion on the capability of central utilities in building the UMPPs. It is surprising to note that 16 respondents (76.2%) out of the total sample respondents 21 opined no opinion. Only 4 respondents (19 %) revealed yes and only one respondent (4.8%) told no.

Though central utilities were fairing well in enhancing capacity addition in generation through many ongoing projects and commissioned power plants during the implementation of project feasibility and bidding process of the UMPPs by government of India, all the 5 UMPPs which were finalized through competitive bidding process was awarded to private sector. It is very surprising that 3 UMPPs, each one were awarded to Reliance Power Limited in the states of Andhra Pradesh, Madhya Pradesh and Jharkhand within a span of 3 to 4 years i.e. from 2006 to 2009, despite the fact that Special Purpose Vehicle (SPV) were constituted by the government to study the feasibility of the project, land survey and acquisitions, water and fuel linkages, coal block allocations, clearances and licenses etc, all the ground work and the transfer of ownership till the project was awarded to the qualified bidder and successfully taken off. Moreover another UMPP was awarded with Merchant Power status to Reliance Power Limited during the same period.

The Researcher identified that the government's process of evaluation and awarding 3 UMPPs to a single power builder having just entered the electricity services in India is far beyond understanding as Reliance Power Limited (RPL) has presently failed to appreciably start both UMPPs at Krishnapatnam in Andhra Pradesh and Tilaiya in Jharkhand states. The present progress at SASAN UMPP in Madhya Pradesh is marginal and the company faces stiff challenges to commission the plant on schedule as per the PPA agreements. The Researcher also identifies it to be a mysterious blunder by the government of India in banking on single company for enhancing 16,000 MW (4x 4000 MW capacity of one UMPP) capacity addition in thermal generation based on coal by awarding 4 UMPPs to RPL with investments to the tune of USD 250 Billion each required during the period 2010 to 2015. Thus it is very much evident from the no opinion of the majority respondents in supporting the above facts in discussing capability of central utilities to build UMPP.

It is suggested that Government of India should devise a better mechanism for award of such huge magnitude mega projects to power builders either in the Public or Private sector with proper evaluation in ensuring technical and financial capabilities along with restrictions on awarding number of similar value projects to single company, so that the competition is fair and equal opportunities are given to all the sectors.

5. Central Utilities developing its generating capacity faster than SEBs.

Table no: 5.5 Central Utilities developing its generating capacity faster than SEBs.

		Central utilities are able to develop its generating capacity faster than the SEBs.				
		State utilities are under stat government control	SEBs are bankrupt and mismanaged	All	No opinion	Total
Sector	State	0	0	2	5	7
		.0%	.0%	28.6%	71.4%	100.0
	Central	1	1	2	3	7
		14.3%	14.3%	28.6%	42.9%	100.0
	Private	0	0	5	2	7
		.0%	.0%	71.4%	28.6%	100.0
Total		1	1	9	10	21
		4.8%	4.8%	42.9%	47.6%	100.0

It is implicit from table no: 5.5 that 47.6 per cent of the total respondents opined no opinion, however 42.9 per cent respondents revealed all supporting the statement central utilities are able to develop its generating capacity faster than the SEBs. This also coincides with the statistical figures of both central and state utilities at National level. The category wise analysis reveals that 71.4 per cent private and 28.6 per cent each state and centre respondents supporting all the statements. 71.4 per cent state, 42.9 per cent centre and 28.6 per cent of the respondents opined no opinion.

The present share of installed capacity of power available with each of the three sectors is as State sector (1950-2010, 60 years of service) 48 per cent equaling to 100,000 MW, next the Central sector (1975-2010, 35 years of service) 31 per cent nearing to 60,000 MW and the Private sector (1991-2010, 20 years of service) 21 per cent about 20,000 MW. The Researcher brought to the surface that Central and Private together 52 per cent i.e. have equaled 100,000 MW out of the total installed capacity 200,000 MW at National level. The prime reasons are not conducive to the revamping of State Electricity Boards and are unable to execute projects like the central utilities.

6. State Utility Model changed in the Energy Sector.

Table no: 5.6 State Utility Model changed in the Energy Sector.

State Utility Model	1	2	3	4	5	Weight Rank
Reduce state expenditures	2 (10)		5 (15)	1 (2)	13 (13)	5 (40)
Enormous budget deficits		4 (16)	1 (3)	16 (32)		4 (41)
Unable to deliver services	2 (10)	2 (8)	12 (36)		5 (5)	3 (59)
Politicization of the departments	1 (5)	15 (60)	2 (6)	3 (6)		2 (77)
Excess involvement of government	15 (75)	1 (4)	1 (3)	1 (2)	3 (3)	1 (87)

In table no.5.6 the respondents gave 1st rank to the factor excessive involvement of government, 2nd rank to politicization of departments, 3rd rank to unable to deliver services, 4th rank to enormous budget deficits, 5th rank to reduce state expenditures regarding state utility model change in the energy sector. It is also evident from the fact that all the above factors had the cumulative effort in unbundling the SEBs as this model was no more meeting the State objectives.

7. Shortage of main power plant equipments as targeted in the Xth & XIth Five Year Plans.

Table no:5.7 Respondents opinion on shortage of main power plant equipments as targeted in the Xth & XIth Five Year Plans.

		Shortage of main power plant equipments (boiler, turbine and generator) is delaying commissioning of power projects as targeted in the X and XI th five year plans.				
		Strongly agree	Agree	Undecided	Strongly disagree	Total
Sector	State	5	1	1	0	7
		71.4%	14.3%	14.3%	.0%	100.0%
	Central Public	5	1	0	1	7
		71.4%	14.3%	.0%	14.3%	100.0%
	Private	6	0	1	0	7
		85.7%	.0%	14.3%	.0%	100.0%
Total		16	2	2	1	21
		76.2%	9.5%	9.5%	4.8%	100.0%

According to table no. 5.7, 76.2 per cent of the total respondents strongly agree that shortage of main power plant equipments (Boiler, Turbine & Generator) is delaying commissioning of power projects as targeted in the Xth and XIth five year plans. The remaining 2 each respondents agree, undecided and 1 respondent strongly disagree with the above statement.

Bharat Heavy Electricals Limited (BHEL) is the only public sector undertaking major entrusted with the manufacturing and supply of boiler, turbine and generator (BTG) meeting the main power equipment needs of the power sector since 1959. The domestic power equipment manufacturing and supply is not at par with the existing demand raised by many power projects being constructed in India was brought to the surface by the Researcher.

The shortage of main power equipments is one of the prime impediments to completion of power projects during the last two decades despite liberalizing the power sector. The above is very much in line with the opinion of the majority of respondents strongly agreeing to the above facts. Many Indian reputed companies like L&T Power, BGR Energy have tied up with global giants Mitsubishi and Hitachi for technological collaboration to compete in the main power equipment market in India, which is now being capitalized by the China's company like Shanghai Electric Corporation, Dongfang, Harbine etc in executing higher capacity 600 MW, 660 MW and 800 MW units in thermal generation. It is also very much evident from the increasing imports of power equipments where China is the major player; this is in line with the table's conclusion.

8. Central Utilities are not participating in Rural Electrification.

Table no: 5.8 Central Utilities are not participating in Rural Electrification.

		The central utilities are not participating in rural electrification.			
		Rural electrification was entrusted to SEBs	All	No opinion	Total
Sector	State	0	5	2	7
		.0%	71.4%	28.6%	100.0%
	Central Public	1	5	1	7
		14.3%	71.4%	14.3%	100.0%
	Private	0	6	1	7
		.0%	85.7%	14.3%	100.0%
Total		1	16	4	21
		4.8%	76.2%	19.0%	100.0%

Respondent's opinion on central utilities are not participating in rural electrification is described in table no.5.8, 76.2 per cent of the total respondents opined all i.e. rural electrification was entrusted to SEBs, Central utilities were meant only for supplementing generation and lack of government policy initiatives are the reasons for central utilities not participating in rural electrification. In this regard the category wise analysis reveals 85.7 per cent private and 71.4 per cent each state and centre respondents opined all factors. Only 4 respondents that is 19 per cent told no opinion. Hence the table concludes that central utilities are inactive in rural electrification. It is suggested to the government to make those policies which encourage the active participation of central utilities in rural electrification.

9. Advantage of power plants located near to coal pits.

Table no: 5.9 Respondent's opinion on the advantage of power plants located near to coal pits.

		Opinion on the advantage of power plants located near to coal pits.				
		Substantial	Considerable	Marginal	No opinion	Total
Sector	State	5	0	0	2	7
		71.4%	.0%	.0%	28.6%	100.0%
	Central Public	5	2	0	0	7
		71.4%	28.6%	.0%	.0%	100.0%
	Private	5	0	1	1	7
		71.4%	.0%	14.3%	14.3%	100.0%
Total		15	2	1	3	21
		71.4%	9.5%	4.8%	14.3%	100.0%

Respondent's opinion on the advantage of power plants located near to coal pits is depicted in table no: 5.9. 71.4 per cent each of the state, central and private respondent's revealed substantial advantage for power plants located near to coal pits, 28.6 per cent central respondents opined considerable and 14.3 per cent of the private respondents opined marginal advantage and 28.6 per cent state and 14.3 per cent private respondents told no opinion.

The table concludes that definitely the power plants located near to coal pits are having advantage as they can save huge amount on transportation cost of coal, which enormously affects the overall cost of electricity generation. It is suggested to the government not to densely populate the coal based thermal power plants in one location because this would lead to higher cost of exporting power and increase in electricity pricing for other regions which are energy deficit, thus not overlooking the advantage because of coal pits.

10. Business opportunities in the power sector after 1991 reforms.

Table no:5.10 Respondent's opinion on business opportunities in the power sector after 1991 reforms.

		Opinion on business opportunities in the power sector after 1991 reforms.				
		0-25%	26%-50%	51%-75%	Above 75%	Total
Sector	State	0	2	2	3	7
		.0%	28.6%	28.6%	42.9%	100.0%
	Central Public	0	1	2	4	7
		.0%	14.3%	28.6%	57.1%	100.0%
	Private	3	2	1	1	7
		42.9%	28.6%	14.3%	14.3%	100.0%
Total		3	5	5	8	21
		14.3%	23.8%	23.8%	38.1%	100.0%

Table no.5.10 speaks about the respondent's opinion on business opportunities in the power sector after 1991 reforms. About 8 respondents (38.1%) of the total sample 21 respondents in which centre 57.7 per cent, state 42.9 per cent and private 4.3 per cent opined above 75% business opportunities in the power sector after 1991 reforms, 23.8 per cent each of the total respondents revealed 26-50% and 51-75% business opportunities in the power sector, only 14.3 per cent of sample respondents told 0-25% business opportunities.

Thus it can be seen from the table that on an average the business opportunities in the power sector after 1991 reforms is really good resulting in participation of so many private companies, formation of joint ventures, synergy among agencies and practice of experimenting new energy models all leading to evolving completely different emerging power mix in India. It is suggested to the government in order to make the business opportunities beneficial and successful it should improve the interfaces and inter linkages among the utilities, regulators, consumers and power markets in the power sector.

11. Contribution of Electricity Acts in revolutionizing the power sector.

Sr. No	Electricity Acts Contribution	Major	Moderate	Minor	No opinion
1	Electricity Act-1887	4.8	42.9	47.6	4.8
2	Electricity Act-1910		61.9	33.3	4.8
3	Electricity Supply Act-1948	42.9	42.9	9.5	4.8
4	Electricity Regulatory Commission Act-1998	71.4	28.6		
5	Central Electricity Act-2003	95.2	4.8		
	Average Percentage	69.81	25.42	3.17	1.60

Electricity Acts	N	Mean	S.D	F-value	P-value	Decision
Private	7	1.5714	.53452	2.192	0.141	N.S
State Public	7	1.4286	.78680			
Central Public	7	1.7143	.48795			

Table no:5.11 Respondent's opinion on the contribution of Electricity Acts in revolutionizing the power sector.

Respondents opinion on the contribution of electricity Acts in revolutionizing the power sector is furnished in table no: 5.11. The table projects that Central Electricity Act-2003 95.2 per cent and Electricity Regulatory Commission Act -1998 71.4 per cent are the major contributors for revolutionizing the power sector. The contribution of other

Acts like, Electricity Act-1910 61.9 per cent, Electricity Act -1887 and Electricity Supply Act-1948 each 42.9 per cent have moderately contributed to the power sector.

The P-value 0.141 in the above ANOVA table is greater than 0.05 level of significance, so it can be concluded that there is no significant average opinion score difference between the three sectors on Contribution of Electricity Acts in revolutionizing the power sector. Hence the hypothesis is accepted and the variables are independent to each other. In this aspect the central public sector opinion is greater than private and state public sectors, which suggests that central public sector has major contribution of Electricity Acts in revolutionizing the power sector.

B. REGULATIONS

The initiation of the Liberalization, Privatization & Globalization (LPG-Policy) in the year 1991 was the prime attempt towards deregulating the Indian Power Sector. Deregulation never meant there would be relaxation in the performance of the Indian Electricity Utilities. Liberalization was brought in to supplement both the State and Central sector utilities in all the three segments generation, transmission and distribution equally to transform and face the infrastructure growth at national as well as global level.

Over the last two decades since 1991 economic reforms the electricity sector in India also experienced major reforms and its impacts are eventually being seen transforming the sector. The major concern being the role of government as an operator, policy maker, felicitator and controller fluctuating like a pendulum without equilibrium. The misconception in India's power sector is that the role of government is diminishing and involvement is decreasing. It is difficult to ascertain and what yard stick is to be used to measure the roles of government cannot be generalized. Every State has its own understanding with the Centre in many matters related to operating and administering the State Utilities despite the central bodies like Central Electricity Authority (CEA), Central Electricity Regulatory Commissions (CERC) and other Central Ministries.

During the period 1990 to 2006, almost every year there was a new addition of a policy to promote competition. In 1950, 63 per cent of the installed capacity was in the private sector and about 37 per cent was in the public sector. The Electricity (Supply) Act 1948 and Industrial Policy Resolution of 1956 facilitated the development of electricity industry in the State sector neglecting the already performing private sector. This clearly reflects that the bent of mind of the policy makers was against corporatization of the Indian Power Sector. Moreover the role of regulation trying to uphold the nationalization spirit could not face competition and in order to escape defeat and collapsing of the Indian economy surrendered to open the falsely protected sector in gradual stages through disguised policies and plans branding them reforms and restructuring. All the above unfertile exercise was a merry go-round of the sector. Competition in the sector could have been created in 1950 itself at least saving 50 years of drained development with ultimately defeated objectives of curbing monopolies and concentration of economic power in the country, otherwise India would have beaten the nations like USA, UK, China and other European countries which boast of being the drivers of global economy today.

12. Key issues before the Regulators.

Table no:5.12 Key issues before the Regulators.

Regulators Key Issues	1	2	3	4	5	Weight Rank
Competition through Open Access	9 (45)	2 (8)	7 (21)		3 (3)	2 (77)
Performance based regulation of inefficient utilities		14 (56)	3 (9)	3 (6)	1 (1)	3 (72)
Development of a sustainable market for electricity	9 (45)	2 (8)	8 (24)	2 (4)		1 (81)
Enhancing regulatory effectiveness	3 (15)	3 (12)		15 (30)		4 (57)
Encouraging procurement from renewable sources			3 (9)	1 (2)	17 (17)	5 (28)

Key issues before the regulators are provided in table no.5.12. The respondents gave 1st rank to the development of a sustainable market for electricity, 2nd rank to competition through open access, 3rd rank to performance based regulation of inefficient utilities, 4th rank to enhancing regulation effectiveness and last rank to encouraging procurement from renewable sources. It is evident from the table that market is becoming a dominant player in the power sector.

The Researcher identified that the Regulation always plays a central role in between policy and reforms. It has a difficult task to simultaneously regulate both policy and reforms which are mutually dependent. Stringent policies are to be deregulated to facilitate the power sector's opening. Without liberalization reforms cannot be initiated. Thus to summarize all the above key issues cannot be parallely addressed by the Regulators. Fixing of one is giving way to slippage in another. However, it is suggested that Role of Regulation is the centre of the circle circumferencing the power sector with all the key indicators at various radiuses essentially needed to be maintained; otherwise the ovality and oblongity may finally lead to collapsibility of the complete circle.

13. Role of Government in the power sector.

Table no:5.13 Respondent's opinion on the Role of Government in the power sector.

Sr. No	Role of Government	Major	Moderate	Minor	No opinion
1	As an Operator	4.8	66.7	28.6	
2	Policy maker	33.3	23.8	42.9	
3	Felicitator	85.7	14.3		
4	Controller	42.9	19	38.1	
5	All the above	52.4	9.5	9.5	28.6

Role of Government	N	Mean	S.D	F-value	P-value	Decision
Private	7	2.0286	.46803	0.726	0.497	N.S
State Public	7	2.2571	.25071			
Central Public	7	1.9714	.61567			

Table no.5.13 speaks about respondent's opinion on the role of government in power sector. It is surprising to note that the central and state utilities who are government companies do not like to be under the control of government as per the factor facilitator 85.7 per cent major and 14.3 per cent moderate. It is also interesting to note that utilities want autonomy at administrative level as per the factor as an operator 4.8 per cent major, 66.7 per cent moderate and 28.6 per cent minor. For all the above factors respondents opined 52.4 per cent major, 9.5 per cent each for moderate, minor and 28 per cent no opinion.

According to the ANOVA test the average opinion score of the State public sector is greater than private and central public sector, which suggests that the state public sector respondents opined that the role of government is major. Further, the P-value 0.497 is not statistically significant concludes that there is no significant difference in the average opinion scores of the three sectors. The hypothesis is accepted and insignificant at 5% level of significance.

14. Coordination of Ministry of Power with other concerned ministries.

Table no:5.14 Respondent's opinion on coordination of Ministry of Power with other concerned ministries.

Sr. No	Coordination of Ministry	Excellent	Very Good	Good	Average	Below Average
1	Ministry of Petroleum and Natural Gas	42.9	23.8	23.8	9.5	
2	Ministry of Coal	52.4	23.8	23.8		
3	Ministry of Energy	52.4	38.1	9.5		
4	Atomic Energy Commission	38.1	28.6	33.3		
5	Ministry of Environment and Pollution		42.9	28.6	28.6	

Coordination of Ministry	N	Mean	S.D	F-value	P-value	Decision
Private	7	3.6857	.62029	1.317	0.293	N.S
State Public	7	3.9429	.82231			
Central Public	7	4.31437	.72899			

It is implicit from table no: 5.14 that coordination of Ministry of Power with Ministry of Coal, Ministry of Energy each 52.4 per cent, Ministry of Petroleum & Natural Gas 42.9 per cent was excellent in the opinion of the respondents. The other ministries like Ministry of Environment & Pollution 42.9 per cent very good and atomic energy commission 33.3 per cent good. The table concludes that coordination among Ministry of coal, energy, petroleum and natural gas is essential for the sound performance of the power sector and it is also proved in the study that respondents gave excellent opinion on the coordination between those ministries.

The Researcher identified that there are many ongoing and likely to start projects getting delayed hence it is suggested to the Ministry of Environment and Pollution to improve coordination with Ministry of Power striving hard to explore setting up power stations across the country as untimely support and delayed clearances should not be impediments to power sector development in India.

The ANOVA Test F value 1.317 and P value 0.293 for the coordination of ministries is found to be insignificant at 5% level of significance. Hence the hypothesis is accepted and variables are independent to each other. For the aspect the coordination between ministry of power and other ministries, the average opinion score of the respondents belonging to Central public is greater than the remaining two sectors which concludes that in the opinion of this sector the coordination of ministry is more precise than the remaining two sectors. But this is not statistically different based on the P-value.

15. National Power Policy by CEA bringing in promising changes.

Table no:5.15 Respondent's opinion on National Power Policy by Central Electricity Authority (CEA) bringing in promising changes.

		National power policy by Central Electricity Authority (CEA) bringing in promising changes.				
		Substantial	Considerable	Marginal	No opinion	Total
Sector	State	5	0	1	1	7
		71.4%	.0%	14.3%	14.3%	100.0%
	Central Public	5	2	0	0	7
		71.4%	28.6%	.0%	.0%	100.0%
	Private	2	3	1	1	7
		28.6%	42.9%	14.3%	14.3%	100.0%
Total		12	5	2	2	21
		57.1%	23.8%	9.5%	9.5%	100.0%

Table no.5.15 infers regarding respondent's opinion on National Power Policy(NPP) by Central Electricity Authority (CEA) bringing in promising changes. About 57.1 per cent of the total respondents opined substantial, 23.8 per cent respondents told considerable and 9.5 per cent viewed marginal for National Power Policy bringing in promising changes. Only 9.5 per cent respondents had no opinion about the promising changes being brought by NPP.

The National Power Policy (2006) came into existence subsequent to the enactment of Electricity Act-2003. Laying guidelines for accelerated development of the power sector, providing supply of electricity to all areas and protecting interests of consumers and other stake holders are the focus areas of the NPP. With the above background and recent formation of NPP and analysis of the table it can be concluded that there is lot NPP has to accomplish in order to bring in promising changes.

The greatest impact of reforms and restructuring in the power sector gave birth to the emerging power mix which gave an opportunity for state, central and private sectors to equally participate in developing the electricity in India, but the NPP was designed with more or less emphasis on favouring the state and central sectors especially in power trading with very marginal entry to private sector. Hence it is suggested to the government to give equal opportunity to the private players.

16. The Sector which has been benefited most through LPG Policy.

Table no:5.16 The Sector which has been benefited most through Liberalization, Privatization & Globalization (LPG) Policy in 1991-92.

		Which sector has benefited most through the LPG (Liberalization, Privatization and Globalization) policy in 1991-92.		
		Private	All	Total
Sector	State	1	6	7
		14.3%	85.7%	100.0%
	Central Public	2	5	7
		28.6%	71.4%	100.0%
	Private	0	7	7
		.0%	100.0%	100.0%
Total		3	18	21
		14.3%	85.7%	100.0%

A whopping majority of 85.7 per cent of the total sample respondents told all i.e., all the three Central Sector, State Sector and Private Sector have been benefited through the LPG Policy in 1991-1992 year. In this regard category wise analysis reveals that private sector cent per cent, state 85.7 per cent and central 71.4 per cent benefited through LPG.14.3 per cent of the total respondents favoured private sector which benefited most through the LPG Policy. It is very much evident from the respondent's opinion that on overall the three Central, State and Private all have more or less equally benefited from the LPG Policy in 1991-92 year.

LPG-Policy marks the revolution of economic reforms in India. Electricity Industry was not an exception to the reaping of benefits from these reforms distributed over the state, central and private sectors. Private Power Policy (1991), Cogeneration (1996), Captive power generation (1997), Mega Power Policy (1998), the amended Electricity Act (1998), enactment of Electricity Act-2003, Ultra Mega Power Policy(2005), National Power Policy(2005), National Tariff Policy (2006), Rural Electrification Policy (2006), Integrated Energy Policy (2006), Power Exchange in India (2007), Point of Connection (2010) are all reforms Act bringing in transition and transformation of the power sector only after the first initiation by the LPG-Policy, hence the table's conclusion also coincides with the benefits reaped by all the sectors after the policy was implemented. (Table no:5.16)

17. Reduction of government's involvement in the utilities making them healthy.

Table no:5.17 Respondent's opinion on the reduction of government's involvement in the utilities making them healthy.

		Will the reduction of government's involvement in the utilities make them healthy.			
		Yes	No	Risk is yet high	Total
Sector	State	6	0	1	7
		85.7%	.0%	14.3%	100.0%
	Central Public	3	1	3	7
		42.9%	14.3	42.9%	100.0%
	Private	7	0	0	7
		100.0%	.0%	.0%	100.0%
Total		16	1	4	21
		76.2%	4.8%	19.0%	100.0%

Respondent's opinion on the reduction of government's involvement in the utilities making them healthy is furnished in table no.5.17. About 76.2 per cent of the total sample respondents in which 100 per cent private, 85.7 per cent state and 42.9 per cent central favored yes i.e., supporting the reduction of government involvement in the utilities making them healthy. It is interesting to note that only one respondent4.8 per cent told no and 4 respondents 19 per cent had no opinion regarding the reduction of governments role in the utilities.

During the last two decades the Government had been continuously criticizing the public sector power boards; it went on propagating that there is lower plant load factor, huge transmission and distribution losses, meager revenue collection and irregular and interrupted supply of power in these boards. So they require reforms in all spheres of its working. They also blamed for corruptions and inefficiency in these power boards and claimed that by dismantling the boards and adopting the policy of liberalization, privatization etc, and the thing will improve. But about 15 years have elapsed after the adoption of the new power policy and 15 years have passed for the start of the dismantling of Orissa and Haryana State Electricity Boards, there is no positive indication in any sphere of its working. The power distribution work also was privatized both in Orissa and Delhi but there is no possibility of any reforms claimed earlier by the government.

There is always a fear that hundred per cent liberalization may lead to fragmentation and decentralization of the power sector as it was at the time of independence, hence it is suggested to the government to have regulatory controls in the key areas of electricity services in India being provided by private companies.

18. Awareness of staff on progressive changes in policies of the power sector.

Table no:5.18 Awareness of staff on progressive changes in policies of the power sector.

Sr. No	Power Sector Policies	Major	Moderate	Minor	No opinion
1	National Electricity Policy	76.2	19	4.8	
2	Electricity Acts	81	19		
3	Power Plant Operations	76.2	14.3	9.5	
4	Trading of Electricity	19	61.9	19	
5	Ministry of Power directives	42.9	28.6	23.8	4.8

Power Sector Policies	N	Mean	S.D	F-value	P-value	Decision
Private	7	2.3143	.32367	1.086	0.359	N.S
State Public	7	2.4286	.58228			
Central Public	7	2.6286	.21381			

Awareness of staff on progressive changes in policies of power sector is depicted in table no 5.18. It is observed from the table that changes in electricity Acts 81 per cent, national electricity policy & power plant operation 76.2 per cent each and ministry of power directives 42.9 per cent are major awareness areas of staff. Moderate awareness of the staff on trading of electricity is 61.9 per cent. The table concludes that awareness of staff on Acts, policies and operation is satisfactory but improvement is required on trading of electricity.

In view of central public sector, the awareness of staff on progressive changes in policies is more than the remaining two sectors but this difference is not statistically different based on the P-value 0.359 in the above ANOVA table. The hypothesis is accepted and these variables are independent to each other.

19. Need for periodic productivity analysis of Indian electricity utilities.

Table no:5.19 Respondent's opinion on need for periodic productivity analysis of Indian electricity utilities.

		Is there need for periodic productivity analysis of Indian Electricity Utilities.			
		Yes	No	No opinion	Total
Sector	State	5	0	2	7
		71.4%	.0%	28.6%	100.0%
	Central Public	5	1	1	7
		71.4%	14.3%	14.3%	100.0%
	Private	4	0	3	7
		57.1%	.0%	42.9%	100.0%
Total		14	1	6	21
		66.7%	4.8%	28.6%	100.0%

Table no: 5.19 illustrates about the respondent's opinion on periodic productivity analysis of Indian electricity utilities. About 66.7 per cent of the total sample in which 71.4 per cent each state & central and 57.1 per cent private respondents told yes supporting the need for periodic productivity analysis of Indian electricity utilities. 28.6 per cent of the total respondents were unable to say anything and one respondent 4.8 per cent was clear to say no need for periodic productivity analysis of the electricity utilities. The table concludes that the respondents feel that periodic productivity analysis is needed for better performance of the power utilities as this would make them more accountable and responsible to deliver better services.

20. Opinion on REC setting electricity tariffs.

Table no:5.20 Respondent's opinion on Regulatory Electricity Commissions (REC) setting electricity tariffs.

		Opinion on regulatory commissions setting electricity tariffs.			
		Annual revenue increased	Remained same	No opinion	Total
Sector	State	4	0	3	7
		57.1%	.0%	42.9%	100.0%
	Central Public	6	0	1	7
		85.7%	.0%	14.3%	100.0%
	Private	3	1	3	7
		42.9%	14.3%	42.9%	100.0%
Total		13	1	7	21
		61.9%	4.8%	33.3%	100.0%

The setting of electricity tariffs by REC led to the increase in annual revenue was opined by 61.9 per cent of the total sample respondents. In this regard sector wise analysis reveals that respondents of central 85.7 per cent, state 57.1 per cent and private 42.9 per cent opined for increase in annual revenue. It is also surprising to note that 33.3 per cent of the total respondents told no opinion and only one respondent 4.8 per cent said it remained same. (Table no:5.20)

Primary cost of generating electricity varies from plant to plant with the type of fuel being used at power station, location of power station to coal peat heads, life of the power plant, transmission power system & evacuation support, overhead expenses and others by the same utility. There is always a gap in tariff determination by the power utilities and REC. Power utilities having advantage of location, fuel, efficiency and grid connectivity could increase their annual revenue based on the tariff by REC but power utilities with disadvantages are selling at under price losing substantial revenue margin.

The Researcher identified that an all India prevailing average ratio of 60:40 for utilities with advantage is as to utilities without advantage very much coincides with the conclusion of the above table.

21. Utilities contribution in "Power to all by 2012".

Table no: 5.21 Respondent's perception on Utilities contribution in "Power to all by 2012".

		What will be your contribution in "POWER to all by 2012".				
		0-25%	26%-50%	51%-75%	Above 75%	Total
Sector	State	1	1	1	4	7
		14.3%	14.3%	14.3%	57.1%	100.0%
	Central Public	0	1	1	5	7
		.0%	14.3%	14.3%	71.4%	100.0%
	Private	5	1	0	1	7
		71.4%	14.3%	.0%	14.3%	100.0%
Total		6	3	2	10	21
		28.6%	14.3%	9.5%	47.6%	100.0%

Respondents perception on Utilities contribution in "Power to all by 2012" is given in table no: 5.21. 10 (47.6%) respondents opined contribution in "Power to all by 2012" above 75 per cent, followed by 6 (28.6%) respondents told contribution range 0-25 per cent, 3 (14.3%) respondents said in between 26-50 per cent and 2 (9.5%) respondents reported contribution in the range 51-75 per cent. Regarding category wise analysis for utilities contribution above 75 per cent respondents revealed that centre 71.4 per cent, state 57.1 per cent and private 14.3 per cent.

The vision "Power to all by 2012" was to be realized through the IXth, Xth and XIth Five Year Plan targets set in generation, transmission, distribution, rural electrification and energizing all households through all the state, central and private sectors operating in the Indian Power Sector. The results achieved in the closing year of the XIth plan speak of the unaccomplishment of set targets by all the state, central and private utilities in the power sector. Thus it is very much evident from the conclusion of the table that combined overall contribution above 75% by the three sectors is not even near to the 50% of the set targets as committed prior to beginning of all the IXth, Xth and XIth Five Year Plans by the government of India. The government not only in the state and central sector but even in the private sector despite series of reforms and restructuring of the power sector failed to ensure achievement of the planned targets leading to shortfall in alleviating energy crisis.

Energy Crisis in India was so acute that the Government thought to add nearly 100,000 MW capacity in power generation within 10 to 15 years which was previously achieved in almost 50 years. The targets so set with the existing State and Central government capacities and potential were very high to achieve despite all the reforms initiatives. Moreover due to the delay in financial closures, linkages, licenses, clearances, fuel supply agreements (FSAs), power purchase agreements (PPAs), shortage of main power equipments. etc many project in the last decade could not be completed in schedule. Hence it is advised that the government should properly plan and fulfill the requirements in order to achieve the set targets.

C. REFORMS

Electricity reforms were initiated and implemented to revive the ailing Indian Power Sector. Though some benefits have been derived the sector is still facing Energy Crisis. The major impact of the reforms was unbundling of SEBs, emerging power mix, development of electricity market and competition in the sector. In India trading of electricity will be an opportunity for business no one might have ever thought of it too early. The reforms opened avenues for many prospective power builders but they were left with promises only.

The State utilities were constituted to shoulder the responsibility of developing India through its contribution in manufacturing sector, energizing pumps for enhancing irrigation yields, improving standard of living in urban & villages by electrifying households, infrastructure growth and finally per capita consumption of electricity. Despite their considerable contributions for over 50 years India still is facing Energy Crisis.

The State utilities have marginally benefited from reforms in autonomy of operation, return on investment, capitalization of market, funds mobilization and overall enterprise efficiency. Despite the global World & Asian bank support inefficiency continues to rot the Indian Power System. It appears the recent national power policies were designed to shift the risk from public enterprises to corporate without real benefits in the true sense because technical, financial, organizational, institutional and socio-political factors are still the vibrant influencing reasons for instability of the sector. It may be too early to conclude the success of power sector reforms; however it has brought in competition in the sector.

22. India's Power Sector even after 50 years of service still energy deficit.

Table no: 5.22 India's Power Sector even after 50 years of service still energy deficit.

India's Power Sector- Energy Deficit	1	2	3	4	Weight Rank
Decision on turning around ailing SEBs was delayed by Government of India	5 (20)		6 (12)	10 (10)	4 (42)
Synergy between government and SEBs was not proper	2 (8)	8 (24)	8 (16)	3 (3)	3 (51)
Inefficient public enterprises management in power sector	3 (12)	11 (33)	7 (14)		1 (59)
Political interference	10 (40)	3 (9)		8 (8)	2 (57)

Table no.5.22 infers regarding respondent's opinion on India's Power Sector even after 50 years of service is still energy deficit. Respondents gave 1st rank to inefficient public enterprises management in power sector, 2nd rank to political interference, 3rd rank to synergy between government and SEBs was not proper and last rank to decision on turning around ailing SEBs was delayed by government of India.

As part of the nationalization policy and the Electricity Supply Act-1948, SEBs were constituted in states and subsequently supplemented by entry of central power utilities in 1975 to develop the Indian Power Sector. The economic crisis in 1991 was rescued by initiating LPG-Policy which opened the power sector dominated by state and central to private power builders. The Electricity Reform Act-2003 further brought in competition by deregulating the sector as the power shortage problem was to be resolved by liberalizing the power market. All the above policy changes were introduced by the Government of India to alleviate the energy crisis due to huge gap in supply and demand of power.

The prime reason for India's Power Sector being energy deficit is inefficient public enterprises management in power sector followed by political interference as reported by the respondents equally concludes with the present scenario related to the unbundling of SEBs and process of restructuring the state utilities are undergoing mandated by the Electricity Act-2003. It is suggested that utilities should become professional in management with business orientation to overcome energy deficit.

23. Power Utilities benefited from the enactment of Electricity Act-2003.

Table no:5.23 Utilities derived benefit from the power sector reforms, after the enactment of Electricity Act-2003.

Sr. No	Power Utilities Benefited	Major	Moderate	Minor	No opinion
1	Autonomy of Operation	95.2	4.8		
2	Return on Investment	61.9	33.3	4.8	
3	Capitalization of Market	66.7	23.8	9.5	
4	Funds Mobilization	9.5	52.4	38.1	
5	Overall efficiency of the Utility	57.1	38.1	4.8	

Power Utilities Benefited	N	Mean	S.D	F-value	P-value	Decision
Private	7	2.2571	.42762	1.592	0.231	N.S
State Public	7	2.5714	.37289			
Central Public	7	2.5714	.33523			

Power Utilities derived benefit from the power sector reforms after the enactment of the Electricity Act-2003 is furnished in table no.5.23. The major benefit that the respondents derived from the reforms is autonomy of operation 95.2 per cent. The researcher found in this study that other major benefits like capitalization of market 66.7 per cent, return on investment 61.9 per cent and overall efficiency of the utilities 57.1 per cent are the major benefits derived from reforms. On the other hand the moderate benefits the respondents derived from funds mobilization 52.4 per cent and overall efficiency of the utility 38.1 per cent.

According to the ANOVA Test the F-value 1.592 and P-value 0.231 for power utilities benefited from power reforms after the enactment of the Electricity Act-2003 is found to be insignificant at 5 % level of significance. Hence the hypothesis is accepted and the variables are independent to each other. As from the above table the mean opinion score 2.5714 of the respondents from state public and central public sector are same and greater than the private sector score 2.2571 where as the standard deviation of State public is greater than the central public so it is concluded that in the opinion of the respondents on utilities benefiting from the power sector reforms, Central public sector is major than the remaining two sectors.

24. Contribution of utilities in developing India.

Table no: 5.24 Respondent's opinion on contribution of utilities in developing India.

Sr. No	Power Utilities Developing India	Major	Moderate	Minor	No opinion
1	Manufacturing sector	95.2	4.8		
2	Standard of living	76.2	23.8		
3	Irrigation/pumps energized	61.9	28.6	9.5	
4	Villages electrified	9.5	81	9.5	
5	Growth in infrastructure sectors	38.1	57.1	4.8	
6	Per capita consumption of electricity	14.3	76.2	9.5	

Power Utilities Developing India	N	Mean	S.D	F-value	P-value	Decision
Private	7	2.3571	.17817	0.362	0.701	N.S
State Public	7	2.5000	.28868			
Central Public	7	2.4524	.43795			

Respondent's opinion on the contribution of utilities in developing India is given in table no.5.24. Respondents identified that utilities major contribution is to manufacturing sector 95.2 per cent, next in order to standard of living 76.2 per cent, irrigation /pumps 61.9 per cent, infrastructure 38.1 per cent, per capita consumption of electricity 14.3 per cent and villages electrified 9.5 per cent. On the other hand moderate opinion of the total respondents is on village electrification 81 per cent, per capita consumption of electricity 76.2 per cent and growth in infrastructure sectors 57.1 per cent.

It can be concluded from the above analysis that village electrification and per capita consumption of electricity are the areas of thrust requiring prime attention of government to immediately implement fast track projects in eliminating the existing gaps. Hence it is suggested that the government should focus on village's electrification so that the standard of living of the people might increase and in turn bring out overall development of the country.

Regarding the dimension utilities contribution in developing India, the State public sector opined more positive than the remaining two sectors, whereas there is no significant average opinion difference between the three sectors as per the P-value 0.701 in the above ANOVA table. Hence the hypothesis is accepted and the variables are independent to each other.

25. Reformation is slow despite World Bank and Asian Development Bank support to the central & state utilities.

Table no:5.25 The pace of reformation is slow despite World Bank and Asian Development Bank support to the central & state utilities.

Slow Reformation	1	2	3	4	5	Weight Rank
No proper accountability	3 (15)	4 (16)	12 (36)	1 (2)	1 (1)	2 (70)
Sluggish departments	1 (5)	3 (12)	4 (12)	1 (2)	12 (12)	5 (43)
Lacking ownership	13 (65)		1 (3)	7 (14)		1 (82)
Reluctant to change		13 (52)	1 (3)	3 (6)	4 (4)	3 (65)
Inefficient management	4 (20)	1 (4)	3 (3)	9 (18)	4 (4)	4 (49)

Respondents gave 1st rank to lack of ownership, 2nd rank to no proper accountability, 3rd rank to reluctant to change, 4th rank to inefficient management and 5th rank to sluggish departments are the reasons for slow reformation despite of World Bank and Asian Bank support to the central and state utilities. It is evident from the table that the prime reason for SEBs failure was the lack of ownership by the public enterprises management governing the state utilities. (Table no: 5.25)

Lack of ownership by the state and central utilities was concluded by the respondents as the prime reason for slow reformation of the sector despite financial support from the World Bank and Asian Development Bank. The Researcher discovered that the above conclusion is in concurrence with the present scenario where the performance of utilities is not appreciable despite all efforts to achieve speedy reformation process as set by the National Policy Makers through the recent Five Year Plans.

26. Even after initiating reforms inefficiency continues to rot the Indian Power System.

Table no:5.26 Respondent's opinion on after initiating reforms inefficiency continues to rot the Indian Power System.

Sr. No	Inefficiency in Power System	Major	Moderate	Minor	No opinion
1	Technical	9.5	57.1	33.3	
2	Financial	95.2	4.8		
3	Organizational	9.5	85.7	4.8	
4	Institutional	42.9	33.3	23.8	
5	Socio-Political	85.7	9.5	4.8	

Inefficiency in Power System	N	Mean	S.D	F-value	P-value	Decision
Private	7	2.3429	.32071	0.065	0.937	N.S
State Public	7	2.4000	.30551			
Central Public		2.3143	.38048			

Respondent's opinion on after initiating reforms inefficiency continues to rot the Indian Power System is shown in table no: 5.26. The major reason for inefficiency is finance 95.2 per cent, socio-political 85.7 per cent and institutional 42.9 per cent. And the moderate reasons are organizational 85.7 per cent and technical 57.1 per cent. It is very much evident from the table that despite the series of reforms the financial strength of the power sector is not healthy as such inefficiency still continues to rot the system. It may be suggested to encourage the domestic and foreign investors to enter into the power sector to turn the sector profitable.

The above P-value 0.937 divulges that there is no significant difference between the average opinion score of the three sectors on the dimension even after initiating reforms inefficiency continues to rot the Indian Power System. Further, the average opinion score 2.400 of the State Public sector is greater than the remaining two sectors which suggests that State public has to improve the power system due to the inefficiency in technical, financial and other aspects in power system.

27. Success of regulators in bringing about reforms in the power sector.

Table no: 5.27 Respondent's opinion on the success of regulators in bringing about reforms in the power sector.

Sr. No	Success of Power Reforms	Major	Moderate	Minor	No opinion
1	Unbundling of State Electricity Boards	95.2	4.8		
2	Power market development	42.9	28.6	28.6	
3	Benefits from competition	42.9	47.6	9.5	
4	Implementation of Electricity Acts and schemes	14.3	81	4.8	
5	Customer satisfaction	14.3	42.9	42.9	
6	Overall development	9.5	47.6	42.9	
	Average Percentage	**36.51**	**42.08**	**21.45**	

Success of Power Reforms	N	Mean	S.D	F-value	P-value	Decision
Private	7	2.2429	.25456	0.120	0.888	N.S
State Public	7	2.2833	.18684			
Central Public	7	2.2286	.20383			

Unbundling of SEBs 95.2 per cent, power market development and benefit from competition 42.9 per cent each are the major success factors as outcome of reforms. Implementation of Electricity Acts and schemes 81 per cent, overall development 47.6 per cent and customer satisfaction 42.9 per cent are the moderate success factors.

It is evident from the table that regulators are keen to improve the situation of power sector by initiating the unbundling of sick SEBs which were impediment to the growth of the sector.

The ANOVA Test F-value 0.120 and P-value 0.888 is found to be insignificant at 5% level of significance for the dimension the success of regulators in bringing about reforms in the power sector. Hence the hypothesis is accepted and the variables are independent to each other. The above table shows that there is no statistically significant difference between the three types of sectors. The average opinion score of the state public is little bit greater than the remaining two sectors. Further, the average scores are very nearer to each other which show that all the three sectors opined all most same.

It is very much imperative from the functions and duties of authority that CEA's main role is purely technical in strengthening the operational and maintenance of the electrical system. To summarize CEA oversees the technical aspects of the electrical system and Regulatory Commissions the commercial or the business aspects of the power sector. Integrated Power System required reforms mutually interdependent interfacing both the technical and commercial aspects to revamp the sector. CEA and Regulatory Commissions both at centre and state are repeatedly falling short of the objectives and targets as set by National Electricity Policy and Plans giving scope to breeding of technical and commercial inefficiency in the Indian Power Sector. Electricity Act-2003 is more or less a regulatory mechanism in issuing, guiding and controlling licenses to the utilities or agencies intending to operate in the generation, transmission, distribution & supply and trading of electricity in the sector. Moreover it through Parts XII to XVI focuses on addressing grievances, disputes, offences & penalties, investigations trying to protect the agencies. Except generation segment the License Raj continues to prevail. Opening the generation segment and at the same time restricting transmission & distribution and supply & trading speaks of marginal liberalization of the sector. To summarize its prime responsibility is issuing license and protecting the agencies with emphasis on promotion of competition in the power sector.

28. The recent reform policies have shifted the risk from Public Enterprises to Private Corporate.

Table no:5.28 The recent reform policies have shifted the risk from Public Enterprises to Private Corporate.

		The recent reform policies have shifted the risk from public enterprises to private corporate.			
		Yes	No	No opinion	Total
Sector	State	5	0	2	7
		71.4%	.0%	28.6%	100.0%
	Central	0	2	5	7
		.0%	28.6%	71.4%	100.0%
	Private	5	0	2	7
		71.4%	.0%	28.6%	100.0%
Total		10	2	9	21
		47.6%	9.5%	42.9%	100.0%

The recent reform policies have shifted the risk from Public Enterprises to Private Corporate is depicted in table no.5.28. About 47.6 per cent of the total sample respondents in which 71.4 per cent each state and private respondents revealed yes thus supporting the statement that the recent reform policies have shifted the risk from

Public Enterprises to Private Corporate. At the same time 42.9 per cent of the total respondents were not in a position to give their opinion on shifting of risk and again 9.5 per cent respondents however were clear in their opinion and told no.

The uncertainty of regulatory reforms, disparity in electricity services, gaps in power supply chain, unelectrified villages, unbundling of SEBs, liberalizing power market, competition in the sector, deregulating power sector, corporatizing electricity services are all the happenings more or less since Economic Reforms in 1991, the Electricity Reforms (2003) to the recent Point of Connection (2010) with the sole objective of promoting participation of the private sector in electricity business in India. This is very much in concurrence from the opinion posed by nearly 50 per cent respondents constituting the state, central and private sector in agreeing with the statement that the recent reform policies have shifted the risk from Public Enterprises to Private Corporate.

29. Domestic Companies investment in power sector during the period 2005-2010.

Table no: 5.29 Domestic Companies investment in power sector during the period 2005-2010.

Power Sector Investments	1	2	3	4	5	6	7	8	9	10	11	12	Weight Rank
Reliance Energy	18 (216)		2 (20)										1 (239)
Essar Power					1 (8)	1 (7)			15 (60)	2 (6)	2 (4)		10 (85)
Lanco Power			10 (100)		4 (32)	2 (14)	2 (12)		1 (4)	2 (6)			4 (168)
TATA Power	1 (12)	13 (143)	3 (30)	3 (27)		1 (7)							2 (219)
ADANI Power		4 (44)			2 (16)		4 (24)	11 (55)					6 (139)
JINDAL Power				1 (9)		2 (14)	1 (6)	2 (10)	3 (12)	10 (30)			11 (81)
GMR Energy				1 (9)	4 (32)	13 (91)		1 (5)	2 (8)				5 (145)
GVK Power				1 (9)	1 (8)	1 (7)	12 (72)	4 (20)		1 (3)	1 (2)		8 (121)

NTPC	1 (12)	2 (22)	3 (30)	12 (108)			1 (6)			2 (6)			3 (184)
APGENCO		1 (11)	1 (10)	2 (18)	8 (64)		1 (6)	3 (15)		1 (3)	4 (8)		7 (135)
PFC	1 (12)	1 (11)	2 (20)	1 (9)	1 (8)						14 (28)	1 (1)	9 (89)
Others										1 (3)		20 (20)	12 (23)

Respondents were asked to rank 12 domestic companies investment according to their order of preference, is given in table no: 5.29. The respondents gave 1st rank to Reliance Energy, 2nd rank to TATA Power, 3rd rank to NTPC, 4th rank to Lanco Power and 5th rank to GMR Energy. The lowest rank to the companies like 11th rank to Jindal Power, 10th rank to ESSAR Power and 9th rank to PFC (Power Finance Corporation). Jindal Power and ESSAR Power (started with captive power) are both new entrants to the power sector and the respondent's opinion also coincided with this.

FDI in the power sector was only 5% of the total investments during the period 2005-2010. The remaining 95% was mobilized through the domestic resources. The major domestic companies in the power sector Reliance Energy (1), Tata Power (2), NTPC(3), Lanco Power (4), GMR Energy (5) and Adani Power (6) brought in huge investments to fund the upcoming projects in the power sector. The private sector utilities were ahead of the state and central utilities in mobilizing funds for their respective projects. The weighted rank provided by the respondents more or less is in close concurrence with the actual investments brought into the sector by domestic companies.

30. Sectors present investment in renewable and alternate energy development.

Table no:5.30 Respondent's opinion on Sectors present investment in renewable and alternate energy development.

Sr. No	SECTORS	Major	Moderate	Minor	No opinion
1	Central	14.3	9.5	76.2	
2	State	14.3	9.5	76.2	
3	Private	90.5	9.5		
4	Public & Private	19	4.8	4.8	71.4

Table no: 5.30 gives a picture about respondents opinion on sectors present investment in renewable and alternate energy development. It is quite evident from the table that private sector 90.5 per cent is contributing in renewable and alternate energy development. The Centre and State sectors each 76.2 per cent are minor contributors to renewable and alternative energy. It is concluded that private sectors are exploring opportunities in renewable and alternative energy development like wind power, solar power but whereas the Central and State sectors are yet to initiate their sincere commitments towards it.

In the wake of the present coal crisis, nuclear power security and safety problems, unavailability of gas it is advised to the State and Central government to start extensively exploring and harnessing the potential of solar and wind energy to meet the power demand in India. As renewable and alternate energy can also resolve the issue of COx, SOx and NOx emission problems to have clear environment in India.

31. Utilities percentage reduction in fiscal deficit after electricity reforms.

Table no:5.31 Utilities percentage reduction in fiscal deficit after electricity reforms.

		What is your % reduction in fiscal deficit after electricity reforms.			
		0-25%	26%-50%	51%-75%	Total
Sector	State	6	1	0	7
		85.7%	14.3%	.0%	100.0%
	Central Public	5	0	2	7
		71.4%	.0%	28.6%	100.0%
	Private	7	0	0	7
		100.0%	.0%	.0%	100.0%
Total		18	1	2	21
		85.7%	4.8%	9.5%	100.0%

Table no.5.31 reflects the utilities percentage reduction in fiscal deficit after electricity reforms. 85.7 per cent of the total sample respondents in which cent per cent private,85.7 per cent state and 71.4 per cent central disclosed that the utilities percentage reduction in fiscal deficit after electricity reform is in between (0-25 %), 4.8 percent told (26-50 %) and 9.5 per cent in the range (51-75%). The table concludes that despite the electricity reforms the percentage reduction in fiscal deficit is in between (0-25%), which needs to be improved substantially. It is suggested that the government should enact policies to control the fiscal deficit and penalize utilities for exceeding the deficit limits as autonomy to utilities is given to eliminate the fiscal deficits.

32. Electricity consumers contributing to losses after power reforms.

Table no: 5.32 Electricity consumers contributing to losses after power reforms.

Losses by Consumers	1	2	3	4	5	6	Weight Rank
Domestic	1 (6)	15 (75)	4 (16)		1 (10)		2 (107)
Commercial	1 (6)	3 (15)	16 (64)	1 (3)			3 (88)
Industrial	1 (6)			13 (39)	6 (12)		4 (57)
Agricultural	17 (102)	3 (15)	1 (4)				1 (121)
Railways				7 (21)	14 (28)		5 (49)
Other Consumers						21 (21)	6 (21)

Respondents gave 1st rank to agriculture, 2nd rank to domestic, 3rd rank to commercial, 4th rank to industrial, 5th rank to railways and 6th rank to other consumers for contributing to the losses after power reforms. The government's policy of free power to farmers for agriculture where the usage is enormously unaccountable has coincided with the opinion of respondents. (Table no: 5.32)

The Researcher identified that in addition to the power system losses consumers are also responsible for power theft, improper utilization of free power, unethical usage of electricity, default consumers, wastage of electrical energy, unwanted overdrawing and draining of power, unawareness of conserving energy which accounts for nearly 30 to 40 per cent all India average contributing to the energy deficit the country is facing. It is very difficult to demarcate the losses of electrical energy accountable to utilities or consumers. However, losses due to consumers are having serious impacts on the operation of the power system. The agricultural and domestic consumers have been rightly ranked by the respondents. Every corner of the country cannot be monitored at any level by any agency or authority. Hence, the loyalty of consumers can help the power sector from minimizing the losses. It is suggested to the consumers or customer of electrical energy users to rise to the expectations of the utilities in the true sense of spirit in battling out the energy crisis in India.

33. Overall performance of utilities in the regime of power sector reforms and restructuring in the state.

Table no:5.33 Respondent's opinion on overall performance of utilities in the regime of power sector reforms and restructuring in the state.

Sr. No	Sectors	Excellent	Very Good	Good	Average	Below Average
1	Central	76.2	14.3	9.5		
2	State	4.8	33.3	61.9		
3	Private	4.8	90.5	4.8		
4	Public & Private	4.8	19	76.2		

Overall performance of utilities in the new regime of power reforms	N	Mean	S.D	F-value	P-value	Decision
Private	7	3.8571	.34932	0.034	0.966	N.S
State Public	7	3.8214	.34503			
Central Public	7	3.8571	.13363			

It is interesting to note that Centre's performance is excellent 76.2 per cent of the total sample respondents, followed by Private's very good 90.5 per cent, Public & Private 76.2 per cent good and State's 61.9 per cent good on the opinion of overall performance of utilities in the new regime of power reforms and restructuring in the state. It may be concluded from the table that State's performance is dwindling day by day.

From the above P-value 0.966 in the ANOVA table it is statistically evident that the three sectors have opined all most same opinion on overall performance in the new regime of the power reforms and restructuring and the score is nearer to 4 which suggests that all these sectors have opined nearer to the option very good. (Table no: 5.33)

CHAPTER –VI

ENERGY MODELS IN INDIA

POWER MIX AND MARKET

(Power Utilities- State, Central and Private Sectors)

In this chapter it is proposed to study A. Power Mix and B. Market emerging in India's Power Sector for power utilities state, central and private sectors.

A. POWER MIX

The greatest impact of reforms and restructuring of the power sector after the enactment of historic Electricity Act-2003, is the evolving power mix in Indian power sector. The power utilities from the State, Central and Private sectors though operate in the same environment but are functionally and administratively being controlled at different levels by respective independent authorities. Independent utilities from time to time came into existence to manage the generation, transmission and distribution segments respectively either by the impact of reforms as seen in case of SEBs which were unbundled or public private partnership models as initial step towards privatization of the sector. Moreover the constitution of Commissions at State and Centre to regulate tariffs and protecting it from private power suppliers to capitalize the market somewhere appears to be the loop hole in the development of the power market.

1. Percentage share of sector segments in supplying electricity in India.

Table no:6.1 Respondents view on percentage share of Power Sector segments in supplying electricity in India.

Sr. No	Power Sector Segments (Average Score)	Central Sector	State Sector	Private Sector	Public Private Partnership	Others
1	Generation	3	3	3	2	
2	Transmission	1	3	1	1.238095	
3	Distribution	0	3	0.238095	0	
4	Rural Electrification	0	3	0	0.142857	
5	Power Market	1	0	1	0	

Table no.6.1 brings out the respondents view on percentage share of Power Sector segments in supplying electricity in India. Generation in the power sector segment was given equal highest average score of 3 by central, state and private sectors. Public Private Partnership (PPP) was the next in generation with average score of 2. The transmission segment was given average score of 3 by the state sector, an average score of one each was given by the central and private sector and little higher than average score of one was awarded by PPP sector. The State sector was the major player in distribution segment with highest average score of 3 just supported with minor average score of 0.238 by the private sector. Again in the rural electrification segment the state sector was the major player with average score of 3 and very marginally supported by PPP with average score of nearly 0.143. The power market segment was equally supported both by the central and private sectors with average score of one each.

Today generation, transmission, distribution, rural electrification and power market are the major power sector segments nurtured and flourished by the state, central and private sectors in India's Power Sector. Prior to entry of central sectors and private sectors all the functions of power supply chain i.e. generation, T&D, rural electrification and power market was shouldered by the SEBs of their respective States. SEBs had wider responsibilities to deliver with prime motto of service to the citizen of India.

The rising demand of power was resolved by introducing central sector with the prime responsibility of enhancing capacity addition in generation to support the SEBs. The transmission segment opening to central sector was subsequently delayed. The 1991 Economic Reforms opened the door for private participation in power sector. The private sector also operates with joint ventures in many segments of the power business. However, the IPP and PPP models were not successful in all the states. The IPPs have started dominating the emerging power mix. The amendments in Electricity Acts have further encouraged competition in the sector. The Electricity Reforms Act 2003 mandates unbundling of SEBs into small entities as GENCOs, DISCOMs, TRANSCOs and TRADECOs to independently take the responsibility for better enterprise management.

The recent National Power Policy (2005), National Tariff Policy (2006), Rural Electrification Policy (2006) further brought in setting up of electricity tariffs and power trading. Again the Power Exchange in India (2007) reforms constituted the central exchanges to trade electricity.

It is suggested there is greater scope for central sector to participate in distribution and rural electrification segment of the power sector. The private sector has been only capitalizing the opportunity in generation segment and can likely focus on other areas where the regulations have made the operation of business smoother.

2. Opinion on energy crisis in India's Power Sector.

Table no:6.2 Respondents view on energy crisis in India's Power Sector.

Sr. No	Energy Crisis	10-15%	15-20%	20-25%	25-30%	30-35%
1	Peak deficit		28.6	66.7		4.8
2	Commercial losses		14.3	28.6	57.1	
3	T&D losses			71.4	19	9.5
4	Operational losses	4.8	19	14.3	52.4	9.5
5	Power shortage			28.6		71.4
	Average Percentage	**0.96**	**12.38**	**41.92**	**25.7**	**19.04**

Respondents view on energy crisis in India's Power Sector is illustrated in table no: 6.2. It is observed from the table that T&D losses 71.4 per cent, peak deficit 66.7 per cent contributing to 20-25 per cent energy crisis. Commercial losses 57.1 per cent and operational losses 52.4 per cent are contributing 25-30 per cent energy crisis and power shortage 71.4 per cent is contributing 30-35 per cent energy crisis. It is evident from the table that the power sector on an average is performing with 30-40 per cent range of energy crisis.

Further peak deficit, commercial losses, T&D losses, operating losses and power shortage all have been the key performance indicators carried over the five decades as legacy of the sector unwilling to change reflecting energy crisis in India as per the energy statistics at national level either in the reports by the government or consultants/institutions privately managed in the country.

It is suggested to the government to devise a measurable mechanism at state and central level to periodically monitor the overall performance of the sector including, both the complete power supply chain by the utilities from all segments and revenue realized against set targets. The performance should be linked to penalties, incentives, budget outlays, policy benefits, power market participation, taxation and duties, fuel allocations, environmental support and other control measures as deemed fit to achieve the standard levels in delivering services, because simply reforming, restructuring and deregulating the sector without accountability is not paying any true dividends.

3. Large gaps remaining in Rural Electrification.

Table no:6.3 Large gaps remaining in Rural Electrification.

Large gaps in rural electrification	1	2	3	4	5	Weight Rank
Failure in implementation of rural electrification schemes	14 (70)	3 (12)	1 (3)	2 (4)	1 (5)	1 (94)
Lack of monitoring on household metering, billing & collection		16 (64)	5 (15)			2 (79)
Under utilization of funds	1 (5)	2 (8)	15 (45)	3 (6)		4 (64)
Inadequate funds flow	5 (25)	1 (4)		15 (30)		5 (59)
All		6 (30)	5 (20)	1 (3)	9 (18)	3 (71)

Respondents gave 1st rank to failure in implementation of rural electrification schemes, 2nd rank to lack of monitoring on house metering, billing & collection, 3rd rank to all the factors, 4th rank to under utilization of funds and 5th rank to inadequate funds flow. All these factors are contributing to large gaps remaining in rural electrification. (Table no:6.3)

The above analysis clearly reveals that failure in implementing rural schemes, lack of monitoring metering, billing & collection, inadequate funds flow and under utilization all are equally attributable in creating large gaps in rural electrification. The Researcher identified that the above has been supported by the Rural Electrification Policy (2006) which was essential to improve the electricity infrastructure in rural areas. There is no doubt that disparity in electricity services cannot be ruled out as rural areas are not at par with the urban areas. The accessibility, availability, quality and reliability of power supply speak about the pathetic situation of remote villages struggling for daily living. Their quest for survival is even worse when load shedding prevails consistently for days together. People below the poverty line are deprived of the basic need as accessibility to electricity is a distant dream. The rural areas are agricultural sector depending upon irrigation throughout the year. Energizing of needy pumps is considered to be a charity by the government which keeps itself safeguarding under the umbrella of subsidies and free power to farmers. Even today the agriculture sector contributes more than the industrial sector in developing and sustaining India's GDP.

India's 70 per cent of the population still lives in rural areas dreaming of better living standards as other citizens are experiencing in urban and sub-urban areas. The percentage of geographical area under rural category is very vast and it requires bigger magnitude projects to battle out the problem of unavailability of power. There are areas in India where power is not seen for months together.

It is suggested that the government immediately drives a plan to meet its immediate mandate of "Lantern to Electric Lamp" through equal participation of all the state, central and private sectors.

4. Need for competition in India's Energy Sector.

Table no:6.4 Respondent's opinion on need for competition in India's Energy Sector.

Sr. No	Energy Sector's Competition	Major	Moderate	Minor	No opinion
1	Increasing demand-supply gap	95.2	4.8		
2	Massive investment requirements	95.2	4.8		
3	Potential benefits from competition	66.7	33.3		
4	Vision Power to all by 2012	85.7	14.3		
5	Emerging Mixes-Power, Energy and Fuel	61.9	28.6	9.5	
6	Low Carbon Electricity	100			

Energy Sector's Competition	N	Mean	S.D	F-value	P-value	Decision
Private	7	2.7143	.26726	1.043	0.373	N.S
State Public	7	2.8810	.12599			
Central Public	7	2.8810	.31497			

Respondent's opinion on need for competition in India's Energy Sector is furnished in table no.6.4. The respondents opinion on low carbon electricity 100 per cent, increasing demand supply gap & massive investment requirements each 95.2 per cent, vision power to all by 2012 85.7 per cent are the major reasons necessitating competition in the energy sector.

Regarding ANOVA Test results it is understood from the above table that the dimension need for competition in India's Energy Sector is insignificant as the P value 0.373 is found to be insignificant at 0.05 level of significance. This explains that it is statistically evident that the respondents of three sectors have opined all most similar opinion on overall Energy Sector's Competition.

5. IPPs making significant addition to the generating capacity in the state.

Table no: 6.5 Independent Power Producers (IPPs) making significant addition to the generating capacity in the state.

		Independent power producers (IPPs) making significant addition to the generation capacity in the state.			
		Yes	No	No opinion	Total
Sector	State	1	2	4	7
		14.3%	28.6%	57.1%	100.0%
	Central Public	1	1	5	7
		14.3%	14.3%	71.4%	100.0%
	Private	5	1	1	7
		71.4%	14.3%	14.3%	100.0%
Total		7	4	10	21
		33.3%	19.0%	47.6%	100.0%

IPPs significant addition to the generating capacity in the state is depicted in table no:6.5. Category wise analysis reveals that 71.4 per cent private and 14.3 per cent each of state and central respondents i.e.7 among the total sample respondents 33.3 per cent told yes, 4 respondents 19 per cent revealed no regarding IPPs significant addition to the generating capacity in the state. It is surprising to note that 10 total sample respondents 47.6 per cent are unable to give any opinion on the above statement. The table concludes that IPPs were having marginal contribution in enhancing the generating capacity in the state.

It is advised to the Government of India that there should be adequate support to translate the policy into reality. There is no doubt that the policy of Independent Power Producers (IPPs) was an effective tool to revamp the sector by enhancing the generation capacity but the State's and Centre's cooperation to private sector was never there in reality. Hence the government both at state and centre should try to actually support the private sector.

6. IPPs policy success to increase the availability of electricity at reduced costs.

Table no: 6.6 Respondent's opinion on the success of Independent Power Producers (IPPs) policy to increase the availability of electricity at reduced costs.

		Did the independent power producers (IPPs) policy succeed to increase the availability of electricity at reduced costs.			
		Yes	No	No opinion	Total
Sector	State	0	1	6	7
		.0%	14.3%	85.7%	100.0%
	Central Public	2	0	5	7
		28.6%	.0%	71.4%	100.0%
	Private	3	3	1	7
		42.9%	42.9%	14.3%	100.0%
Total		5	4	12	21
		23.8%	19.0%	57.1%	100.0%

Table no.6.6 presents respondents opinion on the success of IPPs policy to increase the availability of electricity at reduced costs. 12 among total sample respondents 57.1 per cent revealed no opinion on the statement and 4 respondents 19 per cent told no. It is very surprising that only 5 respondents 23.8 per cent said yes supporting the above statement. It is very much evident from the above analysis that more than 50 per cent of the respondents are unable to analyze the success of IPPs in increasing the availability of electricity at reduced costs.

IPPs were the forerunners in transforming the power sector since Economic Reforms (1991). The conclusion from the above analysis speaks the sad story of the IPPs. This is in right concurrence with the present scenario where IPPs are struggling to perform in the power sector despite reforms to promote, support, encourage, facilitate and compete in the emerging power market.

In view of the above background it is suggested that government should regularly welcome healthy suggestions as part of the feedback mechanism and lessons learnt from the recent past to redefine PPAs and FSAs to streamline the bottlenecks which are impeding the success of IPPs in India.

7. Government really needs to entice private participation in the sector.

Table no:6.7 Government really needs to entice private participation in the sector.

		Does the government really need to entice private participation in the sector.			
		Yes	No	No opinion	Total
Sector	State	2	2	3	7
		28.6%	28.6%	42.9%	100.0%
	Central Public	2	0	5	7
		28.6%	.0%	71.4%	100.0%
	Private	4	1	2	7
		57.1%	14.3%	28.6%	100.0%
Total		8	3	10	21
		38.1%	14.3%	47.6%	100.0%

Government really needs to entice private participation in the sector is described in table no.6.7. Majority of the total sample respondents 47.6 per cent had no opinion, 3 respondents 14.3 per cent told no and 8 respondents 38.1 per cent revealed yes. Thus it is very clear that majority of the respondents are unable to conclude on the government's enticement for private participation in the sector.

It is true nevertheless the need of the hour is to save the sinking power sector from drowning. Private sector as savoir cannot be ignored though they delayed in capitalizing the LPG-Policy and Electricity Reforms Act-2003 but are today holding one tenth of the power sectors supply chain. Their roots are getting deeper and it is a matter of time that they will command the power sector in coming decades.

It is suggested to the government to accommodate private sector at par with the state and central sector eliminating discriminations and conflicts so that the emerging power mix can change the scenario of the country's electricity infrastructure which is becoming essential for India's growth for ever than before.

8. Performance of Public Private Partnership (PPP) in the Liberalized Power Sector(LPS)

Table no:6.8 Respondent's opinion on the performance of Public Private Partnership (PPP) in the Liberalized Power Sector(LPS).

		How is the public private partnership performing in the liberalized Power Sector .				Total
		Excellent	Very Good	Good	Average	
Sector	State	0	2	4	1	7
		.0%	28.6%	57.1%	14.3%	100.0%
	Central Public	1	4	1	1	7
		14.3%	57.1%	14.3%	14.3%	100.0%
	Private	4	2	0	1	7
		57.1%	28.6%	.0%	14.3%	100.0%
Total		5	8	5	3	21
		23.8%	38.1%	23.8%	14.3%	100.0%

Respondent's opinion on the performance of Public Private Partnership (PPP) in the Liberalized Power Sector (LPS) is described in table no. 6.8. 23.8 per cent of the total sample respondents opined performance of the PPP in the LPS is excellent, 38.1 per cent told very good and 23.8 per cent said good. Only 14.3 per cent revealed that the performance of PPP is average. The table concludes that on an overall PPP in LPS are performing well.

9. Will the utilities become free to select their area of business independently in power sector.

Table no:6.9 Freedom to utilities in selecting their area of business independently in power sector.

		Will the utilities become free to select their area of business independently in power sector.			
		Yes	No	No opinion	Total
Sector	State	0	1	6	7
		.0%	14.3%	85.7%	100.0%
	Central Public	2	0	5	7
		28.6%	.0%	71.4%	100.0%
	Private	2	2	3	7
		28.6%	28.6%	42.9%	100.0%
Total		4	3	14	21
		19.0%	14.3%	66.7%	100.0%

Table no: 6.9 furnishes freedom to utilities in selecting their area of business independently in power sector. It is interesting to note that 66.7 per cent of the total sample respondents were unable to give any opinion on freedom to utilities in selecting their area of business independently in power sector. Moreover 14.3 respondents made it very clear that the utilities will never be given freedom to select their area of business independently in power sector. However 19 per cent respondents told yes thus supporting the statement, utilities will become free to select area of business independently.

The above analysis holds good as the policies are not clear in deciding the segment of power sector to be opened to the utilities. The distribution segment is not opened to the central sector utilities, the transmission utility cannot do power trading; the power trading company cannot generate, transmit or distribute power. Above all the sector speaks of deregulation and liberalization with restrictions on freedom to utilities in selecting their area of business independently in power sector is very much evident with the opinion of the respondents.

The Researcher feels that the dual policy of the governments may be revisited by all concerned to redefine rethinking the possible opening of the sector with equal opportunities to any utilities from the state, central and private to take up any business anywhere in India. Then only the sector's all exercise of reforms and restructuring may lead to liberalization and corporatization in the true sense.

10. Can power sector reforms succeed without coal sector reforms.

Table no:6.10 Power sector reforms succeeding without coal sector reforms.

		Can power sector reforms succeed without coal sector reforms.		Total
		Yes	No	Total
Sector	State	1	6	7
		14.3%	85.7%	100.0%
	Central Public	1	6	7
		14.3%	85.7%	100.0%
	Private	0	7	7
		.0%	100.0%	100.0%
Total		2	19	21
		9.5%	90.5%	100.0%

Power sector reforms succeeding without coal sector reforms are shown in table no: 6.10. Power sector reforms cannot succeed without coal sector reforms was the opinion of majority 90.5 per cent respondents of the total 21 sample respondents. In this regard the category wise analysis reveals that 100 per cent private, 85.7 per cent each central and state respondents opined no. Only 2 respondents 9.5 per cent opined yes. The table concludes that the coal sector reforms are very much essential for the success of power sector reforms which coincides with the present coal crisis prevailing in the power sector. Many thermal power projects based on coal due to signing of fuel supply agreements are yet to be commissioned in the country. As 70 per cent of India's power generation is based on coal, its inadequate supply to the thermal plants has lead to underrated power generation adding to the existing energy crisis. Even some of the thermal plants in all the three state, central and private sectors are at the verge of complete closure.

It is suggested to the government that Fuel Supply Agreements (FSAs) between the Power Producers/ Utilities and Coal Suppliers be closed without further delay enabling the operation of the constructed power projects as deemed generation is being lost adding to the power shortage and energy crisis the power sector is already facing.

11. Public opinion on present Power Industry.

Table no: 6.11 Public opinion on Power Industry perceived by the Utilities.

Sr. No	Public opinion on power industry	Major	Moderate	Minor	No opinion
1	An ailing sector	95.2	4.8		
2	Reviving after reforms		4.8	95.2	
3	Detoriating after reforms	100			
4	Unable to face competition and deliver	95.2	4.8		
5	Over all inefficient sector	100			

Public opinion on power industry	N	Mean	S.D	F-value	P-value	Decision
Private	7	2.6000	.00000	0.3	0.744	N.S
State Public	7	2.5714	.07559			
Central Public	7	2.6000	.11547			

Public opinion on Power Industry perceived by the Utilities is portrayed in table no.6.11. It is not surprising to know the public opinion regarding power industry which has been voted, overall inefficient sector and deteriorating after reforms each 100 per cent by the respondents. The other indicators like an ailing sector and unable to face competition 95.2 per cent each are the major opinion of the respondents.

From the above ANOVA table it can be concluded that the opinion on the present power industry as perceived by the respondents on Utilities of the three sectors are very much nearer to each other and there is no statistically significant difference between their average scores. The hypothesis is accepted.

12. Opinion on operating in the new POWER MIX.

Table no: 6.12 Respondent's opinion on operating in the new POWER MIX.

		How are you operating in the new POWER MIX.			
		Successful	Surviving	No opinion	Total
Sector	State	2	5	0	7
		28.6%	71.4%	.0%	100.0%
	Central Public	4	2	1	7
		57.1%	28.6%	14.3%	100.0%
	Private	5	2	0	7
		71.4%	28.6%	.0%	100.0%
Total		11	9	1	21
		52.4%	42.9%	4.8%	100.0%

Respondent's opinion on operating in the new POWER MIX is given in table no: 6.12. Operating successfully was disclosed by 52.4 per cent of the total sample respondents, 42.9 per cent revealed surviving and 4.8 per cent only told no opinion. It is interesting to conclude from the table that in the same new environment of emerging Power Mix 52.4 per cent respondent i.e. the power utilities are successful where as the remaining ones just surviving. It is too early to finally conclude that either all may be successful or may be just surviving in near future.

B. POWER MARKET

Will electricity economics deliver the basic needs of developing Indian Electricity Market? The power market faces the stiff challenges of financial modeling, future energy trends, mastering complex markets, energy crisis & risk management and investment in emerging developing electricity markets. Reforms were initiated with the provisions for tax holidays, import duties relaxation and other licensing benefits to power builders to invest in the power sector and trading of electricity. The State and Central sector utilities electricity suppliers are facing competition from the private sector utilities service providers.

Even though few IPP projects had been conceived in the recent past there has not been any progress mainly on account of the issue of escrow ability and support agreement from the State government. The role of the captive power plants in the Indian Power Sector has changed from self sufficiency to trading of electricity over the years defeating the policy of its existence for the purpose of being a back up in times of power shortages, captive power plants have become the main stay power source for the domestic corporate sector and are being branded as merchant power plants.

Today, all the Indian states are not having equal potential of developing power market to have inter & intra state trading. There are states with huge energy deficits and hardly any state with surplus power to voluntarily share with other neighboring needy states. The operation of national power exchanges needs to be clearly defined. A conducive policy and legal framework is yet to be worked out at national and state level to facilitate the beneficiaries.

13. Rating the essential factors in developing electricity market in India.

Table no:6.13 Rate the essential factors in developing electricity market in India.

Sr. No	Electricity Market	Major	Moderate	Minor	No opinion
1	Electricity economics	95.2	4.8		
2	Financial modeling	81	19		
3	Future energy trends	85.7	14.3		
4	Mastering complex markets	81	19		
5	Energy risk management	76.2	19	4.8	

Table no. 6.13 brings the rating of the essential factors in developing electricity market in India. Electricity economics 95.2 per cent, future energy trends 85.7 per cent, financial modeling & mastering complex markets 81 per cent each and energy risk management 76.2 per cent are the major factors which are contributing to the development of electricity market. It may be concluded that the emerging electricity market's development is based on the essential indicators as described above.

"Electricity Market in India" is the outcome of greatest impact of reforms and restructuring of the power sector. The fire was ignited by the Economic Reforms and the flames are being sustained by the Electricity Reforms in the sector. The transformation of electricity service into electricity industry clearly speaks of the professionalism penetrating into the power sector which is very much evident from the present analysis of the essential factors in developing Electricity Market in India. Electricity economics, financial modeling, future energy trends, mastering complex markets and energy risk management almost all equally are the contributing factors to mould and forge the present Electricity Market in India.

14. Status of power market in the state in the present scenario.

Table no: 6.14 Present status of power market in the state.

		Present status of power market in the state.			
		In developing stage	No initiative by the government	No opinion	Total
Sector	State	5	0	2	7
		71.4%	.0%	28.6%	100.0%
	Central Public	7	0	0	7
		100.0%	.0%	.0%	100.0%
	Private	1	2	4	7
		14.3%	28.6%	57.1%	100.0%
Total		13	2	6	21
		61.9%	9.5%	28.6%	100.0%

Present status of power market in the state is furnished in table no. 6.14. The present power market is in developing stage in the opinion of the 61.9 per cent total sample respondents, in this regard the category wise analysis reveals that cent per cent central, 71.4 per cent state and 14.3 per cent private respondents opined the same. No initiative by the government was revealed by 9.5 per cent of the total sample respondents and 28.6 per cent respondents were unable to give any opinion. The table concludes that power market is a very new concept in providing electricity services in the new emerging power mix and hence it is in developing stage.

15. Impact of reforms & restructuring on power sector.

Table no:6.15 Respondent's opinion on the impact of reforms & restructuring on power sector.

Sr. No	Impact of reforms & restructuring	Increased	Decreased	As it is	No opinion
1	Revenue collection	47.6		52.4	
2	Electricity theft		23.8	76.2	
3	Commercial losses		28.6	71.4	
4	Technical losses		28.6	71.4	
5	Operational efficiency	33.3		61.9	4.8
6	Consumer metering	66.7		33.3	
7	Financial health	38.1		61.9	
8	Demand –Supply gap	4.8	9.5	85.7	
9	Quality and reliability of power supply	19	4.8	76.2	
10	Customer satisfaction	14.3	4.8	81	
	Average Opinion	**22.38**	**10.01**	**67.13**	**0.48**

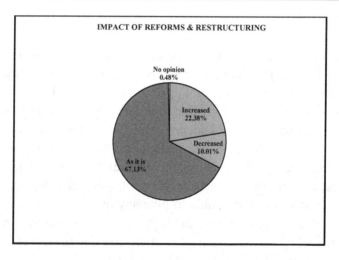

Respondent's opinion on the impact of reforms & restructuring on power sector is presented in table no. 6.15. It is surprising to note that the opinion of the respondents is as it is even after the reforms & restructuring of the power sector, the indicators like demand & supply 85.7 per cent, customer satisfaction 81 per cent, electric theft, quality and reliability of power supply 76.2 per cent each, commercial losses and technical losses 71.4 per cent each, operational efficiency and financial health 61.9 per cent each and consumer metering 31.3 per cent. The above circle diagram indicates the average opinion score of the sample respondents regarding impact of reforms and restructuring on power sector. To summarize about 67.13 per cent revealed as it is, 22.38 per cent opined increased and 10.01 per cent told decreased performance of the power sector.

The table concludes that power sector has improved in consumer metering with 66.7 per cent and in the rest areas it is as it is before the reforms. It is suggested that emerging power mix should redesign the national policies to bring in improvement in all areas which are affecting the performance of the power sector.

16. Opinion on investment in different segments of the electricity sector.

Table no: 6.16 Respondent's opinion on investment in different segments of the electricity sector.

Sr. No	Investment in electricity sector	Major	Moderate	Minor	No opinion
1	Generation	100			
2	Transmission	4.8	90.5	4.8	
3	Distribution	4.8	28.6	66.7	
4	Rural electrification	9.5	4.8	85.7	
5	Technology up gradation	4.8	4.8	85.7	4.8

Table no.6.16 gives the picture of respondent's opinion on investment in different segments of electricity sector. The table reveals that the major investment 100 per cent is done in generation, moderate investment in transmission 90.5 per cent and minor investment in rural electrification, technology up gradation 85.7 per cent each and distribution 66.7 per cent. It is evident from the table that much importance has been given to generation where the investment is skewed and less investment in rural electrification being completely neglected.

17. Utilities participation in the power market after introducing new energy models.

Table no:6.17 Respondent's opinion on Utilities participation in the power market after introducing new energy models.

		Utility participation in the power market after introducing new energy models.				
		Excellent	Very Good	Average	Below average	Total
Sector	State	1	3	3	0	7
		14.3%	42.9%	42.9%	.0%	100.0%
	Central Public	1	4	2	0	7
		14.3%	57.1%	28.6%	.0%	100.0%
	Private	1	3	2	1	7
		14.3%	42.9%	28.6%	14.3%	100.0%
Total		3	10	7	1	21
		14.3%	47.6%	33.3%	4.8%	100.0%

Respondent's opinion on Utilities participation in the power market after introducing new energy models is shown in the table no. 6.17. 14.3 per cent of the total sample respondents told utilities participation in the power market after introducing new energy models was excellent, 47.6 per cent revealed very good,33.3 per cent respondents said average and only 4.8 per cent i.e. one respondent disclosed below average.

It can be concluded from the table that respondents opinion is broadly distributed in the ratio three is to two (3:2) related to utilities participation in the power market when compared to good and average on the whole. Moreover it is too early to conclude as the new energy models have been introduced very recently.

18. Advantage on the TAX holidays and import duties relaxation.

Table no:6.18 Respondent's opinion on taking advantage on the TAX holidays and import duties relaxation.

		Are you taking advantage on the TAX holidays and import duties relaxation.				
		Yes	No	Partial	Not started	Total
Sector	State	0	7	0	0	7
		.0%	100.0%	.0%	.0%	100.0%
	Central Public	0	6	0	1	7
		.0%	85.7%	.0%	14.3%	100.0%
	Private	1	2	3	1	7
		14.3%	28.6%	42.9%	14.3%	100.0%
Total		1	15	3	2	21
		4.8%	71.4%	14.3%	9.5%	100.0%

Respondent's opinion on taking advantage on the TAX holidays and import duties relaxation is depicted in table no: 6.18. Only one respondent 4.8 per cent told yes, 15 respondents 71.4 per cent opined no on taking advantage on the TAX holidays and import duties relaxation, only 3 respondents 14.3 per cent said partial advantage and remaining 2 respondents 9.5 per cent did not start taking advantage. It is evident from the above table that 80 per cent of the respondents are not taking advantage on the TAX holidays and import duties relaxation because the clearances from the government are getting delayed and subsequently the projects are not completed in the stipulated time.

19. ESCROW accounts help in private investments for generation projects.

Table no:6.19 Respondents view on helping of ESCROW accounts in private investments for generation projects.

		Did the ESCROW accounts help in private investments for generation projects.		
		No	No opinion	Total
Sector	State	5	2	7
		71.4%	28.6%	100.0%
	Central Public	4	3	7
		57.1%	42.9%	100.0%
	Private	4	3	7
		57.1%	42.9%	100.0%
Total		13	8	21
		61.9%	38.1%	100.0%

Table no: 6.19 reflects the respondents view on helping of ESCROW accounts in private investments for generation projects. It is unhealthy sign to observe that 61.9 per cent of the total sample respondents revealed no helping of ESCROW accounts in private investments for generation projects and in addition to it remaining 38.1 per cent of the total sample respondents told that they had no opinion about the helping of ESCROW accounts. The above analysis shows that the ESCROW accounts mechanism policy (payment security against insolvency of state utilities) by the government is not a successful story because the state government failed to provide security to the private utilities against payment defaults by the SEBs.

20. International Competitive Bidding route helping to develop the power market.

Table no:6.20 Respondent's perception on International Competitive Bidding (ICB) route helping to develop the power market.

		International competitive bidding route helping to develop the power market.				
		Strongly agree	Undecided	Disagree	Strongly disagree	Total
Sector	State	1	6	0	0	7
		14.3%	85.7%	.0%	.0%	100.0%
	Central Public	0	5	1	1	7
		.0%	71.4%	14.3%	14.3%	100.0%
	Private	3	4	0	0	7
		42.9%	57.1%	.0%	.0%	100.0%
Total		4	15	1	1	21
		19.0%	71.4%	4.8%	4.8%	100.0%

Table no.6.20 presents respondents perception on ICB route helping to develop the power market. It is very surprising to note that respondents strongly agreeing in support of the above statement are only 19 per cent of the total sample respondents. 71.4 per cent respondents opined undecided, 4.8 per cent each disagree and strongly disagree. The Researcher identified that the power utilities are not sure of the ICB route helping to develop the power market, which is in line with the table's conclusion.

21. Will electricity pricing in India just remain a policy or not a reality.

Table no: 6.21 Electricity pricing in India will just remain a policy or not a reality.

		Will electricity pricing in India just remain a policy or not a reality.			
		Yes	No	No opinion	Total
Sector	State	1	0	6	7
		14.3%	.0%	85.7%	100.0%
	Central Public	0	2	5	7
		.0%	28.6%	71.4%	100.0%
	Private	0	3	4	7
		.0%	42.9%	57.1%	100.0%
Total		1	5	15	21
		4.8%	23.8%	71.4%	100.0%

According to the table no. 6.21 about 71.4 per cent of the total sample respondents could not give any opinion on the statement electricity pricing in India will just remain a policy or not a reality. In addition to it no was opined by 23.8 per cent respondents, however only one respondent told yes in support of the statement. It is evident from the table that nearly 95.2 per cent respondents are not confident about the electricity pricing policy becoming a reality in the near future.

Electricity pricing in India is the future challenge to be encountered by the emerging power mix and market. The power supply chain is getting fragmented and decentralized. The functional responsibility matrix is becoming more complex. The bulk power market and retail power market are springing up simultaneously. Power trading and exchanges have their own ambiguities and risks. Utilities and Consumers are coming nearer.

The role of the regulation is diminishing in the sector day by day. On one side Merchant Power is being encouraged and on the other hand RECs are fighting to rationalize the prices. National Tariff Policy (2006) has its own regulations to streamline the pricing mechanism.

The Researcher identified that there has been series of reforms (averagely one new policy enacted annually) since the enactment of Electricity Reforms Act-2003 but the uncertainty of regulatory reforms is supporting the instability and holding the power sector in assessing and determining the unfluctuating electricity prices.

22. Opinion on success of franchisee model in rural areas.

Table no:6.22 Respondent's opinion on success of franchisee model in rural areas.

		Opinion on success of franchisee model in rural areas.			
		Yes	No	No opinion	Total
Sector	State	3	0	4	7
		42.9%	.0%	57.1%	100.0%
	Central Public	1	1	5	7
		14.3%	14.3%	71.4%	100.0%
	Private	4	0	3	7
		57.1%	.0%	42.9%	100.0%
Total		8	1	12	21
		38.1%	4.8%	57.1%	100.0%

Table no. 6.22 brings out the respondents opinion on success of franchisee model in rural areas. The success of franchisee model was opined yes by 38.1 per cent total respondents. Only one respondent told no and moreover 57.1 respondents of the total sample had no opinion about the success of franchisee model in rural areas. It is evident from the above table that utilities are not developing feedback mechanism from the consumers of the schemes being implemented by them. It is suggested that government should analyze the success of implementation of any new model from time to time to take prompt decisions before it dwindles completely.

23. Opinion on selling of power by captive and merchant power producers.

Table no:6.23 Respondents view on selling of power by captive and merchant power producers.

		On selling of power by captive and merchant power plants.			
		Strongly agree	Agree	Undecided	Total
Sector	State	1	0	6	7
		14.3%	.0%	85.7%	100.0%
	Central Public	0	2	5	7
		.0%	28.6%	71.4%	100.0%
	Private	1	0	6	7
		14.3%	.0%	85.7%	100.0%
Total		2	2	17	21
		9.5%	9.5%	81.0%	100.0%

Respondents view on selling of power by captive and merchant power producers is depicted in table no.6.23. Majority of the total respondents 81 per cent view on selling of power by captive and merchant power producers is undecided. 2 respondents 9.5 per cent each opined strongly agree and agree.

Selling of power by captive and merchant power producers is invariably a threat to the state and central sector power utilities which are being respectively governed by SERCs and CERCs. The extent of control by ERCs on captive and merchant power generation and selling is unclear in the sector giving scope for manipulation of electricity prices. Type of consumers was restricted to domestic, commercial, industrial and agricultural but today the SEBs who once upon a time were sellers are the bulk buyers of power from central and private sector utilities. Selling of power by captive and merchant power producers to SEBs cannot be thought of without regulation by the ERCs as the unbundled SEBs even today constitutes the major share in the State sector.

24. Percentage of total power generated by the utilities can be sold directly to consumers of their choice as per the Power Purchase Agreement (PPA)

Table no:6.24 Respondent's opinion on the percentage of total power generated by the utilities can be sold directly to consumers of their choice as per the Power Purchase Agreement (PPA).

		What percentage of total power generated the utilities can sell directly to consumers their choice as per the power purchase agreement (PPA)			
		less than 15%	less than 25%	Others	Total
Sector	State	0	4	3	7
		.0%	57.1%	42.9%	100.0%
	Central Public	0	4	3	7
		.0%	57.1%	42.9%	100.0%
	Private	5	1	1	7
		71.4%	14.3%	14.3%	100.0%
Total		5	9	7	21
		23.8%	42.9%	33.3%	100.0%

Respondents opinion on the percentage of total power generated by the utilities can be sold directly to consumers of their choice as per the Power Purchase Agreement (PPA) is revealed in table no: 6.24. About 23.8 per cent total respondents opined less than 15 %, 42.9 per cent told less than 25% and 33.3 per cent respondents revealed others regarding percentage of selling of power to the consumers of their choice by the power utilities.

25. Respondent's satisfaction on the existing policy on electricity pricing in India.

Table no: 6.25 Respondent's perception on the existing policy on electricity pricing in India.

| | | Are you satisfied with the existing policy on electricity pricing in India. | | | |
		Satisfied	Unsatisfied	No opinion	Total
Sector	State	5	0	2	7
		71.4%	.0%	28.6%	100.0%
	Central Public	4	3	0	7
		57.1%	42.9%	.0%	100.0%
	Private	1	3	3	7
		14.3%	42.9%	42.9%	100.0%
Total		10	6	5	21
		47.6%	28.6%	23.8%	100.0%

Table no.6.25 brings out the respondents perception on the existing policy on electricity pricing in India. It is interesting to note that 10 respondents among the total 47.6 per cent were found to be satisfied with the existing policy on electricity pricing in India. At the same time it is surprising to understand unsatisfactory opinion by 6 respondents 28.6 per cent. Moreover the remaining 5 respondents 23.8 per cent were not having any idea of the existing policy on electricity pricing in India.

The Electricity Regulatory Commissions both at the centre and state are equally responsible to design, determine and implement the tariffs for sell and purchase of power. Utilities which are unable to recover even the cost of generation are naturally not happy with the existing policy on tariff and at the same time utilities which are performing well availing all the advantages of fuel, location, evacuation and efficiency are happy with the same existing policy. The greatest challenge to the ERCs is rationalization of unit cost of power generation throughout the country overcoming all geographical, environmental, technical, commercial and political barriers, which seems to be next to impossible for a country like India with more than 28 states under different ruling governments.

26. Market share in the power sector.

Table no:6.26 Respondent's market share in the power sector.

		What is your market share in the power sector.					Total
		0-15%	16-30%	31-45%	46-60%	Above 60%	
Sector	State	3	0	0	0	4	7
		42.9%	.0%	.0%	.0%	57.1%	100.0%
	Central Public	1	0	0	1	5	7
		14.3%	.0%	.0%	14.3%	71.4%	100.0%
	Private	4	1	1	0	1	7
		57.1%	14.3%	14.3%	.0%	14.3%	100.0%
Total		8	1	1	1	10	21
		38.1%	4.8%	4.8%	4.8%	47.6%	100.0%

Respondent's market share in the power sector is illustrated in table no. 6.26. 0-15 per cent market share was reported by 38.1 per cent total respondents and 4.8 per cent each told in between 16-30 per cent, 31-45 per cent and 46-60 per cent respectively. The major share above 60 per cent was disclosed by 47.6 per cent respondents of the total sample respondents.

The growth of the central sector was commanding after the monopolistic regime of the state sector was over. The success rate in enhancing capacity addition in generation and better performance of power station of the central sector as compared to the state sector has made the central sector achieve major market share in the power sector, which is in line with the respondents reporting of 71.4 per cent for the central sector having share above 60 per cent in the power sector.

PART III

VOICE
OF
CONSUMERS

CHAPTER-VII

INDUSTRIAL –
ELECTRICITY CONSUMERS

An attempt has been made in this chapter to focus on I. Power- Supply, Quality and Billing, II. Power System- Performance and Maintenance and III. Consumer Satisfaction –Services and Problems of Industrial Electricity Consumers.

1. District wise distribution of Industrial Electricity Consumers.

Table no:7.1. District wise distribution of Industrial Electricity Consumers.

District	Frequency	Percent
Visakhapatnam	78	35.9
East Godavari	48	22.1
West Godavari	40	18.4
Krishna	51	23.5
Total	217	100.0

Table no.7.1 describes about four district wise distribution of industrial consumers in Andhra Pradesh. In total 217 industrial consumers are covered from Visakhapatnam, East Godavari, West Godavari and Krishna districts for the sample study. It is observed that nearly 36 per cent (78) of the industrial respondents are from Visakhapatnam district. In East Godavari and West Godavari districts 22.1 per cent (48) and 18.4 per cent (40) of the industrial consumers are covered. The remaining 23.5 per cent (51) respondents are covered from Krishna district.

I. POWER- SUPPLY, QUALITY AND BILLING.

A. SUPPLY

Consistent rate of industrial growth in India primarily depends on the adequate uninterrupted power supply by the utilities. Industrial Sector's performance and operational efficiency is based on the indelible support by power sector in backup power to small and big industrial consumers. In recent times the impact of energy crisis has resulted in huge power supply shortages raising questions about the survival of very small industries without any self resources for power generation, industrial output losses and finally on large the economy of the nation.

Power Crisis has given birth to captive power. The captive power generation has extended to exploit the power supply market by breeding in merchant power concept in the electricity industry in India. Despite initiation of captive and merchant power penetration in the electricity sector the power supply situation has not improved in the country.

Capacity additions through public investments have fallen below the government's target, due to the large public deficit which has hampered the government's ability to invest. More generally, public investments in the power sector have not been commensurate to the needs in the past decade and have suffered from a bias toward the generation of electricity, rather than the transmission and distribution of power. The latter has been corrected in recent years. Participation of Private Sector in Transmission and Distribution Systems is yet to be explored. The creation and commissioning of the National Power Grid is a distant dream.

2. India's power sector support to industrial sector.

Table no:7.2. India's power sector support to industrial sector in the last six years.

Sr. No	Year of supply	Excellent	Very good	Good	Average	Below average
1	2006	47.5	19.4	13.8	16.1	3.2
2	2007	15.7	47.5	20.3	16.1	0.5
3	2008	4.6	27.6	57.1	10.1	0.5
4	2009	3.7	16.1	38.7	37.3	4.1
5	2010	5.5	6.9	12	40.1	35.5
6	2011		3.7	14.7	81.6	

Year	2006	2007	2008	2009	2010	2011
Average Opinion Score	3.92	3.62	3.26	2.78	2.07	1.22

r= -0.98, P-value: 0.001

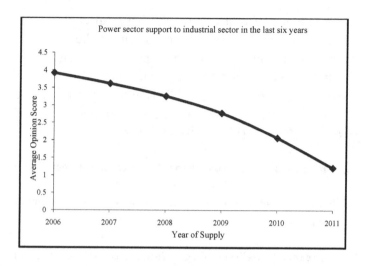

India's Power Sector support to industrial sector in the last six years is depicted in table no.7.2., as it is evident from the graph that the support to industrial sector by power sector in the last six years is declining. The data reveals that 47.5 per cent of the total respondents opined excellent during the year 2006, 47.5 per cent very good in the year 2007, 57.1 per cent opined good in the year 2008, 40.1 per cent said average in the year 2010 and 81.6 per cent revealed average in the year 2011. The average opinion score also declined from 3.92 in 2006 to 1.22 in the year 2011. The table concludes that because of shortage of power the industrial sector did not get support from the power sector.

From the above P-value 0.001 it is concluded that there is a significant decrease in the average opinion score of the respondents on the power sector support to industrial sector for the past six years. Further, it is concluded that there is a significant negative relationship between the year and the corresponding average opinion score. The power sector's support decreases as the year increases.

3. Impact of power shortage on operations of industries in the state.

Table no:7.3 Respondent's opinion on the impact of power shortage on operations of industries in the state.

Sr. No	Industrial Locality	Major	Moderate	Minor	No opinion
1	Urban	77.4	8.8	13.4	0.5
2	Sub-urban	55.8	39.6	4.6	
3	Villages	50.7	21.7	26.3	1.4
4	Others	51.6	4.6	31.3	12.4

Table no.7.3 presents respondents opinion on the impact of power shortage on operation of industries in the state. It is revealed that 77.4 per cent of the industries in urban locality are the major sufferers of power shortage. Industries in sub-urban 39.6 per cent are moderate sufferers and the suffering rate in villages is 26.3 per cent which is minor as compared to other localities. Equally an appreciable majority of industrial consumers from villages 50.7 per cent and others (like remote villages, hamlets, Dalit bastis etc) 51.6 per cent cannot be ignored. Agro, food, vegetables, horticulture, poultry, eggs, fish and aquaculture, dairy milk products, jaggery, sugar mills, rice mills, jute mills, paper and pulp industries. etc, all have their base in and around villages and their contribution to the state economy cannot be undermined.

However, it can be concluded that most of the heavy industries are located in urban and sub-urban areas and this two areas are the major sufferers for the power shortage. It is suggested to the government to take necessary steps to minimize the power shortage so that operation of industries in the state is not affected.

4. Major fuel sources generating cheaper electricity in India.

Table no :7.4 Respondent's opinion on major fuel sources generating cheaper electricity in India.

Major fuel sources	1	2	3	4	5	6	Weight Rank
Coal	7 (42)	7 (35)	9 (36)	9 (27)	24 (48)	161 (161)	6 (349)
Natural Gas	12 (72)	9 (45)	108 (432)	29 (87)	58 (116)	1 (1)	3 (753)
Naptha	1 (6)	5 (25)	36 (144)	144 (432)	25 (50)	6 (6)	4 (663)
Nuclear	7 (42)	9 (45)	55 (220)	28 (84)	89 (178)	29 (29)	5 (598)
Renewable Energy	128 (768)	65 (325)	6 (24)	4 (12)	12 (24)	2 (2)	1 (1155)
Alternative Energy	63 (378)	123 (615)	6 (24)	2 (6)	8 (16)	15 (15)	2 (1054)

Table no.7.4 reveals about respondents opinion on major fuel sources generating cheaper electricity in India. It is to be noted that respondents gave 1st rank to renewable energy, 2nd rank to alternate energy, 3rd rank to natural gas, 4th rank to naptha, 5th rank to nuclear and 6th rank to coal. The above table concludes that renewable energy is the cheapest source of generating electricity and coal is the costliest source of generating electricity. In general renewable energy is the cheapest source of generating electricity and coal is the costliest. The respondent's opinion is also coinciding with the above fact.

The emerging power and energy mix is greatly influencing electricity pricing in the power sector, industrial consumers are the bulk consumers and cheaper electricity prices give them a breathe to survive under the complex mechanism of power market.

5. Investment in different resources for backup power.

Table no: 7.5. Respondent's perception on investment in different resources for backup power.

Backup Power Resources	Frequency	Percentage
Batteries	128	58.99
Diesel Generators	148	68.20
Captive Power	1	0.46
Any other source	29	13.36
None	63	29.03

Respondent's perception on investment in different resources for backup power is shown in table no.7.5. About 68.2 per cent of the respondents are using diesel generators, 59 per cent are using batteries for backup power. It is interesting to note that only 0.46 per cent of the respondents are using captive power because it requires huge amount of investment which is not affordable by most of the respondents. About 29 per cent of the respondents do not have any resources for backup power; this clearly shows that the respondents are poor and unable to afford investment in any resources. This per cent is identified in villages and remote areas where accessibility, availability and affordability of electricity are very poor. The table concludes that nearly one third of the respondents are without any backup power which affects their production and livelihood.

It is suggested to the government to expedite rural electrification and simultaneously strengthen light to medium industrialization, so that the villages are not solely left to agro industries and they too equally develop with potential for livelihood and better standards of living as that of urban and sub-urban.

6. Support of SEBs to industrial consumers in backup power.

Table no:7.6 Respondent's opinion on support of SEBs to industrial consumers in backup power.

		Opinion on support of SEBs to industrial consumers in backup power .				
		Very good	Good	Average	Below average	Total
District	Visakhapatnam	0	8	15	55	78
		.0%	10.3%	19.2%	70.5%	100.0%
	East Godavari	2	4	12	30	48
		4.2%	8.3%	25.0%	62.5%	100.0%
	West Godavari	1	6	10	23	40
		2.5%	15.0%	25.0%	57.5%	100.0%
	Krishna	1	3	12	35	51
		2.0%	5.9%	23.5%	68.6%	100.0%
Total		4	21	49	143	217
		1.8%	9.7%	22.6%	65.9%	100.0%

It is clear from the table no.7.6 that State Electricity Board in Andhra Pradesh is unable to provide backup power to industrial consumers. All the respondents of the four districts like Visakhapatnam (70.5%), Krishna (68.6%), East Godavari (62.5%) and West Godavari (57.5%) opined below average support from SEB. It may be concluded that the State Electricity Boards are not able to generate sufficient power to meet the demands of the industrial consumers.

This is very much in line with the fact that even today in the above districts the distribution power system is under the newly formed DISCOMs from unbundling of SEBs. The reforms and restructuring have only brought in structural changes of the vertically integrated SEBs rather than in efficiency of the power system and consumer support and services. The reforms were intended to benefit the industrial consumers but all are distant dreams as the above analysis with 65.9 per cent of industrial consumers from all the four districts very rightly opined below average.

It is suggested to the central and state governments along with private players to support the industrial consumers in backup power.

7. Industrial output losses because of inadequate power supply by the utilities.

Table no:7.7 Respondent's opinion on industrial output losses because of inadequate power supply by the utilities.

		Industrial output losses because of inadequate power supply by the utilities.					
		Substantial	Considerable	Marginal	No	No opinion	Total
District	Visakhapatnam	50	16	9	3	0	78
		64.1%	20.5%	11.5%	3.8%	.0%	100.0%
	East Godavari	36	6	3	2	1	48
		75.0%	12.5%	6.3%	4.2%	2.1%	100.0%
	West Godavari	27	8	4	1	0	40
		67.5%	20.0%	10.0%	2.5%	.0%	100.0%
	Krishna	36	7	7	1	0	51
		70.6%	13.7%	13.7%	2.0%	.0%	100.0%
Total		149	37	23	7	1	217
		68.7%	17.1%	10.6%	3.2%	.5%	100.0%

Table no. 7.7 gives the picture of industrial output losses because of inadequate power supply by the utilities. All the respondents of four districts 68.7 percent, in this regard East Godavari 75 per cent, Krishna 70.6 per cent, West Godavari 67.5 per cent and Visakhapatnam 64.1 per cent are facing substantial output losses because of inadequate power supply by the utilities. It may be concluded that power shortage affects the production of industries which leads to output losses and in turn affects the economy of the state. Not negligible 17.1 per cent industrial consumers considerably supporting the industrial output losses because of inadequate power supply by the utilities. On an overall nearly 85 per cent of the industrial consumers' opinion is that they are suffering from output losses. Due to the inadequate power supply the industrial consumers are unable to meet the satisfactory productivity ratio.

8. Impact of energy crisis in the last decade (2000-2010 years) on industrial growth in India.

Table no:7.8. Respondent's opinion on the impact of energy crisis in the last decade (2000-2010 years) on industrial growth in India.

| | | Impact of Energy Crisis in the last decade (2000-2010years) on industrial growth in India. | | | | |
		Major	Moderate	Minor	No opinion	Total
District	Visakhapatnam	60	14	4	0	78
		76.9%	17.9%	5.1%	.0%	100.0%
	East Godavari	33	9	5	1	48
		68.8%	18.8%	10.4%	2.1%	100.0%
	West Godavari	28	8	4	0	40
		70.0%	20.0%	10.0%	.0%	100.0%
	Krishna	41	7	3	0	51
		80.4%	13.7%	5.9%	.0%	100.0%
Total		162	38	16	1	217
		74.7%	17.5%	7.4%	.5%	100.0%

Table no.7.8 gives the respondents opinion on the impact of energy crisis in the last decade (2000-2010 year) on industrial growth in India. A majority of 74.7 per cent of the respondents in four districts revealed that energy crisis is major in the last decade. Among the districts Krishna district respondents (80.4%) are the highest in the major opinion, and East Godavari (68.8%) are the lowest in major opinion. The GDP of last decade was averagely growing at 6-7 per cent against the national target of 8-9 per cent; this is very much evident that energy crisis affected the industrial growth in India.

The analysis and conclusion of this table with an overall average of more than 92 per cent of industrial consumers are found supporting the impact of energy crisis both major and moderate is very much in concurrence with the conclusion of table no.7.7.

B. QUALITY

In India every year huge business turnover is being lost due to poor quality of power supply. Moreover consumers dissatisfaction over the voltage variation and damage of electrical equipments cannot be deferred. The policy makers are enforcing regular energy audits to improve the overall quality and reliability of the power system for industrial consumers. Industrial consumers are facing power holidays two to three days a week in many of the developed states in India. Under developing states hardly have average power supply of 8 to 12 hours per day. Some of the states are neither agriculturally sound nor industrially developed. The cyber cities to lantern (kerosene lamps) in villages reflect very clearly the effect of energy disparities in many states of India. Big and small industrial consumers are migrating to electrically developed regions creating unbalance in economic development. Financially weak are closing down. Industrial and agriculture growth both are declining and economic meltdown is seen as the greatest impact of energy crisis in India.

9. Improvement in quality of power by the distribution utilities after reforms.

Table no:7.9. Respondent's opinion on improvement in quality of power by the distribution utilities after reforms.

		Opinion on improvement in quality of power by the distribution utilities after reforms					
		Substantial	Considerable	Marginal	No	No opinion	Total
District	Visakhapatnam	2	20	8	48	0	78
		2.6%	25.6%	10.3%	61.5%	.0%	100.0%
	East Godavari	5	7	13	22	1	48
		10.4%	14.6%	27.1%	45.8%	2.1%	100.0%
	West Godavari	1	5	8	26	0	40
		2.5%	12.5%	20.0%	65.0%	.0%	100.0%
	Krishna	2	3	16	29	1	51
		3.9%	5.9%	31.4%	56.9%	2.0%	100.0%
Total		10	35	45	125	2	217
		4.6%	16.1%	20.7%	57.6%	.9%	100.0%

Respondent's opinion on improvement in quality of power by utilities after reforms is given in table no. 7.9. The majority respondents in West Godavari (65%), Visakhapatnam (61.5%), Krishna (56.9%) and East Godavari (45.8%) districts revealed that there is no improvement in quality of power distributed by the utilities even after the reforms. Only 10 respondents (4.6%) of the total sample revealed substantial, 35 respondents (16.1%) told considerable and 45 respondent's (20.7%) opined marginal improvement in the quality of power by the utilities after the reforms.

It may be concluded that the state utility is only focusing on supply and demand gap rather than improving the quality and reliability of power to industrial consumers.

10. Voltage variation at your terminal is within the statutory limit.

Table no: 7.10. Voltage variation at your terminal is within the statutory limit of the rated value.

		The voltage variation at your terminal is within the statutory limit of the rated value.					
		+5%	+10%	+15%	+20%	None	Total
District	Visakhapatnam	5	23	17	26	7	78
		6.4%	29.5%	21.8%	33.3%	9.0%	100.0%
	East Godavari	6	13	27	1	1	48
		12.5%	27.1%	56.3%	2.1%	2.1%	100.0%
	West Godavari	3	16	20	0	1	40
		7.5%	40.0%	50.0%	.0%	2.5%	100.0%
	Krishna	3	26	17	4	1	51
		5.9%	51.0%	33.3%	7.8%	2.0%	100.0%
Total		17	78	81	31	10	217
		7.8%	35.9%	37.3%	14.3%	4.6%	100.0%

It is evident from the table no. 7.10 that the majority of the respondents in four districts ranged between + 10 per cent to 20 per cent. Krishna district respondents 51 per cent revealed + 10 per cent voltage variation, where as 33.3 per cent of the respondents of Visakhapatnam district revealed + 20 per cent variation. It is to be noted that East Godavari 56.3 per cent and West Godavari 50 per cent respondents revealed + 15 % voltage variation within the statutory limit of the rated value.

It may be concluded that the rated voltage variation is because of the peak demand and variable load on the power system. It is suggested that proper maintenance, renovation, modernization and up gradation of the existing power system can minimize the voltage variation.

11. Recorded damage of electrical equipments.

Table no:7.11 Recorded damage of electrical equipments due to poor quality and unreliable power supply over the last six years.

Sr. No	Electrical Equipments	2006	2007	2008	2009	2010	2011
1	Heavy & light Motors	80	24	47	67	67	84
2	Transformers	19	79	32	86	72	27
3	HT & LT Panels	18	17	67	54	8	40
4	Feeders & distributors	16	46	33	60	81	14
5	Plant equipments	67	37	19	31	25	163

Year	2006	2007	2008	2009	2010	2011
Average Damage	40	40.6	39.6	59.6	50.6	65.6

r= 0.848, P-Value = 0.033

Frequency observation of damaged electrical equipments due to poor quality and unreliable power supply over the last six years is described in table no. 7.11. The frequency distribution of respondents (84) in the damage of heavy and light motors in the year 2011. Damage of transformers opined by (86) respondents for the year 2009. (67) respondents revealed that HT & LT panels damage was in the year 2008. In the year 2010, feeders and distributors damage was more recorded by (81) respondents. The highest majority of the respondents (163) revealed damage of plant and equipments in the year 2011.

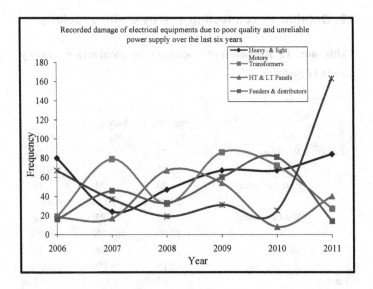

Recorded damage of electrical equipments due to poor quality and unreliable power supply over the last six years

The fluctuations from the graph reveal that the poor quality and unreliable power supply leads to the damage of industrial equipments. This not only affects the equipment but also production schedules and output targets. It is suggested that the power utilities should improve the quality and reliability of power supply which can reduce the damages of equipments and also avoid industrial production losses.

From the above P-value 0.033 it is concluded that there is significant increase in damages year by year. Further, there is a significant relation between year and average damage per year. Hence the hypothesis is rejected and both the variables are dependent to each other.

12. Opinion on conducting energy audits regularly.

Table no:7.12 Respondent's opinion on conducting energy audits regularly.

		Energy audits are regularly conducted.		
		Yes	No	Total
District	Visakhapatnam	23	55	78
		29.5%	70.5%	100.0%
	East Godavari	24	24	48
		50.0%	50.0%	100.0%
	West Godavari	13	27	40
		32.5%	67.5%	100.0%
	Krishna	23	28	51
		45.1%	54.9%	100.0%
Total		83	134	217
		38.2%	61.8%	100.0%

Chi-Sq = 6.753, P-Value = 0.080

Respondent's opinion on conducting energy audits regularly is illustrated in table no. 7.12. There are no regular energy audits as per the total sample respondents' 61.8 per cent. In this regard 70.5 per cent respondent are from Visakhapatnam district. The other district respondents like West Godavari (67.5%), Krishna (54.9%) and East Godavari (50%) revealed that no regular energy audits are conducted.

The above table concludes that because of the scarcity in human resource in the utilities and lack of sincerity among the employees the energy audits are not conducted regularly. It is suggested to the utilities to increase the human resource and enforce the energy audits regularly to improve the quality and overall performance of the power system.

As per the P-value 0.080 of chi-square test it is evident that there is no significant association between the district and conducting the energy audits regularly, which concludes that the opinion of the respondents are not changing as the district changes. Hence, the hypothesis is accepted and both the variables are independent to each other.

13. Loss of business turnover due to poor quality of power supply.

Table no:7.13 Respondent's opinion on lost business turnover due to poor quality of power supply in the year 2010.

		What percentage of expected business turnover was lost due to poor quality					Total
		Nil	0-5%	6-10%	11-15%	16-20%	
District	Visakhapatnam	6	7	5	6	54	78
		7.7%	9.0%	6.4%	7.7%	69.2%	100.0%
	East Godavari	3	3	3	11	28	48
		6.3%	6.3%	6.3%	22.9%	58.3%	100.0%
	West Godavari	2	4	4	5	25	40
		5.0%	10.0%	10.0%	12.5%	62.5%	100.0%
	Krishna	3	2	1	5	40	51
		5.9%	3.9%	2.0%	9.8%	78.4%	100.0%
Total		14	16	13	27	147	217
		6.5%	7.4%	6.0%	12.4%	67.7%	100.0%

A majority of 67.7 per cent of the four district respondents revealed that 16 to 20 per cent business turnover was lost due to poor quality of power supply. Next followed by 12.4 per cent for 11-15 %, 7.4 per cent recorded for 0-5 % business loss and 6 per cent of the total sample respondents revealed 6-10 % business loss. It is surprising to note that 14 (6.5%) respondents did not incur any business loss due to poor quality of power supply. In order to reduce the percentage of business loss it is suggested to improve the quality of power. (Table no: 7.13).

C. BILLING

Independent regulatory commissions were set up to optimize the tariff for industrial consumers but the prevailing situation is worsening. The rate of closing of small scale industries is increasing day by day as the government's actions are bearing no fruits. Sick industries are pleading for extra subsidies to sustain and survive. One of the major factors can rightly be the rise in rapid industrialization rate which is beyond the control of regulation. The attitude of some industrial consumers in not paying their bills timely due to higher tariffs and unwanted thefts were always a major concern for the utilities and authorities. In turn SEBs ended up with huge debts and became bankrupt. To excersie better control unbundling was initiated, however this has only marginalized the losses.

Due to high commercial and industrial tariffs, power shortage, unreliability, and quality concerns, many Indian corporations have set up their own on-site capacity generation capacity to ensure reliability of power supply. One World Bank study concluded that 76% of Indian businesses depend upon on-site primary or backup electricity generators. Captive generating capacity has grown faster than utility capacity in many cases and has provided an additional 15% to 20% of total capacity since the IPP program began in 1991. Diesel represents the most common fuel for captive power generation, although some larger facilities burn coal or gas. The captive power capacity estimates, already significantly high, exclude the use of countless unregulated smaller generation by DG sets (Diesel Generators or so-popularly called "gensets"), numbering in the hundred of thousand, that typically run off diesel.

14. Closing of small industries due to high tariff rates.

Table no:7.14. Respondent's opinion on closing of small industries due to high tariff rates.

		Many small industries are closing down because of higher tariff rates.			
		Yes	No	No opinion	Total
District	Visakhapatnam	72	4	2	78
		92.3%	5.1%	2.6%	100.0%
	East Godavari	40	2	6	48
		83.3%	4.2%	12.5%	100.0%
	West Godavari	33	1	6	40
		82.5%	2.5%	15.0%	100.0%
	Krishna	44	1	6	51
		86.3%	2.0%	11.8%	100.0%
Total		189	8	20	217
		87.1%	3.7%	9.2%	100.0%

Respondent's opinion on closing of small industries due to high tariff rates is placed in table no: 7.14. The data shows that about 189 respondents equaling to 87.1 per cent of the total sample respondents of four districts revealed that many small industries are closed because of higher tariff rates. District wise analysis revealed that a whopping majority of 92.3 per cent of the Visakhapatnam respondents opined that many small industries are closed because of higher tariff rates followed by Krishna 86.3 per cent, East Godavari 83.3 per cent and West Godavari 82.5 per cent respectively.

The table concludes that high tariff rates affect the cost of production and profit earnings. Moreover the small industries are unable to continue their production because of the feasibility in the cost of production. It is suggested to the government that subsidy may be given to the small and financially weak entrepreneurs.

15. Government initiation for survival of small scale private industries.

Table no:7.15 Whether the Government doing anything for survival of small scale private industries.

		If yes, is the govt. doing anything for survival of small scale industries			
		Yes	No	No opinion	Total
District	Visakhapatnam	2	68	2	72
		2.8%	94.4%	2.8%	100.0%
	East Godavari	0	39	1	40
		.0%	97.5%	2.5%	100.0%
	West Godavari	1	27	5	33
		3.0%	81.8%	15.2%	100.0%
	Krishna	0	41	3	44
		.0%	93.2%	6.8%	100.0%
Total		3	175	11	189
		1.6%	92.6%	5.8%	100.0%

Out of 189 respondents who opined that many small industries are closed because of higher tariff rates about 175 respondents (92.6%) gave negative opinion. District wise analysis reveals that except respondents from West Godavari district 81.8 per cent, the respondents from other districts Krishna, Visakhapatnam and East Godavari each above 93 per cent opined regarding the government's failure in doing anything for the survival of small scale industries. It is surprising to note that only 3 respondents (1.6%) out of the 189 opined that the government is taking necessary steps for the survival of the small scale industries.

It is concluded that the government is giving only assurance but not implementing the effective policies for the survival of the industries. It is suggested that it is high time for the government to take necessary steps to protect the small industries that are the backbone of the big industries which in turn would affect the economy of the state. (Table no: 7.15)

16. Introducing of subsidies to protect the survival of financially weak industries.

Table no:7.16 Respondent's opinion on introducing extra subsidies to protect the survival of financially weak industries.

| | | Opinion on introducing of subsidies to protect the survival of financially weak industries. | | | | | |
		0 - 10%	11% - 20%	21% - 30%	31% - 40%	above 40%	Total
District	Visakhapatnam	6	36	30	5	1	78
		7.7%	46.2%	38.5%	6.4%	1.3%	100.0%
	East Godavari	5	29	14	0	0	48
		10.4%	60.4%	29.2%	.0%	.0%	100.0%
	West Godavari	7	24	7	2	0	40
		17.5%	60.0%	17.5%	5.0%	.0%	100.0%
	Krishna	8	28	15	0	0	51
		15.7%	54.9%	29.4%	.0%	.0%	100.0%
Total		26	117	66	7	1	217
		12.0%	53.9%	30.4%	3.2%	.5%	100.0%

Industrial respondents of four districts (53.9%) are not greedy and they are only for basic survival because they revealed only 11 to 20 per cent of subsidies to protect the weak industries. This subsidy by no means is at higher end as compared to the free power given to the farmers. (Table no: 7.16)

The Industrial Policy Resolution of 1948, The Industries (Development & Regulation) Act, 1951 (IDRA), Industry

401

Policy Resolution 1956, The Monopolies & Restrictive Trade Practices Act 1969 (MRTPA), and The Foreign Exchange Regulation Act, 1973 (FERA) were to ensure that operation of the economic system did not lead to concentration of economic power in a few hands and thus industries were protected. Hence, it is suggested to the government to devise a suitable mechanism on subsidy for protecting the sick and financially weak industries.

17. Tariff rate applicable.

Table no: 7.17 Tariff rate applicable to the respondents.

		Which tariff rate is applicable to you.				
		Two Part	Three Part	Maximum demand	Others	Total
District	Visakhapatnam	59	10	5	4	78
		75.6%	12.8%	6.4%	5.1%	100.0%
	East Godavari	41	1	0	6	48
		85.4%	2.1%	.0%	12.5%	100.0%
	West Godavari	34	0	0	6	40
		85.0%	.0%	.0%	15.0%	100.0%
	Krishna	44	1	2	4	51
		86.3%	2.0%	3.9%	7.8%	100.0%
Total		178	12	7	20	217
		82.0%	5.5%	3.2%	9.2%	100.0%

Table no.7.17 gives the tariff rate applicable to the respondents. The majority respondents of Krishna 86.3 per cent, East Godavari 85.4 per cent, West Godavari 85.0 per cent and Visakhapatnam 75.6 per cent told two part tariff rate is applicable to them. The two part tariff rate helps the consumers to minimize their electricity bills and will not cross the maximum consumption limit. On the other types of tariff rates the consumers are at fear to pay more money on electricity consumption. On the other side there is a danger or disadvantage than when they consume less electricity and pay more money on electricity.

Energy Crisis in India

18. Opinion on the present tariff rates.

Table no :7.18 Respondent's opinion on the present tariff rates.

		Opinion on the present tariff rates.				
		Very high	High	Moderate	No opinion	Total
District	Visakhapatnam	53	14	9	2	78
		67.9%	17.9%	11.5%	2.6%	100.0%
	East Godavari	32	9	6	1	48
		66.7%	18.8%	12.5%	2.1%	100.0%
	West Godavari	27	6	7	0	40
		67.5%	15.0%	17.5%	.0%	100.0%
	Krishna	35	10	5	1	51
		68.6%	19.6%	9.8%	2.0%	100.0%
Total		147	39	27	4	217
		67.7%	18.0%	12.4%	1.8%	100.0%

Respondent's opinion on the present tariff rates is furnished in table no: 7.18. Very few respondents (27) opined moderate tariff rate, very high (147) and high (39) of the total sample respondents. District wise analysis revealed that all the respondents of four districts about 67.7 per cent opined very high tariff rates and about 18 per cent opined high tariff rates. It may be concluded that industrial consumers are over burdened on account of the present tariff rates.

In the present scenario the dissatisfaction of the industrial consumers should not be taken lightly by the government. There are Big Industrial (Corporate-Public and Private) consumers who are either State Government/Public sector undertakings or Central Government/Public sector undertakings are getting financial support from national plan outlays, whereas the Private Sector industrial consumers are not getting any support from government and are counting even a penny paid for the electricity consumed. And small industrial consumers are not getting

403

any support from anywhere and are not in a position to manage to survive and hence they are closing down.

II. POWER SYSTEM- PERFORMANCE AND MAINTENANCE

A. PERFORMANCE

Reforms were initiated to improve the power system performance in India because its impact was severely felt on the industrial and infrastructure growth over the last two decades. Many small and big industries are closing down due to poor electricity infrastructure. Industries are migrating to electrically developed regions. The distortions go further. Since the average price per kilowatt-hour is calculated dividing the revenue collected by the quantity sold to a given category of consumer, official statistics probably underestimate the average price paid by agriculture, maybe by half. Indeed, by hiding non-metered or/and non-billed consumption from other sectors into the electricity sold to the farm sectors, the average price is artificially deflated, and the actual amount of subsidies to the farm sector could be over-estimated. This is likely to blur the official appraisal of the amount of subsidies and their actual impact on consumption. The large cross-subsidies from industrial, commercial, and railway hauling to the domestic and agriculture sectors tend to atrophy the paid consumption of the industrial and commercial sectors.

Industry is subject to planned load-shedding, power cuts, voltage collapse and frequency variations, i.e. the high price paid by these customers is not compensated by good-quality supply. On the contrary, the poor quality of electricity service contributed to substantial industrial output losses. The primary effect of under pricing is to distort the overall energy market in favor of electricity. Households, farmers and others who benefit from underpriced electricity consume as much cheap electric power from the grid as possible, and account for the bulk of demand. When the cheap central supply fails, private sources have to make up for the supply gap. Customers who need electricity supply invest in resources such as batteries and diesel generators. In so doing, they cannot benefit from the economies of scale arising from the grid and use systems that are not necessary very efficient in producing electricity.

19. Purchase of bulk power from the utilities.

Table no: 7.19 Respondents purchasing bulk power from the utilities.

		Where from you purchase bulk power.			
		Central Utilities	State Utilities	Private Utilities	Total
District	Visakhapatnam	1 1.3%	75 96.2%	2 2.6%	78 100.0%
	East Godavari	0 .0%	48 100.0%	0 .0%	48 100.0%
	West Godavari	0 .0%	40 100.0%	0 .0%	40 100.0%
	Krishna	0 .0%	51 100.0%	0 .0%	51 100.0%
Total		1 .5%	214 98.6%	2 .9%	217 100.0%

Almost all respondents (214) are purchasing bulk power from the state utilities, except one respondent who belong to Visakhapatnam city purchasing power from the central utility (NTPC, Simhadri Power Plant) and two respondents purchasing from private utilities. These four districts solely depend upon the state utilities for supply of power as only one central sector utility is operating in Simhadri, Parwada mandal in Visakhapatnam district. The Researcher identified that the central generating utility (NTPC) at present allocates 70 per cent of power generated to the state transmission utility and nearly 30 per cent is exported to other states through the central transmission utility. (Table no.7.19)

It is suggested to the government that such locations which are so densely populated by industrial consumers medium and big with substantial power load and electrical energy consumption potential may be declared as "Industrial Power Zone" where any Power Utility from the state, central and private sector can directly sell to them based on their location and nearest power exporting transmission facilities to these zones under short term or long term agreements.

20. Utilities meeting the variable load demand.

Table no: 7.20 Respondent's opinion on utilities meeting the variable load demand.

		Do the utilities meet your variable load demand.				
		Completely	Partially	No	No opinion	Total
District	Visakhapatnam	21	11	45	1	78
		26.9%	14.1%	57.7%	1.3%	100.0%
	East Godavari	12	11	25	0	48
		25.0%	22.9%	52.1%	.0%	100.0%
	West Godavari	10	13	17	0	40
		25.0%	32.5%	42.5%	.0%	100.0%
	Krishna	5	17	28	1	51
		9.8%	33.3%	54.9%	2.0%	100.0%
Total		48	52	115	2	217
		22.1%	24.0%	53.0%	.9%	100.0%

Respondent's opinion on utilities meeting the variable load demand is reported in table no.7.20. Respondents of four districts (53%) opined negative opinion on utilities meeting variable load demand, in this regard Visakhapatnam 57.7 per cent, Krishna 54.9 per cent, East Godavari 52.1 per cent and West Godavari 42.5 per cent. It is interesting to note that 26.9 per cent of the respondents from Visakhapatnam district, 25 per cent each West Godavari, East Godavari and Krishna 9.8 per cent revealed that the utilities are meeting the variable load demand completely and some among the total sample respondents 52 (24%) opined for partial meeting of variable load.

About an average 77 per cent of the industrial consumers concluded that the utilities are not meeting their variable load demand, including the respondents who opined partially. Sometimes the industrial requirements like putting standby manufacturing line in operation, extended hour of working of machines, additional units running, commissioning of plant, other such activities being taken up simultaneously at many manufacturing centre or process plants creates the requirement for variable load other than the daily load consumption. This varies with the nature of industrial consumers small, medium and big depending upon the type of industry like textile, chemical, steel, automobile, manufacturing etc. It may be concluded that depending upon the location, capacity and type of industries, the utilities are accordingly able to meet the variable load demand.

21. Shut downing the plant because of power shortage in the year 2010.

Table no:7.21 Respondent's opinion on shutting down the plant because of power shortage in the year 2010.

		Did you shut down your plant because of power shortage in the year 2010.				
		Completely	Partially	Under rated production	No opinion	Total
District	Visakhapatnam	15	23	32	8	78
		19.2%	29.5%	41.0%	10.3%	100.0%
	East Godavari	12	10	20	6	48
		25.0%	20.8%	41.7%	12.5%	100.0%
	West Godavari	0	12	19	9	40
		.0%	30.0%	47.5%	22.5%	100.0%
	Krishna	9	15	22	5	51
		17.6%	29.4%	43.1%	9.8%	100.0%
Total		36	60	93	28	217
		16.6%	27.6%	42.9%	12.9%	100.0%

Table no: 7.21 gives the picture of shut downing the plant because of power shortage in the year 2010. The data reveals that from the total sample respondents of four districts 93 respondents told under rated production, 60 respondents opined partial production, 36 respondents completely shut downed the production and 28 respondents opined no opinion.

It can be concluded from the table that on an average unappreciable 42.9 per cent of the industrial consumers are operating their plant /manufacturing unit at under rated production. On other hand on account of Power Holiday the production is also being affected. The state utilities are unable to give power throughout the week as such it is affecting the productivity and in turn industrial growth. It is suggested that the centre and state governments should enhance their power capacity in order to meet day to day electricity consumption demand of the industrial consumers.

22. Migration of industries near to electrically developed region.

Table no:7.22 Respondent's opinion on migration of industries near to electrically developed region.

Migration of Industries	1	2	3	4	Weight Rank
Power supply restrictions	29 (116)	24 (72)	90 (180)	74 (74)	4 (442)
No cooperation by the local utilities	28 (112)	99 (297)	73 (146)	17 (17)	2 (572)
Limitation in self-generation/captive power	111 (444)	52 (156)	42 (84)	12 (12)	1 (696)
Regular load shedding	49 (196)	42 (126)	12 (24)	114 (114)	3 (460)

Respondent's opinions on migration of industries near to electrically developed region are revealed in table no.7.22. Respondents were asked to rank the reasons for migrating of industries near to electrically developed regions. To find out the weights of the reasons, Likert's four point scale was used and weighted scores were computed to study in depth of the reasons. In the four point scale the first rank was given 4 weights, second rank was given 3 weights, third rank was given 2 weights and fourth rank is given one weight. 1st rank is given to the reason limitation in self generation or captive power, 2nd rank to no cooperation by local utilities, 3rd rank to regular load shedding and 4th rank to power supply restrictions.

Medium and small scale industries have limitation to set up their captive power. In addition to it no cooperation by the local utilities and regular load shedding are the other factors hampering their daily production and business. Moreover the recent Power Holidays (2-3 days in a week, at present over two years) enforcement by the government in many districts of Andhra Pradesh has worsened the life of medium and small scale industries.

The Researcher observed that Visakhapatnam (Industrial City), Krishna District and East Godavari District (Kakinada-Coastal Industrial Town) are facing severe problem of migration of industries. The Power Holidays in Visakhapatnam has affected the industrial consumers very badly. Big industrial consumers like Hindustan Petroleum Corporation Limited (HPCL), Refinery and Petrochemical Plant, Rashtriya Ispat Nizam Limited (RINL), Visakhapatnam Steel Plant, Bharat Heavy and Pressure Vessels Limited (BHPV, now a subsidiary of BHEL) are all Central Public Sector Undertakings with Navaratna Status, in Visakhapatnam District covered under this study are facing power problem and some of them are surviving meeting their supplementary needs of power from captive power. Presently the RINL Visakhapatnam Steel Plant is expanding its Captive Power capacity to meet the rising demand in the plant. Many small scale industries are closed, some are at the verge of closing, few are existing with no production and many are migrating to the electrically developed regions.

It is suggested to the Government of Andhra Pradesh to immediately remove the Power Holidays, so that the industrial consumers can breathe freely without the power supply restrictions. Migrating of industries is not a good sign for the stability of economic growth in the state.

23. Opinion on state utilities service prior to reforms and restructuring.

Table no:7.23 Respondent's opinion on state utilities service prior to reforms and restructuring.

		How was the service of State utilities prior to reforms and restructuring.			
		Good	Average	Below average	Total
District	Visakhapatnam	8	28	42	78
		10.3%	35.9%	53.8%	100.0%
	East Godavari	7	27	14	48
		14.6%	56.3%	29.2%	100.0%
	West Godavari	9	21	10	40
		22.5%	52.5%	25.0%	100.0%
	Krishna	8	23	20	51
		15.7%	45.1%	39.2%	100.0%
Total		32	99	86	217
		14.7%	45.6%	39.6%	100.0%

Chi-Sq = 13.418, P-Value = 0.037

Respondent's opinion on state utilities service prior to reforms and restructuring is shown in table no. 7.23. About 185 respondents opined average (99) and below average (86) service of the state utilities prior to reforms and restructuring. Only 32 respondents gave good opinion on the service of state utilities.

As from Chi-square value 13.418 and corresponding P-value 0.037 it is evident that the opinion of the respondents on service of the state utilities prior to reforms and restructuring are changing by district. There is a significant impact on the above statement due to the district. Hence the hypothesis is rejected and the variables are dependent to each other.

B. MAINTENANCE

Power system performance and efficiency is directly based on the power maintenance of power lines, equipments and sub-stations. Industrial output losses due to repairs, replacements, shutdowns, breakdowns and failure of power equipments are serious concerns of the industrial consumers. The reformation process is very slow making the maintenance department unhealthier day by day. Power utilities are falling far behind the expectations in maintaining the power system. The industrial consumers are generally HT category type and need extra protection for high voltage energy equipments installed either outside or inside the industry premises. The maintenance of power equipments in the post restructuring period has remained as it is due to which uncontrollable regulation of extra high voltage causes unwanted severe damages to industrial equipments. The industrial electrical equipments like heavy motors, pumps, compressors, EOT cranes, heavy engines, auxiliary power current, station and unit transformers of huge capacity, generators, blowers, ID & FD fans, heavy duty presses, lathes, CNC Machines, robotics, control rooms, PLC circuits, automation system, emergency system, material handling system, conveyors ...and so on etc, requires long period for repairs and replacement with high financial implications.

The impact of maintenance is very serious and huge financial losses are being borne every year continuously over years by the industrial consumers. The state utilities have been banking on the industrial consumers for sell of bulk power to them and as greater percentage of consistent revenue earnings base. The industrial consumers in the state are losing their faith as the things are not being resolved and more complications are breeding in with no alternatives just left to fate and time.

24. Maintenance of power equipments in the post restructuring period.

Table no:7.24 Respondent's opinion on the maintenance of power equipments in the post restructuring period.

		Maintenance of power equipments in the post restructuring period.				
		Improved	Satisfactory	As it is	None	Total
District	Visakhapatnam	4	17	57	0	78
		5.1%	21.8%	73.1%	.0%	100.0%
	East Godavari	0	7	41	0	48
		.0%	14.6%	85.4%	.0%	100.0%
	West Godavari	0	9	31	0	40
		.0%	22.5%	77.5%	.0%	100.0%
	Krishna	0	9	40	2	51
		.0%	17.6%	78.4%	3.9%	100.0%
Total		4	42	169	2	217
		1.8%	19.4%	77.9%	.9%	100.0%

An attempt is made in table no.7.24 to know the respondents opinion on the maintenance of power equipments in the post restructuring period. Majority of 77.9 per cent of the sample respondents revealed that there is no improvement in maintenance of power equipment in the post restructuring period. In this regard district wise analysis revealed that East Godavari 85.4 per cent, Krishna 78.4 per cent, West Godavari 77.5 per cent and Visakhapatnam 73.1 per cent. Though the Indian government initiated the reforms and restructuring process much more is to be done regarding the improvement in the maintenance of power equipments to make the power system healthy.

25. Protection with additional provisions for use of energy at extra high voltage.

Table no:7.25 Respondent's opinion on protection with additional provisions for use of energy at high and extra high voltage.

		Are you protected with additional provisions for use of energy at high voltage.		
		Yes	No	Total
District	Visakhapatnam	22	56	78
		28.2%	71.8%	100.0%
	East Godavari	9	39	48
		18.8%	81.3%	100.0%
	West Godavari	6	34	40
		15.0%	85.0%	100.0%
	Krishna	15	36	51
		29.4%	70.6%	100.0%
Total		52	165	217
		24.0%	76.0%	100.0%

Chi-Sq = 4.081, P-Value = 0.253

Protection of respondents against high and extra high voltage by the utilities is noted in the table no. 7.25. About 165 of total respondents equaling to 76 per cent revealed that they are not protected against high and extra high voltage by the distribution utilities. 52 respondents of the total sample equaling to 24 per cent opined that protection is given by the utilities for high and extra high voltage. Due to the high and extra high voltage problem there is a chance of damaging the industrial equipments, so it is suggested to the government to take appropriate steps in ensuring regular voltage and the safety of the electrical equipment to protect the industrial consumers.

As per the Chi-square analysis for the statement "Protection with additional provision for use of energy at high and extra high voltage by the utilities" there is no significant association between the said statement and district i.e., the opinion of these four districts are almost similar towards the protection with additional provisions and the response is negative. Hence the hypothesis is accepted and both the variables are independent to each other.

26. Condition of all the power equipments installed in the premises.

Table no:7.26 Respondent's perception on the condition of all the power equipments installed in the premises.

Sr. No	Power Equipments	Well maintained	Maintained	Not properly maintained	Not maintained	No opinion
1	Transformers	16.6	14.7	24.9	43.8	
2	EHV apparatus	15.7	11.1	27.2	45.6	0.5
3	Supply cables & lines	12	7.8	20.7	59.4	
4	Energy Meters	9.7	14.7	10.1	65.4	
5	Line Poles	7.8	11.1	11.1	70	
	Average Percentage	12.36	11.88	18.80	56.85	0.10

District	N	Mean	S.D	F-Value	P-value	Decision
Krishna	51	0.20	1.34	0.156	0.926	N.S
Visakhapatnam	78	0.27	1.42			
West Godavari	40	0.11	1.50			
East Godavari	48	0.28	1.38			

Respondent's perception on the condition of all the power equipments installed in the premises is described in table no.7.26. As per the table 56.85 per cent of the respondents from these four districts have said that the power equipments are not well maintained, 18.80 per cent opined not properly maintained, 12.36 per cent respondents revealed well maintained and 11.88 per cent of them opined maintained.

The above table explains the average scores and standard deviations of all the four districts of the respondents on the statement the condition of all the power equipments installed in the premises. Further, the P-value 0.926 of the ANOVA test concludes that there is no significant opinion difference between the four districts and all the districts score are very low. Hence the hypothesis is accepted and the variables are independent to each other.

27. Problem of shortage of electrical materials during repair and replacement.

Table no:7.27 Respondent's opinion on problem of shortage of electrical materials during repair and replacement in recent times.

		Did you ever face problem because of shortage of electrical materials during repair and replacement in recent times.		Total
		Yes	No	Total
District	Visakhapatnam	59	19	78
		75.6%	24.4%	100.0%
	East Godavari	38	10	48
		79.2%	20.8%	100.0%
	West Godavari	32	8	40
		80.0%	20.0%	100.0%
	Krishna	41	10	51
		80.4%	19.6%	100.0%
Total		170	47	217
		78.3%	21.7%	100.0%

Chi-Sq = 0.546, P-Value = 0.909

Respondent's opinion on problem of shortage of electrical materials during repair and replacement in recent times is given in table no.7.27. Vast majority of 78.3 per cent of the total sample respondents opined shortage of electrical materials during repair and replacement time. In this regard the district wise analysis revealed Krishna 80.4 per cent, West Godavari 80 per cent, East Godavari 79.2 per cent and Visakhapatnam 76.5 per cent. The table concludes that there is huge shortage of electrical materials with the utilities. It is suggested that the utilities can maintain an optimum inventory of electrical materials so that the consumers are not affected at the time of repair and replacement.

The Chi-square test value 0.546 and P-value 0.909 are found to be insignificant at 5 % level of significance. Hence the hypothesis is accepted and both the variables are independent to each other. The Chi-square test concludes that there is no significant impact on the statement "Did you ever face problem because of shortage of electrical materials during repair and replacement in recent times" by the district i.e., the opinion of the respondents on the said statement is not significant by district.

28. Frequency of periodic maintenance of industries by the utilities.

Table no:7.28 Respondents opinion on frequency of periodic maintenance of industries by the utilities.

		Frequency of periodic maintenance of industries by the utilities.				
		Once in two months	Once in three months	Once in four months	Above four months	Total
District	Visakhapatnam	3	13	4	58	78
		3.8%	16.7%	5.1%	74.4%	100.0%
	East Godavari	2	0	15	31	48
		4.2%	.0%	31.3%	64.6%	100.0%
	West Godavari	0	0	12	28	40
		.0%	.0%	30.0%	70.0%	100.0%
	Krishna	0	3	13	35	51
		.0%	5.9%	25.5%	68.6%	100.0%
Total		5	16	44	152	217
		2.3%	7.4%	20.3%	70.0%	100.0%

Frequency of periodic maintenance of industries by the utilities is presented in table no. 7.28. About 152 total sample respondents equaling to 70 per cent opined that maintenance of industries by the utilities is done above four months and 44 respondents (20.3%) of total sample revealed once in four months. Least number of respondents i.e. 5 revealed that maintenance is done once in two months. It is suggested to the utilities that maintenance should be done once in three months so that there will be less damage of equipments and minimization of voltage fluctuations. The periodic maintenance of the electrical power equipments by the utilities can enhance the overall efficiency of the power system.

29. Reasons that disturbs production.

Table no:7.29 Respondent's perception on the reasons that disturb the production.

Sr. No	Power Disturbances	Major	Moderate	Minor	No opinion
1	Testing and tripping	18.4	18	62.2	1.4
2	Maintenance Works	19.8	32.3	47	0.9
3	Repairs of equipments, cables and supply lines.	26.3	48.4	25.3	
4	Replacement of equipments	25.8	51.2	23	
5	Repair and extension of line poles	24.9	50.2	24.4	0.5
6	Failure of installed electrical equipments	10.1	36.9	46.5	6.5
7	Disconnections and reconnections	3.7	27.6	59.9	8.8
8	GRID disturbances	1.8	8.8	76.5	12.9

District	N	Mean	S.D	F-Value	P-value	Decision
Krishna	51	1.5637	0.51196	1.9	0.131	N.S
Vishakhapatnam	78	1.7516	0.57565			
West Godavari	40	1.5594	0.60579			
East Godavari	48	1.5625	0.54881			

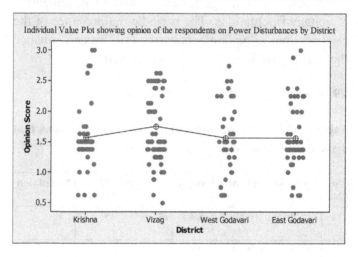

Individual Value Plot showing opinion of the respondents on Power Disturbances by District

Table no.7.29 presents respondents perception on the reasons that disturbs the production. The major and moderate reasons are repairs of equipments, cables & supply lines, replacement of equipments and repair and extension of line poles. Regarding minor reasons are testing and tripping, maintenance work, failure of installed electrical equipments, disconnections and reconnections and GRID disturbances.

The above P-value 0.131 depicts that there is no significant difference in the opinion of the respondents on reasons that disturbs the production of the four districts. The average opinion score of the respondents from Visakhapatnam district is greater than the remaining districts and the remaining three districts opinion is very much nearer to each other, which suggests that Visakhapatnam district has the huge power disturbances when compared with the other districts. The individual plot above shows the same thing.

30. Frequency of electrical inspector visit to the unit.

Table no:7.30 Frequency of electrical inspector visit to the unit in the year 2010.

		Frequency of the electrical inspector visit to your unit in the year 2010.			
		Not even once	One time	Two times	Total
District	Visakhapatnam	52	14	12	78
		66.7%	17.9%	15.4%	100.0%
	East Godavari	28	13	7	48
		58.3%	27.1%	14.6%	100.0%
	West Godavari	22	14	4	40
		55.0%	35.0%	10.0%	100.0%
	Krishna	26	20	5	51
		51.0%	39.2%	9.8%	100.0%
Total		128	61	28	217
		59.0%	28.1%	12.9%	100.0%

Chi-Sq = 8.360, P-Value = 0.213

Frequency of electrical inspector visit to the unit in the year 2010 is illustrated in table no. 7.30. About 59 per cent of the total sample respondents revealed that electrical inspector not even once visited the unit. In this regard district wise analysis varies between 51 per cent Krishna and 66.7 per cent Visakhapatnam. One time and two times visit by the electrical inspector is 28.1 per cent and 12.9 per cent respectively. It may be concluded from the above table that because of lack of manpower, carelessness towards responsibility and sitting in office and completing the work without field work may be the causes for the inspector not visiting the units.

The Chi-square value 8.360 and P-value 0.213 are found to be insignificant at 5 % level of significance, for the statement "How many times the electrical inspector visited your unit in the year 2010". Majority of the four districts respondents have opined that the inspector visited their unit in the year 2010 is not even once. Further, it is statistically evident that the difference is not significant. Hence the hypothesis is accepted and both the variables are independent to each other.

31. Installation of standby power equipments to avoid production loss.

Table no:7.31 Respondent's opinion on standby power equipments installed to avoid loss of production in case of failure of the main power system.

		Do you have standby power equipments installed to avoid loss of production in case		Total
		Yes	No	
District	Visakhapatnam	6	72	78
		7.7%	92.3%	100.0%
	East Godavari	0	48	48
		.0%	100.0%	100.0%
	West Godavari	0	40	40
		.0%	100.0%	100.0%
	Krishna	0	51	51
		.0%	100.0%	100.0%
Total		6	211	217
		2.8%	97.2%	100.0%

Energy Crisis in India

Respondent's opinion on standby equipments installed to avoid loss of production in case of failure of main power system is depicted in table no: 7.31. A whopping majority of 97.2 per cent of the total sample respondents are not having standby power equipments to avoid loss of production. In this regard district wise analysis revealed that cent per cent each of East Godavari, West Godavari and Krishna and 92.3 per cent Visakhapatnam districts respondents opined the same.

It is very difficult to have standby equipments parallel to the main power system to avoid loss of production by the industrial consumers. It may be suggested that those industrial consumers who can afford to have standby equipments may go for it to avoid production loss.

32. Opinion on the healthiness of maintenance department of the utility.

Table no:7.32 Respondent's opinion on the healthiness of maintenance department of the utility.

		How healthy is the maintenance department of the utility					
		Very healthy	Healthy	Marginal	Very Sick	Sick	Total
District	Visakhapatnam	1	10	16	48	3	78
		1.3%	12.8%	20.5%	61.5%	3.8%	100.0%
	East Godavari	0	5	7	31	5	48
		.0%	10.4%	14.6%	64.6%	10.4%	100.0%
	West Godavari	0	4	9	23	4	40
		.0%	10.0%	22.5%	57.5%	10.0%	100.0%
	Krishna	0	4	10	29	8	51
		.0%	7.8%	19.6%	56.9%	15.7%	100.0%
Total		1	23	42	131	20	217
		.5%	10.6%	19.4%	60.4%	9.2%	100.0%

Respondent's opinion on the healthiness of maintenance department of the utility is furnished in table no 7.32. About 60.4 per cent of the total sample respondents told that maintenance department of the utility is very sick,

423

marginal 19.4 per cent, healthy 10.6 per cent, sick 9.2 per cent and very healthy 5 per cent. The table concludes that maintenance department is the backbone of the utility, any disturbance in its operation due to maintenance will affect the entire chain of electricity supply, so utmost care should be taken to maintain the maintenance department.

III. CONSUMER SATISFACTION-SERVICES AND PROBLEMS

A. SERVICES

The energy crisis in India has opened other avenues like diesel power generation, captive power and merchant power for industrial consumers. Unexpectedly the Open Access Policy did not succeed to cheer the industrial consumers. The reforms went undercapitalized bearing no considerable thrust on satisfying the needy industrial consumers. Accessibility and availability of reliable power supply is possible to industrial consumers only with adequate infrastructure facilities in electricity services. A healthy industrial power system operation much depends upon its periodic maintenance, up gradation and communication enabled integrated power system in the state. Heavy industries like manufacturing, automobile, equipments, ship building, process industry (oil& gas, refinery and petrochemicals), steel and mining, smelters.., etc which require bulk power throughout day and night be well protected against severe power cuts due to power crisis. Big industrial consumers need more attention as compared to domestic, commercial, and agricultural consumers. Heavy Industries in the Big Industrial Consumer category are the prime movers of the economy at state and centre.

The distribution utilities need to have more number of Customer Relation Manager (CRMs) to take up the matter one to one for better coordination and services to the industrial consumers.

The Researcher was fortunate to have Visakhapatnam which enjoys the status of City of Destiny in the State to be one of the districts in the sample study, because of its National and Asian recognition as the Industrial City of importance. The sample study could cover all Big Industrial Consumers category from the State, Central and Private Sector similar to the coverage of the utilities from all the sectors.

33. Big industrial consumers turning to captive power.

Table no: 7.33 Big industrial consumers turning to captive power.

		Big industrial consumers are turning to Captive Power.				
		Higher electricity prices	Unreliable supply from network	Become self reliant	All	Total
District	Visakhapatnam	6	10	3	59	78
		7.7%	12.8%	3.8%	75.6%	100.0%
	East Godavari	0	0	6	42	48
		.0%	.0%	12.5%	87.5%	100.0%
	West Godavari	0	0	7	33	40
		.0%	.0%	17.5%	82.5%	100.0%
	Krishna	0	1	7	43	51
		.0%	2.0%	13.7%	84.3%	100.0%
Total		6	11	23	177	217
		2.8%	5.1%	10.6%	81.6%	100.0%

Table no. 7.33 denotes big industrial consumers turning to captive power. Whopping majority of 81.6 per cent of the total sample respondents opined that higher electricity prices, unreliable supply of network, becoming self reliant are the factors contributing for big industrial consumers turning to captive power. The district wise data reveals that East Godavari district respondents (87.5%), Krishna (84.3%), West Godavari (82.5%) and Visakhapatnam (75.6%) of the sample respondents told all the above factors made big industrial consumers turning to captive power. A negligible percentage of 2.8 of the total sample respondents opined higher electricity prices is the reason for big industrial consumers turning to captive power. The table concludes that all the factors are responsible for Big Industrial consumers turning to captive power.

34. Benefits derived from Open Access Policy.

Table no: 7.34 Respondent's perception on the benefits derived from Open Access Policy.

| | | Benefits derived from the Open Access Policy. | | | | | |
		Substantial	Considerable	Marginal	No	No opinion	Total
District	Visakhapatnam	1	1	3	49	24	78
		1.3%	1.3%	3.8%	62.8%	30.8%	100.0%
	East Godavari	4	2	4	23	15	48
		8.3%	4.2%	8.3%	47.9%	31.3%	100.0%
	West Godavari	3	1	5	21	10	40
		7.5%	2.5%	12.5%	52.5%	25.0%	100.0%
	Krishna	2	2	2	2	1	5
		3.9%	3.9%	3.9%	51.0%	37.3%	100.0%
Total		1	6	1	11	6	21
		4.6%	2.8%	6.5%	54.8%	31.3%	100.0%

Respondents perception on the benefits derived from Open Access Policy is given in table no.7.34. Considerable number of the total sample respondents told no (54.8%) and no opinion (31.3%) on the Open Access Policy. Very meager percentage is attributed to the opinions of substantial (4.6%), considerable (2.8%), and marginal (6.5%). It may be concluded that the Open Access Policy is failure in the opinion of the respondents. It is suggested that Open Access Policy should be modified and ensure to benefit the industrial consumers to meet their requirements.

35. Open Access Policy not been successful despite the Electricity Act reforms

Table no:7.35 Open Access Policy not been successful despite the Electricity Act reforms and enabling regulations in the State.

		Why has open access not been successful despite the Electricity Act reforms and enabling regulations in your state.					
		Limited awareness on Open Access to consumers	Limited information on alternate sourcing of power	Fear of discrimination on switching on to various suppliers	All	No opinion	Total
District	Visakhapatnam	23	1	5	41	8	78
		29.5%	1.3%	6.4%	52.6%	10.3%	100.0%
	East Godavari	0	0	9	20	19	48
		.0%	.0%	18.8%	41.7%	39.6%	100.0%
	West Godavari	1	0	7	18	14	40
		2.5%	.0%	17.5%	45.0%	35.0%	100.0%
	Krishna	0	0	5	23	23	51
		.0%	.0%	9.8%	45.1%	45.1%	100.0%
Total		24	1	26	102	64	217
		11.1%	.5%	12.0%	47.0%	29.5%	100.0%

Table no.7.35 presents about Open Access Policy not being successful despite the Electricity Act reforms and enabling regulations in the state. Very few respondents responded to limited awareness on Open Access Policy to consumers (11.1%), limited information on alternate source of power (0.5%), fear of discrimination on switching on to various suppliers (12%) of the total sample. About 47 per cent and 29.5 per cent attributed to all and no opinion. The table concludes that customer awareness on Open Access Policy is limited, lack of information on alternate sourcing of power and fear of discrimination made the Open Access Policy failure.

36. Essential factors for providing industrial growth by the utilities.

Table no: 7.36 Essential factors for providing industrial growth by the utilities.

Power Utilities support to Industrial Growth	1	2	3	4	5	Weighted rank
Adequate infrastructure facilities in electricity services	27 (135)	6 (24)	80 (240)	62 (124)	42 (42)	4 (565)
Accessibility and availability of reliable power supply	8 (40)	91 (364)	64 (192)	41 (82)	13 (13)	2 (691)
States to promote investors	123 (615)	57 (228)	20 (60)	11 (22)	6 (6)	1 (931)
Electricity reforms to be capitalized	60 (300)	43 (172)	13 (39)	73 (146)	28 (28)	3 (685)
Central utilities has to support state industries	6 (30)	22 (88)	59 (177)	7 (14)	123 (123)	5 (432)

Regarding the essential factors contributing for industrial growth by the utilities 1st rank is given to States to promote investors, 2nd rank to accessibility and availability of reliable power supply, 3rd rank to electricity reform to be capitalized, 4th rank to inadequate infrastructure facilities in electricity services and the last rank is given to central utilities support to state industries. It can be concluded that the central and state utilities are unable to invest money in developing the electricity sector and hence encouraging the private investors into the sector. In the opinion of the respondents the central utilities support to state industries is very meager. (Table no:7.36).

Energy Crisis in India

37. Reasons for delay in new connection.

Table no: 7.37 Respondent's opinion on reasons for delay in new connection.

Sr. No	Delay in new connection	Major	Moderate	Minor	No opinion
1	Installation of transformers	51.2	23.5	20.3	5.1
2	Setting up of sub stations	58.5	14.7	19.8	6.9
3	Installation of line poles	53.5	22.1	15.7	8.8
4	Feeder assembly	57.1	31.8	8.3	2.8
5	Processing of request for new connection	83.4	13.4	1.4	1.8

District	N	Mean	S.D	F-Value	P-value	Decision
Krishna	51	2.47	.62	2.44	0.065	N.S
Visakhapatnam	78	2.22	.62			
West Godavari	40	2.49	.68			
East Godavari	48	2.44	.63			

Respondents' opinion on reasons for delay in new connections is illustrated in table no. 7.37. In the opinion of most of the respondents major reason is delay in processing of new connection (83.4%). The other major reasons are setting up of substations (58.5%), feeder assembly (57.1%), installation of line poles (53.5%) and installation of transformers (51.2%).

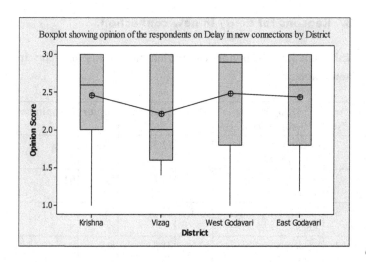

The Box plot opinion of the respondents revealed that the districts like Krishna, West Godavari and East Godavari are more or less same in delay of new connections where as Visakhapatnam district is little better in processing the new connections. It is suggested that the state utilities should take appropriate steps to minimize the processing process of new connections in order to benefit the industrial consumers from the delay in new connection.

The ANOVA Test divulges that there is no significant difference in the opinion of the respondents from the four districts, is almost similar and it is also not statistically significant at 5% level. Hence the hypothesis is accepted and the both variables like districts and reasons for delay in new connections are independent to each other. Further the average opinion score of the West Godavari (2.49) is little bit greater than the remaining three districts which suggest that West Godavari district has little bit greater delay in new connection when compared with the remaining three districts. The above box plot also explains the same; in Visakhapatnam district the score is low which concludes that the delay is low.

38. Big industrial consumers becoming 100 per cent free to select their electricity suppliers.

Table no:7.38 Respondent's opinion on big industrial consumers becoming 100 per cent free to select their electricity suppliers.

		When will big industrial consumers become 100% free to select their electricity suppliers.						Total
		By 2012	2015	2020	2025	2030	No opinion	
District	Visakhapatnam	22	15	7	4	25	5	78
		28.2%	19.2%	9.0%	5.1%	32.1%	6.4%	100.0%
	East Godavari	0	5	2	11	8	22	48
		.0%	10.4%	4.2%	22.9%	16.7%	45.8%	100.0%
	West Godavari	0	6	3	9	5	17	40
		.0%	15.0%	7.5%	22.5%	12.5%	42.5%	100.0%
	Krishna	0	4	3	8	9	27	51
		.0%	7.8%	5.9%	15.7%	17.6%	52.9%	100.0%
Total		22	30	15	32	47	71	217
		10.1%	13.8%	6.9%	14.7%	21.7%	32.7%	100.0%

Respondent's opinion on big industrial consumers becoming 100 per cent free to select their electricity suppliers is given in table no. 7.38. Considerable number of total sample respondents 71 told no opinion, 47 and 32 respondents revealed for the vision 2030 and 2025 year respectively. The district wise analysis reveals that Visakhapatnam district vision is 2030, whereas East Godavari, West Godavari and Krishna districts a majority of the respondents opined no opinion in this regard. The above table concludes that utilities and consumers are the dominant players of the emerging electricity market where the regulation do not want to lose its control over them, which is delaying the customer to select their electricity suppliers. The cold war between the market and regulation is affecting the big industrial consumers.

B. PROBLEMS

The IPPs experience in India since its inception till date is not a success story. Industrial consumers are hoping to benefit from the emerging power mix, developing market and new electricity infrastructure. Moreover many of the States in India have enforced power holidays to manage the power shortage problems. Industrial consumers are burdened with unsubsidized tariffs. The performance of the industrial sector over the last six years has drastically fallen. The establishment of captive power by small scale and medium category industrial consumers is beyond their scope. With great pain somehow they manage with DG sets for short duration power cuts as emergency backup to support uninterrupted production down time. But for days together due to Power Holidays and restricted power supply the situation in the recent years are not favoring the survival of such consumers. They are downsizing and small industries are closing down. Few of them have migrated to more electrically developed regions in other states.

Industrially populated cities or towns should be given priorities by the state government and districts to arrange proper power supply to these consumers and support them during emergency of blackouts and unplanned load shedding. Big industrial consumers with consumption capacity more than 1 MW were supposed to benefit from the existing recently enacted electricity reforms Act, its amendments and new Tariff Policy, Power Policy, Point of Connection. etc.

The power shortage is more alarming for cities or towns which are equally densely populated with domestic, commercial, industrial, agricultural and public consumers. The government and policy makers need to brainstorm and review the developing and developed nation's success story where big and small industries are flourishing in Asia, Europe and America.

39. Players domination in emerging Power Mix in India.

Table no:7.39 Respondent's opinion on players domination in emerging Power Mix in India.

Sr. No	Power Mix Players	Major	Moderate	Minor	No opinion
1	Utilities	43.8	38.2	12.4	5.5
2	Consumers	80.2	10.1	8.3	1.4
3	Regulators	39.2	13.8	43.3	3.7
4	Market	87.1	8.8	2.8	1.4
5	Investors	59.9	17.1	19.4	3.7

Descriptive Statistics

Power Mix Players	Mean	Std. Deviation
Utilities	2.20	.86356
Consumers	2.69	.68148
Regulators	1.88	.98159
Market	2.82	.53846
Investors	2.33	.91315

Respondent's opinion on players domination in emerging power mix in India is described in table no.7.39. The major dominators in power sector are market 87.1 per cent, consumers 80.2 per cent and investors 60 per cent.

It is observed that the role of regulation 39.2 per cent is diminishing.

As per the descriptive statistics the average value of the market 2.82 is greater than the remaining players so it may be concluded that the market dominates the emerging power mix in India followed by consumers 2.69 and investors 2.33.

40. Factors that hamper the business of industrial consumers.

Table no:7.40 Factors that hamper the business of industrial consumers.

Sr. No	Business Industrial Consumers	Major	Moderate	Minor	No opinion
1	Peak load demands	81.1	12.4	3.7	2.8
2	No prior information on long power cuts to reschedule production	79.3	18.9	1.8	
3	Interrupted power supply	59	24.9	13.8	2.3
4	Quality & reliability of power	73.7	23.5	2.8	
5	Services and timely support from the utilities	80.6	11.1	8.3	
6	Power Holidays	73.7	24.4	1.4	0.5
	Average Opinion Score	**74.5667**	**19.2**	**5.3**	**0.9333**

District	N	Mean	S.D	F-Value	P-value	Decision
Krishna	51	2.73	.33	2.718	0.046	S
Visakhapatnam	78	2.58	.42			
West Godavari	40	2.72	.38			
East Godavari	48	2.74	.35			

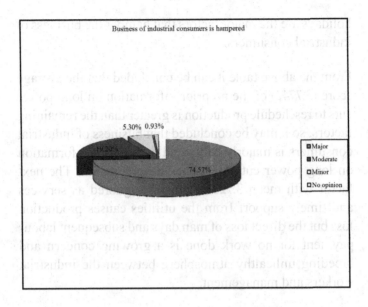

Descriptive Statistics

Business Industrial Consumers	Mean	Std. Deviation
Peak load demands	3.7189	.66615
No prior information on long power cuts to reschedule production	3.7742	.46116
Interrupted power supply	3.4055	.81170
Quality & reliability of power	3.7097	.51239
Services and timely support from the utilities	3.7235	.60633
Power Holidays	3.7143	.51047

Table no.7.40 denotes the factors that hamper the business of industrial consumers. Factors like peak load demands 81.1 per cent, services and timely support from the utilities 80.6 per cent, no prior information on long power cuts to reschedule production 79.3 per cent, an equal per cent of 73.7 per cent to quality and reliability of power and power holidays are the major factors that hamper the business of industrial consumers.

From the above table it can be concluded that the average score (3.7742) of the no prior information on long power cuts to reschedule production is greater than the remaining factors, so it may be concluded that business of industrial consumers is majorly hampered by no prior information on long power cuts to reschedule production. The next factor with mean 3.7235 cannot be ignored as services and timely support from the utilities causes production loss but the direct loss of man days and subsequent labour payment for no work done is a growing concern and breeding unhealthy atmosphere between the industrial workers and management.

It is suggested that the government has to give prior information for long power cuts so that the industrial consumers can reschedule their production. At present the frequency of power holidays are more, hence the government should try to minimize the power holidays.

The ANOVA Test F-value 2.718 and P-value 0.046 signifies that there is a statistically significant relation between the four districts and factors that hamper the business of industrial consumers. The average score of the Krishna district (2.73) and West Godavari (2.72) and East Godavari (2.74) district is very much nearer to each other.

41. Deregulation in electricity sector brings power efficiency.

Table no: 7.41 Respondent's opinion on deregulation in electricity sector brings power economic efficiency into the market.

		Deregulation in electricity sector bring power economic efficiency into the market.			
		Yes	No	No opinion	Total
District	Visakhapatnam	28	42	8	78
		35.9%	53.8%	10.3%	100.0%
	East Godavari	16	9	23	48
		33.3%	18.8%	47.9%	100.0%
	West Godavari	12	10	18	40
		30.0%	25.0%	45.0%	100.0%
	Krishna	11	17	23	51
		21.6%	33.3%	45.1%	100.0%
Total		67	78	72	217
		30.9%	35.9%	33.2%	100.0%

Chi-Sq = 33.866, P-Value = 0.000

Table no.7.41shows a mix opinion of the respondents on deregulation in electricity sector brings power economic efficiency into the market. The respondents of Visakhapatnam district 53.8 per cent of them told no, and 35.9 per cent told yes, Krishna 33.3 per cent for no, and 21.6 percent for yes, West Godavari 25 per cent for no and 30 per cent for yes, and East Godavari 18.8 per cent no, 33.3 per cent yes. It is to be noted that 72 total sample respondents equaling to 33.2 per cent did not give any opinion towards it.

The Chi-square value 33.866 and P-value 0.000 found that there is a statistically significant association between the statement "Deregulation in electricity sector bring power economic efficiency into the market" and the districts. As per the P-value 0.000 of the chi-square test it is statistically evident that as the respondents from district to district the opinion is different on the said statement.

42. Industrial consumers able to purchase electricity directly from the IPPs.

Table no: 7.42 Respondent's opinion on industrial consumers able to purchase electricity directly from the Independent Power Producers (IPPs).

		Will industrial consumers be able to purchase electricity directly from the Independent Power Producers(IPPs).			Total
		Yes	No	No opinion	
District	Visakhapatnam	28	46	4	78
		35.9%	59.0%	5.1%	100.0%
	East Godavari	10	13	25	48
		20.8%	27.1%	52.1%	100.0%
	West Godavari	8	16	16	40
		20.0%	40.0%	40.0%	100.0%
	Krishna	9	18	24	51
		17.6%	35.3%	47.1%	100.0%
Total		55	93	69	217
		25.3%	42.9%	31.8%	100.0%

Chi-Sq = 41.968, P-Value = 0.000

The table no.7.42 shows that about 162 of the total sample respondents have no and no opinion for industrial consumers able to purchase electricity from Independent Power Producers (IPPs). The breakup analysis of district wise shows that respondents of Visakhapatnam district 59 per cent of them told no, and 35.9 per cent said yes, West Godavari 40 per cent for no and 20 per cent for yes, Krishna 35.3 per cent for no, 17.6 per cent for yes, and

East Godavari 27.1 per cent for no and 20.8 per cent for yes. It may be concluded that industrial consumers are less visionary about getting power directly from IPPs.

The Chi-square value 41.968 and P-value 0.000 reveals that there is significant association between the variables at 5 % level of significance. Hence the hypothesis is rejected. Further the opinion of the respondents from the four districts on the statement "will industrial consumers be able to purchase electricity directly from the independent power producers" statistically different i.e., both the statement and the district are dependent.

The three districts i.e. East Godavari with Godavari Gas Power Plant under Spectrum Power Generation Limited at Kakinada, GVK Power Plant under GVK Power at Samalkota, Gautami Power Plant under Gautami Power at Samalkota, Reliance Power Plant under Reliance Power at Samalkota and GMR Vemagiri Power Plant under GMR Vemagiri Power Generation Limited at Rajhamundry, and Konnassema Power Plant under Konnasema Gas Power Limited, West Godavari, and Kondapalli Power Plant under Lanco Power Limited at Vijaywada, Krishna District. All these Private Power Companies Reliance, Lanco, GVK, Spectrum, Gautami, GMR and Konnaseema Power are operating in the Krishna- Godavari Basin (KG) of Andhra Pradesh.

However, except Kakinada which is populated with medium category industrial consumers, with two or three Big Fertilizer Companies like Nagarjuna and Godavari Fertilizers, both the districts East Godavari and West Godavari are more densely populated with agricultural industries. The industrial consumers from the above districts though have many IPPs but are unable to purchase direct power from them. The recent electricity reforms Act though have facilitated the provision but implementation and its feasibility in the State or Country needs to be seen.

43. Benefits from the emerging electricity market.

Table no: 7.43 Benefits from the emerging electricity market in India.

		Benefiting from the emerging electricity market in India.			
		Yes	No	No opinion	Total
District	Visakhapatnam	17	48	13	78
		21.8%	61.5%	16.7%	100.0%
	East Godavari	12	13	23	48
		25.0%	27.1%	47.9%	100.0%
	West Godavari	10	13	17	40
		25.0%	32.5%	42.5%	100.0%
	Krishna	9	18	24	51
		17.6%	35.3%	47.1%	100.0%
Total		48	92	77	217
		22.1%	42.4%	35.5%	100.0%

Chi-Sq = 24.077, P-Value = 0.001

Respondent's opinion on benefits derived from the emerging electricity market in India is illustrated in table no.7.43. A majority of the respondents i.e. 169 total sample respondents revealed no and no opinion on the above factor. Only 48 total respondents are agreeing that they are benefited from the emerging electricity market in India. The electricity market in India is so volatile with series of reforms one after the other within unlimited time gap, enabling to bring benefits to the Industrial consumers.

The Chi-square value 24.077 and P-value 0.001 are found to be significant at 5% level of significance. The hypothesis is rejected and the variables are dependent to each other. Further the opinion of the respondent from four districts on the statement "Are you benefiting from the emerging electricity market in India" is statistically significant i.e., the opinion on this particular statement is changing district by district.

44. Industries across the country are facing power shortage problem.

Table no: 7.44 Respondents opinion on industries across the country are facing power shortage problem.

Sr. No	Regions	Major	Moderate	Minor	No opinion
1	Eastern	82.5	8.3	5.1	4.1
2	Western	42.4	18.4	33.6	5.5
3	Northern	63.1	16.1	17.5	3.2
4	Southern	48.4	37.8	10.6	3.2
5	North Eastern	77.9	10.1	8.8	3.2

Descriptive Statistics

Regions	Mean	Std. Deviation
Eastern	3.6912	.75251
Western	2.9770	.99276
Northern	3.3917	.88638
Southern	3.3134	.78966
Northeastern	3.6267	.77807

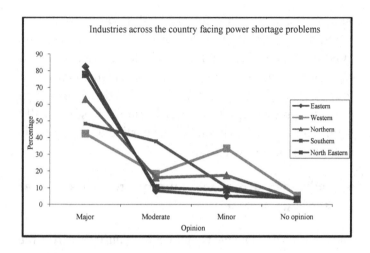

Industries across the country facing power shortage problems

Respondent's opinion on industries across the country is facing power shortage problems are brought out from table no. 7.44. It is observed from the table that eastern region 82.5 per cent, north eastern region 77.9 per cent and northern region 63.1 per cent are major problem of power shortage, when compared to industries in southern region 48.4 per cent and western region 42.4 per cent. It is suggested that the energy flows across the country should be rationalized to remove the regional disparities in access of electricity by industrial consumers.

As per the graph diagram it is evident that eastern region is facing major power shortage problems.

The average opinion score of eastern region is greater than the remaining regions across the country when compared with the remaining regions and the western region is less than the remaining regions. This concludes that eastern region has huge power shortage problems rather than other regions and the western region has low power shortage problems than other regions.

CHAPTER-VIII

DOMESTIC & COMMERCIAL – ELECTRICTY CONSUMERS

An attempt has been made in this chapter to focus on I. Power- Supply, Quality and Billing, II. Power System-Performance and Maintenance and III. Consumer Satisfaction –Services and Problems of Domestic & Commercial electricity consumers.

1. District wise distribution of Domestic & Commercial Consumers.

Table no:8.1 District wise distribution of Domestic & Commercial Electricity Consumers.

		Consumer		
		DOMESTIC	COMMERCIAL	Total
District	Visakhapatnam	120	60	180
		26.3%	26.3%	26.3%
	East Godavari	112	56	168
		24.6%	24.6%	24.6%
	West Godavari	110	55	165
		24.1%	24.1%	24.1%
	Krishna District	114	57	171
		25.0%	25.0%	25.0%
Total		456	228	684
		100.0%	100.0%	100.0%

Table no: 8.1 describes about four district wise distribution of Domestic & Commercial consumers in Coastal Andhra Pradesh. In total 684 respondents were selected in which 456 respondents belong to domestic category and 228 respondents are from commercial category who are spread in four districts like Visakhapatnam, East Godavari, West Godavari and Krishna districts. It is observed that 120 domestic and 60 commercial respondents covered from Visakhapatnam district. In East Godavari 112 domestic and 56 commercial respondents, West Godavari 110 domestic and 55 commercial respondents, Krishna 114 domestic and 57 commercial respondents are covered for the sample study.

I. POWER –SUPPLY, QUALITY AND BILLING

A. SUPPLY

India's Power System is facing acute power crisis as the availability of power averagely on daily basis is in between 13-18 hours in almost all the states in India. The situation is worse for the electrically underdeveloped states like Jharkhand, Bihar, Chhattisgarh, Madhya Pradesh, Uttar Pradesh, West Bengal and nearly all the North-Eastern States. The power generating stations are dominated in Eastern Region (ER) and hence bulk of power is to be exported to Western Region (WR) and Northern Region (NR) through the grids to meet the daily power needs and peak demand of energy.

Domestic and Commercial category is the major consumer of electricity in India. Making electricity available right from remote villages, small towns, suburban, urban areas to big metropolitan cities is always a great challenge to the power utilities and electricity suppliers. Moreover when the power sector is energy deficit the fulfillment of responsibility is below expectations of the consumers. The power system faces regular power cuts due to shutdown, burnout and tripping of transformers, voltage problems and grid failure. Inefficiency of the power system is affecting the customers. The power supply service to electricity consumers is not satisfactory. Consumers have started depending on alternate sources of power supply by DG (diesel generating) sets, invertors and home-ups. The diesel power generation in the country is growing at an alarming rate of 4 to 6 per cent.

The definition of consumer classification is not that exhaustive to include organized and unorganized consumers from all the sections of society like industry, domestic, commercial, businesses, educational, institutional, corporate offices, public places and offices, residential (individuals, public and private), shops-big & small, hawkers and not to forget all agricultural sector especially the irrigation system which is affected severely because of poor quality of power supply (not undertaken due to limitation of time in sample study)., railways traction etc.

2. Daily availability of power in the area

Table no:8.2 Respondents opinion on daily availability of power in the area.

		What is the daily availability of power in your area.				
		0-6 hours	7-12 hours	13-18 hours	19-24 hours	Total
District	Visakhapatnam	0	14	161	5	180
		.0%	7.8%	89.4%	2.8%	100.0%
	East Godavari	1	28	135	4	168
		.6%	16.7%	80.4%	2.4%	100.0%
	West Godavari	2	33	105	25	165
		1.2%	20.0%	63.6%	15.2%	100.0%
	Krishna District	1	18	124	28	171
		.6%	10.5%	72.5%	16.4%	100.0%
Total		4	93	525	62	684
		.6%	13.6%	76.8%	9.1%	100.0%

Daily availability of power in the respondent's area is depicted in table no.8.2. A vast majority of 76.8 per cent of all district respondents expressed that daily availability of power is in between 13-18 hours. In this regard the distribution of respondents district wise were Visakhapatnam 89.4 per cent, East Godavari 80.4 per cent, Kakinada District 72.5 per cent and West Godavari 63.6 per cent.

| | | What is the daily availability of power in your area. | | | | |
		0-6 hours	7-12 hours	13-18 hours	19-24 hours	Total
Consumer	DOMESTIC	3	57	360	36	456
		.7%	12.5%	78.9%	7.9%	100.0%
	COMMERCIAL	1	36	165	26	228
		.4%	15.8%	72.4%	11.4%	100.0%
Total		4	93	525	62	684
		.6%	13.6%	76.8%	9.1%	100.0%

It is interesting to note from both the tables the district as well as consumer that majority of consumer respondents (525 out of 684) have reported availability of power in between 13-18 hours in their area, followed by 93 respondents equaling to 13.6 per cent revealed about the availability of power in between 7-12 hours. The category wise analysis reveals that a majority of 78.9 per cent domestic and 72.4 per cent commercial respondents reported 13-18 hours of power availability in their area. The above table concludes that majority of the people are suffering with acute power cut in their area.

The Researcher identified that the Energy Profile of India is not uniformly distributed across the country. Due to the nonexistent of an integrated power system grid connecting all the regions Eastern Region (ER), Northern Region (NR), North Eastern (NE), Western Region (WR) and Southern Region (SR) many problems of reducing planned and unplanned load shedding is not being resolved. Hence it is suggested to the government to expedite the formation of National GRID and 100 % linkages to all power stations to meet the power supply – demand gap and to provide power to both rural and urban areas for at least about 20 hours per day.

3. Frequency of power cut due to the various causes.

Table no: 8.3 Respondent's opinion on experience of power cut due to the various causes.

Sr. No	Causes for power cut	Very Frequently	Frequently	Occasionally	Rarely	No opinion
1	Shut down of sub-stations	6.3	16.1	28.7	42.5	6.4
2	Burn out of transformers	10.7	14.3	31.7	32.7	10.5
3	Tripping of transformers due to over load	11.4	19.2	36.8	21.3	11.3
4	Other causes of transformer failure	11.7	24.9	28.2	20.2	15.1
5	Voltage problem	28.7	24.3	24	17.3	5.7

Respondent's opinion on experience of power cut due to various causes is furnished in table no.8.3. Very frequently shutting down of sub-stations is the minor cause recorded by 6.3 per cent of the total sample respondents. Other causes of transformer failure 24.9 per cent and voltage problems 24.3 per cent are the causes for frequent power cut reported by the respondents. About 31.7 per cent of the respondent's revealed burn out of transformers is the cause for occasional power cuts. The above analysis gives a strong inference that in addition to the power crisis, the poor performance and unappreciable maintenance of the power equipments the distribution system is unable to provide uninterrupted power supply.

District	N	Mean	Std. Deviation	F-Value	P-Value	Decision
Visakhapatnam	180	2.1756	.50457	36.083	0.0000	S
East Godavari	168	2.4417	.77656			
West Godavari	165	1.7333	1.00227			
Krishna District	171	1.6690	.84305			

The above table divulges that there is a significant average difference among the opinion of the respondents from all the four districts on the causes of power cut as their ANOVA test value (36.083) and P-value (0.000) is significant at 5% level of significance. Hence the hypothesis is rejected. The average opinion score of the East Godavari district 2.4417 is greater than the remaining districts which conclude that East Godavari district has more power cut than the remaining districts followed by Visakhapatnam district, whereas the Krishna district 1.6690 has the less average value which concludes that when compared with these four districts this Krishna district has less power cut.

Consumer	N	Mean	Std. Deviation	Z-Value	P-value	Decision
DOMESTIC	456	2.0320	.86186	1.055	0.292	NS
COMMERCIAL	228	1.9588	.84429			

To know the average significant difference between the domestic consumers and commercial consumers Z-test is administered. The above Z-value (1.055) and P-value (0.292) suggests that the average opinions of both types of respondents are not significant i.e., their opinion is unanimous. Further, the average opinion score of the domestic customers is little bit higher than the commercial customers, which suggests that domestic customers have more power cuts than commercial.

4. Alternate source of power supply.

Table no: 8.4 Respondent's opinion on alternate source of power supply.

Alternate Power Supply	Frequency	Percentage
Personnel DG set installed	72	10.53
Inverters	307	44.88
Home-UPS	288	42.11
No source	215	31.43

Table no: 8.4 illustrates about the alternate source of power supply of respondents who are having at residential and commercial establishments. The inverters are being used as alternate source of power supply by 44.8 per cent of the total respondents, followed next by 42.11 per cent respondents using home-UPS and 10.53 per cent have personnel DG sets installed at their premises. It is interesting to note that 31.43 per cent of the respondents reported no alternative source availability with them.

The table concludes that nearly 70 per cent of the respondents depend upon alternate source of power supply, however at the same time above 30 percent of the respondents are unable to afford any alternate source of power supply both in the domestic as well as commercial consumer segments. The Researcher identified that because of power shortage, diesel power generation in India is increasing at 4-5 per cent national growth rate which is very much in line with the above table's conclusion. It is suggested to the government to expedite projects in renewable energy segment as India has great potential for wind and solar energy, creating and giving equal opportunity to all the players in the power sector.

5. Saving of energy by standby mode.

Table no: 8.5 Respondent's opinion on saving of energy by standby mode.

		Opinion on energy saving by not allowing power to be consumed in stand-by-mode.		
		Yes	No	Total
District	Visakhapatnam	169	11	180
		93.9%	6.1%	100.0%
	East Godavari	150	18	168
		89.3%	10.7%	100.0%
	West Godavari	132	33	165
		80.0%	20.0%	100.0%
	Krishna District	141	30	171
		82.5%	17.5%	100.0%
Total		592	92	684
		86.5%	13.5%	100.0%

Chi-square: 17.951, P-value: 0.000

Table no: 8.5 depicts saving of energy by standby mode. The Chi-square test value 17.951 and P-value 0.000 for the districts showed significant difference in the opinion of respondent's district wise. Where the Chi-square value 0.308, P-value 0.579 for the domestic and commercial respondents revealed no significant difference in the opinion of both domestic and commercial respondents as saving of energy by standby mode.

Consumer		Opinion on energy saving by not allowing power to be consumed in stand-by-mode.		Total
		Yes	No	
Consumer	DOMESTIC	397	59	456
		87.1%	12.9%	100.0%
	COMMERCIAL	195	33	228
		85.5%	14.5%	100.0%
Total		592	92	684
		86.5%	13.5%	100.0%

Chi-square: 0.308, P-value: 0.579

Majority of the respondents i.e., 592 (86.5%) out of the total sample respondents 684 said yes to saving of energy by not allowing power to be consumed in standby mode. In this regard a whopping majority of 87.1 per cent domestic and 85.5 per cent commercial respondents revealed positive opinion.

The Researcher brought to the surface that though the consumers' willingness to save energy by switching of the electrical appliances (like light, fan, AC, TV, computers, mobile chargers, HVAC, etc) was reported with considerable percentage appears to be only assurances by them. Thus to conclude consumers have a wider role to play in saving and conserving energy in all segments of society and country at large. This is an area where neither the government authorities nor the distribution utilities can do much about it. Draining of power when the electrical appliance keeps consuming power with its non utilization by the consumer is really unpardonable.

However, it is suggested that the consumers should develop a habit to switch off appliances daily. Over the time it will become part of their way of life and keep sharing, educating, motivating, and inspiring others, to save energy and its impact on society.

According to Chi-square value 0.308 and P value 0.579 it may be concluded that there is no much variation in domestic & commercial consumer's opinion.

6. Time taken by electricity utilities to attend the supply faults.

Table no: 8.6 Respondent's opinion on attending the supply faults by the electricity utilities.

		The time taken by electricity utilities to attend the supply faults.				
		Within a day	2 to 3 days	4 to 5 days	above 5 days	Total
District	Visakhapatnam	53	59	61	7	180
		29.4%	32.8%	33.9%	3.9%	100.0%
	East Godavari	10	83	67	8	168
		6.0%	49.4%	39.9%	4.8%	100.0%
	West Godavari	70	59	26	10	165
		42.4%	35.8%	15.8%	6.1%	100.0%
	Krishna District	89	54	24	4	171
		52.0%	31.6%	14.0%	2.3%	100.0%
Total		222	255	178	29	684
		32.5%	37.3%	26.0%	4.2%	100.0%

Chi-square: 107.042, P-value: 0.000

Table no. 8.6 reflects four district respondent's opinion on attending the supply faults by the electricity utilities. Except 29 respondents out of the 684 total sample respondents who said above 5 days, 178 (26%) respondents told within 4 to 5 days, 255(37.3%) respondents viewed within 2 to 3 days and 222 (32.5%) respondents opined within a day.

According to the Chi-square value 107.042 and its corresponding P-value 0.000 is found to be significant at 5% of level of significance. Hence this hypothesis is rejected and there is significant difference in the opinion of the district respondents.

Consumer		Is the time taken by electricity utilities to attend the faults.				Total
		Within a day	2 to 3 days	4 to 5 days	above 5 days	
Consumer	DOMESTIC	158	166	113	19	456
		34.6%	36.4%	24.8%	4.2%	100.0%
	COMMERCIAL	64	89	65	10	228
		28.1%	39.0%	28.5%	4.4%	100.0%
Total		222	255	178	29	684
		32.5%	37.3%	26.0%	4.2%	100.0%

Chi-square: 3.138, P-value: 0.371

The category wise analysis reveals that about 36.4 per cent and 34.6 per cent domestic respondents opined 2-3 days and within a day respectively on attending the supply faults. Regarding commercial respondents 39 per cent and 28.1 per cent opined 2 to 3 days and within a day respectively.

Respondent's opinion on attending the supply faults by the electricity utilities is significantly differing district wise because all the districts are not having similar customer services. Districts which are more electrically developed with proper infrastructure have better services because of more number of customer centers distributed within the districts covering all the locations urban, sub-urban, villages and remote villages equally.

As per the analysis of consumer category there is no significant difference of opinion because both the consumers either domestic or commercial are given similar customer services in attending faults without any special preference or provision classifying the consumer category. The table concludes that there is no variation in domestic & commercial consumer's opinion. This is very much coinciding with the present scenario of consumers irrespective of any districts in the State.

7. Opinion on getting a new electricity connection.

Table no: 8.7 Respondent's opinion on new electricity connection.

		What is your opinion on getting a new electricity connection.				
		Within a month	1to 2 months	3to 4months	above 4 months	Total
District	Visakhapatnam	53	63	58	6	180
		29.4%	35.0%	32.2%	3.3%	100.0%
	East Godavari	8	72	81	7	168
		4.8%	42.9%	48.2%	4.2%	100.0%
	West Godavari	61	53	37	14	165
		37.0%	32.1%	22.4%	8.5%	100.0%
	Krishna District	69	71	21	10	171
		40.4%	41.5%	12.3%	5.8%	100.0%
Total		191	259	197	37	684
		27.9%	37.9%	28.8%	5.4%	100.0%

Chi-square: 96.363, P-value: 0.000

Table no.8.7 depicts respondent's opinion on new electricity connection. There is significant difference in opinion of the respondents belonging to all the four districts on the above statement "What is your opinion on getting a new connection?" as their P-value 0.000 shows significant. The chi-square value and the corresponding p-value divulge that the opinion on getting a new electricity connection is changing significantly by the type of consumers.

		What is your opinion on getting a new electricity connection.				
		Within a month	1to 2 months	3to 4months	above 4 months	Total
Consumer	DOMESTIC	130	201	100	25	456
		28.5%	44.1%	21.9%	5.5%	100.0%
	COMMERCIAL	61	58	97	12	228
		26.8%	25.4%	42.5%	5.3%	100.0%
Total		191	259	197	37	684
		27.9%	37.9%	28.8%	5.4%	100.0%

Chi-square: 36.555, P-value: 0.000

It is evident from the table that 44.1 per cent domestic consumers got new connection within 1 to 2 months but at the same time 42.5 per cent commercial consumers got new connections within 3 to 4 months, which concludes that commercial new connections are taking more time than domestic consumer's connections. Moreover both domestic and commercial respondents opinion on getting new connection within one month showed little variance, where as above 4 months is almost equal i.e. 5 per cent each.

Thus from both, the Chi-square analysis applied to district wise and consumer category wise it can be inferred that consumers irrespective of their category and as well as district there is significant difference of opinion in getting new connection. The Researcher identified that the above is in close concurrence with the existing fact that commercial consumers do not enjoy any preference over domestic consumers for obtaining new electricity connection.

8. Electricity Utility that provides best services in the area.

Table no: 8.8 Respondent's perception on the best electricity services in the area.

		Which utility provides the best electricity services in your area.				
		Central	State	Private	Public & Private	Total
District	Visakhapatnam	8	169	2	1	180
		4.4%	93.9%	1.1%	.6%	100.0%
	East Godavari	3	148	14	3	168
		1.8%	88.1%	8.3%	1.8%	100.0%
	West Godavari	8	113	27	17	165
		4.8%	68.5%	16.4%	10.3%	100.0%
	Krishna District	8	117	24	22	171
		4.7%	68.4%	14.0%	12.9%	100.0%
Total		27	547	67	43	684
		3.9%	80.0%	9.8%	6.3%	100.0%

Chi-square: 69.449, P-value: 0.000

Respondent's perception on the utility which provides best electricity services in the area is given in table no: 8.8. According to the Chi-square test value 69.449 and P-value 0.000 on the respondent's opinion on the utility which provides best services to them is found to be significant at 5 per cent level of significance. Hence the hypothesis is rejected. Further there is significant difference in the opinion of the respondents belonging to districts for the above statement.

| | | Which utility provides the best electricity services in your area. | | | | |
		Central	State	Private	Public & Private	Total
Consumer	DOMESTIC	23	363	35	35	456
		5.0%	79.6%	7.7%	7.7%	100.0%
	COMMERCIAL	4	184	32	8	228
		1.8%	80.7%	14.0%	3.5%	100.0%
Total		27	547	67	43	684
		3.9%	80.0%	9.8%	6.3%	100.0%

Chi-square: 14.663, P-value: 0.002

According to the table, domestic 79.6 per cent and commercial 80.7 per cent of the respondents opined that the state utility is providing best service to them. 14 per cent of commercial and 7.7 per cent domestic respondents revealed that private utilities are providing services next to state utility.

According to the Chi-square test value 14.663 and P-value 0.002 on the respondent's opinion on the utility which provides best services to them is found to be significant at 5% level of significance. Hence the hypothesis is rejected. Further there is significant difference in the opinion of the respondents belonging to domestic and commercial category for the above statement.

As per the Chi-square value 69.449 and P-value 0.000 above in the district wise, there is significant difference because best electricity services are available in electrically well developed districts by the utilities. This is also supported by the fact that irrespective of consumer category i.e. both domestic and commercial consumers equally are availing better electricity services in developed districts like Visakhapatnam from the state utilities. The other districts East Godavari, West Godavari and Krishna districts are having power mix of state and private sector utility. The central utility is only in power generation but not in distribution of power directly to the consumers in all the above districts, which very well supports the perception of the respondents as per the table. The above facts are also in line with the conclusion from the table no. 8.6.

B. Quality

The power supply quality & reliability is a chronic problem in the power system. The reforms could bring changes in managerial and administrative controls of the state owned organizations delivering electricity services but failed to improve the shortages in power supply, efficiency in operation, quality of power, operation & maintenance, metering and billing system. Consumers both in the domestic as well as commercial are suffering from poor quality of power supply damaging their home appliances and electrical equipments.

Commercial consumers lose potential business hours daily due to power cuts and voltage problems. Consumer grievances related to loss of damages and electrical safety both at residential and commercial establishments needs immediate attention by the authorities.

As a bird cannot fly with single wing, similarly India's Power Sector with its two wings one being the Power Utilities and other Electricity Consumers cannot fly to success unless both of them are in complete harmony with each other.

Monitoring the performance of electric utilities is becoming very essential and it is high time that performance benchmarking approach has not been defined and developed reflecting major key performance indices (KPIs) in the day to day operations of the power utility including technical, operational and financial.

9. Main causes of power cuts.

Table no: 8.9 Respondent's view on causes of power cuts.

Sr. No	View on power cuts	1	2	3	4	Weighted Rank
1	Shortage in power supply	319 (1276)	112 (336)	92 (184)	161 (161)	1 (1957)
2	Inefficient distribution system	78 (312)	303 (909)	207 (414)	96 (96)	2 (1731)
3	Operation & maintenance problems	90 (360)	186 (558)	309 (618)	99 (99)	3 (1635)
4	Poor quality of power	200 (800)	82 (246)	75 (150)	327 (327)	4 (1523)

Table no.8.9 infers about the respondents view on causes of power cuts. Respondents gave 1st rank to shortage in power supply, followed by 2nd rank to inefficient distribution system, 3ʳᵈ rank to operation & maintenance problems and the last 4ᵗʰ rank to poor quality of power. The table concludes that the shortage in power supply and inefficient distribution system are the major causes as per the domestic and commercial consumers for power cuts which also coincides with the conclusion of table no: 8.2 regarding poor availability of daily power.

10. Opinion on quality of power supplied daily.

Table no: 8.10 Respondent's opinion on quality of power supplied daily.

Sr. No	Power quality	Yes	No
1	Low voltage	71.9	28.1
2	High voltage	58.6	41.4
3	Normal voltage	43.7	56.3
4	Fluctuations	60.1	39.9
5	Frequencies	37.9	62.1

Respondents opinion on quality of power supplied daily is shown in table no: 8.10. Low voltage was reported by 71.9 per cent of the total respondents, followed by 60.1 per cent respondents suffered from fluctuations, 58.6 per cent for high voltage and 56.3 per cent respondents said the power voltage is not normal. It is very much evident from the above table that the power supply is having voltage problem and fluctuating between low and high voltage throughout the day. It is suggested that power distribution system should improve its power supply regulation with a steady voltage which will help the consumers to protect their electrical equipments from damaging.

The above is not the problem faced by domestic and commercial consumers but it also extends to the industrial consumers very much proved in the analysis and conclusion of the table no.7.11 from Chapter VII on Industrial Electricity Consumers, was correlated by the Researcher.

11. Facing fault in the metering system.

Table no: 8.11 Respondent's opinion on facing fault in the metering system.

Sr. No	Meter faults	Very Frequently	Frequently	Occasionally	Rarely	No opinion
1	Meter not working with connected load	13	23.7	23.7	21.2	18.4
2	Meter working without connected load	9.5	16.5	28.5	23.5	21.9
3	Tripping of meters due to over load	9.5	17.1	34.1	25.3	14
4	Meter reading not proportionate with energy consumption	12.7	24	31	21.8	10.5

Respondent's opinion on facing fault in the metering system is furnished in table no. 8.11. An equal per cent of 23.7 each complained for frequently and occasionally fault of meter not working with connected load. About 28.5 per cent of the total respondents opined that meter working without connected load occasionally. 34.1 per cent of them complained occasional tripping of meters due to over load. And 21.8 per cent of the respondents said rarely the meter reading not proportionate with energy consumption.

District	N	Mean	Std. Deviation	F-Value	P-Value	Decision
Visakhapatnam	180	1.9111	.99216			
East Godavari	168	2.2976	1.06663	16.254	0.0000	S
West Godavari	165	1.6576	.97109			
Krishna District	171	1.6257	.96344			

To know whether there is any significant difference in the average opinion of the respondents belonging to four districts on the dimension meter faults ANOVA test is conducted. The above P-value 0.000 suggests that there is a statistically significant average difference between the four districts on the said dimension. Further, the average opinion score of the East Godavari district is greater than the remaining districts which conclude that East Godavari district has huge meter faults than other districts followed by Visakhapatnam district.

Consumer	N	Mean	Std. Deviation	Z-Value	P-value	Decision
DOMESTIC	456	1.7840	.96772	-3.232	0.001	S
COMMERCIAL	228	2.0526	1.13075			

The above table illustrates that there is a significant difference in the average opinion score of the respondents belonging to both types. Also, the Commercial consumer's average score is very much higher than the domestic consumers and the difference is statistically significant difference at 5% level of significance. Further it suggests that Commercial consumers have opined that they are facing problems due to meter faults

12. Damage and loss of electrical appliances due to poor quality of power.

Table no: 8.12 Damage and loss of electrical appliances due to poor quality of power supply in recent years.

		Did any damage and loss of electrical appliances have taken place due to poor quality of power supply in recent years.		
		Yes	No	Total
District	Visakhapatnam	140	40	180
		77.8%	22.2%	100.0%
	East Godavari	141	27	168
		83.9%	16.1%	100.0%
	West Godavari	104	61	165
		63.0%	37.0%	100.0%
	Krishna District	119	52	171
		69.6%	30.4%	100.0%
Total		504	180	684
		73.7%	26.3%	100.0%

Chi-square: 21.784, P-value: 0.000

Damage and loss of electrical appliances due to poor quality of power supply in recent years is furnished in table no.8.12. The district wise analysis shows that East Godavari 83.9 per cent, Visakhapatnam 77.8 per cent, Krishna District 69.6 and West Godavari 63 per cent respondents opined yes for damage and loss of electrical appliances due to poor quality of power supply in recent years. About on an average 73.7 per cent considerable respondents from the districts under sample study revealed that they were suffering from poor quality of power supply.

The above P-value 0.000 suggests that there is a significant association between the district and the statement "Did any damage and loss of electrical appliances have taken place due to poor quality of power supply in recent years" i.e., the opinion of the respondents changes on the above statement when the district changes at 5% level of significance.

		Did any damage and loss of electrical appliances have taken place due to poor quality of power supply in recent years.		
		Yes	No	Total
Consumer	DOMESTIC	336	120	456
		73.7%	26.3%	100.0%
	COMMERCIAL	168	60	228
		73.7%	26.3%	100.0%
Total		504	180	684
		73.7%	26.3%	100.0%

Chi-square: 0.0000, P-value: 1.000

The Researcher identified that it is very much evident and interesting to note from the table no. 8.12 that both the consumer's domestic and commercial equally opined 73.7 per cent yes and 26.3 per cent no for the above statement. The above table's conclusion also coincides with the conclusion of table no: 8.10. To summarize nearly 75 per cent of the consumers are facing damage of electrical appliance because of poor quality of power supply. It is suggested to improve the performance of distribution utilities in order to provide good quality of power supply to minimize and avoid damage and loss of electrical appliances of the consumers.

According to Chi-square value 0.000 and corresponding P-value 1.000 of domestic and commercial consumers there is no significant impact on the statement "did any damage and loss of electrical appliances have taken place due to poor quality of power supply in recent years" due to type of consumer. Hence the hypothesis is accepted and there is no significant difference in the opinion of consumer respondents.

13. Consumers who suffered because of poor quality of power supply.

Table no: 8.13 Effect of poor quality of power supply on consumers.

Sr No	Electrical Energy Consumers	Major	Moderate	Minor	No opinion
1	Educational institutions	64.2	24.4	9.9	1.5
2	Shopping malls	41.7	33.5	22.4	2.5
3	Offices	45.6	34.5	18.3	1.6
4	Residential	67.3	20.8	10.1	1.9

Consumers affected because of poor quality of power supply are detailed in table no: 8.13. Residential 67.3 per cent, educational institutions 64.2 per cent, offices 45.6 per cent and shopping malls 41.7 per cent are the major sufferers and affected by poor quality of power supply. The sufferings of commercial consumers always have a financial impact on their business whereas the domestic consumers at the same time do suffer but may not have any business losses. Therefore the sufferings of the electrical energy consumers like educational institutions, shopping malls, offices and residential will differ from major, moderate to minor accordingly. However it can be concluded from above table that on an average 55 per cent consumers are suffering because of poor quality of power supply.

Poor quality of power supply is also one of the major attributes to the rising frequency of power cuts. The Researcher emphasized that the conclusion of the table no.8.45 discussing the impact of power cuts on day to day living is again supported by the fact established by the analysis of table no.8.13. The conclusion of the above table is supported very much by the respondents of electrical energy consumers is equally evident with the analysis and conclusion of table no.8.12.

14. Utilities providing better quality and reliable power.

Table no:8.14 Respondent's opinion on utilities providing better quality and reliable power.

Sr. No	Power Utilities	Yes	No
1	Central	29.1	70.9
2	State	83.9	16.1
3	Private	27.2	72.7
4	Public& Private	22.2	77.8

Respondent's opinion on utilities providing better quality and reliable power is given in table no.8.14. A whopping majority of 83.9 per cent of the respondents including both from domestic and commercial revealed the State utilities are providing better quality & reliability of power. 70.9 per cent respondents disclosed no for central utilities, private utilities were not supported for providing better quality & reliable power by 72.7 per cent of the respondents and moreover public & private too was declined support by saying no by 77.8 per cent of the respondents. The table concludes that the state utilities are providing better quality and reliable power.

The Researcher identified that the power transmission & distribution (T&D) system in Andhra Pradesh is dominated by and under the monopoly of APTRANSCO and APDISCOMs new entities constituted on unbundling of SEBs. Entry of central utilities, private and public & private in the distribution system in Andhra Pradesh state is yet to become a reality.

C. BILLING

The reforms initiated hundred per cent metering system to improve the billing and receivables from consumers. At national level nearly 50 per cent of the energy consumed is not billed. Power utilities need to increase the service centers and consumers have to be loyal in paying their bills. The financial health of the utilities directly depends upon rate of return. Utilities are unable to recover the cost of electricity generation and in addition to it subsidies & cross-subsidies are worsening the situation of state owned service providers. Though default consumers are being penalized government should design mechanism to curb these practices.

15. Average monthly electricity energy consumption.

Table no: 8.15 Pattern of average monthly electricity energy consumption.

		Your pattern of average monthly electricity energy consumption.				
		101-200units	201-300units	301-400units	Above 400units	Total
District	Visakhapatnam	5	28	68	79	180
		2.8%	15.6%	37.8%	43.9%	100.0%
	East Godavari	14	40	83	31	168
		8.3%	23.8%	49.4%	18.5%	100.0%
	West Godavari	41	37	47	40	165
		24.8%	22.4%	28.5%	24.2%	100.0%
	Krishna District	55	56	33	27	171
		32.2%	32.7%	19.3%	15.8%	100.0%
Total		115	161	231	177	684
		16.8%	23.5%	33.8%	25.9%	100.0%

Chi-square: 127.732, P-value: 0.000

Average monthly electricity consumption of the respondents is shown in table no. 8.15.

The pattern of average monthly electricity energy consumption is changing significantly by district as the P-value 0.000 in the above table is significant at 5% level of significance.

		Your pattern of average monthly electricity energy consumption.				
		101-200units	201-300units	301-400units	Above 400units	Total
Consumer	DOMESTIC	100	98	168	90	456
		21.9%	21.5%	36.8%	19.7%	100.0%
	COMMERCIAL	15	63	63	87	228
		6.6%	27.6%	27.6%	38.2%	100.0%
Total		115	161	231	177	684
		16.8%	23.5%	33.8%	25.9%	100.0%

Chi-square: 47.490, P-value: 0.000

About 36.8 per cent of the domestic and 27.6 per cent of the commercial respondents are consuming 301-400 units of electrical energy. And 19.7 per cent of the domestic and 38.2 per cent of the commercial respondents are consuming above 400 units monthly. The above table concludes that because of the modern equipments majority of the domestic consumers are consuming in between 301 to 400 units monthly. The commercial consumers in order to attract the customers spend more power on decoration of the shop with lighting. As such they are consuming more than 400 units per month.

The Researcher also identified that commercial consumers who are falling within 201-300 units and 301-400 units can consume more but are unable to do so because of frequent power cuts and power shortage during the peak period especially in evening being the business hours.

The Chi-square value 47.490 and the corresponding P-value 0.000 divulges that the pattern of average monthly electricity energy consumption is changing significantly by type of consumer as the p-value in the above table shows significance at 5% level of significance. Hence the hypothesis is rejected and both the variables are dependent to each other.

16. Regular payment of monthly bill.

Table no: 8.16 Payment of monthly bill regularly.

| | | Do you pay the monthly bill regularly. | | Total |
		Yes	No	
District	Visakhapatnam	132	48	180
		73.3%	26.7%	100.0%
	East Godavari	115	53	168
		68.5%	31.5%	100.0%
	West Godavari	127	38	165
		77.0%	23.0%	100.0%
	Krishna District	152	19	171
		88.9%	11.1%	100.0%
Total		526	158	684
		76.9%	23.1%	100.0%

Chi-square: 21.875, P-value: 0.000

Respondent's opinion on the regular payment of monthly bill is described in table no.8.16. The most loyal district in paying the monthly bill as per respondents 88.9 per cent Krishna district and respondents 31.5 per cent from East Godavari district admitting not paying the monthly bill regularly. It is a good sign to see that average loyalty of consumers stood at 76.9 per cent.

The above P-value 0.000 concludes that there is a significant difference in opinion by the type of district on the statement "Do you pay the monthly bill regularly" i.e., Krishna district respondents are more precise than the remaining three district respondents to pay the monthly bill regularly followed by Visakhapatnam and West Godavari.

| | | Do you pay the monthly bill regularly. | | |
		Yes	No	Total
Consumer	DOMESTIC	365	91	456
		80.0%	20.0%	100.0%
	COMMERCIAL	161	67	228
		70.6%	29.4%	100.0%
Total		526	158	684
		76.9%	23.1%	100.0%

Chi-square: 7.609, P-value: 0.006

A whopping majority of 80 per cent of the domestic respondents revealed that they are very regular in paying their monthly electricity bill, where as 20 per cent of them said no. In the case of commercial respondents 70.6 per cent of them revealed that they are paying regularly the electricity bill. But 29.4 per cent of them are irregular payers.

The above P-value 0.006 concludes that there is a significant difference of opinion by the type of consumer on the statement "Do you pay the monthly bill regularly" i.e., domestic consumers are more precise than the commercial consumers to pay the monthly bill regularly. With the above analysis it can be concluded that substantial percentage of consumers are paying the monthly bill regularly. Further there is scope for improvement and it is suggested to the consumers to dedicate themselves in making it hundred per cent in the state.

17. Frequency of default monthly bills with fine.

Table no:8.17 Payment of monthly bills with fine during last year.

		If no, how many times did you pay the monthly bills with fine during last year.				
		1-2 times	3-4 times	4-5	above 5 times	Total
District	Visakhapatnam	32	14	2	0	48
		66.7%	29.2%	4.2%	.0%	100.0
	East Godavari	12	33	8	0	53
		22.6%	62.3%	15.1%	.0%	100.0
	West Godavari	13	13	8	4	38
		34.2%	34.2%	21.1%	10.5%	100.0
	Krishna District	6	6	7	0	19
		31.6%	31.6%	36.8%	.0%	100.0
Total		63	66	25	4	158
		39.9%	41.8%	15.8%	2.5%	100.0

Payment of monthly bills with fine during last year is depicted in table no: 8.17. An unappreciable of all districts average of 41.8 per cent for paying the monthly bills with 3-4 times fine during the year is brought to the surface as per the analysis of the above table. Moreover 15.8 per cent of all districts respondents paying the monthly bills with 4-5 times make the situation very unpleasant.

		If no, how many times did you pay the monthly bills with fine during last year.				
		1-2 times	3-4 times	4-5 times	above 5 times	Total
Consumer	DOMESTIC	50	30	8	3	91
		54.9%	33.0%	8.8%	3.3%	100.0%
	COMMERCIAL	13	36	17	1	67
		19.4%	53.7%	25.4%	1.5%	100.0%
Total		63	66	25	4	158
		39.9%	41.8%	15.8%	2.5%	100.0%

Both the domestic and commercial respondents disclosed 1 -2 times 39.9 per cent, 3-4 times 41.8 per cent, 4-5 times 15.8 per cent and above 5 times 2.5 per cent as their frequencies in paying their monthly electricity bills with fine. Category wise analysis reveals that commercial consumers 53.7 per cent with 3 to 4 times paid monthly bills with fine, which is very high as compared to domestic consumers 54.9 per cent with 1 to 2 times.

Collecting fine as penalty and restoring connection is not improving the response and loyalty of the consumers. So it is suggested that the government and the distribution utilities can devise for more stringent penalty measures to control delay in collection of monthly electricity bills as this stagnates the proper cash flow of the utilities and affects the financial health of the power sector.

18. Reasons for not paying electricity bills within due date.

Table no: 8.18 Respondent's reasons for not paying electricity bills within due date.

		Your reasons for not paying electricity bills within due date.				
		Bills delayed	Heavy rush in line	Pending clarification in faulty bills	Dependency on others for payment	Total
District	Visakhapatnam	6	16	22	4	48
		12.5%	33.3%	45.8%	8.3%	100.0%
	East Godavari	3	35	14	1	53
		5.7%	66.0%	26.4%	1.9%	100.0%
	West Godavari	8	13	11	6	38
		21.1%	34.2%	28.9%	15.8%	100.0%
	Krishna District	4	8	7	0	19
		21.1%	42.1%	36.8%	.0%	100.0%
Total		21	72	54	11	158
		13.3%	45.6%	34.2%	7.0%	100.0%

Respondent's reasons for not paying electricity bills within due date is shown in table no: 8.18. A majority of 66 per cent respondents from East Godavari district said heavy rush in line being the reason for not paying electricity bills within due date. 45.8 per cent respondents reported pending clarification in faulty bills being the cause from Vishakhapatnam district. 21.1 per cent each respondents from West Godavari and Krishna district told delaying of bills to be the other reason for not paying the electricity bills within due date. Moreover it is interesting to note that 7 per cent of the total respondents depend on others for paying their bills.

		Your reasons for not paying electricity bills within due date .				
		Bills delayed	Heavy rush in line	Pending clarification in faulty bills	Dependency on others for payment	Total
Consumer	DOMESTIC	16	28	39	8	91
		17.6%	30.8%	42.9%	8.8%	100.0%
	COMMERCIAL	5	44	15	3	67
		7.5%	65.7%	22.4%	4.5%	100.0%
Total		21	72	54	11	158
		13.3%	45.6%	34.2%	7.0%	100.0%

As far as domestic consumers are concerned about 42.9 per cent said pending clarification in faulty bills. And 65.7 per cent of commercial consumers revealed heavy rush in line. As the commercial consumers are very busy and heavy rush in line made them default in payments.

The Researcher observed that consumer service centers / billing centers are not uniformly distributed in urban and suburban areas of the districts studied. In case of villages and remote villages, one service center on average caters to the needs of nearly fifteen villages consumers in and around it. It is suggested that the issue of bills and collection needs immediate attention as the facility of payment through net banking, ATM centers, and service centers is only available in urban & suburban areas, where as the villages are deprived of proper services by the utilities. Hence the government is advised to establish few service centers in villages and collaborate with existing banks for extending net banking in villages.

19. Waiting time at the counters for the payment of bill.

Table no:8.19 Respondents opinion on waiting time at the counters for the payment of bill.

		Generally how much waiting time is required at the counters for the payment of bill.				
		Less than 20 minutes	21 -40 min	41-60 min	above 60 min	Total
District	Visakhapatnam	1 .6%	50 27.8%	98 54.4%	31 17.2%	180 100.0%
	East Godavari	4 2.4%	39 23.2%	79 47.0%	46 27.4%	168 100.0%
	West Godavari	26 15.8%	60 36.4%	53 32.1%	26 15.8%	165 100.0%
	Krishna District	47 27.5%	72 42.1%	32 18.7%	20 11.7%	171 100.0%
Total		78 11.4%	221 32.3%	262 38.3%	123 18.0%	684 100.0%

Respondent's opinion on waiting time at the counters for the payment of bill is given in table no. 8.19. The table reveals that an average of 11.4 per cent respondents had to wait for paying their bill less than 20 minutes, 32.3 per cent waited for 21-40 minutes, 38.3 per cent waited for 41-60 minutes and 18 per cent of them waited for above 60 minutes.

		Generally how much waiting time is required at the counters for the payment of bill.				
		Less than 20 minutes	21 -40 min	41-60 min	above 60 min	Total
Consumer	DOMESTIC	54 11.8%	156 34.2%	179 39.3%	67 14.7%	456 100.0%
	COMMERCIAL	24 10.5%	65 28.5%	83 36.4%	56 24.6%	228 100.0%
Total		78 11.4%	221 32.3%	262 38.3%	123 18.0%	684 100.0%

Chi-square: 10.314, P-value: 0.016

Nearly 40 per cent of the domestic respondents opined that they need 41-60 minutes of time at the counter for the payment of bill, where as commercial respondents 36.4 per cent also needed the same time. The least per cent of 11.8 and 10.5 per cent of domestic and commercial respondents respectively took less than 20 minutes for the payment of bill. From the table it can be concluded that waiting time by the respondents at the counter for paying the bill consumes more time.

The Study observed that in the present scenario time is the greatest constrain for any individual and people are unable to spend more time on anything. The waiting time is obviously more in districts with high population density and less customer centers. So it is suggested that the government should open more number of customer centers to reduce the waiting time for bill payment.

For the statement "Generally how much waiting time is required at the counters for the payment of bill" the domestic respondents opined that less waiting time is required at the counters for the payment of bill whereas the commercial consumers opined little bit huge time to wait and their opinion is statistically significant difference. As per the Chi-square value 10.314 and p-value 0.016 it can be concluded that both domestic and commercial consumers irrespective of their consumer category are losing much time waiting at the counter for paying the bill. Hence, the consumer has significant impact on the variable.

20. Utilities action against default consumers.

Table no:8.20 Utilities action against default consumers.

Sr. No	Utilities action against default consumers	Frequency	Percentage
1	Temporarily disconnecting supply	478	69.88
2	Permanently terminating supply	133	19.44
3	Recovery with penalty	404	59.06
4	Punishment	133	19.44
5	Pending to be resolved	296	43.27

Utilities action against default consumers is shown in table no. 8.20. A majority of 69.88 per cent of the total sample respondents reported that supply connections are temporarily disconnected, 59.06 per cent revealed that recovery is done with penalty, 43.27 per cent were of the opinion that dispute cases in bill payments are pending to be resolved, 19.44 per cent respondents each told permanently terminating supply and punishment by utilities action against default consumers.

In addition to the existing power crisis the disloyalty of the consumers is worsening the unhealthiness of the power sector. No government or utility would appreciate to enforce and penalize their customers but the fact that all India average for collection efficiency is only 50 per cent i.e. only 50 per cent of the total energy sold is recovered, thus not even meeting the cost of generation. The Researcher brought out the above truth and appreciated the default consumers as respondents to reveal the truth of being penalized by the utilities for defaulting. It is suggested that more interaction is necessary between utilities and consumers to understand the problem of both so that the deficiency in the collection system can be minimized and simultaneously default consumers should transform themselves into regular payers.

21. Opinion on electricity pricing in India.

Table no:8.21   Respondent's opinion on electricity pricing in India.

Sr. No	Electricity pricing	Strongly Agree	Agree	Undecided	Disagree	Strongly Disagree
1	Consumers want cheaper prices	58.8	34.2	4.1	2	0.9
2	Existing tariff to be decreased	45.9	42.7	7.5	2.3	1.6
3	Unit slabs to be increased	42.1	33.9	13.9	7.3	2.8
4	Increase in subsidy	40.6	28.9	17	8.9	4.5

Respondent's opinion on electricity pricing in India is presented in table no. 8.21. It is found from the study that out of the total sample respondents of 684, about 58.8 per cent of them strongly agree for cheaper prices, 45.9 per cent for existing tariff to be decreased, unit slabs to be increased by 42.1 per cent and 40.6 per cent opined for increase in subsidy. Whereas 42.7 per cent of the respondents agree for existing tariff to be decreased, i.e.13.9 per cent respondents undecided for unit slabs to be increased, 8.9 respondents and 4.5 respondents disagree and strongly disagree respectively for increase in subsidy.

District	N	Mean	Std. Deviation	F-Value	P-Value	Decision
Visakhapatnam	180	1.3722	.60693	7..506	0.0000	S
East Godavari	168	1.2470	.68560			
West Godavari	165	1.0515	.74208			
Krishna District	171	1.0599	.92298			

The above table illustrates that there is a significant difference in the opinion of the respondents from four districts on the statement "Electricity Pricing". Further the above average values shows that the Visakhapatnam district respondents opined that the electricity pricing is to improve more in all the dimensions when compared with the opinion of the respondents belonging to the remaining three districts followed by East Godavari.

Consumer	N	Mean	Std. Deviation	Z-Value	P-value	Decision
DOMESTIC	456	1.1656	.70691	1.806	0.072	N.S
COMMERCIAL	228	1.2270	.85048			

The above Z-Value (1.806) and its correspondent P-value 0.072 depicts that there is no significant difference in the opinions of the respondents belonging to both types of consumers on electricity pricing i.e., both the consumers opined unanimously. The table concludes that a majority of the respondents want electricity at cheaper price. Further, the average opinion score 1.2270 of commercial consumers is greater than the domestic consumers which shows that commercial consumers have opined positively on electricity pricing.

II. POWER SYSTEM- PERFORMANCE
AND MAINTENANCE

A. Performance

It is over two decades since LPG Policy in 1991 year to the recent mandate of government "Power to all by 2012", the performance of the power distribution system despite reforms and restructuring is not as per the demand of the domestic and commercial consumers. The step towards privatizing electricity in the state is just a misnomer rather than a reality. The unbundling of SEBs was done with the objective to improve the distribution services to the consumers. Despite formation of independent distribution company from SEBs in the state there is lot to be done in this segment. Performance of utilities in delivering services to the satisfaction of the consumers presents a gloomy picture.

Power Transmission and Distribution System is the backbone of India's Power Sector with generating power stations, sub-stations, load dispatch centres, transformer and feeder installations,...etc being the essential limbs. Improper functioning of any of the parts leads to the overall under performance of the power system. Despite policy changes, deregulation, reform initiatives, restructuring of the state utilities, implementation of government schemes, valuable inputs to the sector through constituted government committees as findings and recommendations of survey, research reports, analysis of the electricity industry by domestic as well as foreign consultants, outcomes of seminars, public debate and open hearings, international and national meets on energy and power, and so many in the process of revamping the sector, the performance of India's Power System is undoubtly unappreciable over the years.

22. Improvement in the power distribution system.

Table no: 8.22 Respondent's perception on improvement in the power distribution system.

		Over a decade, do you see any improvement in the power distribution system.		
		Yes	No	Total
District	Visakhapatnam	111	69	180
		61.7%	38.3%	100.0%
	East Godavari	83	85	168
		49.4%	50.6%	100.0%
	West Godavari	125	40	165
		75.8%	24.2%	100.0%
	Krishna District	98	73	171
		57.3%	42.7%	100.0%
Total		417	267	684
		61.0%	39.0%	100.0%

Chi-square: 25.603, P-value: 0.000

Table no.8.22 explains the respondent's perception on improvement in the power distribution system. For the statement "Over a decade, do you see any improvement in the power distribution system" the respondents belonging to all the four districts opined significantly different. Further, the respondents from West Godavari district opined more positively towards the power sector when compared with the remaining districts followed by Visakhapatnam related to the improvement in the power distribution system over a decade.

		Over a decade, do you see any improvement in the power distribution system.		
		Yes	No	Total
Consumer	DOMESTIC	272	184	456
		59.6%	40.4%	100.0%
	COMMERCIAL	145	83	228
		63.6%	36.4%	100.0%
Total		417	267	684
		61.0%	39.0%	100.0%

Chi-square: 0.995, P-value: 0.318

It is clear from the table that about 63.6 per cent of the commercial respondents and 59.6 per cent of the domestic respondents opined yes for seeing improvement in the power distribution system.

It is concluded that a majority of 61 per cent of the total sample respondents opined positively towards power distribution system. But still 39 per cent of them are having negative opinion. So it is suggested to the government to frame those policies which satisfy the majority of the respondents for improvement in the power distribution system.

For the statement "Over a decade, do you see any improvement in the power distribution system" there is no significantly different opinion of both the type of consumers. Hence the hypothesis is accepted and both the variables are independent to each other. Further, the commercial respondents opined more positively towards the power sector than the domestic consumers but the opinion is not significantly different.

23. Reasons for improvement of power distribution system.

Table no:8.23 Reasons for improvement of power distribution system.

Sr. No	Power Distribution	1	2	3	4	5	Weighted Rank
1	Reforms & restructuring of power sector	140 (700)	65 (260)	67 (201)	124 (248)	21 (21)	3 (1430)
2	Private sector giving better services	78 (390)	149 (596)	132 (396)	50 (100)	8 (8)	1 (1490)
3	Improvement in services by state utilities	64 (320)	138 (552)	151 (453)	61 (122)	3 (3)	2 (1450)
4	Rising demand from the consumers for good quality services	126 (630)	65 (260)	59 (177)	159 (318)	8 (8)	4 (1393)
5	All	118 (590)	19 (76)	107 (321)	112 (224)	61 (61)	5 (1272)

Reasons for improvement of power distribution system are furnished in table no: 8.23. To find out the weights of the reasons, Likert's five points scale was used and weighted scores were computed to study in depth of the reasons. In the five point scale the first rank was given 5 weight, second rank was given 4 weight, third rank was given 3 weight, fourth rank was given 2 weight and fifth rank was given 1 weight. Private sector giving better services attained 1st rank, 2nd rank was awarded to improvement in services by state utilities, 3rd rank was given to reforms & restructuring of power sector, rising demand from the consumers for good quality services stood at 4th rank and all the factors collectively responsible for improving the power sector was ranked 5th by the respondents.

24. Opinion on wastage of electrical energy.

Table no:8.24 Respondent's opinion on wastage of electrical energy.

Sr. No	Electrical Energy Losses	Yes	No
1	Excess illumination in commercial buildings	89.3	10.7
2	Display of advertisement boards	75.4	24.6
3	Lighting decorations	78.5	21.5
4	Customer attraction shows at complexes	71.1	28.9
5	Brand/mall publicity	74.3	25.7
6	Unethical usage	76.3	23.7

Respondent's opinion on wastage of electrical energy is shown in table no: 8.24. Wastage of energy by excess illumination in commercial buildings was reported by 89.3 per cent of the total sample respondents, followed by 78.5 per cent saying yes to lighting decorations, unethical usage was another major cause for wastage of electrical energy reported by 76.3 respondents, display of advertisement boards 75.4 per cent and brand/mall publicity 74.3 per cent by the respondents. 28.9 per cent respondents do not consider customer attraction shows at complexes to be wastage of electrical energy. However 71.1 per cent of them do consider it wastage. The table concludes about 75 per cent of the respondent's average opinion is that all the above factors account for wastage of electrical energy. The present modernization of cities with multiplexes, malls, shopping centers, restaurants, amusement parks and other functions & commercial brand promotions consume enormous unaccountable electrical energy for unproductive purpose.

The Researcher observed that there is lot of criticism the SEBs, the State and Central government utilities have been facing for the huge losses in India's Power System over a long period of time. The consumers too are to be equally blamed for their irresponsibility in usage of electricity. The above analysis reflects a very true picture of wastage of electrical energy in the country. Hence it is suggested that both domestic and commercial consumers should act on saving of electrical energy to battle out the present energy crisis being faced by all the states in India along with the efforts of the government and power utilities.

25. Power loss due to negligence in switching off the appliances.

Table no:8.25 Power loss due to negligence in switching off the appliances.

Sr. No	Premises/ Establishments	Major	Moderate	Minor	No opinion
1	Residents	67	15.5	16.1	1.5
2	Offices	41.5	37.4	18.6	2.5
3	Institutions	40.6	36.7	19.2	3.5
4	Complexes	49.9	27.5	17.8	4.8
5	Public Places	79.1	14.5	3.2	3.2

Power loss due to negligence in switching off the electrical appliances is discussed in table no: 8.25. The major power loss happens at public places due to negligence in switching off the appliances as per 79.1 per cent respondents. The next major power loss occurs at residences was the opinion of 67 per cent respondents. Moreover complexes 49.9 per cent, offices 41.5 per cent and institutions 40.6 per cent are the premises /establishments where major power loss takes place.

Generally people's attitude on public property is different from the private or own property. They show utmost care towards own property. In the study it is proved that nearly 80 per cent of power is lost at public places.

26. Overall functioning of the integrated power system.

Table no:8.26 Respondent's opinion on the overall functioning of the integrated power system.

		What is your opinion on the overall functioning of the integrated power system					
		Excellent	Very Good	Good	Average	Below average	Total
District	Visakhapatnam	4	14	35	89	38	180
		2.2%	7.8%	19.4%	49.4%	21.1%	100.0%
	East Godavari	0	11	52	70	35	168
		.0%	6.5%	31.0%	41.7%	20.8%	100.0%
	West Godavari	7	27	67	39	25	165
		4.2%	16.4%	40.6%	23.6%	15.2%	100.0%
	Krishna District	9	33	64	53	12	171
		5.3%	19.3%	37.4%	31.0%	7.0%	100.0%
Total		20	85	218	251	110	684
		2.9%	12.4%	31.9%	36.7%	16.1%	100.0%

Respondent's opinion on the overall functioning of the integrated power system is shown in table no.8.26. It is alarming to see the table's analysis that the total respondent's opinion on the overall functioning of the integrated power system in all districts is average 36.7 per cent and below average 16.1 per cent. In addition to it only 2.9 per cent opined excellent which is a matter of serious concern for the power sector.

		What is your opinion on the overall functioning of the integrated power system					
		Excellent	Very Good	Good	Average	Below average	Total
Consumer	DOMESTIC	14	59	151	166	66	456
		3.1%	12.9%	33.1%	36.4%	14.5%	100.0%
	COMMERCIAL	6	26	67	85	44	228
		2.6%	11.4%	29.4%	37.3%	19.3%	100.0%
Total		20	85	218	251	110	684
		2.9%	12.4%	31.9%	36.7%	16.1%	100.0%

Chi-square: 3.283, P-value: 0.512

It is observed from the table no.8.26 that out of the 684 respondents,251 equaling36.7 per cent opined that overall functioning of the integrated power system is on an average, 31.9 per cent said good, 16.1 per cent revealed below average, 12.4 per cent told very good and a negligible percentage of 2.9 opined excellent. Consumer category wise analysis reveals that domestic respondent's opinion is more positive than commercial respondents regarding overall functioning of the integrated power system. Thus the table concludes that the integrated power system is performing averagely. It is suggested to the government to take necessary measures to improve the performance of the integrated power system.

The calculated Chi-square 3.283 and its corresponding P-value 0.512 exemplifies that there is no significant association with the respondent's opinion on overall functioning of the integrated power system by both the consumers. Hence the hypothesis is accepted and there is no relation between the variables and they are independent. It may be concluded that both the category of consumer respondents opined more or less same.

27. Response of authorities in case of emergency/ electrical short circuit.

Table no:8.27 Response of authorities in case of emergency/ electrical short circuit.

		What is the response of authorities in case of emergency/electrical short circuit.					
		Excellent	Very Good	Good	Average	Below average	Total
District	Visakhapatnam	4	17	27	87	45	180
		2.2%	9.4%	15.0%	48.3%	25.0%	100.0%
	East Godavari	1	8	31	93	35	168
		.6%	4.8%	18.5%	55.4%	20.8%	100.0%
	West Godavari	5	30	41	68	21	165
		3.0%	18.2%	24.8%	41.2%	12.7%	100.0%
	Krishna District	11	25	53	64	18	171
		6.4%	14.6%	31.0%	37.4%	10.5%	100.0%
Total		21	80	152	312	119	684
		3.1%	11.7%	22.2%	45.6%	17.4%	100.0%

Response of authorities in case of emergency/electrical short circuit is revealed in table no.8.27. It is unsatisfactory to note from the above table that the response of authorities in case of emergency/electrical short circuit is average 45.6 per cent and below average 17.4 per cent as reported by all the district respondents.

		What is the response of authorities in case of emergency/electrical short circuit.					
		Excellent	Very Good	Good	Average	Below average	Total
Consumer	DOMESTIC	13	51	96	222	74	456
		2.9%	11.2%	21.1%	48.7%	16.2%	100.0%
	COMMERCIAL	8	29	56	90	45	228
		3.5%	12.7%	24.6%	39.5%	19.7%	100.0%
Total		21	80	152	312	119	684
		3.1%	11.7%	22.2%	45.6%	17.4%	100.0%

Chi-square: 5.265, P-value: 0.261

It is evident from the table no.8.27 that an overall 45.6 per cent of the sample respondents opined response of authorities in case of emergency/electrical short circuit is on an average and 17.4 per cent told below average. About 22.2 per cent and 11.7 per cent of the respondents opined good and very good response respectively. Thus the table concludes that the response of authorities in case of emergency is average. It is suggested to the utilities to improve the response of authorities.

The calculated Chi-square value 5.265 and P-value 0.261 proved that there is no significant relation between the opinion of the both category of respondents and authorities response in case of emergency /electrical short circuit. Hence the hypothesis is accepted and both the variables are independent to each other. Further both the consumers opined unanimously.

28. Agencies contribution in overall development of the electricity sector.

Table no:8.28 Contribution of agencies in overall development of the electricity sector in India.

Sr. No	Developing Electricity in India	1	2	3	4	5	6	Weighted Rank
1	Central Utilities	209 (1254)	220 (1100)	112 (448)	38 (114)	40 (80)	65 (65)	2 (3061)
2	State Utilities	253 (1518)	220 (1100)	89 (356)	40 (120)	58 (116)	24 (24)	1 (3234)
3	Private Utilities	86 (516)	89 (445)	325 (1300)	110 (330)	48 (96)	26 (26)	3 (2713)
4	Regulators/ Government	33 (198)	36 (180)	89 (356)	269 (807)	174 (348)	83 (83)	4 (1972)
5	Investors	28 (168)	92 (460)	36 (144)	182 (546)	287 (574)	59 (59)	5 (1951)
6	Consumers	74 (444)	26 (130)	35 (140)	45 (135)	77 (154)	427 (427)	6 (1430)

Table no: 8.28 reflects contribution of agencies in overall development of the electricity sector in India. The State Utilities was given 1st rank, 2nd rank to the Central Utilities, 3rd rank to the Private Utilities, 4th rank to regulators/government, 5th rank to investors and 6th rank to consumers. It is evident from table that the State Utilities were pioneer in taking up the development of electricity sector in India; however the Central Utilities though they entered late in the power sector were not far behind the State Utilities in their contribution.

The Researcher brought out an interesting observation that during the pre-independence period 1900 to 1950 year private companies were providing electricity services very fragmentally to handful of limited affluent customers who could afford to pay for this luxury commodity, 1950-2000 was the era of monopoly by the SEBs, though Central Utilities had entered the power sector in 1975 with restricted area of service in generation only. The period from 1991 Economic Reforms (LPG Policy) to Electricity Act -2003 Reforms saw many initiatives rolling by the Government of India to restructure and redefine the ailing power sector. The period after Electricity Act-2003 is totally changing the power mix of the sector and challenges of contribution to the recent mandate Power to all by 2012 continues.

29. Benefits of privatizing electricity in the state.

Table no:8.29 Respondent's opinion on the benefits of privatizing electricity in the state.

Sr. No	Benefits of Privatization	1	2	3	4	5	Weighted Rank
1	Improved quality and reliability of power supply	169 (845)	106 (424)	88 (264)	88 (176)	233 (233)	5 (1942)
2	Efficient Power Management	85 (425)	157 (628)	116 (320)	249 (498)	77 (77)	4 (1976)
3	Competitive prices	92 (460)	99 (396)	320 (960)	116 (232)	57 (57)	3 (2105)
4	Improved maintenance and safety	87 (435)	261 (1044)	78 (234)	160 (320)	98 (98)	1 (2131)
5	Better customer services	251 (1255)	62 (248)	85 (255)	71 (142)	215 (215)	2 (2115)

Table no: 8.29 speaks about the respondent's opinion on the benefits of privatizing electricity in the state. 1st rank was given to improved maintenance and safety, better customer services was awarded 2nd rank, 3rd rank went to competitive prices, 4th rank was attained by efficient power management and 5th rank to improve quality and reliability of power supply were all given preferences by the respondents as the benefits of privatization. The table concludes that benefits of privatization had very less influence on improvement of quality and reliability of power and on efficient power management. However, there is improvement in maintenance and safety, customer services have become better and competition in prices.

B. MAINTENANCE

Consumers are deprived of power supply for long time due to maintenance works. The installed power equipments are not being periodically maintained and frequency of failures are very high. One of the prime reasons is inadequate manpower and material resources with the utilities. The incoming power supply lines are loosely connected to the line poles overcrowded with many connections making it very difficult for the respective consumer to identify their own connections. There are areas the system maintenance is a big question.

The geographical area to be covered, number of distribution stations and power equipments lay out in the supply line are more for the domestic consumers as compared to the commercial consumers because of their localized concentration in a market place. Thus the maintenance of the power system providing power supply for domestic consumers need more manpower and service centers. On the other hand in villages and remote areas in spite of less power equipments the minimal maintenance is also not being done reflecting the irresponsibility of the state utility in distribution segment. It appears that autonomy and accountability invariably tend to diverge from the main objective of maintaining efficient power system and delivering satisfactory customer services. Liabilities had been the legacy of the state utilities but the introduction of utilities /service providers from the private sector has begun to give it a new face of orientation. Something which had been damaged over the decades will need at least years to have a new leaf of life.

30. Deprived of power supply during repairs.

Table no:8.30 Deprived of power supply during repairs.

		During maintenance repairs for what period you are deprived of power supply.				Total
		0-2hours	3-5hours	6-8 hours	above 8 hours	
District	Visakhapatnam	1	15	65	99	180
		.6%	8.3%	36.1%	55.0%	100.0%
	East Godavari	1	30	50	87	168
		.6%	17.9%	29.8%	51.8%	100.0%
	West Godavari	25	58	48	34	165
		15.2%	35.2%	29.1%	20.6%	100.0%
	Krishna District	45	62	37	27	171
		26.3%	36.3%	21.6%	15.8%	100.0%
Total		72	165	200	247	684
		10.5%	24.1%	29.2%	36.1%	100.0%

Table no.8.30 enumerates that 36.1 per cent and 29.2 per cent of the total sample respondents reveals above 8 hours and 6-8 hours respectively regarding power cut during repairs. The Visakhapatnam 55 per cent and East Godavari 51.8 per cent were the major districts deprived of power supply above 8 hours during maintenance period.

		During maintenance repairs for what period you are deprived of power supply.				Total
		0-2hours	3-5hours	6-8 hours	above 8 hours	
Consumer	DOMESTIC	56	117	132	151	456
		12.3%	25.7%	28.9%	33.1%	100.0%
	COMMERCIAL	16	48	68	96	228
		7.0%	21.1%	29.8%	42.1%	100.0%
Total		72	165	200	247	684
		10.5%	24.1%	29.2%	36.1%	100.0%

Chi-square: 8.779, P-value: 0.032

The category wise analysis shows that 42.1 per cent commercial and 33.1 per cent domestic, 29.8 commercial and 28.9 per cent domestic respondents opined above 8 hours and 6-8 hours respectively regarding power cut during repairs. The table concludes that a majority of the respondents of both categories opined that they had to wait for more than 8 hours if there was any maintenance repair.

The Chi-square value 8.779 and its corresponding P-value 0.032 suggest that for the statement "During maintenance repairs for what period you are deprived of power supply" both the types of consumers opined similar way. And it is found to be significant at 5% level of significance. Hence the hypothesis is rejected and variables are dependent to each other.

31. Sudden failure in power supply due to GRID disturbance.

Table no:8.31 Respondent's opinion on sudden failure in power supply due to GRID disturbance.

		Sudden failure in power supply due to GRID disturbance.					
		Once in a month	Quarterly	Half Yearly	Yearly	above one year	Total
District	Visakhapatnam	1	3	36	25	115	180
		.6%	1.7%	20.0%	13.9%	63.9%	100.0%
	East Godavari	0	11	24	24	109	168
		.0%	6.5%	14.3%	14.3%	64.9%	100.0%
	West Godavari	6	32	24	19	84	165
		3.6%	19.4%	14.5%	11.5%	50.9%	100.0%
	Krishna District	8	38	25	22	78	171
		4.7%	22.2%	14.6%	12.9%	45.6%	100.0%
Total		15	84	109	90	386	684
		2.2%	12.3%	15.9%	13.2%	56.4%	100.0%

Sudden failure in power supply due to GRID disturbance is elicited in table no.8.31. The opinion of district wise respondents on GRID disturbance taking place above one year causing sudden failure in power supply is reported as East Godavari 64.9 per cent, Visakhapatnam 63.9 per cent, West Godavari 50.9 per cent and Krishna district 45.6 per cent.

		Sudden failure in power supply due to GRID disturbance.					
		Once in a month	Quarterly	Half Yearly	Yearly	above one year	Total
Consumer	DOMESTIC	9	56	76	59	256	456
		2.0%	12.3%	16.7%	12.9%	56.1%	100.0%
	COMMERCIAL	6	28	33	31	130	228
		2.6%	12.3%	14.5%	13.6%	57.0%	100.0%
Total		15	84	109	90	386	684
		2.2%	12.3%	15.9%	13.2%	56.4%	100.0%

Chi-square: 829, P-value: 0.934

The table gives information that 56.1 per cent domestic and 57 per cent of commercial respondents revealed that sudden failure in power supply due to GRID disturbances is above one year. A negligible percentage of 2.6 commercial and 2 per cent domestic consumer respondents opined once in a month.

The Chi-square value of 829 divulges that there is no significant relationship in the opinion of the total respondents with regard to sudden failure in power supply due to GRID disturbance. P-value 0.934 is more than the standard value of significance level 0.05. Hence the hypothesis is accepted and both the variables are independent to each other. Further both the types of consumers opined in a similar passion about the said statement.

32. Periodic maintenance of power equipments.

Table no: 8.32 Periodic maintenance of power equipments.

		What is the frequency of periodic maintenance of power equipments.				
		Once in a month	Two months	Three months	Yearly	Total
District	Visakhapatnam	0	5	77	98	180
		.0%	2.8%	42.8%	54.4%	100.0%
	East Godavari	1	5	67	95	168
		.6%	3.0%	39.9%	56.5%	100.0%
	West Godavari	9	25	51	80	165
		5.5%	15.2%	30.9%	48.5%	100.0%
	Krishna District	18	38	37	78	171
		10.5%	22.2%	21.6%	45.6%	100.0%
Total		28	73	232	351	684
		4.1%	10.7%	33.9%	51.3%	100.0%

Periodic maintenance of power equipments is furnished in table no. 8.32. Very less percentage for once in a month 4.1 per cent and two months 0.3 per cent has been reported by the total respondents. 33.9 per cent for three months and 51.3 per cent for yearly are the average opinion of the district respondents on frequency of periodic maintenance of power equipments. So it can be concluded from the table that nearly 50 per cent of the respondents have to wait for one year (long period) for maintenance of power equipments.

		What is the frequency of periodic maintenance of power equipments.				
		Once in a month	Two months	Three months	Yearly	Total
Consumer	DOMESTIC	17	53	161	225	456
		3.7%	11.6%	35.3%	49.3%	100.0%
	COMMERCIAL	11	20	71	126	228
		4.8%	8.8%	31.1%	55.3%	100.0%
Total		28	73	232	351	684
		4.1%	10.7%	33.9%	51.3%	100.0%

Chi-square: 3.420, P-value: 0.331

More than half of the consumers belonging to both the domestic and commercial 51.3 per cent opined that the frequency of periodic maintenance of power equipments is being done yearly. In this regard the category wise analysis reveals that 55.3 per cent commercial and 49.3 per cent domestic opined yearly maintenance.

It is suggested to the utilities to increase the manpower in the maintenance department so that with good frequency of periodic maintenance the life of the power equipments increases, its working efficiency increases, electrical safety aspects are improved and overall the power system becomes healthy giving better power supply, quality and reliability.

The Chi-square value 3.420 and P-value 0.331 is found to be insignificant at 0.05 level of significance, this indicates no significant association between the opinion of the respondents between domestic and commercial. Hence, both the category expressed same opinion. The hypothesis is accepted and the variables are independent. The frequency of periodic maintenance of power equipment being yearly brings out the fact that the utilities are not having adequate manpower to carry out the maintenance works with more frequency within the year.

33. Maintenance of power equipments in their area.

Table no:8.33 Respondent's opinion on the maintenance of power equipments in their area.

Sr. No	Power Equipments	Well Maintained	Maintained	Not properly maintained	Not maintained	No opinion
1	Transformers	24	18.7	34.4	20.9	2
2	Sub –stations	19.7	20.5	31.7	24.3	3.8
3	Line poles	11.3	19.6	21.1	44.3	3.8
4	Feeders	7.9	12.4	20.9	47.7	11.1
5	Energy meters	14.9	20.8	18.1	36.1	10.1
	Average Percentage	**15.56**	**18.4**	**25.24**	**34.66**	**6.16**

It could be seen from the data presented in the table no.8.33 that 34.4 per cent and 31.7 per cent of the total respondents opined that the transformers and substations are not properly maintained. Regarding line poles 44.3 per cent, feeders 47.7 per cent and energy meter 36.1 per cent of the sample respondents told not maintained.

District	N	Mean	Std. Deviation	F-Value	P-Value	Decision
Visakhapatnam	180	.5400	1.33235			
East Godavari	168	.1619	1.09412	31.471	0.0000	S
West Godavari	165	1.0158	1.00583			
Krishna District	171	1.2538	1.05201			

The ANOVA Test value and its corresponding P-value exemplifies that there is a significant difference in the opinion of the respondents belonging to all the four districts for the statement "What is your observation on the maintenance of nearby power equipments installed in your area". Further, the opinion of the respondents belonging to Krishna district is greater than the remaining districts followed by West Godavari district. i.e., for these two districts the power equipments are well maintained when compared with the other districts.

Consumer	N	Mean	Std. Deviation	Z-Value	P-value	Decision
DOMESTIC	456	.7044	1.10669	2.881	0.004	S
COMMERCIAL	228	.8123	1.38228			

Similarly, for the Z-test value 2.881 the P-value 0.004 suggests that there is a significant mean difference in the opinion of the consumers belonging to both types. Further, the average opinion of the consumers belonging to commercial opined positively on the power sector when compared with the domestic.

34. Preference on the timings to carry out periodic maintenance work.

Table no:8.34 Respondent's preference on the timings to carry out periodic maintenance work.

		Which part of the day would you recommend to carry out periodic maintenance work.				
		6.00AM-.10.00AM	12Noon-.4.00PM	10.00PM-.6.00AM	Others	Total
District	Visakhapatnam	13	72	31	64	180
		7.2%	40.0%	17.2%	35.6%	100.0%
	East Godavari	34	39	24	71	168
		20.2%	23.2%	14.3%	42.3%	100.0%
	West Godavari	24	75	28	38	165
		14.5%	45.5%	17.0%	23.0%	100.0%
	Krishna District	19	104	12	36	171
		11.1%	60.8%	7.0%	21.1%	100.0%
Total		90	290	95	209	684
		13.2%	42.4%	13.9%	30.6%	100.0%

Chi-square: 66.401, P-value: 0.000

Table no.8.34 provides the respondents preference of the timings to carry out periodic maintenance work of the sample study. Different district respondents opined significantly different on the statement "Which part of the day would you recommend to carry out periodic maintenance work". Further, 42.4% of the respondents opined that their convenient time is 12Noon to 4pm.

		Which part of the day would you recommend to carry out periodic maintenance work.				
		6.00AM-.10.00AM	12Noon-.4.00PM	10.00PM-.6.00AM	Others	Total
Consumer	DOMESTIC	45	219	53	139	456
		9.9%	48.0%	11.6	30.5%	100.0%
	COMMERCIAL	45	71	42	70	228
		19.7%	31.1%	18.4	30.7%	100.0%
Total		90	290	95	209	684
		13.2%	42.4%	13.9	30.6%	100.0%

Chi-square: 26.533, P-value: 0.000

42.4 per cent of the total respondents recommended 12 Noon -4 PM. In this regard the category wise analysis revealed domestic 48 per cent and commercial 31.1 per cent.

From the Chi-square value 26.533 generated and P-value 0.000, it may be concluded that periodic maintenance of work and category has significance relation. The null hypothesis is refuted at 5 per cent level of significance. Hence both the variables are dependent. The above P-value concludes that there is statistically significant difference in the opinion of the respondents belonging to both the types on the statement "Which part of the day would you recommend to carry out periodic maintenance work".

35. Opinion on Utilities maintenance resources.

Table no: 8.35 Respondent's opinion on Utilities maintenance resources.

Sr. No	Utilities Maintenance Resources	Adequate	Inadequate	No opinion
1	Trained manpower	34.2	59.6	6.1
2	Lineman & meter readers	30.8	60.5	8.6
3	Equipments/tools and tackles	30	54.1	15.9
4	Electrical materials used for repairs and replacements	27	56	17
5	Infrastructure and service centers	23	58.2	18.9

Table no. 8.35 explains the respondent's opinion on utilities maintenance resources. According to the table all the utilities maintenance resources like trained manpower 59.6 per cent, lineman and meter readers 60.5 per cent, equipments/tools and tackles 54 per cent, electrical materials used for repairs and replacements 56 per cent and infrastructure and service centers 58.2 per cent are inadequately maintained.

District	N	Mean	Std. Deviation	F-Value	P-Value	Decision
Visakhapatnam	180	-.3244	.73024			
East Godavari	168	-.4238	.57234	7.483	0.000	S
West Godavari	165	-.2885	.57312			
Krishna District	171	-.1111	.58976			

For the dimension "What is your opinion on resources in maintenance by utilities" the respondents belonging to all the four districts opined negatively and their opinion is statistically significant different. As their average value proves that the resources in maintenance by utilities are inadequate so power sector has to improve in this regard.

Consumer	N	Mean	Std. Deviation	Z-Value	P-value	Decision
DOMESTIC	456	-.3044	.61909	1.406	0.161	N.S
COMMERCIAL	228	-0.2518	.65379			

The average opinion score of the respondents belonging to commercial is little bit greater than the domestic consumers. There is no significant difference in the opinion of the consumers on the statement "What is your opinion on resources in maintenance by utilities" according to Z value 1.406 and P value 0.161. Hence the hypothesis is accepted.

36. Opinion on incoming power supply lines.

Table no: 8.36 Respondent's opinion on incoming power supply lines.

Sr. No	Incoming power supply conditions	Yes	No
1	Overcrowding of line pole with many connections	87.1	12.9
2	Wires loosely connected and juggled	81.9	18.1
3	Meter and main fuse outside with weather protection	67	33
4	Can you identify your incoming power supply line?	29.4	70.6

Respondent's opinion on incoming power supply lines is described in table no: 8.36. It is very much surprising that nearly 70.6 per cent respondents were unable to identify their incoming power supply line. Moreover 87.1 per cent respondents say overcrowding of line pole with many connections, for 81.9 per cent of them wires loosely connected and juggled and regarding meter and main fuse outside with weather protection 67 per cent said yes. The table concludes that reflecting the unsatisfactory arrangement of basic requirements of supporting incoming power supply lines to residential premises and commercial establishments in various districts and the state.

The Researcher with the background of the field survey during the sample study visited towns, cities, residential colonies, government housing boards, VUDA colony, tall apartments, public buildings, blocks, houses cluster in villages, homes of below poverty line (BPL) in remote areas. etc expressed that the overcrowding of line pole with many connections, wires loosely connected and juggled, meter and main fuse location and identification of power supply lines are unsatisfactory in arrangement not solely due to the electrical department but due to the constrain of town, city and village planning.

Hence it is suggested that town, city and village layout planning, overall plot plan with electrical power system layout, installation of transformers, feeders and distribution boards equipments with safety, proper routing of line poles, crossovers, under cables etc should be given more emphasis by the concerned district authorities before developing plots, roads, drains and other infrastructure to minimize the haphazard arrangement of electricity incoming supply lines to premises/establishments.

It is also suggested to the public/citizens to construct their houses, buildings, market complexes, etc with proper layout, design and duly approved by the concerned authorities to contribute to the minimizing of haphazard arrangement of incoming power supply lines.

37. Raids to detect electricity theft cases in the post-restructuring period.

Table no: 8.37 Respondent's perception on raids to detect cases of electricity thefts in the post-restructuring period.

		Number of raids to detect cases of electricity thefts in the post-restructuring period.				
		Increased	Decreased	As it is	No opinion	Total
District	Visakhapatnam	29	31	103	17	180
		16.1%	17.2%	57.2%	9.4	100.0%
	East Godavari	13	31	99	25	168
		7.7%	18.5%	58.9%	14.9%	100.0%
	West Godavari	11	40	91	23	165
		6.7%	24.2%	55.2%	13.9%	100.0%
	Krishna District	22	43	76	30	171
		12.9%	25.1%	44.4%	17.5%	100.0%
Total		75	145	369	95	684
		11.0%	21.2%	53.9%	13.9%	100.0%

Chi-square: 21.566, P-value: 0.010

Table no.8.37 describes the respondent's perception on raids to detect cases of electricity thefts in the post-restructuring period. There is significant difference in opinion of the respondents belonging to all the four districts on the statement "Number of raids to detect cases of electricity thefts in the post-restructuring period" as their p-value shows significant.

		Number of raids to detect cases of electricity thefts in the post-restructuring period.				
		Increased	Decreased	As it is	No opinion	Total
Consumer	DOMESTIC	50	105	242	59	456
		11.0%	23.0%	53.1%	12.9%	100.0%
	COMMERCIAL	25	40	127	36	228
		11.0%	17.5%	55.7%	15.8%	100.0%
Total		75	145	369	95	684
		11.0%	21.2%	53.9%	13.9%	100.0%

Chi-square: 3.240, P-value: 0.356

From the table no.8.37 it is observed that a little more than fifty three per cent i.e. 53.9 per cent of the respondents opined that number of raids to detect electricity thefts is as it is. In this regard 21.2 per cent and 11 per cent opined decreased and increased respectively.

The Chi-square value 3.240 and P-value 0.356 suggests that there is no significant difference between number of raids and category at 5 per cent level of significance. Hence the hypothesis is accepted and the variables are independent to each other.

III. CONSUMER SATISFACTION- SERVICES AND PROBLEMS

A. Services

The services rendered by power utilities are not an easy task. More power markets are needed in India. The energy flows across the country needs to be optimized if the energy starved areas are to benefit from the pooling and exporting of power from surplus areas. The global alliance model did not take off in revamping India's power sector. The only motive of business somewhere clouds the real service moral of company's operating utilities who commit promising agendas to bring satisfaction to the electricity consumers.

The consumers are not aware of the power supply chain and its importance to understand the Energy Crisis, India's Power System is facing despite reform and restructuring. Due to lack of awareness on many fronts like energy conservation measures, controlling wastage of electrical energy, safety of electrical power equipments installed, performance and maintenance, billing and metering system, tariff and electricity pricing, etc the government's targets, mission, vision and plans are not becoming objectively successful in the real sense.

Impact of power cuts on day to day living is very much seen in children's education, lack of communication network, pumping and water problems, unrest and health problems, recreation and loss of business almost in all the areas as per the consumers either in the domestic or commercial category. The impact of power cut in the evening hours from 6.00 PM TO 10.00 PM severely affects the children's education (suitable daily study time) and commercial consumers (small business enterprises like grocery, flour mills, cloth merchant, vegetable and sweet vendors, departmental and general stores, etc) i.e. market is completely disturbed. Small business enterprises have to spend on diesel or battery sources as an alternate source of power to facilitate their business the only means for survival.

38. Rating the services rendered by the utility.

Table no: 8.38 Respondent's rating the services rendered by the utility.

Sr. No	Utility Services	Excellent	Very Good	Good	Average	Below average
1	Timely distribution of Bills	34.9	20.2	25	19.3	0.6
2	Accuracy& correctness of bills	14.9	26.2	21.6	35.8	1.5
3	Promptness in providing new connections	11.8	12.9	24	41.4	9.9
4	Quality of power supply	6.1	10.2	17.3	48.8	17.5
5	Utilities concern for customers	5.1	9.6	12.3	43.1	29.8
6	Repairs and replacements in time	5	8.3	9.5	33	44.2
	Average Percentage	12.97	14.57	18.28	36.90	17.25

Respondents' rating the services rendered by the utility is depicted in table no.8.38. The ratings are decided by five types like, excellent, very good, good, average and below average. It is observed from the table that regarding timely distribution of bills 34.9 per cent of the respondents opinion is excellent whereas for accuracy & correctness of bills 35.8 per cent, promptness in providing new connections 41.4 per cent, quality of power supply 48.8 per cent and utilities concern for customers 43 per cent of the respondents perception are an average. 44.2

per cent respondents have considerably rated repairs and replacement in time services by the utilities as below average.

Overall the table concludes that the total sample respondents' rating the services of utilities is average with 36.90 per cent. Hence it is suggested that the utilities should take utmost care in providing good services to the customers by changing in policies and procedures.

District	N	Mean	Std. Deviation	F-Value	P-Value	Decision
Visakhapatnam	180	2.4630	.96615			
East Godavari	168	2.3571	.83668			
West Godavari	165	2.9354	.76011	24.767	0.000	S
Krishna District	171	3.0244	.91514			

For the dimension "Rating the services rendered by the utility" the respondents from Krishna district rated more positively than the remaining three districts followed by West Godavari district. The P-value 0.000 shows that there is a statistically average significant difference in the opinion of the respondents belonging to all the four districts.

Consumer	N	Mean	Std. Deviation	Z-Value	P-value	Decision
DOMESTIC	456	2.7442	.85526	1.089	0.277	N.S
COMMERCIAL	228	2.5855	1.03126			

The above Z-test value 1.089 and its corresponding P-value 0.277 show that there is no statistical significant difference in the opinion of both the type of consumers. Further the domestic consumers rated little bit positively than the commercial consumers but the difference is not statistically differed. The hypothesis is accepted.

39. Global alliance bringing benefits to India's Power Sector.

Table no:8.39 Respondent's perception on Global alliance bringing benefits to India's Power Sector.

		Global alliance bring benefits to India's Power Sector.			
		Yes	No	No Opinion	Total
District	Visakhapatnam	158	21	1	180
		87.8%	11.7%	.6%	100.0%
	East Godavari	149	18	1	168
		88.7%	10.7%	.6%	100.0%
	West Godavari	131	30	4	165
		79.4%	18.2%	2.4%	100.0%
	Krishna District	133	36	2	171
		77.8%	21.1%	1.2%	100.0%
Total		571	105	8	684
		83.5%	15.4%	1.2%	100.0%

Respondents perception on Global alliance bringing benefits to India's Power Sector is furnished in table no: 8.39. Except 15.4 per cent respondents an appreciable majority of respondents 83.5 per cent of all districts disclosed their support for global alliance bringing benefits to India's Power Sector.

		Global alliance bring benefits to India's Power Sector.			
		Yes	No	No Opinion	Total
Consumer	DOMESTIC	392	57	7	456
		86.0%	12.5%	1.5%	100.0%
	COMMERCIAL	179	48	1	228
		78.5%	21.1%	.4%	100.0%
Total		571	105	8	684
		83.5%	15.4%	1.2%	100.0%

The domestic respondents 392(86%) and commercial 179 (78.5%) together 571 (83.5%) told yes. The table concludes that overall opinion of the respondents is that global alliance brings benefits to India's Power Sector. India is facing fiscal deficit averagely in the range 4-6%, so global alliance can help the country to mobilize huge foreign direct investments (FDIs) & better technology for financing projects and upgrading running power plants thus helping the sector to compete, develop, grow and become healthy in delivering better services to the nation.

40. Opinion on more power markets are needed in India.

Table no: 8.40 Respondent's opinion on the need of more power markets India.

| | | Your opinion on more power markets are needed in India. | | | |
		Yes	No	No Opinion	Total
District	Visakhapatnam	168	10	2	180
		93.3%	5.6%	1.1%	100.0%
	East Godavari	149	17	2	168
		88.7%	10.1%	1.2%	100.0%
	West Godavari	132	24	9	165
		80.0%	14.5%	5.5%	100.0%
	Krishna District	142	25	4	171
		83.0%	14.6%	2.3%	100.0%
Total		591	76	17	684
		86.4%	11.1%	2.5%	100.0%

Table no.8.40 brings out respondent's opinion on the need of more power markets in India. A whopping majority of 591 district respondents equaling to 86.4 per cent opined the need for more power markets in India. In this regard Visakhapatnam 93.3 per cent was ahead of all districts. East Godavari 88.7 per cent was followed by Krishna district 83 per cent. The last district West Godavari 80 per cent was also not far behind in expressing the need for more power markets in India.

		Yes	No	No Opinion	Total
Consumer	DOMESTIC	404	38	14	456
		88.6%	8.3%	3.1%	100.0%
	COMMERCIAL	187	38	3	228
		82.0%	16.7%	1.3%	100.0%
Total		591	76	17	684
		86.4%	11.1%	2.5%	100.0%

Your opinion on more power markets are needed in India.

The majority of the respondents in domestic 88.6 per cent and commercial 82 per cent respectively opined positively for more power markets are needed in India. It is interesting to note that only 11.1 per cent told no and 2.5 per cent had no opinion. The table concludes that the need of more power markets in India is required which is very much evident from the recent constitutions of National Power Exchange centers and State trading centers in the country.

41. Reforms helped to optimize the energy flows across the country.

Table no: 8.41 Respondent's perception on the reforms that helped to optimize the energy flows across the country.

		Yes	No	No Opinion	Total
District	Visakhapatnam	107	72	1	180
		59.4%	40.0%	.6%	100.0%
	East Godavari	100	67	1	168
		59.5%	39.9%	.6%	100.0%
	West Godavari	101	59	5	165
		61.2%	35.8%	3.0%	100.0%
	Krishna District	140	28	3	171
		81.9%	16.4%	1.8%	100.0%
Total		448	226	10	684
		65.5%	33.0%	1.5%	100.0%

Header above table: Has the reforms helped to optimize energy flows across the country.

Respondent's perception on the reforms that helped to optimize the energy flows across the country is illustrated in the table no: 8.41. 226 respondents equaling to 33 per cent all districts is not a neglected majority whose perception that the reforms did not help in optimizing the energy flows across the country cannot be ignored.

| | | Has the reforms helped to optimize energy flows across the country. | | | |
		Yes	No	No Opinion	Total
Consumer	DOMESTIC	277	171	8	456
		60.7%	37.5%	1.8%	100.0%
	COMMERCIAL	171	55	2	228
		75.0%	24.1%	.9%	100.0%
Total		448	226	10	684
		65.5%	33.0%	1.5%	100.0%

65.5 per cent of the total sample respondents in which 75 per cent commercial and 60.7 per cent domestic are of the positive opinion that optimization of energy flows across the country has taken place after the reforms. It is interesting to note at the same time that 33 per cent respondents said that there is no optimization of energy flows and only 1.5 per cent very meager had no opinion.

The table finally concludes that though optimization is going on yet much has to be done to remove the regional disparities in accessing the basic means of living electrical energy throughout the width and breadth of the country. The Researcher observed through the existing energy profile of India that energy flow needs to be expedited by the government and utilities to bring balance between the surplus and deficits state in the country.

B. PROBLEMS

In addition to the load shedding, power holidays and elimination of metering and billing system there is disparity in electricity services being provided to consumers from different localities in the state as well as country. The removal of regional disparities in accessibility of electricity when the power sector is energy deficit is a major problem to be addressed on continual basis. The electricity industry and services to the consumers operate under many reformed /amended policies and Acts. The awareness level among the consumers is not appreciable. Understanding know how and practice of conserving energy, minimizing wastage of electrical energy, ethical usage of power, sincerity in paying electricity bills, discouraging theft of power, reducing power losses at offices, residences, public places etc can help the sector to compensate the rising demands.

42. Problems in obtaining electricity connection in your unit.

Table no:8.42 Respondent's opinion on the problems in obtaining electricity connection.

		Did you face any problems in obtaining electricity connection in your unit.		
		Yes	No	Total
Distric	Visakhapatnam	151	29	180
		83.9%	16.1%	100.0%
	East Godavari	141	27	168
		83.9%	16.1%	100.0%
	West Godavari	97	68	165
		58.8%	41.2%	100.0%
	Krishna District	103	68	171
		60.2%	39.8%	100.0%
Total		492	192	684
		71.9%	28.1%	100.0%

Chi-square: 50.429, P-value: 0.000

Respondent's opinion on the problems in obtaining electricity connection is described in table no. 8.42. The district wise analysis reveals that 83.9 per cent each Visakhapatnam and East Godavari, followed by Krishna district 60.2 per cent and West Godavari 58.8 per cent faced problems in obtaining electricity connection in their unit. The Chi-square value 50.429 and P-value 0.000 shows that the perception of the respondents belonging to all the four districts is statistically dissimilar on facing problems in obtaining electricity connection in their unit. It is found to be significant at 5 per cent level of significance. Hence the hypothesis is rejected.

Consumer		Did you face any problems in obtaining electricity connection in your unit.		Total
		Yes	No	Total
Consumer	DOMESTIC	330	126	456
		72.4%	27.6%	100.0%
	COMMERCIAL	162	66	228
		71.1%	28.9%	100.0%
Total		492	192	684
		71.9%	28.1%	100.0%

Chi-square: 0.130, P-value: 0.718

It is observed from the table that out of the total 684 respondents about 492 respondents equaling to 71.9 per cent had positive opinion on the problems obtaining the electricity connection. The remaining 162 respondents equaling to 28.1 per cent are having negative opinion. The category wise analysis reveals that 72.4 per cent domestic and 71.1 per cent commercial respondents are having positive opinion on the problems obtaining the electricity connection.

The table concludes that a whopping majority 71.9 per cent of the respondents are facing problems in obtaining the electricity connection. For the statement "Did you face any problems in obtaining electricity connection in your unit" the consumers of both the types opined unanimously, as their P-value 0.718 shows insignificant. Hence the hypothesis is accepted and variables are independent to each other.

43. Service providers attending complaints and resolving them within time limits.

Table no: 8.43 Respondent's perception on service providers attending complaints and resolving them within time limits.

Sr. No	Consumer Complaints	Within 4Hours	Within 8Hours	Within 16hours	Within 24Hours	Above 24Hours
1	Fuse Calls	51	18.1	20.5	8.8	1.6
2	Over head line break downs	15.1	34.2	24.1	20.2	6.4
3	Underground cable faults	12.1	15.8	26	32.7	13.3
4	Transformer failure	9.8	11.3	13.5	33.6	31.9
5	Voltage problem	19.6	19.9	8.9	31.4	20.2
6	Repair and replacement of meters	8.2	4.7	5.4	15.5	66.2

Table no: 8.43 reflects respondent's perception on service providers attending complaints and resolving them within time limits. Except repair and replacement of meters fault which are attended in above 24 hours has been reported by majority of the respondents 66.2 per cent, other faults like fuse calls within 4 hours by 51 per cent respondents, overhead line break downs majority of the respondents 34.2 per cent said within 8 hours, underground cable faults within 24 hours by 32.7 per cent, transformer failure within 24 hours by 33.6 per cent and voltage problem within 24 hours told by 31.4 per cent respondents.

The complaints discussed here are due to the faults arising in the distribution power system of the utilities and may also be due to the electrical appliances being used by the consumers. The consumers are at liberty to purchase electrical equipments from any manufacturer either registered /approved/certified vendor by concerned electrical authority /certification body or not. This usage of domestic electrical appliances have given scope for faults arising at residences like blowing of fuse due to over load, sometimes short circuit because of improper wiring, tripping of other equipments, including sometimes even the failure of certified appliances. In this regard the power system should also take measures to see the electrical safety of the consumers. The utilities performance and maintenance of power equipments are the concerns of the consumers despite technological up gradation in the power distribution system. The failure of power equipments, improper maintenance and inadequate manpower (like lines man, pole man, fuse call attendant, meter man, etc) are the essential factors responsible for delay in timely attending the faults has been also brought to the surface by the Researcher.

44. Awareness of Electricity Acts and Policies being implemented to reform and restructure the Indian Electricity Sector.

Table no:8.44 Respondent's awareness on Electricity Acts and Policies being implemented to reform and restructure the Indian Electricity Sector.

Sr. No	Electricity Acts & Policies	Major	Moderate	Minor	No opinion
1	Electricity Act-2003	31.1	19.2	18.4	31.3
2	National Electricity Policy	20	28.2	16.2	35.5
3	Rural Electrification Policy	19.2	22.2	20.2	38.5
4	Central Electricity Regulatory Commission(CERC)/ SERC	18.9	22.2	16.7	42.3
5	Accelerated Power Development & Reform Program (APDRP)	20.3	21.5	15.5	42.7
	Average Percentage	21.9	22.66	17.4	38.06

Respondent's awareness on Electricity Acts and Policies being implemented to reform and restructure the Indian Electricity Sector is revealed in the table no.8.44. It is surprising to note that the majority of the total sample respondents had no opinion on the following Electricity Acts 31.3 per cent, National Electricity Policy 35.5 per cent, Rural Electrification Policy 38.5 per cent, CERC/ State Electricity Regulatory Commission (SERC) 42.3 per cent and Accelerated Power Development &Reform Program 42.7 per cent. The table concludes that majority of the respondents had no opinion and next is with moderate awareness on the above Acts and Policies.

District	N	Mean	Std. Deviation	F-Value	P-Value	Decision
Visakhapatnam	180	1.8500	1.07003	28.226	0.000	S
East Godavari	168	2.5238	1.13175			
West Godavari	165	2.8242	1.14738			
Krishna District	171	2.8421	1.27588			

For the dimension "Awareness of electricity Acts and policies being implemented to reform and restructure the Indian Electricity Sector" the four district respondents opined significantly as their ANOVA value 28.226 and its P-value 0.000 shows significant. Further, the average perception score of the Krishna district is more than the remaining three districts followed by West Godavari district which suggests that these two district respondents awareness is more precise than the remaining two district respondents.

Consumer	N	Mean	Std. Deviation	Z-Value	P-value	Decision
DOMESTIC	456	2.3377	1.23323	-5.709	0.000	S
COMMERCIAL	228	2.8202	1.14505			

As per the mean value 2.8202 and its corresponding standard deviation 1.14505, the commercial consumers are little more familiar with the above said electricity Acts and policies than the domestic consumers. The perception on this familiarity is statistically significant different for these two types of consumers at 5 per cent level of significance. Hence the hypothesis is rejected.

It can be summarized from the above analysis that on an average nearly 40 per cent of the consumers are unaware of the Electricity Acts and policies which are implemented to reform and restructure the Indian Electricity Sector. As the sample study covered specifically only three major type of consumers domestic, commercial and industrial in the districts, leaving the agricultural consumers due to the limitation and vastness of the study (however, there were domestic consumers who were farmers/agriculture consumers residing in villages near to sub-urban areas of the districts covered during the sample study, thus not completely ignoring them), the Researcher believes that the above percentage may be even higher and in between 70-80 per cent at national level keeping in mind the literacy rate in India. Hence, it is suggested that the government and power utilities have more interactive sessions in exchanging views, ideas, suggestions, recommendations, so that all these basic inputs can further be redefined, realized and re-implemented with betterment to continually revamp the sector.

45. Impact of regular power cuts on your day to day living.

Table no: 8.45 Impact of regular power cuts on your day to day living.

Sr. No	Impact of power cuts	Major	Moderate	Minor	No opinion
1	Children's Education	88.6	5.8	3.7	1.9
2	Lack of communication network	46.3	40.4	11.3	2
3	Pumping/water problems	41.4	39.8	15.8	3.1
4	Unrest and health problems	40.1	38.9	16.4	4.7
5	Recreation	39.6	32.9	21.1	6.4
6	Loss of business	63.5	21.2	10.5	4.8

Table no.8.45 elucidates the respondent's opinion on impact of regular power cuts on day to day living. Opinion on power cuts of the respondents is listed as major, moderate, minor and no opinion. The impact of regular power cut on respondents day to day living is major in all the factors like children's education 88.6 per cent, lack of communication network 46.3 per cent, pumping/water problems 41.4 per cent, unrest and health problems 40.1 per cent, recreation 39.6 per cent and loss of business 63.5 per cent.

District	N	Mean	Std. Deviation	F-Value	P-Value	Decision
Visakhapatnam	180	2.4389	.42094			
East Godavari	168	2.2966	.60146	4.494	0.004	S
West Godavari	165	2.2081	.66422			
Krishna District	171	2.3450	.67436			

The above P-value 0.004 illustrates that there is a significant difference in the average perceptions of the respondents from all the four districts. The average opinion score of the respondents from Visakhapatnam district is more positive, which suggests in Visakhapatnam district the respondents opined that they are facing huge problems due to the power cuts such as children's education, lack of communication network etc.

Consumer	N	Mean	Std. Deviation	Z-Value	P-value	Decision
DOMESTIC	456	2.3279	.53683	0.187	0.851	N.S
COMMERCIAL	228	2.3187	.71316			

Both domestic and commercial consumers opined unanimously for the dimension "Impact of power cuts" as their average values shows positive which suggests that they are facing huge problems due to this power cuts. The

P-value 0.851 is found to be insignificant at 5% level of significance. Hence the hypothesis is accepted and both the variables are independent to each other.

Daily availability of power in the area vide the analysis of table no.8.2 is in between 13-18 hours which gives a clear evidence of power cuts for 5-10 hours every day averagely. The conclusion of the table no.8.45 related to impact of power cuts on day to day living considerably is in very close concurrence to the above discussion was brought to light by the Researcher. Again moreover it was also identified and correlated by the Researcher the analysis and conclusion of the table no.8.4, pertaining to the usage of alternate source of power supply by the consumers because of power cuts, in the above context.

With all the above facts it is suggested to the government and state distribution utilities to consider the scheduling time period of power cut so that the impact of power cuts on day to day living is minimized, as power cuts cannot be completely avoided amidst the energy crisis the state is facing.

46. Suitable time for planned power cut in your area.

Table no: 8.46 Suitable time for planned power cut in respondent's area.

		What should be the suitable time for planned power cut in your area.					
		4.00 AM -6.00 AM	10 AM- 12 Noon	12 Noon to 2.00 PM	11.00 PM to 1.00 AM	No opinion	Total
District	Visakhapatnam	10	33	29	53	55	180
		5.6%	18.3%	16.1%	29.4%	30.6%	100.0%
	East Godavari	11	46	24	30	57	168
		6.5%	27.4%	14.3%	17.9%	33.9%	100.0%
	West Godavari	16	49	16	44	40	165
		9.7%	29.7%	9.7%	26.7%	24.2%	100.0%
	Krishna District	25	51	24	27	44	171
		14.6%	29.8%	14.0%	15.8%	25.7%	100.0%
Total		62	179	93	154	196	684
		9.1%	26.2%	13.6%	22.5%	28.7%	100.0%

Chi-square:31.9, P-value: 0.000

Details regarding suitable time for planned power cut in respondents area is presented in table no.8.46. The perception of the respondents on the statement "what should be the suitable time for planned power cut in their area" is significantly different by their district which they are living as their p-value shows significant at 5% level of significance.

		What should be the suitable time for planned power cut in your area.					
		4.00 AM -6.00 AM	10 AM- 12 Noon	12 Noon to 2.00 PM	11.00 to 1.00 AM	No opinion	Total
Consumer	DOMESTIC	37	123	68	106	122	456
		8.1%	27.0%	14.9%	23.2%	26.8%	100.0%
	COMMERCIAL	25	56	25	48	74	228
		11.0%	24.6%	11.0%	21.1%	32.5%	100.0%
Total		62	179	93	154	196	684
		9.1%	26.2%	13.6%	22.5%	28.7%	100.0%

Chi-square: 5.492, P-value: 0.240

It is observed that a higher average 28.7 per cent of the total sample respondents had no opinion on suitable timings followed by 26.2 per cent 10 AM-12Noon,22.5 per cent 11PM to 1.00 AM, 13.6 per cent 12 Noon to 2.00 PM and least per cent of 9.1,4.00 AM to 6.00 AM.

The generated Chi-square value 5.492 and P value 0.240 for the above dimension is found to be insignificant at 5 per cent level of significance. The opinion of the consumers of both the types is not significantly differing on the suitable time for planned power cut in their area. Hence the hypothesis is accepted.

All the districts are not equally electrically developed. Districts which are more electrically developed are industrial intensive and consumption pattern of consumers is very high and distributed over the complete day. In urban and city areas the business activities either commercial or non-commercial continues till the late evening hours. In villages and remote villages the major activities of irrigation and other non –industrial usage is almost in the day time. From the above background it becomes very clear that the opinion of the districts is bound to differ, which is in line with the analysis and conclusion of the statement "suitable time for planned power cut in your area" under discussion.

It is practically very difficult for the power utilities to address all the consumers with their respective choice of time for the planned power cut to take place. However, the utilities can look into the majority of the consumer's preference so that primarily the basic needs for living and business are not affected. At the same it is suggested that the government should seriously keep on pursuing the issue of power shortage to minimize the power cuts frequency and time period for bringing satisfaction to the consumers.

47. Opinion on introducing SMART CARDS.

Table no:8.47 Respondent's opinion on introducing of SMART CARDS.

		Opinion on introducing of SMART CARDS (pre paid cards) under house hold reforms thus eliminating the metering and billing system.					
		Strongly Agree	Agree	Undecided	Disagree	Strongly Disagree	Tota
District	Visakhapatnam	26	9	28	54	63	180
		14.4%	5.0%	15.6%	30.0%	35.0%	100.0%
	East Godavari	6	13	41	53	55	168
		3.6%	7.7%	24.4%	31.5%	32.7%	100.0%
	West Godavari	14	58	38	19	36	165
		8.5%	35.2%	23.0%	11.5%	21.8%	100.0%
	Krishna District	22	65	40	18	26	171
		12.9%	38.0%	23.4%	10.5%	15.2%	100.0%
Total		68	145	147	144	180	684
		9.9%	21.2%	21.5%	21.1%	26.3%	100.0%

Chi-square: 139.875, P-value: 0.000

Table no.8.47 explains the opinion of the respondents on introducing of SMART CARDS under house hold reforms thus eliminating the metering and billing system. The opinion of the respondents belonging to all the four districts are significantly different on introducing of SMART CARDS (pre paid cards) under house hold reforms thus eliminating the metering and billing system. Hence the hypothesis is rejected.

		Opinion on introducing of SMART CARDS (pre paid cards) unde house hold reforms thus eliminating the metering and billing system.					
		Strongly Agree	Agree	Undecided	Disagree	Strongly Disagree	Total
Consumer	DOMESTIC	47	101	105	96	107	456
		10.3%	22.1%	23.0%	21.1%	23.5%	100.0%
	COMMERCIAL	21	44	42	48	73	228
		9.2%	19.3%	18.4%	21.1%	32.0%	100.0%
Tota		68	145	147	144	180	684
		9.9%	21.2%	21.5%	21.1%	26.3%	100.0%

Chi-square: 6.492, P-value: 0.165

The opinion is divided into strongly agree, agree, undecided, disagree and strongly disagree. It is clear from the table that about 26.3 per cent of the total respondents strongly disagree for introducing the SMART CARD under house hold reforms. Next followed by 21.5 per cent undecided, 21.2 per cent agree, 21.1 per cent disagree and 9.9 per cent strongly agree.

The table concludes that nearly 50 per cent of the total sample respondents disagree for the introduction of SMART CARDS under house hold reforms. SMART CARDS introduction is an initiative under the Energy Management implementation programme by the Government of India. This can be an effective tool to curb down unaccountable usage of electrical energy and simultaneously a protective mode for improving collection efficiency. Presently, on an average at all India level 50 per cent of energy sold is not billed. Both, the power utilities operating the distribution system (including billing and metering system) and the loyalty of the consumers' willingness to pay for the services in time is equally responsible for unhealthiness of power sector.

So it is suggested that the consumers should come forward with proactive approach to accept the usage of SMART CARDS thus supporting the government in its programme to improve the collection efficiency in every state. The Researcher is of the opinion that a substantial improvement in collection efficiency to the range between 80-90 percent at national level can help the power utilities to operate in future without subsidies and at economical price of electricity energy per unit recovering the complete cost of power generation including the ROR for its sustainability and survival of the sick utilities in the sector.

For the statement "Opinion on introducing of SMART CARDS (pre paid cards) under house hold reforms thus eliminating the metering and billing system" both the types of the consumers opined commonly. The Chi-square value 6.492, P-value 0.165 is found to be insignificant at 5% level of significance. Hence the hypothesis is accepted and both the variables are independent to each other.

48. Challenges to reduce wastage of energy by the utilities.

Table no: 8.48 Challenges to reduce wastage of energy by the utilities.

Sr. No	Reducing Energy Wastage	1	2	3	4	5	Weighted Rank
1	Regular energy audits required	258 (1290)	80 (320)	133 (399)	180 (360)	33 (33)	2 (2402)
2	Consumer awareness programmes	126 (630)	287 (1148)	170 (510)	89 (178)	12 (12)	1 (2478)
3	Rewards for loyal consumers	98 (490)	211 (844)	268 (804)	98 (196)	9 (9)	3 (2343)
4	Enforcement by regulators	162 (810)	101 (404)	101 (303)	301 (602)	19 (19)	4 (2138)
5	All	35 (175)	5 (20)	10 (30)	18 (36)	120 (120)	5 (381)

Challenges to reduce wastage of energy by the utilities are brought out in table no: 8.48. In respondents opinion consumer awareness program would be the prime force to reduce wastage of energy given first rank, respondents gave 2nd rank to conducting of regular energy audits, rewards for loyal consumers attained 3rd rank, 4th rank was taken by enforcement by regulators and all stood last. However as all the factors are essential but there is great emphasis on awareness programs and energy audits according to the above table. It is suggested to the government to conduct more awareness programs and regular energy audits.

49. Opinion on services provided by utilities in the state.

Table no: 8.49 Respondent's opinion on the services provided by the utilities in the state.

Sr. No	Consumers Locality	Excellent	Very Good	Good	Average	Below average
1	Urban	27.2	25	33.2	14	0.6
2	Sub-urban	6.1	25	36.4	27.5	5
3	Villages	1.3	6.7	21.8	45.2	25
4	Remote villages	0.7	3.9	6.4	26.6	62.3
5	Other backward areas	0.7	2.6	5.1	11	80.6

Table no: 8.49 describes respondent's opinion on the services provided by the utilities in the state. Services in the other backward areas as per 80.6 per cent respondents followed by remote villages 62.3 per cent are below average. The villages get average service was disclosed by 45.2 respondents. Services in urban and suburban is very good was revealed by 25 per cent each respondents and also good by 33.2 and 36.4 respondents respectively. About 27.2 per cent of the total sample respondents told services in urban to be excellent.

Energy Crisis in India

The table concludes that the utilities are good in providing services in urban and suburban areas but villages, remote villages and other backward areas are being neglected by the utilities. It is suggested to the Government of India to design a new mechanism of ascertaining best services provided to all areas especially villages and remote villages.

The Researcher found from the sample study analysis that there is perfect correlation between the respondents representing the Power Utilities (from all the state, central and private sector) providing services and the Domestic & Commercial consumers residing at various localities in different districts in the state with varying level of loyalty, which is very much evident from the conclusion of Chapter VIII, (Domestic & Commercial Electricity Consumers), table no. 8.18 and 8.49 and Chapter V(Generation, Transmission and Distribution) table no.4.25

CHAPTER IX

COMMERCIALIZATION OF ELECTRICITY

Citizen Vs Consumer

Indian Electricity Sector has journeyed from nationalization to commercialization of electricity. Will commercializing electricity bring any promising changes in the overall scenario of the Indian Power Sector?

Who is a Global Consumer? Are Indian citizens becoming global consumers due to participation of global stakeholders in Energy Industry in India? Consumer pricing is no more purely based on national policies and issues. Many international trade rules, excise duties, customs and taxations are applicable to arrive at the cost of producing power and finally consuming it as useful energy.

From management's perspective a citizen is a consumer. The social perception is built on the ideologies of citizens. Nation has to safe guard citizens. Citizens have to build the nation.

"Consumer is the King", is the new mantra of Global Markets. How far it holds well in India? Are the Indian citizens seating on the throne of market? Election campaigns are the only period when the contestants are the well wishers of the citizens.

Once elected to power, they have their own mandates for the nation. This is the oldest philosophy all over the world.

Can any national Policy demarcate between Citizen, Consumer and Customer precisely? A citizen is both the consumer as well as the customer. All the worry is about mapping customer to prices and citizen to services.

I can make an impartial inference that all the war in the energy sector is about "Services Vs Prices".

Today's concept of market is that every consumer is a customer. Do we get a good service by paying good price in the energy sector? Service is having different dimension with respect to the category of consumer. The impacts of service performance is more in the retail consumer segment.

In Retail consumers of power the residential or the household sector is a mammoth sector. If you clearly define, it is almost the entire nation. Every citizen is having a household connection.

The issues are right from supply to end usage. Electricity Bill has been always a subject of anti people.

People never like tariff hike. Government sees people as customers. The concept of profit is at its own motives.

Do you think just by relaxing the policy huge investments can be arranged by private organizations at par with the government organizations?

Policy -3C's

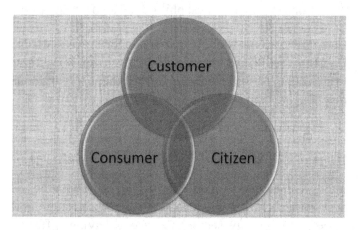

In this part an attempt has been made through chapters on electricity consumers to focus on Power- Supply, Quality and Billing, Power System- Performance and Maintenance and Consumer Satisfaction –Services and Problems of Industrial, Domestic and Commercial Electricity Consumers.

How consumers are availing the services and their satisfaction levels was very well captured in this case study. The application of statistical tools and mathematics gives empirical figures and rankings to the outcome of the questionnaire representing the issue of the citizens of India. Every question is an important aspect of the power sector in discussion.

My narration is more like a commentary based on the field survey, feedback & data collected and analyzed on the issues prevailing in the energy and power sector in India.

Energy & Power together is responsible for the good rate of economy of the nation. The growth rate in power and energy will definitely reflect in the rate of economy the nation is growing.

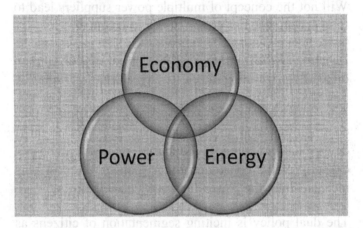

The main objective of the amendment seems to be to push the commercialization of electricity, opening up the distribution sector before the profit motive of corporate houses. The priorities of Government seems to be in favour of high income groups where people want 24X7 quality power supply without bothering for tariff.

The Government is talking of two different tariffs one for common man and other for people willing to pay 50% extra during peak hours for uninterrupted power supply. The Government is revising the tariff policy leading to peak load tariff and normal tariff.

Power sector is facing serious challenges such as large scale financial losses, rising tariffs, deteriorating performance of existing plants, fuel availability and quality related concerns and poor quality of supply and service. The proposed amendments aim at making fundamental changes to the sector structure and organization, but it is not clear how these changes will help in tackling the issues mentioned above.

Will not the concept of multiple power suppliers lead to total privatization of power supply in country?

I wish to know from my readers, "What is your opinion on totally privatizing the electricity services in India?".

Why are we making two divisions of citizens? One common man and another rich man. Is policy on tariff determination going to be based on the purchasing capacity of the consumer rather than on the cost plus mechanism of the power generating utilities?

The dual policy is inciting segmentation of citizens as rich and poor customers. The poor customers are having wider consumer base.

Is electricity going to be completely commercialized in India? Will everybody give up the subsidies on power?

Rights Vs Price, you have to pay the price for your rights. This is the environment a citizen is sailing from dawn to dusk. The question is good service at what price.

Commerce Vs Business, though it looks similar is at crossroads. Commercial regulations are not always welcomed by the business fraternity. Expecting business with service motto only may not be an idealistic perception today.

Funding without timely returns is one of the major concerns of any investor in India's Energy Sector. Though the mechanisms were designed it has its own reasons of failure. Nothing took off as it was envisaged in during the blue prints of reforms and restructuring in power sector.

Investor Vs Returns, is another area where the energy policy fails to completely safeguard the investors against huge risks. Who will mitigate them? Who will take the overall responsibility? Risk management sounds to be good only in the theoretical books but not really in the arena of Indian Power Sector.

What should be considered during formulating a power policy in India?

Politics Vs Economics, is the guiding factor for the manifestos and mandates in the power sector by the ruling party leading the government. The situation becomes more complex in a multi party collated form of government.

Almost every state in India has two to three leading parties on average.

Political Synergy practically does not last long in a democratic set up. Thus India is losing opportunities of technological advancement because of weaker technological synergies in energy and power sector.

The experience and effect of market power in a scarce market has not been considered in formulating the proposal. As India is energy starved nation, reducing price of power through competition is impractical.

The multiple licensee system will help only "cherry picking" and the deterioration of the incumbent public sector licensee, which will be the only responsible for supplying electricity to the unprivileged common man. This simply means nationalizing the losses and privatizing the profits. The competition is possible only in a situation of surplus, not scarcity of electricity, which the country was facing.

As per census 2011 figures, close to 45% of rural India lack access to electricity. More than 33% of Indian households are still have no access to electricity. Moreover, even in cities, households suffer on account of shortage of power.

At present nearly 40 % population of country does not have access to power as they cannot afford power even at existing rates. Therefore giving multiple licenses of supply will lead to chaos, heavy losses of Discoms, endless litigations and sky level tariff hike for common people.

The practical impact of proposed amendments will be inability of the State Discoms to make investments for extending power supply to 80 million un-electrified households and making it impossible to achieve the Govt. of India objective/ target of 24×7 supply for all consumers by 2018-19.

It is a well known fact that the stability of the power sector on a whole has gone down since the enactment of Electricity Act 2003, though there are achievements in some areas. From a common man's view point, the electricity is fast becoming a costly affair going beyond his hold. How to perfectly define who is a common man?

In the name of competition and efficiency in the supply of electricity with more than one supply licensee offering supply of electricity to consumers in the same area, separation of carriage and content in the distribution sector is being looked at. Multiple supply licensees at the same area of operation is aimed at retail competition thus to tide over the impractical proposal of multiple distribution licensees existing in Act 2003.

Even though there is a dream of improving quality and reducing cost through market competition, the reality is different. As per the amendment anybody applying for a licensee has the right to get a license and there is every chance of non-serious players to come in as licensee and collect security deposits and fly away.

Supply Vs Distribution, the amendment is silent on the mechanism of setting off the power flow between supply licensees and distribution licensee. Since incumbent licensee has the responsibility of serving power to every consumer as a last resort it has to formulate its power purchase plans. But it will fall in trouble due to black box strategies of other licensees.

Even though electricity is a matter on the concurrent list in the Constitution, the powers of the State Governments, which are already shackled to a large extent by virtue of

Electricity Act 2003, are seen likely to be curtailed by the proposed amendments.

This will severely affect the Centre –State relations which are against the vision of your good governance.

In India, the situation in power sector, such as consumer mix, consumer spread, sources of generation, ownership pattern etc. are vastly different from states to states. The priorities and strategies of development of the states will be different and will also be having their own stake in deciding the structure of the sector, development strategies and Tariff design including decisions on subsidies and cross subsidies of Electricity.

Hence making the policy decisions of Central Government as mandatory is against the federal set up of governance and is not proper. The proposed system of separating out supply from wires business involves a foolproof and dispute free system of energy accounting and loss determination.

Energy accounting and loss determination itself would make the proposed system unmanageable and full of disputes. An elaborate and computerized energy accounting and loss accounting systems are nowhere in existence and without these the commercial aspects of energy supply simply cannot be settled.

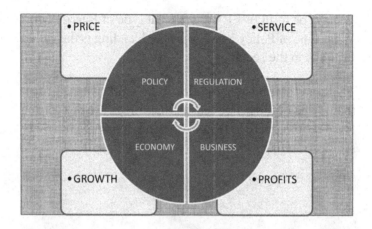

The wheel of policy, regulation, economy and business can come out with many combinations of price, service, profits and growth in the energy sector.

Commercialization cannot be decided in an isolation framework. An integrated approach is required in deciding the type of electricity services models India wishes to adopt for reenergizing the country.

Energy Economists in India need to focus more on R& D in the sector. Electricity is not a commercial commodity which can be traded as you like and whenever you like. It is the life line of the nation.

It is a well known fact that the impossible is often the untried.

What type of power India needs today? Which is economical? Which is available in abundance?

What type of POWER MIX? What type of Energy Mix? What type of Policy Mix? A proper blending is the call of the hour in the sector.

There are several possibilities to be worked out. In fact that is one of the prime reason that things are not getting fixed permanently in the volatile and dynamic electricity sector in India.

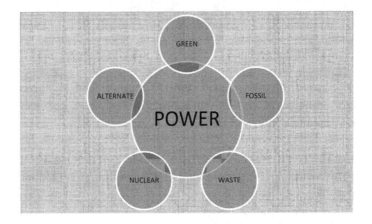

How to meet the country's RE goals? Where is an effective framework for Renewable Purchase Obligations (RPO) in India?

Just like the Coal Sector which was once at commanding heights, now the Energy Industry is banking on the RE Sector.

India is going Green. Will Green Energy replace 100% Fossil Energy? It is time which perhaps may decide the course of Energy in India.

Today, the journey of lighting from GLS-CFL-LED itself is reflection of the changes the power industry has undergone by innovation in power systems.

LED promises to save enormous electrical energy in India. If implemented could save 100 billion units annually.

Every unit of electricity saved by a consumer counts. This culture of conserving and saving energy needs greater emphasis, awareness and encouragement for true implementation all over the country. The present rate is unappreciable compared to the Global standards.

Is the road map prepared by the Electricity Act and National Action Plan on Climate Change (NAPCC) to increase the RE generation in India?

Renewable Energy Certificates (REC) concept has its own doubts of success. Who will address the critical mismatches in the mechanism?

Policy Makers Vs Regulators, the road never converges. Why the gap continues to crop up uncertainties in the energy sector? Nearly 75% of the States in India have failed to meet the RPO targets?

Do you think in the regime of deregulation, liberalization, privatization, globalization, corporatization and commercialization of electricity services conditional contracts and incentives will be obliged by MNCs or TNCs in India?

Are not we inviting them to the wrong ceremony? Only a "Green Agenda" will not solve the national issues of energy crisis in India.

People are ready and willing to pay electricity bills in rural areas. The question is of poor infrastructure, means and pay points to facilitate their receivables. The modes are to be developed to connect to the prospective electricity consumers in rural areas in India.

How to reach rich India's poorest electricity consumers?

SECTION-C

SUMMARY & CONCLUSION

"Energy builds Infrastructure
&
Infrastructure builds Energy".

No one can deny this. One is incomplete without the other.

Why electricity consumption rate doesnot follow the economic growth rate in India?

Affordability Vs Access, gaps needs immediate attention both at the Centre as well as State. Why India failed in rapdly unifying, developing and electrifying rural areas of the country?

Irrigation Vs Industry, which shoud be given preference by the poicy makers. Why revenue collection from electricity consumers in India is not happening properly? Deregulation never meant relaxation in penalties to the defaulters.

Will the commercialization of electricity make its controls free from the Constitutional Rights or obligatins? Do you think at this point of discussion and debate the "Concurrent List" needs redefinition and revision?

Can the role of Central Government be eliminated completely in the electricity services in India?

India in the new world speaks and dreams of emerging economy mix. The energy industry is the totality of all of the industries involved in the production and sale of energy, including fuel extraction, manufacturing, refining and distribution. Modern society consumes large amounts of fuel, and the energy industry is a crucial part of the infrastructure and maintenance of society in almost all countries.

In particular, the energy industry comprises: the petroleum industry, including oil companies, petroleum refiners, fuel transport and end-user sales at gas stations, the gas industry, including natural gas extraction, and coal gas manufacture, as well as distribution and sales, the electrical power industry, including electricity generation, electric power distribution and sales, the coal industry, the nuclear power industry, the renewable energy industry, comprising alternative energy and sustainable energy companies, including those involved in hydroelectric power, wind power, and solar power generation, and the manufacture, distribution and sale of alternative fuels and traditional energy industry based on the collection and distribution of firewood, the use of which, for cooking and heating, is particularly common in poorer countries.

The point of discussion is that there should be proper mapping, planning and fulfillment for, "Policy for Energy and Energy for Policy".

I am sharing with you the prime paradox of the whole crisis. As stated above the infrastructural support to energy sector have been very poorly aligned in India. Even today right from exploration of oil & gas, mining of coal & lignite, to evacuation of power from energy utilities to the supply lines to retail consumers has its daily challenges.

Neither the infrastructure is coming up as planned nor the energy capacity addition as envisaged. Under these shortfall targets what strategies could be taken up to bridge the unanticipated gaps of failure.

Who will benefit?

Sphere of Consumers

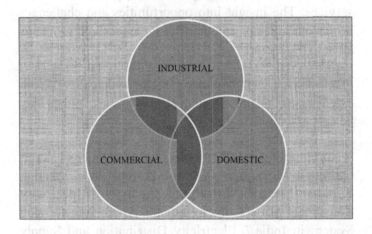

My readers need not be perplexed to hear from the author sad stories and incidents of the sector. In one more recent review made by me you will find that the Delhi Electricity Regulatory Commission is set to hold the public hearing for tariff determination for financial year 2015 next month.

What I am trying to emphasize is that this is the most vibrant and vulnerable sector in India.

This case study has been intended to give new directions for further research.

The Case Study "ENERGY CRISIS IN INDIA" with reference to Power Utilities and Electricity Consumers in the selected Districts of Coastal Andhra Pradesh, was limited to only four districts of Andhra Pradesh.

This is a model analytical study in the sector. Many such study can be designed, surveyed and analyzed for continual feedback on the sector's governance, performance and services. The insight into opportunities and challenges brings out the gaps and maps of the issues and problems alive in the sector.

It reveals the gaps between policies and reality. As an extension to this present study, the following studies may be carried out.

1. Rural Electrification in India,2. Performance of Power Utilities in India, 3. Evaluation of Power Policies in India, 4. Indian Electricity Market, 5. Analysis of Electricity Consumers' Satisfaction in India, 6. Power Transmission System in India,7. Electricity Distribution and Supply Chain in India, 8. Pricing of Electricity in India, 9. Public Vs Private Power Utilities, 10. Conventional Fuels Vs Renewable

A more intensive study at micro level may be carried out in many areas. India needs to promote research in energy and power sector with great thrust and drive throughout the country.

Energy Training Centers should primarily make a place in every district of the country.

Urban Vs Rural, gaps in electricity services should be eliminated by developing at par infrastructures and integrated power systems.

This analytical study attempted to overview the performance of the Indian power sector with greater emphasis on electrifying rural India since British Rule when electricity was a luxury and the subsequent developments after Independence with the philosophy of nationalization marching ahead surrendering to corporatization of electricity services.

The journey of electricity in India beginning with the lantern street lamps to the illuminating Cyber cities of today has its own saga of pros and cons.

India till the implementation of the Industrial Policy supported by subsequent growth and development was Rural India only. The rapid industrialization began after 1965-70 to become self reliant primarily in manufacturing sector.

Even today the agriculture sector dominates the share in India's GDP. Despite industrialization nearly over half a century the country's major population lives in rural areas. It is very difficult to demarcate rural and urban keeping in view the proximity of each. The lack of electricity accessibility in rural areas is one of the predominant reasons for poor rate of literacy in backward states.

The potential and vigor of the young minds is being nipped in the bud. The policy of establishing small scale agro industries to stop migration of people from villages for lively hood has been brutally murdered with no power supply support.

Moreover the dependency on fossil fuels for heating and cooking could not be eliminated despite promises at the State and Centre. Struggling to survive is the dividends of all the efforts in electrifying India.

To sum up, Rural Electricity Consumers awareness level on policy matters and implementation strategy had been invariably poor. The State Electricity Boards never had their engineering to improve the overall integrated power systems connecting all the villages to the main grid.

Why India is unable to generate power as per inherited potential?

The existing public electricity-supply industry needs to be put in order first to allow the private sector to operate. To ensure an optimal allocation of capital and energy resources, the size of electricity markets at the state level is still too small.

Efforts must be made to improve the development and the management of the power sector at the Union level. The central government has underestimated the specific regulatory needs for competition to expand and for the grid to develop in a sustainable manner.

Is Indian government concentrating to adopt a comprehensive reform plan for the electricity supply industry? Simply introducing competition to the electricity sector and no concern for improving its overall performance is as good as not hearing the voices of citizens of India.

Is India taking into account the goals of electricity access, energy security, environmental protection and economic growth?

India is lagging behind in ownership to deliver public services? Though India has more or less a system for service but it is not efficiently working out the plans to achieve the goals of millions and millions of citizens.

How to make the states accountable for the performance of their public electricity system?

Efficiency by providing additional financial incentives to better-performing states on the basis of a transparent set of criteria is again tainted with duality in policy. Absolute priority should be given to achieving full cost recovery within a defined time frame.

How to have an uncontaminated policy in the power sector? This is necessary because so-called non-technical losses which are actually unpaid or stolen electricity are largely the result of political interference or of negligence by the state governments.

Why State governments should be provided incentives to enforce the law and to clamp down on non-paying consumers? Is it not their responsibility?

States should be accountable for the cost of transmission and distribution (T&D) losses in their budgets and to establish tariffs based on a low level of T&D losses.

There is helplessness that electricity theft cannot be controlled in India. We the citizens of India can prove this hypothesis to be certainly wrong. Let us all take a pledge not to cheat the nation in energy and power.

We the citizens of India can definitely change the scenario of the country which is branded as energy deficit in the world. The citizens have to hold the hand of the government for a win-win situation.

This would reinforce the responsibilities of regulators to monitor T&D losses and differentiate between technical and non-technical losses. A legal framework should be established to sanction the loose handling of tariffs and power theft, and providing targets and incentives for the states. No progress can be achieved without improved revenue collection from final consumers.

Why we are unable to set and adhere to a firm timetable for introducing market mechanisms in India? An implementation timetable should provide for establishing the regulatory framework, reforming subsidies, curbing power theft and developing innovative solutions for private sector distribution.

Why not have two power markets? The focus should be on development of a power market at the central level and should clearly identify the steps to be taken at the state level. A number of such mechanisms have nominally been implemented, but future implementation will need clearly-designed monitoring criteria.

Does concentrating political accountability in a single energy ministry help the energy sector? Do you think integration of political accountability into a single energy ministry is essential?

Only an integrated authority can exploit economies of scale through co-operation and integration at the Union level has always been debated in India. But again the vastness and complexities from interfacing issues related to cross-functioning departments remains incomprehensible.

Many of our intellectual citizen's feel that the mobilization of investment capital is to be done by the centralized public utilities. The strategy of increasing generation capacity through large-scale IPPs has not proved successful despite the big story of reforms and restructuring in India.

The gap has been partially covered by the development of self-generation and by central public-sector investments. It would be beneficial to have a mix of large and small public-utility capacity, at least temporarily, to reduce the supply-demand gap.

Are we actually facilitating and encouraging grid access for surplus electricity from captive producers, while encouraging private investment in generation? Use of existing capacity should be maximized to make a significant contribution from the private sector to the emerging electricity market.

Who will create the framework for a power market at the international level? This recommendation complements the above call for more integration. India is still far from the point where a competitive global market can govern the supply-demand balance.

Are we really seeing the benefits of liberalization? However, India's eventual target should be an electricity market. Why only at the aggregated Union level are there sufficient demand and supply?

The first steps toward such a national market would be increased investment in the Union-level electricity grid, and giving more freedom for market players to exchange and trade across state borders.

Is India religiously implementing measures to improve business practices of the emerging electricity supply industry in the public sector?

Why more attention is not being paid to developing human skills and personal accountability at all levels of the state and central government?

Do you think because of India's large population, consumption of electricity per capita is among the lowest in the world? Or this is because of unavailability of power.

I have a scientific analysis behind my sharing that population is an only a misnomer in the whole process of defending statements in safeguarding the failures of the sector.

Projections & Commitments are always being mismatched. There are promising projections of an average annual growth rate of 5% to 5.5 % for the next 20 years for India's GDP and of 5.5% to 6.0% for electricity generation, corresponding to a threefold rise in electricity supply over the period. These projections need high levels of investment throughout the entire sector.

Which should be more rate of power generation or rate of national growth? I earnestly wish my readers to spend some valuable time in understanding the economics of growth in India.

Indian electricity policy aims to provide cost-effective, affordable and secure access to electricity for all. Given the large rural population, rural electrification always remains with grievances and dissatisfaction.

Global Power Policy should favor ecology or economy? Both are essential for a nation to be healthy. Where do India stands in this regard? This is for my readers to brainstorm so that the intension of this book can be justified.

What can be a better way of learning and sharing than this? Everybody has the ability and idea to excel. Let us integrate the individual potentials to realize the nation's dream of power to all.

This analytical review focuses on the electricity supply chain industry. It explores the linkages between price, demand and supply. It recounts the emergence of a competitive power market so far and examines possible future development of this market.

All the recommendations are the voices of Indian power consumers. The reviews of the citizens are in fact practically required to bring things on the surface by analyzing the Indian electricity sector. More and more similar type of studies across the country now and then should be undertaken for continual improvement and development.

India faces many challenges on the energy front, but must deal simultaneously with economic, social, political, pollution and environmental challenges as well.

These are valuable considerations which are essential on energy policy formulation. The wider access to modern commercial energy sources, the reduction of airborne pollutants in cities, and improvements in the reliability and the quality of energy services are strong drivers of Indian energy policy.

In addition to general policy issues, the study reviewed India's electricity-supply industry and its various market components or sub-sectors, examining the demand side of the power market, then distribution, transmission and generation.

"Urban Vs Rural", brings out the disparities in electricity services in India. Rural electrification is considered in its own rights, as it involves specific market dynamics. It invariably appears that "Inconvenience is highly regretted", is the apology to safeguard from the failures in rural India.

This book does not believe in demoralizing any individual or his dignity of labour during the entire analysis. I personally have due regards to the whole system we are part of it. What is being explored here is that how betterment can be sustained in crisis?

I am not promoting any pre-determined model of market and regulatory organization against the national laws of services. It does however try to identify possible areas of improvement of the existing set-up, in order to restore the sector's health, introduce more competition and satisfy the country's growing electricity needs.

What Indians understand by General Electricity Policy? The Government of India, in conjunction with state governments, should use indicative planning and the normal techno-economic project clearances to guide technical choices and the power mix, define and implement the principles on which tariffs are set and tariffs themselves, and do so increasingly through independent regulatory commissions, increase the level of public funds in the sector to encourage development, create an environment that will attract private players.

Even today most of the electricity-supply industry in India remains in the public sector. Why there are announcements of huge coal based power plants and renewable in the public sector despite the liberalization policy?

Does India fear to completely rely on Private Utilities in energy sector?

Public Utilities Vs Private Utilities, can they merge into one identity as National Energy Utilities. If not, then what is the stand of national policy with two different perspectives?

The central government, through public companies, owns and operates one-third of the power generation and interstate exchanges. At the state level, SEBs own and operate most of the remaining two-thirds of the generation capacity, as well as single-state transmission and distribution systems. States define their own tariff structures.

State-wide electricity systems are relatively small, in line with the low country per capita electricity consumption. The sector would benefit from further national integration and the economies of scale that would accompany it.

Although the central government is politically committed to reforming the regulatory framework to facilitate the development of a power market, implementation of the reform policies has been slow.

Is power technology competency and capability to bring in rapid implementation not being taken care of by the policy makers in India?

Power-sector policies are designed and implemented by the Ministry of Power at the national level and by ministries in charge of power or energy at the state level. Political intervention in electricity matters is common at the national level.

Fuel-supply issues for power generation projects may also need clearance from the Ministry of Coal (and the Ministry of Railways) or the Ministry of Petroleum and Natural Gas, whose opinions often differ from those of the Ministry of Power. Political intervention motivated by social concerns is frequently exerted and can frustrate efforts to rationalize electricity prices.

How to stop "Stealing of Electricity"? Can we go for prepaid meters as the revolution in communication sector like the pre-paid mobile connections? It can be one of the proven means to minimize the loss of revenue collection from legal connections.

The side effects of this way of subsidizing energy consumption are significant. Overpricing of industrial electricity hampers competitiveness. In other sectors, under pricing of electricity is a direct incentive to waste power.

In theory, cost-reflective tariff structures do not differentiate between final uses of electricity. The lowest tariffs apply to customers with the highest consumption and load factors (industrial customers). Households, on the contrary, pay the highest rate due to their low load factor, limited consumption and the relatively higher cost of distribution.

State governments should promote and foster payment for electricity by all customers. Legal action must be taken at the state level to prevent theft so that electricity suppliers have increased assurance that all customers will pay.

Tariff should be designed to recover costs on the basis of the electricity which is sold and paid for only, separating the cost of stolen electricity from the tariff structure. Otherwise, paying customers could end up being burdened with the costs of non-paying customers.

To avoid such a difficulty, the unit price should perhaps be capped temporarily.

Subsidy reform will undoubtedly result in tariff increases. To gain acceptance from consumers, the increases should be accompanied by significant improvements in the reliability, quality and accessibility of electricity supply. Restoring the investment capability of SEBs – or their unbundled sub-divisions – should be a priority.

An active communications programme to explain the rationale behind subsidy reform and market pricing must accompany the reform.

Cost-based electricity pricing needs to be implemented for all users. This requires an accurate data collection system and information on costs. If policy-makers find it appropriate to maintain partial subsidies for a particular category of consumers, the mechanism should be transparent and carefully monitored.

The subsidy should also be allocated directly from the state budget to avoid burdening the utilities. It should expire within a set time frame. Access to electricity for low-income households should be carried out through direct support, or by mechanisms such as lifeline rates.

Demand-side management and load management should be more actively pursued at the state levels for all sectors, particularly industry and agriculture, to reduce peak supply shortages and increase the cost-efficiency of the system.

For such measures to be successful, metering and pricing policies based on daily demand profiles should be implemented for agricultural use puts a heavy financial burden on the electricity sector and incidentally threatens water resources in the long-term. Low cost recovery translates into degradation of service, which in turn requires costly investments in stand-by capacity in the industrial and commercial sectors and by large domestic consumers.

Confronted by high prices and unreliable supply from the network, big industrial consumers increasingly turn to "captive-power", which now represents more than one-third of their consumption.

Every industrial consumer lost by the SEBs further worsens their financial situation since it reduces their sales base to low-paying customers. Subsidies artificially sustain demand from the consumers already connected to the grid, but a large unmet demand exists because of grid deficiencies and the inability of insolvent utilities to invest in additional connections.

This policy recommendation applies to schemes such as Kutir Jyothi, facilitating access to electricity to low income groups. State governments should expedite reforms in the distribution sector, separating distribution from other activities carried out by SEBs. This process could be monitored at the central level. States should be accountable for the performance of their public electricity systems, particularly revenue collection by distributors.

Distributing entities should be placed on a commercial footing and improved revenue collection should be rewarded. Best practices should be disseminated to other states.

In the state of Orissa, the privatization of distribution fell short of expectations. Changing the tariff methodology was insufficient to allow for increasing revenue collection. It is hard to say whether this was due to a lack of political support or to inappropriate regulation.

The central government should rapidly provide financial incentives for states to create innovative institutional and regulatory structures that improve revenue collection.

Once the revenue collection has improved, but only then, corporatized public distributors should be privatized.

Managing the distribution sector efficiently requires appropriate information about electricity consumption. Accordingly, a consolidated consumption database should be created and made transparent through improved metering. The management of distribution should be monitored using criteria based on the optimal use of resources.

Indicators should include sales per kilometer of distribution line, average capacity of sub-stations, final marginal cost per kWh distributed, and equipment turnover rates. The distribution grid must be expanded.

An accurate database on consumption, including such items as technical losses, must be made available to all market players. No such database exists in India.

In its policies for electricity reform, the central government identified the need to separate distribution from other activities carried out by SEBs. But, few states have implemented this policy.

The commercial and the technical elements of distribution could be easily separated. Billing customers and taking payment could be handled by a separate entity from the one responsible for the distribution of electric power to consumers.

Average electricity consumption per square kilometer is very low in India compared with averages in OECD countries. This may justify the development of distributed generation rather than centralized power generation. The substantial auto-production capacity that already exists in the industry may be connected to the grid and emerge

Given current losses in the transmission sector, investments in transmission are likely to be far more cost-effective than investments in generation. They should be given the highest priority by the central government. As a means to achieve a national electricity market, POWERGRID should be given a clear mandate and adequate capital to set up a national transmission grid. Private-sector participation should be encouraged to supplement public efforts through specific investment schemes such as build-operate and transfer (BOT).

The central government's plans are essential to guide investments in transmission since the large development needs of the system entail high investment risks. But, unlike the existing plans which do not refer explicitly to cost as an optimization criterion, future plans should use economic criteria extensively.

An independent central system operator could be assigned the responsibility for operation, maintenance and development of the very-high-voltage transmission network (400 kV and above, both inter and intrastate). This operator should co-operate closely with another entity responsible for merit-order dispatching of all Indian electricity generation, including auto-production as distributed generation in the years to come.

However, the bulk of power generation currently uses a centralized grid and is fuelled mostly by domestic hydro and coal concentrated in specific areas. This is why transmission is a key component of India's electricity supply industry. For the time being, interstate transmission is dictated by supply-demand imbalances between states. For the last 20 years, public expenditures in transmission have not been commensurate with generation expenditures.

This increased T&D losses already considerably burdened by power theft and reduced pooling of Indian power-generation resources, and thus led to an unreliable transmission system.

The concept of regional planning and operation was adopted in the 1960s. Five regions were identified. The current development of domestic resources (hydro and coal) for the Indian electric power system is a first step in the gradual integration of the regional systems into an India-wide power system.

Plans to build large power plants, particularly if they are fuelled by liquefied natural gas (LNG) which itself needs large infrastructure, will make an integrated national power system even more necessary.

SEBs tends to favor state-level solutions to reduce power shortages. They prefer to add generation capacity instead of developing interstate and inter-regional electricity trade.

This is largely due to the soft budgetary constraints on SEBs and their insufficient use of cost criterion in investment decisions.

A central transmission company (CTU), responsible for developing the interstate transmission grid and power exchange, was established in 1989 as a public enterprise.

It is called POWERGRID Corporation of India. The CERC is now formulating an interstate transmission tariff and a grid code.

For the time being, transmission pricing, operation and investment at the state level remain the responsibility of SEBs.

In 1999-2000, of total Indian generation capacity amounting to 113 GW, 15 GW were auto-production1. Of the remaining 98 GW, coal-fired generation accounted for 61%, hydro 24%, gas 10%, nuclear 3% and oil 2%. Given India's vast coal resources, and its large untapped hydroelectric potential, these two resources are likely to provide the bulk of additional generation capacity in future.

Almost two thirds of the generation capacity in India is owned and operated by the states through electricity boards or electricity departments. Despite the opening of generation to IPPs in 1991, the private sector provides less than 10 GW of total generation capacity. The capacity of central generating companies has developed rapidly since their corporatization and now represents around one-quarter of total capacity.

These large power plants allocate their supply to more than one state through the interstate transmission grid. Bulk-power exchanges are still limited to supply from central generating units and surplus power exchanges from one state to another.

Generation capacity is not centrally dispatched. Individual state power markets are too small for true competition among large IPPs since they cannot absorb large new generation additions rapidly.

Existing generation suffers from several recurrent problems. The efficiency and the availability of the coal power plants are low by international standards. A majority of the plants use low-heat-content and high-ash unwashed coal.

This leads to a high number of airborne pollutants per unit of power produced. Moreover, past investments have skewed generation toward coal-fired power plants at the expense of peak-load capacity. In the context of fast-growing demand, large T&D losses and poor pooling of loads at the national level exacerbate the lack of generating capacity.

In the longer term, consumers who are connected directly to the transmission grid should be free to buy from any supplier.

Transmission pricing should anticipate the emergence of an interstate and intrastate competitive power market.

What should be the principles for pricing? The transmission system operator should provide access to the grid without discriminating among types of users. There should be no discrimination among customers when connecting new customers to the transmission network. Use-of-system charges should not restrict, distort or prevent competition in the generation, supply or distribution of electricity.

It is often called captive production in India. In India, investments in auto-production are made primarily for standby purposes or as a substitute to electricity provided through the grid.

Making it possible for private investors to develop IPPs was one of the first elements of the liberalization process initiated by the central government in 1991.

The IPP policy has met with only mixed success in India.

Here is a question for all of us witnessing this energy crisis in India at this point of chaos, "Was liberalization with deregulation and privatization the only way to bring in the reforms and restructuring?"

I am sure the voices of citizens are mix of various school of thoughts and perceptions.

About 250 projects were identified, mostly in memorandums of understanding with state authorities early in the liberalization process. Most of the projects never reached the competitive-bidding stage and sites were not prioritized.

Disputes over these projects have hampered the development of newer, more viable ones; the time and effort required to develop new IPP projects in India proved too great for some foreign investors, and many reduced their Indian exposure.

Among recurring difficulties are the lack of prior clearance of the projects by the authorities, problems in securing fuel supply agreements and the bankruptcy of SEBs; the lack of prior prioritization of the possible projects has led investors to perceive a high commercial risk in an overcrowded market-place.

Furthermore, the IPP policy has done little so far to increase the availability of electricity and reduce costs. In 2000, the Ministry of Power created a special group to review transparency in the bidding process.

Lack of transparency has resulted in power purchase agreements (PPAs) that did not always meet the objective of increased power availability at lower prices. The only IPP projects that came online, apart from Dabhol, were small in scale, because of the limited size and the insolvency of the states' power markets. Many of these IPPs use naphtha, a costly oil product, as a fuel.

How to address the criticality of insolvency? In addition, the high commercial risk perceived by investors increases interest rates. Only about a dozen projects generating around 3,000 MW came online.

Public enterprises, such as the National Thermal Power Corporation, represent an increasing share of incremental capacity. Facing financial difficulties, the SEBs slowed their investments in incremental capacity in the 1990s and the public sector's withdrawal from generation has not been compensated by private investments. The gap between supply and demand has worsened.

Interstate sales of bulk-power are priced using a cost-plus mechanism. Availability based tariff (ABT) is now under discussion led by the CERC, and could be implemented in the near future.

The tariff is intended to deal with current issues facing the power system, such as improving the availability of generation units, penalizing unscheduled interchanges, and establishing a level playing field for merit-order dispatching to be applied to state owned capacity versus bulk-power supplied by other states or by central generating companies.

This tariff was devised as a first step toward a competitive bulk-power market. The efficiency of the device is questionable because the ABT is a relatively complex tariff. The time is now ripe for integration of the generation mix on an India-wide basis.

Future plans should use economic criteria and least-cost utility planning to determine the optimal electric power system at the country level. Due consideration should be given to India's large-scale hydroelectric potential and sizeable coal resources, to the emergence of a market for imported natural gas and imported coal, to the need to keep the nuclear option open, and to the environmental effects of various technologies.

The existence in neighboring countries of a potential for surplus power from hydroelectricity or natural gas should also be considered. Development plans for coal and electric power should be coordinated to decide whether to transport coal or electricity. The gas industry should also be consulted, as it seeks to develop the gas network.

The central government should facilitate investments by national generating companies and promote competition among them.

Generation dispatching should be carried out at the national level. Dispatching is already done regionally through several mechanisms including Regional Load Dispatch Centers (RLDC), but it should be further implemented at the national level.

The central government should use appropriate tariffs to accelerate the implementation of a framework for dispatch of surplus electricity to the grid from auto-producers.

Generation projects for state markets should be limited in size. They should concentrate on renovating existing state capacity and on the developing of peaking capacity (combustion turbines and peaking hydroelectric power plants) and grid-connected renewable (such as wind and solar).

All these measures highlight the need for further integration of the power generation sector on a national basis. There is a clear need for better co-ordination among the various ministries in charge of energy matters.

National integration of the power generation sector and co-ordination among the various energy sectors will do better if technical, economic and environmental criteria outweigh political criterion in the decision process.

The risk of market concentration at the state level calls for the development of a national market for generators. The creation of this power market at the national level requires mechanism.

It will be difficult however to avoid such an intermediate step toward a fully-competitive power market. Electricity-market institutions are still in their infancy in India, and international experts agree that the transition to a fully-competitive market is a long-term process involving gradual changes.

A number of the difficulties in the generation link of the power chain will gradually be resolved as end-user payment for electricity improves. If it happens, this will boost the financial flow, improve the solvency of the purchasing utilities and reduce the commercial risk perceived by private investors.

A large part of the Indian population lives in rural areas. According to official statistics, most villages are electrified1. However, few households in these villages actually have access to the electricity grid2.

The investment required to connect the remaining households to the main electricity grid is very large. Population density is low in rural areas, and a large part of the rural population has low income. Most Indian villages already have a main connection to the grid. The feeder – or medium-voltage line – that links the village to the network may actually be a very small part of the investment required to supply electricity to the households of a given village.

Electricity consumption for agriculture in rural zones is heavily subsidized. The average price paid by the agriculture and irrigation sector is reported to be equivalent to USD 0.5 cent/kWh. This was only 12.5% of the unit cost of supply.

Low revenues from agriculture consumers limit the incentives for SEBs to develop consumption and to ensure good-quality power supply in electrified villages. Some consumers seeking more reliable service simply generate their own electricity an agreement on the bulk-power tariffs. Accordingly, the discussions on the ABT should be accelerated and its implementation expedited.

Why India is not becoming attractive to foreign investors? What are the major risks? Can we not diminish some of the risks? Is India not prepared to take the challenges of reenergizing?

Why IPP projects are not undergoing a transparent bidding? Viability of Projects is becoming another major issue of concern in the sector. Projects should be better prepared before calls for tender are issued.

Fuel supply agreements are crucial and should be secured in advance, contracts, once signed, must be upheld, commercial risk could be mitigated by prioritizing projects at the central government level and by providing state guarantees through organizations such as the Power Trading Corporation (PTC), tariffs orders should be implemented over a sufficiently long period of time to offer a stable environment to investors.

India could benefit more from IPPs by rapidly making the bidding processes more transparent and fully competitive to avoid a later inflation of project costs.

Why Power Policy did not think about power equipments manufacturing capacities and automation systems up gradation early to the reforms Act implementation?

Competition at the level of equipment supply should also increase. India should foster international technology co-operation to increase access to cheaper, cleaner and more efficient power technologies.

India's Rural Electrification is facing the real energy crisis. This field survey had many respondents from the remote hamlets revealing their daily struggle with the quality of power supply they receive.

Poor farmers are mercilessly waiting for the golden dawn. Irrigation has become bane to them. They do not have alternate means of survival. Though they feed the whole nation they are not fed by proper electricity supply.

What the rural schemes are doing? The definition of an electrified village does not account for the number of household connected but just the fact that an electricity line extends to that particular village.

Reforming subsidies and improving the payment rate for electricity already delivered is as important for rural electrification as for the generation, transmission and distribution sectors overall.

Much of rural electrification could take place outside the main grid, using decentralized supply or small-scale local grids and alternative energy sources such as biomass and wind. These solutions may require the creation of large credit facilities to stimulate investment.

The Government of India should encourage and experiment with innovative institutional models to supply electricity to rural consumers, such as co-operatives.

From the time of India's independence in 1947, the demand for electricity has grown rapidly. Final consumption of electricity has increased by an average of 7% per year since 1947. This sustained growth is the result of economic development and the increase in electrical appliances.

It has been accompanied by a gradual shift from noncommercial sources of energy, such as biomass, in the household and commercial sector as well as the reduction in the use of coal for process heat in industry and kerosene for household lighting.

Of total final sales of 332 TWh in 1999-2000, industry accounted for just over one third, agriculture for 30% and the household sector for 18%. But for many years, electricity supply has fallen short of demand and the sustainability of this trend is very uncertain. Though the overall demand-supply gap decreased from an estimated 8.1% in 1997-98 to 5.9% in 1998-99, it rebounded to 6.2% in 1999-2000. Peak power shortages fell from 18% in 1996-97 to 12% in 1999-2000.

The duration and number of blackouts and brownouts are beyond acceptable limits, leading to shortfalls of up to 15% of demand. Consumption is largely constrained by the supply.

It seems that the seasonal variation in the load between summer and winter is limited, and changes during the day are not high either as compared to other countries.

Inadequate power transmission and distribution result in shortages which in turn affect consumption patterns and induce commercial users and the most affluent domestic customers to rely on standby/in-house investments in auto-production capacity. Because of unsatisfied demand, increases in electricity prices would

Is it desirable to develop a regional electricity grid connecting India, Bhutan, Nepal and Bangladesh? The land-locked countries can benefit from the above.

In this decade there had been lot of collaborative issues in air for relationship between India and China especially in the emerging energy sector. China has slowly made India its market for power equipments. It has gained by having openings for sales and service too in India.

The need for reforming the sector was felt because the state –owned vertically integrated electricity supply industry was becoming inefficient and bankrupt. Hence private investment was encouraged to address shortages and power cuts.

Is it not ridiculous to comprehend that the independent power producers (IPPs) are selling power under PPAs to the largely unreformed SEBs despite the era of liberalization? Despite deregulation the government has fixed the consumer of IPPs. That is where the story of crisis is whirling without any realistic benefits from the reformative Acts.

Can the Electricity Boards save millions by subsidizing energy efficiency in India? Where does the subsidy go? Does it reach the desired citizens?

Energy efficiency is a concept advocated by environmental groups all over the world to reduce energy consumption and save non-renewable energy sources. Now, economists too see sense in that. Several electric utilities in the United States, Germany, UK, Canada and other countries have already adopted the concept.

The business principle behind the concept is that if the marginal cost of setting up new generation unit exceeds that of carrying out energy efficiency measures, the latter should be preferred. In the case of SEB, this principle can also be translated to mean that energy efficiency should be preferred over purchase of costlier power from thermal plants as the Board subsidizes power to several groups.

What should be the cost of power? The SEB now spends more than Rs. 4.00-Rs 5.00 a unit for power from thermal projects. The average cost of the power sold by it is about

Rs. 3.30 a unit. However, its sells power at an average rate of Rs. 2.50 – Rs 2.75 a unit. So, if the SEBs manages to reduce consumption of one unit, it stands to save about Re 1 to Rs 0.75.

How the actual savings can be made even higher?

What should finally be the actual realization on one unit of power sold? The actual realization is less than Rs. 2.00 to Rs 2.50 a unit in India. Domestic consumers on an average pay only Rs. 1.00 to Rs 1.50 a unit. Power Dependence on costly thermal power can be reduced if peak load is brought down.

Today, about 20 per cent of the demand in the State is for lighting. The Board's difficulties in managing peak loads in the evenings also arise from this. Energy efficiency can be of great help in this area.

Compact fluorescent lamps (CFL) are one of the major technologies available in this field to achieve energy efficiency. A CFL lamp, consuming just about 9 watts, can replace a 60 watts incandescent bulb. This means an energy saving of more than 85 per cent. Similarly, halogen lamps, which is suitable for outdoor lighting, uses 40 per cent less energy and generally lasts two to four times longer than regular bulbs. And again LED the best today.

As the total power used for lighting is five to six million units a day, energy efficiency measures can theoretically achieve a saving of about four million units. However, achievement of a saving of four million units in lighting alone would be impractical. Some lighting loads like neon signs and factory lighting might have to be excluded from the calculation.

CFL Vs LED, another transition with bottlenecks of finances and policies. The distribution of it to all and 100% replacement has all its challenges.

Replacement of existing incandescent and fluorescent lamps with CFL and LED by customers would happen only gradually. So, the SEB would have to vigorously promote the use of energy efficient lighting by offering subsidies as is done by power utilities in other countries.

The State Central Governments can also offer subsidies as energy efficiency saves natural resources and makes money available for funding development in areas other than power generation.

Let us look at the below analysis on energy saving.

Currently, the market price of a 9 watt CFL in India with adapter is about Rs. 350 apiece. (This can directly fit into existing light holders.) Aesthetically more appealing units would cost Rs. 750 or more.

A CFL lamp has nearly ten times the life time of an incandescent lamp. During its life time (8000 hours), each will save about 500 units. At Rs. 1.30 a unit, this means a saving of Rs. 650. Add to this, the cost of ten incandescent lamps (about Rs. 100).

One stands to benefit Rs. 400 for an investment of Rs. 350. There is a tremendous saving for commercial establishments who pay about Rs. 6 a unit (though the

Board would lose revenues over there). CFLs are good even for textile shops.

Today, CFL are being replaced by LED. Technologies are available in the international market for not less than 1000 products ranging from computers to small appliances that are energy efficient. Devices like dimmer switches (good for bedrooms, dining rooms etc.) and timers (suitable for latrines in offices and public places) can also save energy.

A sodium vapour lamp with reflectors on streets gives optimum light. (Only a portion of the light from incandescent street lights, seen in panchayat areas, reaches the road. CFL with suitable reflectors would be good alternative if theft can be prevented).

If the lighting load of six million units a day is reduced by just two million units a day, the State will save enormous energy.

Much more electrical energy can be saved by encouraging replacement of electrical heating with solar heating (in hotels, for example) and use of high efficiency motors and processes in factories and other work places (energy auditing).

However, instead of subsidizing energy conservation and efficiency, the Government and Board are now promoting consumption by offering free electricity to small homes and farmers.

A better strategy would have been to subsidize high efficiency pumps and drip irrigation (which saves both power and water) and homes that consume less than, say,

10 units a month through the use of energy efficient lights and devices.

Each SEB's were very conservative in their approach restricting themselves to discharging their responsibilities limited to their respective states. Linking all the Indian villages with the national grid is a huge task to be accomplished. Only the route through incentives and enforcement may not be the right means to attract power providers without intuitional commitment and service orientation.

It is high time the government should realize that villages are not commercial and business centre's but are the backbone of the country. It is surprising to note that almost all the power stations have been constructed on villagers land sacrificing their property and pain of rehabilitation to contribute in developing the national infrastructure projects and in return the government penalizes them to starve for power.

Saving Energy is as good as Generating Energy. There are hundreds of ways to save energy.

On the whole justice needs to be done before it is too late. It is time for spiritual brainstorming along with strategic thinking to resolve the issues of electrifying India. Review of government annual reports, statistics, consultant's analysis, consortiums, seminars, meets, papers and research all reveal the fact that India's GDP, Electricity and Infrastructure are averagely growing with a rate in between 5 per cent to 9 per cent annually.

Electricity is a prime mover to sustain infrastructure and consequently GDP. India properly needs to map industry and resources to develop several economic centers throughout the nation encompassing all the rural areas. Agriculture and Industry are the two faces of the coin economic development. One is incomplete without another. Maintaining equilibrium is very essential before and after flooding liberalized policies bringing turbulence to the whole system.

Power Utilities should start considering rural citizens as prospective electricity customers. Retail electricity market needs more attention by the government as villagers will never be bulk buyers of power for their basic needs like industrial consumers.

Operating emerging power markets is a great challenge to the power sector. Satisfying both Rural and Urban power demands simultaneously with rationalized tariff needs optimization strategies to be implemented by the government without sacrificing the economics of scale.

Utilities action against default consumers for temporarily disconnecting supply and recovery with penalty is not improving the collection efficiency. In addition to the existing power crisis the disloyalty of the consumers is worsening the unhealthiness of the power sector. No government or utility would appreciate to enforce and penalize their customers but the fact that all India average for collection efficiency is only 50 per cent.

It is suggested that more interaction is necessary between utilities and rural consumers to understand the problem of both so that the deficiency in the collection system can be minimized and simultaneously default consumers should transform themselves into regular payers.

Power system performance and efficiency is directly based on the proper maintenance of power lines, equipments and sub-stations. Industrial output losses due to repairs, replacements, shutdowns, breakdowns and failure of power equipments are serious concerns of the rural consumers. The reformation process is very slow making the maintenance department unhealthier day by day.

Power utilities are falling far behind the expectations in maintaining the power system. The rural consumers are generally LT category type and even do not need extra protection for high voltage energy equipments installed either outside or inside their premises. The maintenance of power equipments in the post restructuring period has remained as it is due to which uncontrollable regulation of extra high voltage causes unwanted severe damages to industrial equipments.

It is suggested to the utilities that maintenance should be done once in three months so that there will be less damage of equipments and minimization of voltage fluctuations. The periodic maintenance of the electrical power equipments by the utilities can enhance the overall efficiency of the power system.

As far as Rural Electrification is concerned large gaps have remained due to failure in implementation of rural electrification schemes and lack of monitoring on house metering, billing and collection. There is no doubt that disparity in electricity services cannot be ruled out as rural areas are not at par with the urban areas.

It is suggested that the government immediately drives a plan to meet its immediate mandate of "Lantern to Electric Lamp" through equal participation of all the state, central and private sectors to fulfill the dreams of millions of citizens living in rural India.

The outlays for rural electrification both at the Centre and State should mandatorily be fixed in reasonable proportion to the urban areas. Public Power Utilities and Private Sector Corporate should hold the minimum responsibility of electrifying villages surrounding to its power station within a radial span of 25 km to 50 km as per the generation capacity of the unit, such provisions should statutorily be included in the Power Purchase Agreement (PPA) for Independent Power Producers (IPPs).

Rather than waiting for long transmission lines to be completed and networked with the national and state power grids, the areas within the reach of power stations must be thought of direct distribution by the utilities. Such new provisions are to be implemented to rapidly electrify the villages.

Government should encourage participation of electricity consumers from all segments in policy making and schemes to be implemented. It is time all the agencies, stakeholders and citizens together need to dive deep into it with interactive sessions of brainstorming for finding resolutions to the issues of energy crisis in rural areas.

More number of Rural Energy Centers is to be opened for improving the electrification system in villages. A revolutionary drive in the nation is essential to make electricity accessible to all the citizens of the country.

Economic Centers are not uniformly distributed in India. The present growth of industrialization is taking place only in electrically developed regions. Many of the developed states are unable to provide consistently reliable power supply.

It is not surprising to note that the major share of power is generated in the eastern region but is transmitted to the western region. The gap in regional disparities in generating and distributing is to be bridged at the earliest despite two decades of reforms.

LPG-Policy (Liberalization, Privatization and Globalization) marks the revolution of economic reforms in India. Electricity Industry was not an exception to the reaping of benefits from these reforms distributed over the state, central and private sectors.

Private Power Policy (1991), Cogeneration (1996), Captive power generation (1997), Mega Power Policy (1998), the amended Electricity Act (1998), enactment of Electricity Act-2003, Ultra Mega Power Policy(2005), National Power Policy(2005), National Tariff Policy (2006), Rural Electrification Policy (2006), Integrated Energy Policy (2006), Power Exchange in India (2007), Point of Connection (2010) are all reforms Act bringing in transition and transformation of the power sector only after the first initiation by the LPG-Policy implemented. Though the electricity revolution has started with the Xth and XIth Five Year Plans the result of the new emerging power and energy mix is yet to be seen. The XII th plan just remained a warm up trial prior to fighting out the real issues in the battle field of energy and power.

Will the XIII th plan do any extraordinary contribution?

"Competency Vs Contribution", is very well visible in zigzag fashion in the power sector. I am of the opinion that India faces acute problems in commitments towards policies because of the incompetency and lack of sincere dedication in contribution.

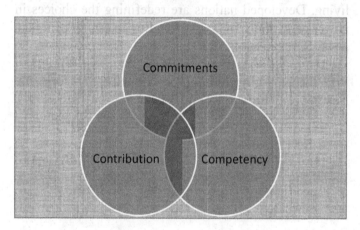

The sphere of these 3 C's is very much instrumental in effectively implementing the policies. The non awareness on the policies is not desirable if the country wishes to gain from the citizens of India.

Knowledgeable Citizens can understand the real problems of the country. Country is a mammoth resource to produce live, grow, develop and sustain. And all these only by the usage of energy.

Indian Citizens are to be integrated globally. India is in transition. The transformation is based on the possible transitions happening in the energy sector. More and more growth is required.

The simplest of simplest life is becoming dependable on energy needs day by day.

Today, Global Energy Crisis is concern of everyone. World's dependencies on Electric Power is again questioning the sustainability of modern, better and clean living. Developed nations are redefining the choices in power generation. India is struggling to craft a complete power supply chain.

Will the emerging Indian Power Sector transform the Destiny of Energy in Rural India?

THANKS GIVING

Let us understand the fact that, "Had there been no Energy Crisis in India, the cause may not have been questioned by anyone?".

As all Indians are looking for a feasible remedy, the challenge is to select an optimal energy model, in this regard the analytical study has attempted to throw some indelible light on the darkness of the Indian Energy Sector.

I am presenting this study on behalf of the millions and millions of citizens of India who eagerly are waiting to witness the transition from darkness to lightness. Many more cyber cities are the dreams of Indians.

I am thankful to the entire team whoever joined hands in supporting me right from the concept of the study to the present form it is being shared with society in the form of an organized commentary on Indian Electricity Services.

Politics Vs Economics, is the prime mover for any national development in the World. I believe every stakeholder is contributing to develop and sustain the Indian Power Sector within the limitations and restrictions of scope and availability.

Policy, regulation, legislation, controls, monitoring, implementation, projects, institutions, structures, frameworks, services, finances, revenues, losses, profits, and so on are struggling to excel with infinite permutations and combinations.

Research & Development (R&D) in India is not to be neglected in core sectors. R&D is a continual tool towards betterment of the complete supply chain of electricity supply. Ministry of New & Renewable Energy is taking initiatives to conduct solar training programmes.

Power Consumption Vs Power Conservation, the balance can be made only by awareness, education and training programmes throughout the World.

Energy is always a Global issue.

Projects Vs Operations, speaks the saga of transition from power project concept to operational power plant with all difficulties and struggles from the zero date of project. Till the Commercial Operation Date (COD) is not achieved the constructional, environmental, societal, political and linkages issues remain active in the sector.

I have a deep sense of gratitude towards all power project developers, promoters, constructors, owners, who toil with all turbulences, clearances, licenses, approvals, authorizations, certifications and so on before the dreams turn into reality.

In addition to it the contribution by logistics providers the railways, ports and transporters is commendable in building India. No doubt this is all time a praiseworthy area for the operations of the entire supply chain of oil, gas, coal, fuels and other consumables in the energy sector.

Villages Vs Smart Cities, today speaks the race and pace in modernization of India. The recent mandate is target of 1,00,000 MW grid connected Solar Power.

I sincerely admit to have learnt from the visionaries, economists, reformers, scientists, developers, researchers, engineers, administrators, consultants, evaluators, designers, manufacturers, builders, constructors, and many more who formally or informally have been sharing their knowledge and wisdom on the subject.

Every citizen should be concerned about energy security of country. Had the reforms and restructuring been not initiated power supply's privatization might have not taken place. The crux of the matter is not privatization only. The issue is of the service satisfaction of electricity consumers. Has the gap between supply and demand of power bridged

Let all of us thank the transformation and transition in the Indian Energy Sector which is taking place with great drive in National Solar Mission.

Can India meet the target of generating 1,75,000 MW of Renewable Power by 2022?

The plan titled "Perspective Transmission Plan for 20 Years" is being proposed to be executed. The total investment envisaged is around Rs 2.6 lakh crore during the 13th plan period.

Can Renewable Energy end Carbon Emissions completely? Citizens should be thankful to India for its vigorous initiatives in green power corridors.

Finally to summarize every minute effort should be analyzed, recognized and acknowledged which adds to the betterment of India's Energy Sector.

Will Green Energy dominate the Power Sector in India?

I believe, "Learning by criticism brings in excellence". We all should thank this type of debate, discussions, brainstorming and analysis. It brings out innovations and refinement in thinking and decision making.

The perception of constructive criticism should be to find avenues for strengthening the Indian Power System.

I am grateful to all the analysts in the energy and power sector who have sacrificed their valuable time in researching and innovating better ways of improving the power systems in the world.

I am equally indebted to the great scientists, educationists and reformists who have lived their lives to light the world.

I am obliged to understand their pain in transforming the darkness of the world into lightness forever.

I hope every reader should participate in saving electrical energy.

This book, "Energy Crisis in India", is a drive to alleviate the energy crisis. I sincerely request my readers and their associates to join me and the nation in saving energy.

Finally from the bottom of my heart we will all remain indebted to the, "People who Power the World".

Dr Shree Raman Dubey

BE. MBA. Ph.D

ACRONYMS

ABT	Availability Based Tariff
AEC	Atomic Energy Commission
APDRP	Accelerated Power Development and Reform Program
AREP	Accelerated Rural Electricity Program
APSEB	Andhra Pradesh State Electricity Board
AT&C	Aggregate Technical & Commercial Losses
ATE	Appellate Tribunal for Electricity
BEE	Bureau of Energy Efficiency
BLOT	Build Lease Operate Transfer
BOOT	Build Own Operate Transfer
BPL	Below Poverty Line
CAGR	Compounded Annual Growth Rate
CEA	Central Electricity Authority
CERC	Central Electricity Regulatory Commission
CESC	Calutta Electric Supply Company
CIL	Coal India Limited
CPP	Captive Power Producer
CPRI	Central Power Research Institute
CPSU	Central Public Sector Undertaking

CTU	Central Transmission Utility
DAE	Department of Atomic Energy
DDT	Dividend Distribution Tax
DPR	Detailed Project Report
DVC	Damodar Valley Corporation
DISSCOMS	Distribution Company
EA 2003	Electricity Act 2003
ERC	Electricity Regulatory Commission
FBR	Fast Breeder Reactors
FBT	Fringe Benefit Tax
FDI	Foreign Direct Investment
FIPB	Foreign Investment Promotion Board
FOIR	Forum of Indian Regulators
FTP	Foreign Trade Policy
GDP	Gross Domestic Product
GENCO	Generation Company
HVDC	High Voltage Direct Current
HVDS	High Voltage Direct System
ICB	International Competitive Bidding
IES	Indian Electricity Sector
IEX	Indian Energy Exchange
IPP	Independent Power Producer
IPS	Indian Power Sector
IPTC	Independent Power Transmission Company
IREDA	Indian Renewable Energy Development Agency Ltd
JV	Joint Venture
KVA	Kilo Volt Ampere

kW	Kilowatts
LPG	Liberalization, Privatization and Globalization
LPS	Liberalized Power Sector
MAT	Minimum Alternate Tax
MoA	Memorandum of Agreement
MoC	Ministry of Coal
MNRE	Ministry of New & Renewable Energy
MoP	Ministry of Power
MoPNG	Ministry of Petroleum and Natural Gas
MPP	Merchant Power Plant
MoU	Memorandum of Understanding
MU	Million Units
MYT	Multi Year Tariff
MNES	Ministry of Non Conventional Energy Sources
MNRE	Ministry of New and Renewable Energy
MTPA	Million Tonnes per annum
MW	Mega Watts
NCMP	National Common Minimum Program
NEP	National Electricity Policy
NEEPCO	North Eastern Electric Power Corporation Ltd
NELP	New Exploring Licensing Policy
NGO	Non Government Organisation

NHDC	Narmada Hydroelectric Development Corporation Ltd
NHPC	National Hydroelectric Power Corporation Ltd
NLC	Neyveli Lignite Corporation Ltd
NLDC	National Load Despatch Centre
NPCIL	Nuclear Power Corporation of India Limited
NPTI	National Power Training Institute
NTP	National Tariff Policy
NTPC	National Thermal Power Corporation Limited
PFC	Power Finance Corporation Limited
PLF	Plant Load Factor
PMGY	Pradhan Mantri Gramodaya Yojana
PPA	Power Purchase Agreement
PPP	Public Private Partnership
POWERGRID	Power Grid Corporation of India Limited
PSA	Power Sale Agreement
PSU	Public Sector Undertaking
PTC	Power Trading Corporation India Limited
R-APDRP	Restructured Accelerated Power Development and Reform Programme
REC	Rural Electrification Corporation Ltd.
REL	Reliance Energy Limited
RPL	Reliance Power Limited
RGGVY	Rajiv Gandhi Grameen Vidyutikaran Yojna

RLDC	Regional Load Despatch Centre
R&D	Research & Development
R&M	Renovation & Modernization
R&R	Rehabilitation & Resettlement
REST	Rural Electricity Supply Technology
ROE	Return on Equity
ROI	Return on Investment
SCADA	Supervisory Control and Data Acqisition
SEB	State Electricity Board
SEC	Solar Energy Centre
SERC	State Electricity Regulatory Commission
SEZ	Special Economic Zone
SLDC	State Load Despatch Centre
STU	State Transmission Utility
TERI	The Energy and Research Institute
T&D	Transmission and Distribution
THDC	Tehri Hydro Development Corporation Limited
TRANSCO	Transmission Company
TSA	Transmission Service Agreement
TSC	Transmission Service Charge
TSP	Transmission Service Provider
UI	Unscheduled Interchange
UMPP	Ultra Mega Power Project
VAT	Value Added Tax
VEI	Village Electrification Infrastructure

BIBLIOGRAPHY

1. Kulkarni, V. S. "Power Sector: Policies and Perspectives in the Post-Reform Period." Abhijeet Publication, New Delhi (2004): 319-331.

2. Bosi, Martina. "An Initial View on Mehodologies for Emissions Baselines: Electricity Generation Case Study, IEA Information Paper." Energy and Environment Division, IEA (2000).

3. Burdon, I. P. "Options for mid-merit power generation in the UK electricity market." Power Engineering Journal 12.3 (1998): 115-122.

4. Genoud, Christophe, and Matthias Finger. Regulatory Convergence?: The Example of the European Electricity Sector. IDHEAP, Institut de hautes études en administration publique, 2002.

5. Sury, M. M. India: A Decade of Economic Reforms 1991-2001. New century Publications, 2001.

6. Bharadwaj, Anshu, and Rahul Tongia. "Distributed Power Generation: Rural India-A Case Study." Submitting for publication (2003).

7. Arentsen, MAARTEN J., J. W. Fabius, and ROLF W. Künneke. "Dutch business strategies under regime transition." European Energy Industry Business Strategies (2001): 151-195.

8. Mahalingam, Sudha. "Unbundling trouble." Frontline 14.8 (1997): 84-89.

9. Dubash, Navroz K., and Sudhir Chella Rajan. "The politics of power sector reform in India." World Resources Institute. Washington, DC Processed (2001).

10. Ahluwalia, Sanjeev S., and Gaurav Bhatiani. "Tariff Setting in the Electric Power Sector-Base paper on Indian Case Study." TERI Conference on Regulation in Infrastructure Services, New Delhi. 2000.

11. Purkayastha, Prabir. "Power Sector Policies and New Electricity Bill: from Crisis to Disaster." Economic and Political Weekly (2001): 2257-2262.

12. Jamasb, T., R. Mota, and D. Newbery. "M. Pollitt (2005),"Electricity Sector Reform in Developing Countries: A Survey of Empirical Evidence on Determinants and Performance"." World Bank Policy Research Working Paper No 3549.

13. Okten, Cagla, and Peren Arin. "How Does Privatization Affect Efficiency, Productivity and Technological Choice? Evidence from

Turkey." Unpublished manuscript, Louisiana State University (2003).

14. Choukroun, Sylvie. "Enron in Maharashtra: power sector development and national identity in modern India." PhD diss., University of Pennsylvania, 2002.

15. Anderson, Dennis, Ralph Turvey, and Charles Taylor. "Study of electricity tariffs in Andhra Pradesh." International Bank for Reconstruction and Development, Washington (1975).

16. Sant, Girish, Shantanu Dixit, and Subodh Wagle. "The Enron Controversy."Techno-Economic Analysis and Policy Implications, Prayas, Pune (1995).

17. Surry, J. "From Public to Private Ownership: Objectives and Rationale." The British Electricity Experiment Privatisation: The Record, The Issues, The Lessons, Earthscan, London (1996).

18. Reddy, M. Thimma. "Development in the Power Sector in Andhra Pradesh."Prayas-Focus on Global South--Event on Power Sector Reforms, Mumbai(2000).

19. Reddy, C. R., and G. Raman. "Reddy and U. Prabhakar Reddy," Power Sector Reforms,". Southern." Economist (2003): 5-8.

20. Pollitt, M. "Issues in Electricity Market Integration and Liberalization, in A European

Market for Electricity?." Bergman, L. et al., Monitoring European Deregulation 2 (1999).

21. Bidwai, Praful. "The other Enrons." Frontline 19.4 (2002): 100-106.

22. Sankar, T. L., and U. Ramachandra. "Regulation of the Indian power sector."ASCI Journal of Management 29.2 (2000).

23. Mahalingam, S. "Power to the Regulator." Frontline 15.10 (1998): 110-115.

24. Gupta, A. "A Requiem for Reform." Business Today 11 (2002): 60-64.

25. La Porta, Rafael, and L. Florencio. "de-Silanes (1999),"." The Benefits of Privatization: Evidence from Mexico", Quarterlv Journey of Economics 4.

26. Tongia, R. "Demand and Supply of Power in India: An Analysis of the Electric Power Grid (working paper). Electrical and Computer Engineering/Engineering and Public Policy. Pittsburgh." Car negie Mellon University, Pittsburgh (1998).

27. Dunkerley, J. C. "China's Energy Strategy: Economic Structure, Technological Choices, and Energy Consumption by Xiannuan Lio." ENERGY JOURNAL-CAMBRIDGE MA THEN CLEVELAND OH- 17 (1996): 109-110.

28. Ahluwalia, M. S. "Report Of The Expert Group (on) Settlement Of SEB Dues."New Delhi, Ministry of Power (2001).

29. Kannan, K. P., and N. Vijayamohanan Pillai. "The Aetiology of the Inefficiency Syndrome in the Indian Power Sector." Center for Development Studies, Trivandrum (2002).

30. Arulraj, A., and D. Raja Sekaran. Performance of thermal utilities in Indian energy sectors. Serials Publications, 2009.

31. BRADSHAW, TEDK, and W. O. O. D. R. O. W. CLARK II. "SOME CASE STUDIES." Electricity reform: social and environmental challenges. 1998.

32. Tongia, Rahul, and V. S. Arunachalam. "India's Nuclear Breeders: Technology, Viability, and Options." Indian Academy of Science, 1997.

33. Sant, Girish, and Shantanu Dixit. "Agricultural pumping efficiency in India: the role of standards." Energy for Sustainable Development 3.1 (1996): 29-37.

34. Singh, Joga. "Plant size and technical efficiency in the Indian thermal power industry." Indian Economic Review (1991): 239-252.

35. Brown, Richard E., and Mike W. Marshall. "The cost of reliability."Transmission & Distribution World 53.14 (2001): 13.

36. Ranganathan, V. "World Bank and India's Economic Development." Economic and Political Weekly (2003): 236-241.

37. Gangakhedkar, Rajesh, and R. K. Mishra. "Public–Private Partnership in Power Sector: A Focus on Ultra Mega Power Projects." Journal of Infrastructure Development 4.1 (2012): 27-39.

38. Yadav, H. S., and M. S. Yadav. "Elasticity and Substitution of Factors in Power Industry in Madhya Pradesh." Indian economic journal 53.1 (2005): 109.

39. Upadhyay, Anil K. "Power sector reforms: Indian experience and global trends."Economic and Political Weekly (2000): 1023-1028.

40. Parikh, Kirit S. "The Enron story and its lessons." Journal of International Trade & Economic Development 6.2 (1997): 209-230.

41. Baijal, Pradip. "Restructuring power sector in India: a base paper." Economic and Political Weekly (1999): 2795-2803.

42. Drillisch, Jens, and Christoph Riechmann. Liberalisation of the Electricity Supply Industry-Evaluation of Reform Policies. Energiewirtschaftliches Inst., 1998.

43. Mukherji, Rahul. "Managing competition: Politics and the building of independent regulatory institutions." India Review 3.4 (2004): 278-305.

44. Bhattacharyya, Subhes C. "The Electricity Act 2003: will it transform the Indian power sector?." Utilities Policy 13.3 (2005): 260-272.

45. Ranganathan, V. "Determining T&D Losses in India: Their Impact on Distribution Privatisation and Regulation." Economic and Political Weekly(2005): 657-668.

46. Sinha, Shirish, Joy S. Clancy, Nico G. Schulte Nordholt, Kaushik Deb, and Leena Srivastava. "Energy sector reforms and rural energy access in India: the emerging issues." Transition towards sustainable development in South Asia(2003): 43-60.

47. Godbole, Madhav. "Electricity Act, 2003: questionable wisdom." Economic and Political Weekly (2003): 4104-4110.

48. ARASU, FR JG VALAN. "Future Prospects of the Power Sector in India."Studies In Indian Economy 1 (2005): 73.

49. D'Sa, Antonette, KV Narasimha Murthy, and Amulya KN Reddy. "India's Power Sector Liberalisation: An Overview." Economic and Political Weekly (1999): 1427-1434.

50. Tongia, Rahul, and Rangan Banerjee. "Price of power in India." Energy Policy26.7 (1998): 557-575.

51. Sankar, T. L. "Towards a People's Plan for Power Sector Reform." Economic and Political Weekly (2002): 4143-4151.

52. Beato, Paulina, and Jean-Jacques Laffont. Competition in public utilities in developing countries. Inter-American Development Bank, 2002.

53. Dubash, Navroz. "Institutional transplant as political opportunity: the practice and politics of Indian electricity regulation." CLPE Research Paper 31 (2008).

54. Dussan, Manuel I. Electric power sector reform in Latin America and the Caribbean. Infrastructure and Financial Markets Division, Social Programs and Sustainable Development Department, Inter-American Development Bank, 1996.

55. Dubash, Navroz K., and D. Narasimha Rao. "Regulatory practice and politics: Lessons from independent regulation in Indian electricity." Utilities Policy 16.4 (2008): 321-331.

56. Mahalingam, Sudha. "Economic reforms, the power sector and corruption." The Politics of the Economic Reforms in India, New Delhi: Sage (2005): 197-226.

57. Khanna, Madhu, and David Zilberman. "Adoption of energy efficient technologies and carbon abatement: the electricity generating sector in India."Energy Economics 23.6 (2001): 637-658.

58. Sinha, Archana. Privatisation of the power sector in India: a preliminary appraisal. Indian Social Institute, 2003.

59. Bialek, Janusz. "Recent blackouts in US and Continental Europe: Is liberalisation to blame?." (2004).

60. Shukla, P. R., Subodh K. Sharma, and P. Venkata Ramana. Climate change and India: issues, concerns and opportunities. Tata McGraw-Hill Pub. Co., 2002.

61. Bhargava, Nisha, and Shakuntala Gupta. "The Punjab State Electricity Board: Past, Present and Future." Punjab University research Journal (Arts), XXXIII (2) (2006): 93-104.

62. Badiani, Reena, and Katrina K. Jessoe. "Electricity Subsidies, Elections, Groundwater Extraction and Industrial Growth in India." (2010).

63. Razavi, Hossein. Financing energy projects in emerging economies. Pennwell Corporation, 1996.

64. Churchill, Anthony A., and Robert Saunders. "Financing the energy sector in developing countries." Energy world 177 (1990): 8-12.

65. Salies, Evens, and Catherine Waddams Price. "Charges, costs and market power: the deregulated UK electricity retail market." The Energy Journal (2004): 19-35.

66. Nikomborirak, Deunden, and Wanwiphang Manachotphong. "Electricity reform in practice: The case of Thailand, Malaysia, Indonesia and the Philippines."Intergovernmental group of experts on Competition Law and Policy in United Nations Conference on Trade and Development, geneva, Switzerland. Retrieved May. Vol. 20. 2007.

67. Bambawale, Malavika Jain, Anthony L. D'Agostino, and Benjamin K. Sovacool. "Realizing rural electrification in Southeast Asia: lessons from Laos." Energy for Sustainable Development 15.1 (2011): 41-48.

68. Wisuttisak, Pornchai. "Regulation and competition issues in Thai electricity sector." Energy Policy (2012).

69. Besant–Jones, J. E., and R. Bacon. "Global Electric Reform, Privatisation and Liberalisation of the Electric Power Industry in Developing Countries." Energy and Mining Board Discussion Paper Series, Paper 2 (2002).

70. von Hippel, David, et al. "Northeast Asia regional energy infrastructure proposals." Energy Policy 39.11 (2011): 6855-6866.

71. Gao, Hang, and Johannes Van Biesebroeck. "Effects of deregulation and vertical unbundling on the performance of China's electricity generation sector." (2011).

72. Nagayama, Hiroaki. "Japanese Electricity Industry: Recommendations for Restructuring." The Electricity Journal 24.10 (2011): 79-90.

73. Wu, Yanrui. "Electricity Market Integration: Global Trends and Implications for the EAS Region." (2012).

74. Giulietti, Monica, Luigi Grossi, and Michael Waterson. "Price transmission in the UK electricity market: Was NETA beneficial?." Energy Economics 32.5 (2010): 1165-1174.

75. Kwoka, John. "Restructuring the US electric power sector: A review of recent studies." Report Prepared for the American Public Power Association, http://www. appanet. org/files/ PDFs/RestructuringStudyKwoka1. pdf (2006).

76. Phadke, Amol, and Sudhir Chella Rajan. "Electricity reforms in India: not too late to go back to the drawing board." Economic and Political weekly (2003): 3061-3072.

77. Chang, Youngho. "The New Electricity Market of Singapore: Regulatory framework, market power and competition." Energy policy 35.1 (2007): 403-412.

78. Karmacharyaa, S. B., and L. J. de Vriesa. "Electricity Sector Reform in India: Case Study of Orissa, Delhi and Karnataka Electricity Sector."

79. Jung, Hyun Soo, Jin-sang Lee, and Jung-Ho Kim. "The Implementation of PPP and IPP in the Ethiopian Energy Sector." 한국아프리카학회지 36 (2012): 269-294.

80. Kessides, Ioannis N. "The Impacts of Electricity Sector Reforms in Developing Countries." The Electricity Journal 25.6 (2012): 79-88.

81. Yi-chong, Xu. "The myth of the single solution: electricity reforms and the World Bank." Energy 31.6 (2006): 802-814.

82. Eberhard, Anton, and Katharine Nawaal Gratwick. "IPPs in Sub-Saharan Africa: determinants of success." Energy policy 39.9 (2011): 5541-5549.

83. Sen, Anuradha. "Integrated Resource Planning In Power Sector." Available at SSRN 916502 (2006).

84. Sinha, Shirish, et al. "Energy sector reforms and rural energy access in India: the emerging issues." Transition towards sustainable development in South Asia (2003): 43-60.

85. Thomas, Steve, Jayantha Gunasekara, and Ruana Rajepakse. Turning off the lights: the threat to community electricity in Sri Lanka. ITDG Publishing, 2005.

86. ARASU, FR JG VALAN. "Future Prospects of the Power Sector in India."Studies In Indian Economy 1 (2005): 73.

87. Lee, Seung-Hoon. "Electricity in KOREA."

88. Gore, Olga, et al. "Russian electricity market reform: Deregulation or re-regulation?." Energy Policy (2011).

89. Pagani, G. A., and M. Aiello. Energy market trading systems in g6 countries. Tech. Rep. JBI preprint 2010-6-01, JBI, University of Groningen, 2010.

90. Griffin, James M., and Steven L. Puller, eds. Electricity deregulation: choices and challenges. Vol. 4. University of Chicago Press, 2005.

91. Dubash, Navroz. "Institutional transplant as political opportunity: the practice and politics of Indian electricity regulation." CLPE Research Paper 31 (2008).

92. Dubash, Navroz K., and Narasimha Rao. "Emergent regulatory governance in India: comparative case studies of electricity regulation." a conference on "Frontiers of Regulation: Assessing Scholarly Debates and Policy Changes," University of Bath. September. 2006.

93. Sood, Yog Raj, Narayana Prasad Padhy, and H. O. Gupta. "Wheeling of power under deregulated environment of power system-a bibliographical survey."Power Systems, IEEE Transactions on 17.3 (2002): 870-878.

94. Remme, Uwe, et al. Technology Development Prospects for the Indian Power Sector. No. 2011/4. OECD Publishing, 2011.

95. Banerjee, Arindam. "A Study on Foreign Direct Investment (FDI) in Power Sector in Indian Scenario." IME Journal: The Research Journal of Institute of Management Education 6.1 (2012).

96. Khatik, S. K., and R. V. Saxena. "Analysis of Enterprise Resource Planning Execution in Power Distribution Utilities in India." Advances In Management(2012).

97. Goyal, Mohit, Hemant Dujari, and Sarthak Misra. "Indian UMPP dream turned sour: A case study based discussion." Energy Policy (2012).

98. Ghose, M. K. "Sustainable Technologies for Energy Management to Meet the Coal Demand in the Indian Context." Energy Sources, Part B: Economics, Planning, and Policy 7.3 (2012): 213-221.

99. Khajuria, A., and N. H. Ravindranath. "Climate Change in Context of Indian Agricultural Sector." J Earth Sci Climate Change 3.110 (2012): 2.

100. Bhakar, R., N. P. Padhy, and H. O. Gupta. "Network Pricing in India: Policies and Practices." Energy Sources, Part B: Economics, Planning, and Policy 7.3 (2012): 265-274.

101. Reddy, V. Siva, S. C. Kaushik, and N. L. Panwar. "Review on power generation scenario of India." Renewable and Sustainable Energy Reviews 18 (2012): 43-48.

102. Chatterjee, Elizabeth. "Dissipated energy: Indian electric power and the politics of blame." Contemporary South Asia 20.1 (2012): 91-103.

103. Siddiqui, Md Zakaria, Gauthier de Maere d'Aertrycke, and Yves Smeers. "Demand response in Indian electricity market." Energy Policy (2012).

104. Bisht, Medha. "Bhutan–India Power Cooperation: Benefits Beyond Bilateralism." Strategic Analysis 36.5 (2012): 787-803.

105. Walton, C. Dale. "A Review of "India as an Asia Pacific Power"." Comparative Strategy 31.2 (2012): 194-195.

106. Shailaja, G., and K. Rajender. "Performance of Power Sector in Andhra Pradesh: A Study of APGENCO Limited." The IUP Journal of Infrastructure10.1 (2012): 65-73.

107. Acharjee, P. "Strategy and implementation of Smart Grid in India." Energy Strategy Reviews (2012).

108. Chaudhary, Ankur, Ambuj D. Sagar, and Ajay Mathur. "Innovating for energy efficiency: a perspective from India." Innovation and Development 2.1 (2012): 45-66.

109. Sengupta, Sandeep. "India: the next superpower?: managing the environment: a growing problem for a growing power." (2012).

110. Kundu, Goutam Kumar, and Bidhu Bhusan Mishra. "Impact of reform and privatisation on employees a case study of power sector reform in Orissa, India." Energy Policy (2012).

111. Kessides, Ioannis N. "The Impacts of Electricity Sector Reforms in Developing Countries." The Electricity Journal 25.6 (2012): 79-88.

112. Singh, S. N., and R. K. Jha. "A design of utility/ DG interfaced adaptive solar (pv) home green power generator and socio-economic impact in Indian rural society."

113. Joseph, Das. "Agricultural Crisis in India: The Root Cause and Consequences."Available at SSRN 2167261 (2012).

114. Sinha, Bikramjit, and Kirti Joshi. "Analysis of India's solar photovoltaics research output." Annals of Library and Information Studies (ALIS) 59.2 (2012): 106-121.

115. Ashok, S., and R. Banerjee. "Load-management applications for the industrial sector." Applied energy 66.2 (2000): 105-111.

116. Smith, Thomas B. "Electricity theft: a comparative analysis." Energy Policy32.18 (2004): 2067-2076.

117. Singh, Anoop. "Power sector reform in India: current issues and prospects."Energy policy 34.16 (2006): 2480-2490.

118. Pachauri, Shonali, and Daniel Spreng. "Direct and indirect energy requirements of households in India." Energy policy 30.6 (2002): 511-523.

119. Thakur, Tripta, et al. "Impact assessment of the Electricity Act 2003 on the Indian power sector." Energy Policy 33.9 (2005): 1187-1198.

120. Sharma, Ashok. "India and energy security." Asian Affairs 38.2 (2007): 158-172.

121. Martin G.Glasesar, "Outlines the Public Utility Economics", The McMillan Company, New York,1927.

122. Young, H.P., "Electric Power System Control", Chaman Publishers Ltd., London,1950.

123. Eli, Winston, Clemens, "Economics and Public Utility", Appletinon Century Crafts, Inc., New York, 1950.

124. Zaborsky, John, "Electric Power Transmission", Ronald Press Publications, New York,1954.

125. Drake, Mayall, Kirchmayer and Wood, "Optimum Operation of a Hydro Thermal System", AIEE, Transmission,Vol.81, Pt.III, 1962.

126. Skrotzki, "Electric Transmission and Distribution", McGraw-Hill Publications, New York, 1964.

127. Nelson, D.C., "A Study of the Electricity of Demand for Electricity by Residential Consumers: Sample Markets in Nebraska", Land Economics, Wisconsin Press, Madison, WI, 1965.

128. Baxter,R.E and Rees,R., "Analysis of Industrial Demand for Electricity", Economic Journal, Basil Blackwell Ltd, England, 1968.

129. Cargill, Thomas F., and Robert A. Meyer, "Estimating the Demand for Electricity by Time of Day", Applied Economics, Chapman & Hall, London,1971.

130. Wilson, John W., "Residential Demand for Electricity", Quarterly Review of Economics and Business, University of Illinois, Urban Champaign, 1971.

131. Halvorsen, Robert Francis, "Residential Demand for Electricity", Ph.D. Thesis, Harvard University, New York,1972.

132. Anderson, Kent P., "Residential Demand for Electricity :Econometric Estimates for California and the United States", The Rand Corporation, Santa Monica, 1972.

133. Anderson, Dennis., "Models for Determining Least Cost Investments in Electricity Supply", The Bell Journal of Economics and Management Science, Vol.3, (Spring .1972).

134. Engel-Kron, Robert and Hunt, "Electric Power Statistics Equipment of Turbine and Chemical Departments", Mir Publications, Moscow, 1974.

135. Howthakker,H.S., Verleger P.K .Jr ., and Sheehan, D.P., "Dynamic Demand Analysis for Gasoline and Residential Electricity", American Journal of Agricultural Economics, American Agricultural Economics Association,Iowa, 1974.

136. Macraks,Michael   S.,(Ed.),   "Energy: Demand,Conservation and Institutional Problems", MIT Press, Cambridge, 1974.

137. Smith,V,Kerry, Cicehetti,C.J., and Gillen,W.J., "Measuring the Price Elasticity of Demand for Electric Power : The U.S. Experience", Paper delivered at French —American Workshop on Energy System Forecasting Planning and Pricing, University of Wisconsin, Madison 1974.

138. Griffin, James M., "The Effects of Higher Prices on Electricity Consumption", The Bell Journal of Economics and Management Science, Autumn, 1974.

139. Baughman, Martin and Paul Joskow, "The Effects of Fuel Prices on Residential Appliance Choice in the United States", Land Economics, Wisconsin Press, Madison, WI, 1975.

140. Telson Michal.L ., "The Economics of Alternative levels of Reliability for electric power generation systems", The Bell Journals of Economics, Vol.6, 1975.

141. Anderson,K.P., "Price Electricity of Residential Energy Use", Rand Corporation, Santa Monica, 1974.

142. Sultan, R.G.M., "Price in the Electrical Oligopolv", Vol. J., Graduate School of Business Administration, Harvard University, Boston, 1974.

143. Sarikas, R.H., Herz, H., "Electric Rate Concepts and Structures", Springfield,NTIS, 1976.

144. Cicchetti, C.J., Gillen, W.J., Smolensky, P., "Marginal Cost and Pricing of Electricity –An Applied Approach", Ballinger Publisher & Co., Cambridge, 1977.

145. Munasinghe,M., Warford J.J., "Shadow Pricing and Power Tariff Policy", The World Bank, Washington, D.C., 1978.

146. Robert and Hunt, "Electric Power System Components, Transformers and Rotating Machines", Vannostrand Publications, New York, 1979.

147. Mekay,D.J., "Introduction of Peakload Pricing in Europe", Rand Corporation, Santa Monica, 1979.

148. Action J.P., and others, "British Industrial Response to the Peakload Pricing of Electricity", Rand Publications, Santa Monica, 1980.

149. Cervero, R., "Peakload Transit Pricing-Theory and Practice", University of California, California, 1981.

150. Wood, D., "Electricity Pricing", Business School, Manchester,1981.

151. Action, J.P., "Promoting Energy Efficiency Through Improved Electricity Pricing", A Mid Project Report, Rand Corporation, Santa Monica, 1982.

152. Webb, Michael, "The Determination of Reserve Generating Capacity Criteria in Electric Supply System", Applied Economics,1977.

153. Munasinghe, Mohan., "The Economics of Power System Reliability and Planning", IBRD,D.C.20433, U.S.A, 1979

154. Margh,W.D., "Economics of Electric Utility Power Generation", Oxford University Press, 1980.

155. Munasinghe, M., Warford,J.J., "Electricity Pricing-Theory and Case Studies", Baltimove Johns, University Press, Hopkins,1982.

156. Kehlhofer,R.H., "Combined Cycle Gas and Steam Turbine Power Plants", The Fairmound Press, Lilburm, G.A., 1991.

157. Stultz,S.C and Kitto,J.B (eds), "Steam- its generation and use", 40ᵗʰ ed., The Babcock & Wilcox Co., Barberton, OH, 1992.

158. Winter, John .V and Corner, David.A., "Power Plant Setting",Van Nostrid Reinhold Environmental Engineering Series, New York,1992.

159. Lucio Monari, "A Reality Check on subsidizing Power for Irrigation in India", The World Bank Group Private Sector and Infrastructure Network., Note Number 244, April 2002.

160. Pierre Audinet, "Electricity Prices in India", Energy Prices and Taxes, 2ⁿᵈ Quarter 2002, IEA, 2002.

161. Andres Loza, "An Evaluation of the Reforms in the Argentinean Power Sector in the Nineties.",Energy Discussion Paper No: 2.62-2/04, International Energy Initiative, Latin America Office, Brazil, July 2004.

162. Eva NIESTEN, "Regulatory Institutions and Governance Transformations in Liberalising

Electricity Industries", Annals of Public and Cooperative Economics, Vol.77, No.3,Rotterdam School of Management, Erasmus University Rotterdam, The Netherlands, September 2006.

163. Pond, Richard., "Liberalisation, privatisation and regulation in the UK electricity sector." Working Lines Research Institute, London Metropolitan University, London EC3N2EY, UK, November 2006.

164. Caroline Varely, Jeffery Logan and Jonathan Sinton, "China's Power Sector Reforms", International Energy Agency (IEA),Head of Publications Service, OECD/IEA, France, 2006.

165. Kwoka, John. "Restructuring the US electric power sector: A review of recent studies." Report Prepared for the American Public Power Association, Northeastern University, November 2006.

166. National Association of Regulatory Utility Commissioners (NARUC's), "The Role of Consumer Organisations in Electricity Sector Policies and Issues", USAID Consumer Report,2006.

167. Jesse Berst, Philip Bane, Michael Burkhalter, Alex Zheng, "The Electricity Economy", Global Smart Energy, Global Environment Fund, August 2008

168. Sten Bergman, Saifur Rahman, Jaakko Helleranta, Ada Karina Izaguirre, Maria Shkaratan and Prasad Tallapragada V.S.N, "Monitoring Performance of Electric Utilities: Indicators and Benchmarking in Sub-Saharan Africa", Electric Utility Capacity Assistance Project (EUCAP),The World Bank, 2009

169. Govinda R. Timilsina, Lado Kurdgelashvili and Patrick A. Narbel, "A Review of Solar Energy: Markets,Economics and Policies", Policy Research Working Paper 5845, The World Bank, Development Research Group, Environmental and Energy Team, October 2011.

170. Frost and Sullivan, "China and India tipped to lead boom in gas,nuclear and renewable", Power Engineering International, Vol.20, Issue 10, PennWell Global Energy Group, U.S.A, November 2012.

171. Michael Herson, "Global Fuel Trends: Fuel for thought", Power Engineering International, Vol.20, Issue 10, PennWell Global Energy Group, U.S.A, November 2012.

172. Government of India, Planning for Power Development in India: A Hand Book of Information', Central Water and Power Commission, Ministry of Irrigation and Power, Simla, 1955.

173. Government of India, 'Report on the Evaluation of Power Electrification Programme', Planning Commission, New Delhi, 1960.

174. Government of India, 'Report of the Committee on the Working of State Electricity Boards',(Venkataraman Committee), New Delhi, 1964.

175. Government of India, 'Report on Survey of Labour Conditions in Electric Power Stations, 1965-66', Labour Bureau, Ministry of Labour, New Delhi, 1966.

176. Government of India, Report on the State Electricity Board'(submitted to the Administrative Reforms Commission), Central Electricity Authority, New Delhi, 1969.

177. Government of India, 'Electricity and Economic Development in Madras State', Research Programmes Committee, Planning Commission, New Delhi, 1969.

178. Government of India, 'Report of the Fifth Finance Commission', Planning Commission, New Delhi, 1969.

179. State Planning Commission, 'The Perspective Plan for Tamil Nadu-Prosperity Through Power', Report on the Taskforce on Fuel and Power, 1972-1984, The Author, Madras, 1972.

180. Ramanuj Das, 'Electricity Loss ', Low Publico, Hyderabad, 1975.

181. Pachauri, R.K., 'Energy and Economic Development in India', Preegal Publications, New York, 1978.

182. Wagre, D.M., and Rao, N.V., 'Power Sector in India', Popular Prakasan, Bombay, 1978

183. Government of India, 'Report of the Committee on Power', department of Power, Ministry of Energy, New Delhi, 1980.

184. Ramana Rao, T.V., ' A Study on Industrial Relation in APSEB', Unpublished Thesis, Andhra University, Visakhapatnam, 1981.

185. Government of India, "State Electricity Board-Financial Performance Review", Central Electricity Authority, Controller of Publications, Delhi, 1982.

186. Chelapathi Rao, G.V., 'Materials Management in State Electricity Board', Administrative Staff College of India, Hyderabad, 1984.

187. Rambabu, D., ' A Study on Material Management in Andhra Pradesh State Electricity Board', Unpublished Thesis, Andhra University, Visakhapatnam, 1985.

188. Government of India, 'Twelfth Electric Power Survey of India', Power Survey Directorate, Central Electricity Authority, New Delhi, 1985.

189. Kothari's Industrial Directory of India, 'Industry Profile-Electricity' Kothari Enterprises, Madras, 1990, pp.6-1.

190. Government of India, 'Fourteenth Electric Power Survey of India', Central Electricity Authority, Department of Power, Ministry of Energy, New Delhi, 1991.

191. Ghuman,B.S., "Public Enterprises in India : Phases of Reform in the 1990s". Asian Journal of Public Administration, Vol21, No 2, (December 1999), 220-233.

192. Study produced by the International Energy Agency's Office of Non-Member Countries. Electricity in India, Providing Power for the Millions, November 2000.

193. Rao, K.P., "Power Tariff blues of Andhra Pradesh",The Hindu, Daily, Chennai,June 27, 2000.

194. Amulya K.N.Reddy, "Indian Power Sector Reform for Sustainable Development :The Public benefits Imperative, Energy for sustainable Development, Vol.2, New Delhi, 2000.

195. Padmanaban,S and Sarkar,Ashok ., " Electricity Demand Side Management (DSM) In India –A Strategic And Policy Perspective", Distribution Reform, Upgrades and Management (DRUM) Training Program, US Agency for International Development (USAID), New Delhi, India, 2001.

196. Tongia, Rahul (Dr), "The Political Economy of Indian Power Sector Reforms", India Infrastructure Report, 2002.

197. Thakur, Tripta (Dr), "Productivity and Efficiency analysis of the Indian State Electricity Boards". Department of Electrical Engineering, MAHIT Bhopal, 2002

198. International Energy Agency, "Electricity in India: Providing Power for the millions", April 2002.

199. Massimo Filippini and Shonali Pachauri, "Elasticities of Electricity Demand in Urban Indian Households". Centre for Energy Policy and Economics, Swiss Federal Institutes of Technology, CEPE Working Paper Nr.16, March 2002.

200. Santhakumar, V, "Impact of the distribution of the cost of reform on social support for reforms: A Study of power sector reforms in Indian States", India Development Foundation, Gurgaon, Haryana, India, 2003.

201. Government of India, The Electricity Act-2003.

202. Pandey, Ajay, "Reforms in Electricity", Tariff Policy in the Electricity Sector: A review, Indian Infrastructure Report,2004.

203. Lamb, Peter M., "The Indian Electricity Market: Country Study and Investment Context",

Working Paper #48, Program on Energy and Sustainable Development at Stanford University, Stanford, 2005.

204. Navroz K. Dubash, "The New Regulatory Politics of Electricity in India: Independent, Embedded or Transcendent?" Paper presented at a workshop on "The Politics of Necessity", Oxford, 2005.

205. Mishra, R.K and Kiranmai .J, " Restructuring of S.L.P.Es' in India-A Macro Analysis", The Journal of Institute of Public Enterprise, Vol.29, No. 3&4, Osmania University Campus, Hyderabad, India, September 2006.

206. Singh Kulwant and Kumar Surinder, "Power Sector Reforms: A Comparative Analysis of Punjab, Haryana and Delhi Power Systems", The Journal of Institute of Public Enterprise, Vol.29, No. 3&4, Osmania University Campus, Hyderabad, India, September 2006.

207. Ramana, D.V, "Electricity Sector Reforms and Accounting –Some Observations from the First Phase of Reforms in Orissa", The Journal of Institute of Public Enterprise, Vol.29, No. 3&4, Osmania University Campus, Hyderabad, India, September 2006.

208. Government of India, 'Study on Impact of Restructuring of SEBs', (the National Report submitted by Indian Institute of Public Administration), Ministry of Power, New Delhi, 2006.

209. The Electricity Governance Initiative (EGI), "Benchmarking best practice and promoting accountability in governance of the electricity sector" Summary Report, The Forum on Electricity Governance, 29-31 March 2006, Bangkok, Thailand.

210. Government of India, Ministry of Power, A Study on "Impact of Restructuring of SEBs" report prepared the 27th September, 2006, by Indian Institute of Public Administration.

211. Das, Kanti Tushar (Dr) and Mishra, Lopamudra (Dr), "Political Economy of Power Sector Restructuring in ORISSA", Department of Business Administration and Department of Economics, PTRAW, Sambalpur University, Orissa, 2006.

212. Ahmed Waquar, "Neoliberalism And Contested Policies Of The Power Industry In India" The Industrial Geographer, Volume 5, issue 1, p. 44-57, Penn State University, University Park, PA 16802, USA., 2007.

213. Singh Anoop, "Policy Environment and Regulatory Reforms for Private and Foreign Investment in Developing Countries: A Case of the Indian Power Sector", Asian Development Bank Institute, Discussion Paper No: 64., New Delhi, April 2007.

214. The National coordination committee of Electricity Employee & Engineers examined the report. 2007.

215. The Hindu, Survey of Indian Industry, 2008.

216. Government of India, The Planning Commission, "Report of HIGH LEVEL PANEL on Financial Position of Distribution Utilities", December, 2011 New Delhi

217. KPMG Consultant, "Power Sector in India", White paper on Implementation Challenges and Opportunities, Energy Summit, Nagpur, January 2010.

218. Report by CRISIL Infrastructure Advisory (CRIS)

219. Maureen L.Cropper, Alexander Limonov, Kabir Malik, and Anoop Singh, "Estimating the Impact of Restructuring on Electricity Generation Efficiency: The Case of the Indian Thermal Power Sector", NBER Working Paper No. 17383, NATIONAL BUREAU OF ECONOMIC RESEARCH, Cambridge, September 2011.

220. Gupta Vebhav, "Power Exchanges a Boon or Bane : A Case –Study of Indian Power Sector", International Journal of Scientific & Engineering Research,Volume 2, Issue 10, October 2011, ISSN 2229-5518.

221. Uwe Remme, Nathalie Trudeau, Dagmar Graczyk and Peter Taylor, "Technology Development Prospects For The Indian Power Sector." International Energy Agency, 2011.

222. Brain Min and Miriam Golden, "Theft and Loss of Electricity in an Indian State", University of Michigan and University of California, Los Angeles, Princeton University. 2012.

223. A report on "Comparative study on power situation in the Northern and Central states of India" by PHD Research Bureau, PHD Chamber of Commerce and Industry, PHD House, August Kranti Marg, New Delhi, September 2011.

224. Government of India, Ministry of Power, Report of The Working Group on Power for Twelfth Plan (2012-2017), New Delhi, January 2012.

225. "Power To The People Investing In Clean Energy For The Base Of The Pyramid In India",India's Centre for Development Finance at the Institute for Financial Management and Research (CDF-IFMR) and the World Resources Institute's New Ventures Program

226. Dr Anshu Bhardwaj and Dr Rahul Tongia, "Distributed Power Generation :Rural India –A Case Study. This work was supported in part by the United Nations Foundation. Carnegie Mellon University, 5000 Forbes Avenue, Pittsburgh, PA 15213, USA

227. Rajesh Gangakhedkar and R.K.Mishra, "The evaluation of UMPP in India", New Delhi, 2012.

228. McKinsey & Company, "Powering India-The Road to 2017", 2012.

Printed in the United States
by Bookmasters

Printed in the United States
By Bookmasters